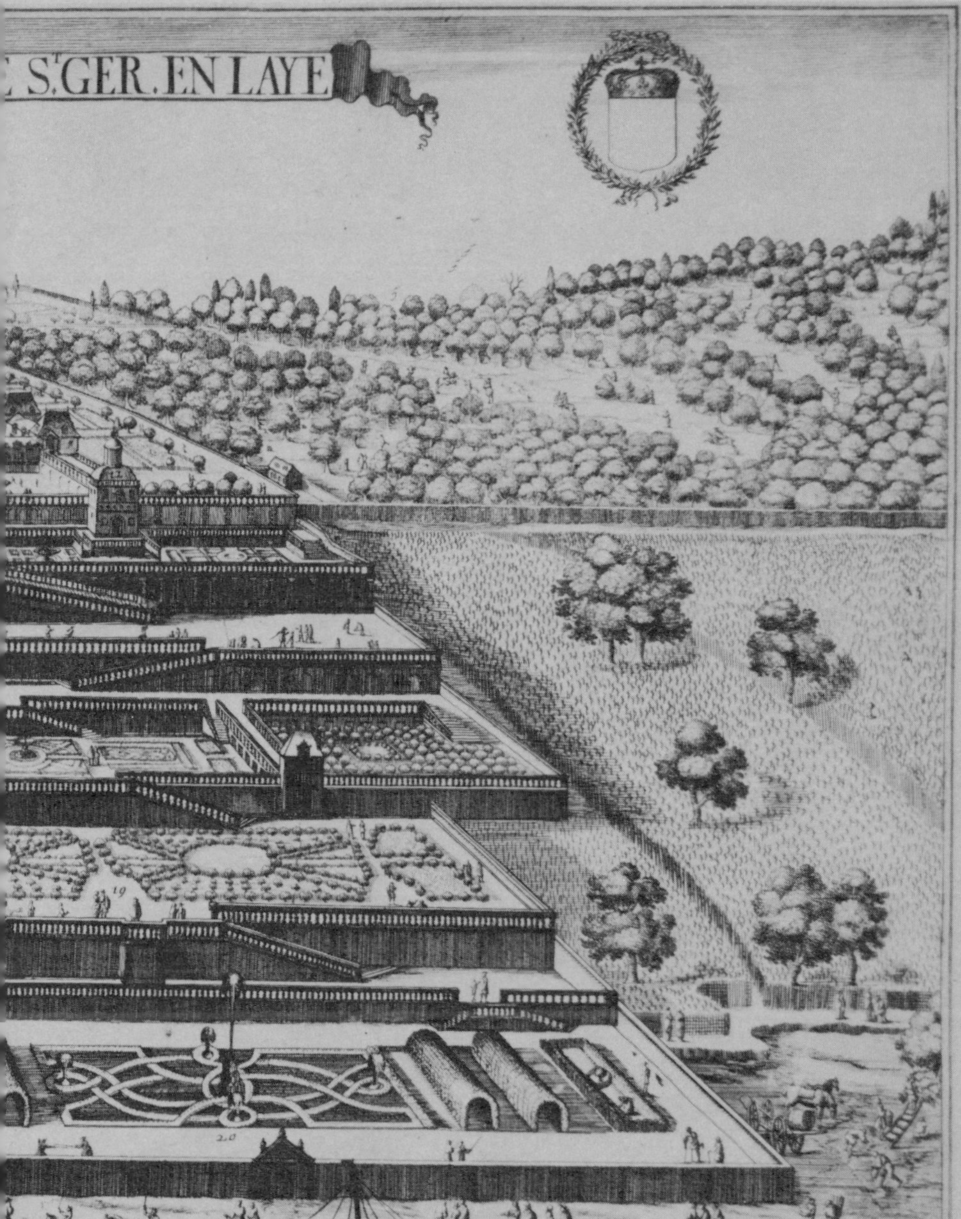

E S.t GER. EN LAYE

rotte d'Orphée
leux bosquets
rdin dentre les deux bosquets
rdin en pante
rdin des cañaulx

21 La Riuiere de Seine

A Paris rue St Jacques proche St Yves chez

The Lion and the Lilies

THE LION & THE LILIES

The Stuarts and France

EILEEN CASSAVETTI

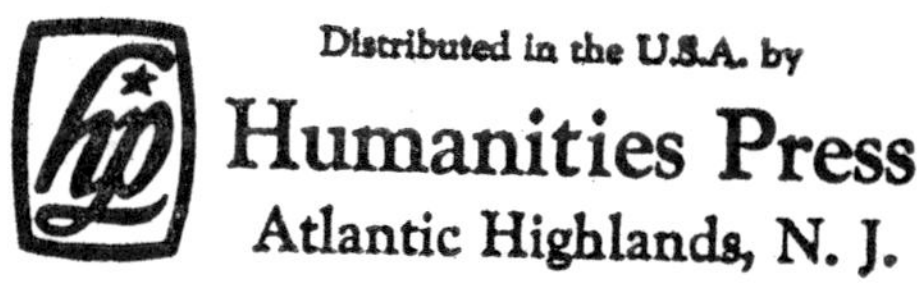

MACDONALD AND JANE'S · LONDON

FIRST PUBLISHED IN GREAT BRITAIN IN 1977 BY
MACDONALD AND JANE'S PUBLISHERS LIMITED
PAULTON HOUSE
8, SHEPHERDESS WALK
LONDON NI 7LW
PRINTED AND BOUND IN GREAT BRITAIN BY
REDWOOD BURN LIMITED
TROWBRIDGE AND ESHER

ISBN 354 041 363

FOR PATRICK, ANDREW, FRANCESCA AND HUGO

TABLE OF CONTENTS

List of Illustrations

ALL THE RESEARCH for this book was done in France. In Paris I worked in the Archives Nationales where I am indebted to the help and advice given by Monsieur Bernard Mahieu and Madame Favier; in the Archives du Ministère des Affaires Etrangères at the quai d'Orsay, and at the Bibliotheque Nationale. For help and permission to reproduce prints I am grateful to Monsieur Jean Adhémar, Conservateur en Chef du Cabinet des Estampes at the Bibliothèque Nationale.

For the earlier part of the book I must thank Monsieur Jean-Yves Ribault, Directeur des Services d'Archives Départementales du Cher at Bourges, and for the later chapters I consulted the Archives Départementales de Vaucluse and the Musée Calvet at Avignon.

I should also like to thank the following for giving me access to family documents and rare books on the subject of the Stuarts in France and for permission to reproduce portraits and prints in their possession, some of them hitherto unpublished: the Marquis de Vogüé, his brother the Comte Antoine de Vogüé and their uncle the Comte Robert-Jean de Vogüé; the Comte de Miramon-Fitzjames; the Duke and Duchess of Alba: the Duc de la Force and the Comtesse de Caumont La Force: the Duc de Rohan; the Prince and Princess de Rohan in Vienna, head of the Austrian branch of the Rohan family: and for her constant interest, help and encouragement during the last three years of her life, the late Comtesse Jean de Pange, née the Princess Pauline de Broglie. My thanks are due to my editor, Felix Brenner, for his enthusiasm, attention to detail and the hard work he has put in this book. Lastly I am most grateful to my eldest son Patrick Cassavetti for his patience and skill in photographing eight of the portraits and prints illustrating the text, including the portrait of the Old Pretender which has never before been reproduced and is by permission of the Baron de Chillaz, President of the Foundation of the Scots College in Paris.

The author and publishers also wish to thank the following for their help and kind permission to reproduce the illustrations in the text:

Her Majesty the Queen

The Duke and Duchess of Alba
The Bibliotèque Nationale, Paris
The Archives du Cher, Bourges
The Collège Ecossais, Paris
The Musée Condé, Chantilly
The Dulwich College Gallery, London
The family Caumont La Force
The Goodwood Estate, Chichester
The National Portrait Gallery, London
Comte Victor de Pange
The Scottish National Portrait Gallery, Edinburgh
The family de Vogüé

Rochecolombe, Ardèche. 1970—
rue St Jacques, Paris 1976.

THIS BOOK is not intended to be another political history of the royal house of Stuart, which has been dealt with excellently countless times by specialists of varying nationalities, notably the nineteenth century German historians Von Ranke and Von Klopp. It is instead the first general history of the Stuart connection with France; a chronicle of the personalities who made up this extraordinary family throughout their chequered career from their rise in France in the eleventh century to their assumption of power, first in Scotland and then in England, and to their exile and extinction in France at the end of the *ancien régime*. Often they were inept bunglers who brought misfortune upon their own heads by being over-emotional and by taking personal affront at any criticism of their obstinately upheld doctrine of the divine right of kings. They were a brave, loyal and magnanimous lot for the most part, who seldom bullied or persecuted their subjects and, in spite of their fatal mistakes in policy, left behind a legacy of patronage of the arts and sciences.

I first became aware of the Stuarts when I was sent to a school in Renfrewshire founded by James VI's tutor, George Buchanan, the stern Presbyterian misogynist who had received his own education at the Scots College in Paris. Summers spent in the Western Highlands and Islands sailing perilously in small boats across the stormy Minch made the Jacobite adventure a reality for me. But it was on coming to live in Paris that a whole new chapter of the Stuart story revealed itself. It began with proximity. The great dome of the most beautiful baroque church in Paris, the Val de Grâce, is within sight of my window. Here its founder, Anne of Austria, worshipped, as did Henrietta Maria, Charles I's widow. Here, in the year of the secret Treaty of Dover, 1670, the heart of Charles II's sister, Henriette Anne, Duchesse d'Orleans, was buried. Across the road, in what was once the English Benedictine monastery, the embalmed bodies of James II and his youngest daughter, Louise Marie Stuart, lay for nearly ninety years, in expectation of being transported to final burial in

Westminster Abbey. Instead, they suffered the fury of the Revolutionary mob, and their bodies were thrown into the *fosse commune*. Farther down the rue St Jacques in an inner courtyard, behind a fish shop, is the once elegant, now dilapidated eighteenth-century convent of the Visitation. Bonny Prince Charlie's only child, Charlotte, Duchess of Albany, and her mother, the Prince's discarded Scottish mistress, Clementina Walkinshaw, lived there in shabby obscurity for twenty years at the expense of the Cardinal Duke of York.

In 1972 I bought an old house in Ardèche, the province bordering on the Cévennes—as wild and romantic as Scotland or Greece and as hot as Provence. Not long after I discovered that the ruined château dominating the twelfth-century village was owned by the Vogüé family, who also own the last surviving property of the Stuarts in France, the Renaissance château of La Verrerie at Aubigny in Berry. The archives of La Verrerie, dating back to the fifteenth century, were hidden in an attic and so remained intact during the French Revolution, when those of so many noble families were destroyed. Through the kindness and interest of the Marquis de Vogüé and his brother, Comte Antoine, I was able to consult those papers for the early part of this book. For the medieval section and for the material up to the end of the seventeenth-century I researched the Series J in the cartons *France-Ecosse* in the Archives Nationales in Paris. To peruse these documents dealing with the early Scottish Stuart kings, the Scots Guards and the old alliance, which are among the most precious records in the Trésor des Chartes, was an awe-inspiring and moving experience. From the seventeenth-century onwards, illuminating material on the exiled Stuarts at St Germain-en-Laye is found in the Series K, including the Chaillot mss, giving details of the widowed Henrietta Maria's domestic arrangements at Chaillot as well as many autograph letters of James II, Mary of Modena, James III and Princess Louise Marie Stuart. In addition to these documents, the vast collection of autograph letters and secret memoirs in the quai d'Orsay archives relating to the Stuarts in the seventeenth and eighteenth centuries made me consider the whole Stuart story from a new angle—the French viewpoint of the usefulness of the Stuarts in promoting French interests, which forms a recurrent theme throughout the history of the family.

The story begins with the exploits of a modest but remarkable man, Sir John Stuart of Darnley, in Renfrewshire, who became Constable of the Scottish Army in France after Agincourt, and who died in 1429, hero of the French resistance to the English invaders just before Joan of Arc raised the siege of Orléans. It continues with the fortunes and misfortunes of the family in Scotland and England and the collapse of the young Chevalier, the last Stuart claimant to the throne of Great Britain, after his defeat at

Culloden, the last battle to be fought on British soil. It ends with Henry, Cardinal Duke of York, at his death in Rome in 1807, who styled himself Henry IX. He lies buried in St Peter's with his brother who called himself Charles III and their father the Jacobite James III in a tomb paid for jointly by the Pope and George IV.

The Stuart story has the fascination of failure. They left practically nothing tangible behind; but, in reading their correspondence, and the later Stuarts were all prolific letter-writers, one hears their voices. In the 'sweet, low voice' ascribed by Ronsard to Mary, Queen of Scots, the loud broad Scots accent of James I, the dignified stammer of Charles I, the seventeenth-century court French of Henriette Anne d'Angleterre, the perfectly enunciated and written English of James III and the strange Scots-Irish accent in French and English, as well as the lamentable spelling of his son, they emerge as vivid though exasperating human beings, set apart by their obsessive belief in their divine right to rule. The direct line of the Stuarts died out, but nearly every ruling or ex-ruling house in Europe today is proud to claim its share of Stuart blood, either as descendants of the Protestant Elizabeth of Bohemia, daughter of James I and grandmother of George I of Hanover, or of the Catholic French-educated Henriette Anne Stuart, Duchesse d'Orléans, the favourite sister of Charles II.

Part One

The Early Stuarts in France and Scotland, 1419–1603

I

IN OUR GREAT WANT AND NECESSITY

THE LITTLE TOWN of Aubigny-sur-Nère, south of the Loire and halfway between Orléans and Bourges, has changed very little in outward appearance since it first became a Scottish outpost in France in the darkest days of the Hundred Years' War. The sturdy grey château, with its fifteenth-century turrets and high pointed gables in the main street of the town, and the Château of La Verrerie in the green wooded countryside of Berry to the south, still bear the chequered arms of the Stuarts of Darnley quartered with the fleur-de-lys of France, in recognition of the vital contribution the Stuarts made to the survival of the French between their disaster of Agincourt in 1415 and the appearance of Joan of Arc at the siege of Orléans in 1429. At Agincourt almost the entire French nobility had been wiped out, and those who had not been killed were captured and held to ransom. After that, Normandy and Aquitaine had been entirely overrun by the English invaders and their allies, the Burgundians. The kingdom of France, depleted of men and money, shrank to the three central provinces of Anjou, Poitou and Berry. The government of the mad King Charles VI was on the point of collapse; his vicious Queen, Isabeau of Bavaria, was in league with England's ally, the Duke of Burgundy; and their last surviving son, the Dauphin Charles, hated by his mother, barely escaped with his life and fled to Bourges when the Burgundians occupied Paris in May 1418.

Timid and introverted though he was, the sixteen-year-old heir to the throne was determined to fight for his inheritance. From Bourges he launched a desperate appeal to Scotland to honour the old alliance between the two countries by sending him reinforcements without delay. He specially requested that the veteran Constable of the Scottish Army, Sir John Stuart of Darnley, 'in our great want and necessity', should lead this force of mercenaries against the enemies who were threatening his kingdom with annihilation. The Constable was a hardened campaigner against the English, and had fought several times before in France. His second cousin, the third Stuart King, James I, had been captured on his way to France thirteen years before and was still held prisoner in London by Henry V.

Darnley was fifty-four years old and in those days could quite honourably have claimed the *repos du guerrier,* but this was neither his inclination nor his fate. When he left Castle Darnley in Renfrewshire in the autumn of 1419, the Constable took a decisive step in his own life by putting down lasting roots in the country he went to help; though, in one sense, he was only reaching back to his origins, for the Stuart Kings had had their beginnings in France.

The Stuarts went from France to Scotland in the eleventh century and, as allies or as exiles, they kept returning to France during the next 600 years—years of almost constant collaboration with the French, even when four of them sat on the throne of Britain. They gave ten sovereigns to Scotland, one of whom was also Queen of France, and six to Great Britain. They came in the wake of the Norman conquerors of England, but they were not Normans. They were a noble Celtic family from Dol-de-Bretagne, kinsmen of the rulers of Brittany.

The first of these soldiers of fortune was Alain the Sénéchal of Dol, a sad little town between St Malo and Mont St Michel, near the site of the forest of Broceliande of Arthurian legend. The first Stuarts were adventurers, moody and restless by temperament but of undisputed loyalty to the causes they espoused. Alain of Dol soon realized there was no future for him at the court of the former Duke of Normandy, William the Conqueror, and went north to Scotland to offer his services to King Malcolm Canmore and his English Queen Margaret. Towards the end of his life romantic wanderlust seized him again, and he left Scotland to join Godfrey de Bouillon and Raymond de Toulouse on the First Crusade in 1095, dying during the Siege of Jerusalem in 1099.

A quarter of a century later Walter Fitzalan, a great-grandson of Alain of Dol, was made High Steward of Scotland when King David I established the French feudal system in the lowlands. With this hereditary highest office of state went a substantial grant of lands in the rich Clyde valley, among them Darnley and Paisley, where the next High Steward founded an abbey in 1164 as an offshoot of the great Benedictine centre of learning at Cluny in France. In this abbey all the early Stuarts were buried. The following year, in 1165, the High Steward was sent as Ambassador to France to sign the first Franco-Scottish military alliance, pledging mutual support against their common enemy, territorially ambitious England.

This High Steward's grandson Walter fought during the Scottish wars of liberation against Edward I and Edward II and, as Robert the Bruce's chief supporter, played a leading part in the victory at Bannockburn. He married Bruce's only daughter, Marjory, and in 1316 became the father of Robert II, the first of the long line of Stuart kings. The young Robert's apprenticeship was long and hard, as Robert the Bruce was succeeded in 1329 by David, his weak and ineffectual son by a second marriage. In 1333 David Bruce's army was defeated and the boy King was forced into exile in France by Edward III and did not return until 1341. During the rule of the English puppet King Edward Baliol, Robert Stewart fought bravely as a partisan leader, and, many years later, when David Bruce died childless in 1371, he succeeded. As Robert II he promptly renewed the alliance with France and both he and his son, Robert III, sent Scottish troops to help the French in the Hundred Years War, which Edward III and the Black Prince had begun in the middle of the fourteenth century, and which had been dragging on ever since. Henry V was crowned King of England in 1413, and immediately concentrated all his energy upon crushing France completely.

When the Dauphin's call for help came in 1419, the twenty-five-year-old Scottish King, James I, had already spent thirteen years in the Tower of London, along with several French princes of the blood. He had been en route to France in protective exile against his uncle, the ambitious Duke of Albany, when his escort was surprised by Henry IV's men. Now Henry V, the victor of Agincourt, was his master and Scotland was ruled by the unscrupulous Robert Stuart, Duke of Albany. In spite of his devious dealings with the Burgundian court, the Regent Albany did, however, adhere to the terms of the old alliance. In October 1419, after the murder of John, Duke of Burgundy, Albany sent a force of mercenaries to the Dauphin under Sir John Stuart of Darnley and two other Stewarts, the Earls of Buchan and of Wigton. They sailed from Dumbarton in the Firth of Clyde to La Rochelle, the only port in France left unoccupied by the English.

On 24 October 1419 the three veterans rode into Bourges at the head of 6,000 men-at-arms and mounted archers, to be greeted by the Dauphin and his pathetically young captains. These were the sons of the great nobles captured or killed at Agincourt. The eldest, Philippe, Comte de Vertus, brother of Henry V's most important prisoner in England, the Duc Charles d'Orléans, was just twenty-one, while Charles de Bourbon, the Comte de Clermont, and the Duc d'Alençon were fifteen and fourteen respectively. To these young men the tall lean figure of the Scottish Constable, with his grizzled red hair and shrewd yet kindly eyes, must have seemed the father figure each one of them so sorely lacked. Thaumassière, the historian of Berry, describes their arrival in Bourges: 'In France there came to the assistance of the Dauphin, Scottish lords with a great army, the leaders of which were the Earls of Buchan and Wigton and Sir John Stuart, Constable of the Scottish Army; all of whom fought fiercely against the English as their King was held prisoner in England. And the following year, 1420, the King of England brought a great army into France[1].'

In May 1420, after the English had forced the surrender of the key town of Melun, near Paris, the humiliating treaty of Troyes was drawn up. By this document Henry V disinherited the Dauphin and at the same time married his sister, Catherine of Valois. By the terms of the treaty the heirs to this union were to be the next legitimate Kings of France.

The English King also ordered that the Scottish officers captured at Melun be brought to his presence to witness the signing of the Treaty of Troyes. Once they had been humiliated in this way, instead of their being exchanged, according to all the laws of chivalry, he commanded that they be hanged as traitors to their King James I, so as to demoralize the Scots fighting for the Dauphin under Darnley.

The situation was so desperate that the Dauphin had to send the Constable back to Scotland to raise more troops and money. During his absence the Regent Albany died, and the political unrest that followed delayed Darnley's return until the New Year of 1421. With these reinforcements he met the Dauphin at Poitiers at the end of January and learned that the French had lost their most experienced commander, Philippe de Vertus. His place had been taken by his young half-brother, Dunois, the Bastard of Orléans, who was to prove himself John Stuart's most trusted lieutenant.

There was no time to lose. Dunois's spies reported that the English were descending towards the Loire from Normandy. It was vital that the French take the offensive to stem their advance. So, as soon as the frost and fog of winter abated, a combined army of 4,000 Scottish men-at-arms and mounted archers and 2,000 French troops marched north to seek out their Anglo-Norman adversaries. Easter was early that year, and on Saturday 22 March they were attacked by a superior English force at Baugé in Anjou, about thirty-six miles north of Tours.

In this battle the English commander, the Duke of Clarence, brother and heir-apparent to Henry V, was killed. A cousin of the Scottish Constable, a fighting priest John Kirkmichael, later Bishop of Orléans, was the first to break a lance on the Duke, whom he recognized by the jewelled crown on his helmet. Clarence was then unhorsed and wounded by another Scot, who left the Earl of Buchan to finish him off with his mace. The Constable took Thomas de Beaufort, the eighteen-year old Earl of Somerset and future brother-in-law of King James, as his prisoner, exchanging him later for Arnauld de Barbazan, the heroic governor of Melun. About 2,000 English were killed and 200 noble prisoners taken for ransom in this first French victory since the disaster of Agincourt. Because it had been a surprise attack on the part of the English, the victorious Scots and French were doubly jubilant.

After the dead had been counted, the Earls of Buchan and Wigton, as highest in rank, sat down in their tent and laboriously wrote out in French a report to the Dauphin on how the day had gone:

> Most High and Mighty Prince,
>
> May it please you to know that we arrived on Friday last at the town of Baugé with the intention of attacking the English, your and our ancient enemies, on the field of La Lande Charles, and today we sent our beloved cousin, the Constable of the Scottish Army, John Stuart of Darnley and the Maréchale de La Fayette to examine the said field with several other lords where we intended fighting our enemies next Monday because Easter was too high a festival. But today our said enemies arrived before this town before sunset and as soon as we knew of it we threw ourselves upon them and, thanks be to God, the victory is ours. The Duke of Clarence and the Earl of Quint (Kent) are killed and the Earl of Sumbrecit (Somerset) is taken. Finally, all the power of your enemy's army is either taken or killed. And for this reason, most high and mighty prince, we pray you ardently that it will please you to come into Anjou so as to go forth into Normandy, for with the help of God everything is yours . . . We know nothing more to say to you at present except to pray you to let us know your intentions by this pursuivant.
>
> Written at this town of Baugé on Easter Eve at midnight.
>
> Your very humble servants, the Earls of Buchan and Wigton[2].

This crushing defeat of the English at Baugé was not only the turning point in the Hundred Years War for the French, it also forced Henry V to sign a truce with Scotland promising to release the Scottish King, now in the sixteenth year of his captivity.

In contemporary French documents it is to John Stuart, Constable of the Scottish Army, that the credit for this signal victory is given. He was rewarded in the first instance by the gift of Concressault in Berry and by the distinction of having his personal astrologer, a privilege normally reserved for princes of the blood. This 'souverain astrologue Maître Germain Thibouville', who was also a skilled physician, predicted the imminent deaths of both the mad Charles VI of France and of Henry V, both of whom obligingly disappeared from the scene within the next eighteen months. The citation mentions 'the victory of Baugé in which battle the said John Stuart conducted himself as a valiant and courageous knight, serving us with goodwill and generous spirit, both he and his said company, that we shall always be indebted to him who by the grace of God, gave us victory that day against our ancient enemies[3]'.

Then, on 26 March 1422, the Dauphin made over to 'his dear and beloved cousin, John Stuart, Seigneur of Darnlee and of Concressault', the royal château, town and seigneurie of Aubigny-sur-Nère, which he himself had inherited in 1416 from his great-uncle Jean, Duc de Berry, the greatest patron of the arts of his time, who, during his last years, commissioned the work that has immortalized his name: 'Les Très Riches Heures du Duc de Berry'.

In the letters of donation the French sovereign records the following for posterity:

> John Stuart, Seigneur of Darnley, at our prayer and request, came from Scotland and brought with him a great company of men-at-arms and archers, to put into effect the ancient alliance of the Kingdoms of France and Scotland, in our great want and necessity and because he served us well and continues to serve us day by day against the English our ancient enemies and against our rebellious subjects, showing a great love and affection for us and has engaged diligently himself and all those of his company for a space of about three years for our benefit and that of our kingdom especially at the Battle of Baugé where he showed himself to be a valiant and courageous knight . . . that he may be more inclined to remain in our service for which he left his wife, his children and other relatives and friends, we have, with the advice of those of our blood and after deliberation with our Great Council, granted, ceded and transferred for ever to this our cousin John Stuart and his heirs male descending in direct line, the town, lands, château and demesne of Aubigny-sur-Nère. Without reserving anything except the faith, homage and sovereignty due to us for the said town, lands and château of Aubigny.
>
> Given at Bourges on 26th day of March 1422 and of our reign the first[4].

Negotiations for the release of James I were still under way when Henry V died of dysentery outside Paris at the beginning of the following August. His departure from life was followed two months later by the death of Charles VI. So the nine-month old son of the dead English King, and grandson of the French King, was proclaimed King of England and France at Notre Dame.

During 1423 John Stuart's main concern was to push back the English invaders infiltrating more and more into Anjou, Poitou and Berry. In June of that year the inhabitants of Orléans thronged the streets to watch the erect figure of the Scottish Constable march through their city at the head of his troops, armed with swords, bows and guisarmes (double-edged pikes), and wearing the traditional Scottish colours of red, green and white. At the end of the march the notables of Orléans offered them a brilliant reception, serving them with Loire fish and claret. The Constable was crossing the Loire with the aim of reducing the provinces of Auxerre and Nevers to obedience, but the campaign that augured so well took a disastrous turn. On 30 July an English force led by the Earls of Salisbury and Suffolk and Lord Willoughby de Broke arrived to relieve the

Burgundians the Constable was besieging in the town of Cravant. The Spanish and Lombard mercenaries who were fighting with the Scots deserted the Constable when they saw the large English force. John Stuart rallied his men but was outnumbered. He lost an eye and was captured by a Burgundian noble. The English commander Suffolk, reporting to the English Council of Regency in Paris, estimated the French and Scottish casualties as 3,000 killed or captured. 'The flower of the enemy,' he wrote triumphantly, 'is dead or taken, first of whom is their commander, the Constable of the Scottish Army.'

Some time elapsed before the ransom money was paid by the uncrowned French King, after which he granted Sir John leave to carry out his vow and make a pilgrimage to Jerusalem. In August 1424, during his absence, the English Regent Bedford attacked the Franco-Scottish forces at Verneuil in Normandy. Bedford was as brilliant a tactician as he was a wily politician, and with a comparatively small force routed his opponents with an impressive list of enemy dead and captured. Both the Earls of Buchan and Wigton were killed, and among the French commanders the Duc d'Alençon, the Maréchal de La Fayette and the Sire de Gaucourt, all of whom had witnessed the donation of Aubigny to the Constable, were taken prisoner.

At the beginning of that year Bedford had finally selected a suitable English bride for James I, according to the conditions laid down for his release in the terms of the Scottish treaty. She was Lady Jane Beaufort, a niece of Cardinal Beaufort, son of John of Gaunt and grandson of Edward III. Though intended as a marriage of convenience, it turned out to be one of those rare things, a royal love match. James recorded for posterity in his poem *The Kingis Quair*—'suddenly my heart became her thrall forever of free will, for of menace there was no token in her sweet face'.

At the end of February 1424 the pair were married in what is now Southwark Cathedral, and, after eighteen years' imprisonment, James I returned to Scotland with his English bride. His long captivity had allowed him to develop his taste for books and music, and at thirty he was a sensitive, cultivated man determined to be wise ruler and a good husband and father to his children. The court lived at Perth, where foreign envoys were agreeably surprised by the degree of comfort and civilization they found in that northern landscape. James tried to keep on good terms with England as well as with France, and for the first years of his reign this tactful attitude worked.

By 1426, when the Scottish Constable returned from his pilgrimage, he found Charles VII in almost as desperate straits as he had been in when he first summoned the Scottish mercenaries in 1419. At sixty the Constable was the sole survivor of the commanders who had fought at

Baugé. In the spring of that year he took the remnants of his Scottish troops to join the Breton Constable Arthur de Richemont in an attempt to push the English out of Brittany. Finally, at the end of 1426, they defeated the enemy at Mont St Michel and forced them to withdraw into Normandy.

For this John Stuart was rewarded with the royal fief of Evreux in Normandy and, in February 1427, by the unprecedented honour of quartering the arms of the Stuarts of Aubigny with the royal arms of France, 'that his services may be for ever remembered he and his descendants may bear forever in their arms the escocheons of France in the first and last quarters thereof, three fleur-de-lys of gold in a field of azure[5]'.

The Stuart family was now established at Aubigny, and the Constable's daughter Jeanne married Bernard d'Armagnac, leader of the anti-Burgundian faction in France. Charles VII was anxious to renew the alliance with Scotland in a tangible fashion, and in 1428 sent Sir John Stuart to James I to arrange a marriage between his five-year-old son, the Dauphin Louis, and the four-year-old Princess Margaret Stuart. As fellow-envoys Charles sent Regnault de Chartres, the Archbishop of Reims, and the poet Alain Chartier. At the Scottish court Chartier described the old alliance as 'inscribed not upon sheepskin parchment but engraved upon the living flesh of men: written not in ink, but in blood'. The effect of the three ambassadors' visit was to make James drop the negotiations he had been considering with England, to renew the existing military alliance between France and Scotland and to discuss terms for his daughter's marriage to the heir to the French throne.

On 17 July 1428 King James formally announced his consent to the Stuart-Valois marriage and at the same time signed the renewal of the military alliance[6]. He agreed to send the princess to France the following spring with an army of 6,000 men. The most difficult question was what the French King was prepared to make in the way of a marriage settlement. The three envoys had to stay in Scotland while three Scots—Sir Patrick Ogilvy and the Bishops of Aberdeen and Lothian—were sent to Charles VII to demand the strategically important province of Saintonge, famous for its wine, and surrounding the King's only free port of La Rochelle. The bargaining was long and hard and the treaty was only ratified at Chinon at the end of October 1428[7]. By this time the English under the Earl of Salisbury had begun the siege of Orléans, to which more and more English reinforcements were being drafted. The Scottish Constable had settled his long-neglected family affairs during the summer in Scotland and was impatient to get back to the fight in France. He had to wait, however, until the return of the Scottish envoys from Chinon.

The only representation of Sir John Stuart of Darnley and d'Aubigny was painted in the sixteenth century. The quartered arms of Stuart and the House of France can be seen at the lower left.

James decided in the circumstances that he could not send his daughter as early as he had promised but he did let Sir John sail in January, taking with him all the Scottish troops he could muster for the defence of Orléans. Symphorien Guyon's history of the siege of Orléans refers to 'Sir John Stuart commanding 400 very valiant men-at-arms, being joined on 8 February by a large reinforcement led by well-equipped warriors, among them Messire William Estuart, brother of the Constable and many more knights and esquires, accompanied by about a thousand fighting men'. This contingent managed to get into the city while part of the English attacking force was in winter quarters. Two days later it was learned that the veteran of Agincourt, Sir John Fastolfe, was bringing a convoy of Lenten provisions to the besiegers from Paris. The Scottish Constable and Dunois, the Bastard of Orléans, held an emergency council of war and decided a sortie must be made to intercept it without delay. They set out from the city with about 1,000 men between them, arranging that William Stuart and Hugh Kennedy should follow them the next day.

On 12 February Sir William's detachment reached a place called Rouvray St Denis, some twenty-four miles north of Orléans, when they sighted the English convoy approaching from the direction of Etampes. As the long line of provision waggons came into view, the Comte de Clermont's troops were seen coming from the west. This was the moment for concerted action but, for some unfathomable reason, Clermont held back and did not attack. Fastolfe seized his chance and entrenched his waggons in a large square with two openings, one wide, one narrow. He planted pointed stakes in the ground and drew up his men behind them to wait for the combined attack. The Scots insisted upon attacking on foot, while the French argued for an attack on horseback. To end the dispute Sir John Stuart ordered his 400 Scots to fight on foot and led the assault. It had been agreed that only the archers should dismount. Dunois followed him on horseback with La Hire, Kennedy and William Stuart close behind him. The Scottish archers aimed for their sitting target, but as soon as Fastolfe realized that Clermont and his Auvergnat troops were hanging back, he ordered his men to surround the Scots. He gave the order 'no quarter' and, as the Comte de Clermont was seen to ride away in the direction of Blois, the Scots were set upon without mercy and cut to pieces. Dunois was wounded at the outset by an arrow in the foot, but two of his own archers helped him to remount and thereby saved his life.

Symphorien Guyon continues his account: 'In the ensuing battle, Sir John Stuart coming to the relief of his brother who was being hard pressed by the English, pulled him out of danger and, though wounded himself, made a most gallant and persevering resistance. But at length, surrounded on all sides by his enemy and covered with wounds, the old warrior sank to the ground. His brother William who had retired from the battle, seeing what was happening, flew to confront the enemy once more and was himself slain.'[8]

There was no pursuit, as the English were for the most part foot-soldiers. They had managed to keep intact most of their provisions, the greater part of which were barrels of wine and salted herrings, which gave the name of the Battle of the Herrings[9] to the fatal encounter at Rouvray St Denis.

Dunois ordered the bodies of the Scottish Constable and his brother to be given honourable burial behind the High Altar of Orléans Cathedral, where the *messe écossaise* ordered in the Constable's will was sung annually on the anniversary of the battle up till the time of the French Revolution. The ten critical years he had spent fighting for his adopted country were among the blackest in French history, and although he died at the age of sixty-four defeated in his last battle, the independence of France; for which he had striven, was, unknown to him, already in sight, with the appearance of Joan of Arc less than two months after his death.

Chroniclers of the siege of Orléans describe the Scottish Constable as the best friend France ever had, La Thaumassière saying that 'he raised the affairs of France and brought back to the French the courage to defend themselves and chase the English from their country'.[10]

The year 1429 marked the rebirth of the French monarchy and of France as a power in Europe. It also, through the French alliance, confirmed the rise of the House of Stuart across the channel during the next 200 years.

2

THE STUARTS OF AUBIGNY

On the day John Stuart was killed at the Battle of the Herrings, Joan of Arc was already on her way from Lorraine, convinced of her divine mission to save France. On 12 February 1429 she went to the Governor of Vaucouleurs in the Vosges and said to him: 'In the name of God do not tarry but send me to the Dauphin. For today our noble Dauphin has suffered a great defeat near Orléans and is in danger of greater if you send me not to him.' At her insistence the stolid Baudricourt gave her a page's dress and a good horse and sent her on her way to Chinon. When she reached the château on 6 March she found the court plunged in despair. The Dauphin, prostrate by the death of the Scottish Constable, was threatening to abandon his kingdom and talked wildly of fleeing to Scotland or to Spain.

Joan went straight up to Charles, who had refused to receive her and had disguised himself among his courtiers, knelt before him and said: 'Most noble Dauphin, I have come from God to help you and your kingdom. I come to tell you on behalf of My Lord that you are the true heir to the throne of France and the true son of the late King[1].' This was the miraculous sign for which the neurotic young man had been praying all the years his mother had taunted him with his possible illegitimacy. Psychological trick or not, it had the desired effect, and when Joan went on to ask him for men and arms and the Duc d'Alençon to lead this force with her to relieve Orléans, Charles agreed.

The first problem was how to get food into the besieged city. Each of his captains in turn told the Dauphin it was impossible to get a convoy through the English lines. Joan, however, insisted that they would take food into Orléans and not an Englishman would hinder them. Charles sent Sir Patrick Ogilvy, John Stuart's successor as Scottish Constable to escort this convoy, which passed the English fortifications and reached Orléans on 29 April. The following day Joan and her army forced an entrance into the besieged city. The effect produced by Joan on the

English was no less hypnotic than on her followers. During the following week she directed attacks on the forts that commanded the city on the river side to the south in the suburb still known as Olivet. The first of these attacks against the Fort St Loup was entirely successful. The English section commander, Talbot, was too far away to save this vital position, the loss of which proved to be a turning point in the siege. On 6 and 7 May there was bitter fighting, during which Joan was wounded in the shoulder by an arrow, and some of the English soldiers shouted out 'The witch is dead'. But when they saw that she returned to the attack without faltering, the more superstitious of the English were struck with terror, and on the evening of 7 May the entire English garrison surrendered. On 8 May the English commanders gave the order to abandon the siege, which had lasted seven months.

Later that same day, Joan, accompanied by the Bishop of Orleans, Jean St Michel—none other than John Kirkmichael, the fighting priest of Baugé—led a victory thanksgiving procession into the cathedral. Immediately behind them the blazing standards of the victorious captains filled the nave with brilliant colour as the leaders and men crowded into the great building. Dunois, D'Alençon, La Hire, Gilles de Raïs, Patrick Ogilvy, Hugh Kennedy and John Wishart knelt with Joan in front of the High Altar, close to the tomb where Sir John Stuart and his brother William lay buried. As the *Te Deum* was being sung, the English retaliated in the only way left to them by burning their forts and stores and putting up some show of resistance to the north of the city. But the victors of Orléans were unwilling to risk a pitched battle with the victors of Agincourt, and so the English were able to retire to the north of the Loire.

Having taken Orléans, Joan's next mission was to crown the Dauphin King of France at Reims. On 17 July 1429, surrounded by the Scottish archers of his bodyguard, and with Joan at his side, Charles the Dauphin was anointed and crowned as Charles VII, with one of the consecrating prelates the Scottish Bishop of Orléans. Joan's next task was to persuade the King to march on Paris to drive out the English, but the enterprise failed. From the following spring onwards things began to go badly for Joan. Charles, tricked by the Duke of Burgundy, the ally of the English Regent John of Lancaster, Duke of Bedford, lost his nerve and withdrew into Touraine. Even the Duc d'Alençon deserted her, and she found herself hard pressed, fighting on the outskirts of Paris with her diminishing band of *fidèles*, including the Scots who had fought with her at Orléans—Ogilvy and Kennedy. She made a brave last sortie to surprise an English force that had been plundering the countryside round Paris. This was her last victory. Unfortunately the greed for plunder by the victors cut off some of the French and on 24 May Joan was taken prisoner

A fifteenth century illuminated manuscript by Jean Fouquet portrays the kneeling Charles VII as one of the Magi accompanied by his armed escort of the Garde Ecossaise

at Compiègne and transferred first to Beaulieu and then Beaurevoir where she was sold to the English by the Burgundians in November.

After months of incessant questioning by the inquisitorial court at Rouen, shamefully abandoned by the King she had crowned, Joan was condemned to be burned as a relapsed heretic, 51 weeks after her capture. Six months later the young son of Henry V was crowned King Henry of France and England. The date was 16 December 1431.

By consenting to the burning of Joan of Arc, the Duke of Bedford improved English morale for a while and maintained English supremacy in France. But a notary in the English service said he returned from viewing the heap of ashes which was all that remained of the saviour of France: 'We are all lost men for a saintly woman has today perished.' That heap of ashes did not inspire Charles VII and his bickering friends to put aside their differences and make a concerted effort to expel the English. It took four years of seemingly endless sorties and parlaying for Philip, Duke of Burgundy, to finally lose patience with his English allies. A congress was called in Arras in August 1435 at which Philip urged the Duke of Bedford to come to terms with Charles and forget the Treaty of Troyes and its claims for the crown of France for Henry VI and his heirs. Bedford left the meeting in a rage; took himself to Rouen and died nine days later. His life work collapsed with his death. Charles VII reluctantly agreed to Philip's stern and humiliating demands and a provisional treaty of peace was signed. The Treaty of Arras was just as cynical as most arrangements of this sort, and the Duke of Burgundy proceeded to beseige the English in Calais at once. The small English forces performed a brilliant military feat in prolonging the struggle for eighteen years. Only at the end of that exhausting period was it tacitly understood that the two crowns would never be united.

Once the Treaty of Arras was signed, the French King decided it was time the marriage agreed between his heir and the Scottish King's eldest daughter should take place. In April 1436 a fleet of twenty French ships arrived in the Clyde estuary to escort the twelve-year-old bride to France. At Dumbarton the King of Scotland, James I, bade farewell to Margaret his frail poetic daughter, with whom he had so many tastes in common. The parting was a sad one, tinged with foreboding, although the prospect before the little princess of being the future Queen of France was a splendid one. The convoy sailed in three galleys and six barges. The English put to sea with no fewer than 180 vessels to try to intercept them, but they were so occupied in plundering Flemish and Spanish wine ships off the coast of Brittany that the bridal convoy got through safely, landing at the Ile de Ré, just off the coast at La Rochelle.

The wedding was fixed to take place at Tours on 25 June. The princess, attended by her own and French ladies-in-waiting, had spent the last few weeks at Poitiers while the necessary formalities and papal dispensations with regard to age were completed[2]. On the afternoon of 24 June she made her entry into Tours with her French and Scottish entourage, and was led by the Lord High Admiral of Scotland, the Earl of Orkney to meet her future mother-in-law, Queen Marie of Anjou. The Queen then sent for her son to come and meet his bride. He did so without much enthusiasm, followed by his own knights and squires. The Dauphin Louis was a surly suspicious youth of thirteen, devoid of the rudimentary manners expected of a courtier. He did, however, manage to rise to the occasion, and when the two children met, they put their arms round one another and kissed each other gravely.

The King arrived so late on the wedding day that he did not have time to change his grey travelling clothes. He went straight to the bride's room, where she was being dressed for the ceremony, embraced the little fair-haired girl and appeared to be delighted with his daughter-in-law[3]. In contrast to his disagreeable son, Charles VII showed tenderness and affection for her as long as she lived. At the marriage feast the Dauphine Marguerite, the Queen, her mother Yolanda of Aragon, Queen of Sicily, the Duchesse of Vendôme and the Earl of Orkney, sat at the King's table. The Dauphin Louis presided at another table, where Sir Walter Ogilvy of Angus and the other Scottish lords were the guests of honour. The marriage was not to be consummated for two years, as the bride was only twelve. In July the Dauphin was given a separate household, while his wife remained with the Queen and her ladies.

In February 1437 the Dauphine's father James I, who had sought to curb the lawlessness of the great nobles by increasing the power of the Scottish Parliament known as the Three Estates, was stabbed to death at Perth by his own kinsmen Sir Robert Stewart and Sir John Graham, descendants of Euphemia Ross, the second wife of his grandfather Robert II. This murder plunged Scotland once again into a state of confusion, as the heir, the Dauphine's only surviving brother, James II, was only six years old. The most powerful Scottish noble, the Earl of Douglas, was made Regent and promptly renewed the treaty with France, sending a force of mercenaries to help Charles VII expel the Spaniards from Languedoc. The new Constable of the Scottish army was John Stuart's son, Sir Alan Stuart of Darnley. With his help, the French King fulfilled one of the chief aims of Joan of Arc by taking Paris on 12 November 1437, entering his capital in triumph for the first time since his flight from the Burgundians in 1418. He rode into the city accompanied by the Dauphin Louis and the Dauphine Marguerite d'Ecosse.

Shortly afterwards Alan Stuart returned to Scotland but was killed in a brawl at Linlithgow. His brother Alexander inherited the Darnley estates. John, the youngest son of Sir John Stuart of Darnley, had remained in France to do homage to Charles VII and thus became the second Seigneur of Aubigny. He married a French heiress, Beatrix d'Apchier, who had grown up in the household of the Armagnac granddaughter of the old Duc de Berry. They had several daughters who married French noblemen, and one son Béraud, who carried on the Stuart military tradition in France.

When the marriage of the Scottish princess and the Dauphin was finally consummated in 1438, it was a complete fiasco. The Dauphin, the future

Louis XI, was devious and moody, with peculiar obsessions. He disliked women and treated his young wife with cruelty and neglect. In spite of the affection shown to her by the other members of the royal family, she was deeply unhappy and homesick, though Scotland, torn by internal strife, was no refuge. Like her father in his captivity, she wrote poetry, but in her case it was to solace her empty marriage. She became more and more introspective and strange in her habits; she was terrified that her husband was trying to poison her, and took to drinking vinegar instead of wine and eating green unripe apples instead of the rich dishes prepared at the court. As though his neglect were not enough, the Dauphin took a perverse delight in accusing Marguerite of entertaining poets and musicians in her apartments at unseemly hours, and of being seen kissing her father's friend, the now old and ugly Alain Chartier.

Marguerite's younger sister Isabel had a happier fate. When her fiancé, the heir to the Duc de Bretagne died before their marriage, the old Duc François promptly married her himself. The marriage of the second daughter of James I took place in November 1442 in the province of Ile-et-Vilaine, of which Dol of the Stuarts is the capital. As Duchesse Isabeau de Bretagne she became co-ruler of the Duchy, which remained independent of France until her granddaughter, the Duchesse Anne, married first Charles VIII and on his death Louis XII, and, as Queen of France brought Brittany as her dowry to the French crown. Isabel, unlike her sister the Dauphine, outlived her old husband for many years and had many lovers. She lived to see the birth of her great-granddaughter, the Princesse Claude de France, who passed on to her son, Henri II, her russet hair and long-featured sombre Stuart features. The circle was completed in the next generation by the marriage of Henri's son, the Dauphin François to the half-French, half-Scottish Mary, Queen of Scots.

By 1444, though no conclusive treaty had been signed, a truce had been agreed between France and England to allow the two countries to trade with each other after more than a century's fighting. Another nine years were to pass, however, before the French victory over the English under Talbot, the veteran of Baugé and Orléans, at Castillon-la-Bataille on the Dordogne brought the Hundred Years' War to an end in 1453.

During the truce Charles VII was faced with the problem of trying to control the mercenaries he had called in to help him fight the English. He took the bold step of giving his difficult son the task of welding these roving bands of marauders into a disciplined army for the defence of the country instead of alienating the native population. The decision proved to be a brilliant one. With all his faults of character, the Dauphin Louis had a flair for organization and for dealing with military adventurers of this sort. In 1445 the two companies of the Scots Guards and the Hundred Scottish-

Men-at-Arms were formed. They were recruited mainly from the survivors or descendants of the original men-at-arms and mounted archers brought to France in 1419 by Sir John Stuart of Darnley. Now known and registered on muster rolls each October as the Garde Ecossaise and the Cent Gens d'Armes Eccossais, these exiled Scots became the personal bodyguard of the Dauphin Louis. Their main duties apart from fighting were in connection with coronations, state entries and royal funerals.

These Scots Guards were both foot and horse soldiers. In ceremonial processions such as state entries into towns the sovereign was immediately preceded by the Hundred Men-at-Arms, while the Scots Guards rode behind, so that he was always protected by two bodyguards. The traditional colours of the company were red, white and green. A miniature by Jean Fouquet in Etienne Chevalier's *Book of Hours* depicts Charles VII kneeling before the Virgin and Child at Bethlehem surrounded by his Scots Guards wearing striped red, white and green sleeveless surcoats over their armour and red, white and green plumes on their helmets.

In August 1445 the newly formed Garde Ecossaise had the sad duty of carrying the twenty-year-old Dauphine Marguerite to her grave in the Cathedral of Châlons-sur-Marne[4]. The court had been spending the summer in Champagne, and for once the Dauphine seemed to be enjoying life, dancing in ballets and taking part in other festivities. Suddenly she collapsed and was dead within twenty-four hours. The King, who was devoted to his daughter-in-law, risked a scandal by ordering an inquest, but no trace of the poison he suspected was to be found. The Dauphin was as indifferent to her in death as he was in life, and the verdict was that the unhappy princess had died of grief. Later that year her body was moved to Touraine and buried in the Church of St Laon at Thouars before Christmas[5].

None of the ballads she is known to have written in the same style as her father have survived. The enigma of the tragic poet-princess continues to fascinate French scholars of the period, who hope one day to discover some fragments of her verse. The Duchesse Isabeau of Brittany is credited with at least two poems written in French lamenting the untimely death of her sister[6].

Their brother, the Scottish King was fourteen when the Dauphine Marguerite died, having been born, one of twin brothers, in October 1430. He was the only son of James I to survive, and grew up in an atmosphere of violence dominated throughout his youth by members of the Douglas family. These descendants of the second wife of Robert II continued to deny James II his right to the Stuart crown, and were constantly intriguing with the English against the Franco-Scottish alliance. When he attained his majority in 1448, James dealt summarily with his troublesome relations, who had signed a treaty with England during his minority, and then in 1449, to strengthen his links with the continent, he married Mary of Gueldres. Through the influence of the Stuarts of Aubigny the French alliance with Charles VII was renewed; and through his sister Isabeau, James could count on the backing of the powerful ruler of Brittany. He selected suitable husbands for his younger sisters, marrying Eleanor to Duke Sigismund of Austria and Joanna, who had been born dumb, to Lord Dalkeith, whom he created Earl of Morton to ensure some trusted male support for the Stuart Kings in Scotland. By Mary of Gueldres he had four sons. The eldest, who became James III, was born on 10 June 1451, the same day of the month as his unfortunate namesake the Jacobite James III born in 1688. Then followed Alexander, Duke of Albany; David, Earl of Moray; and John, Earl of Mar, all names which crop up again and again in the history of the Stuart family.

In the year his son and heir was born James II founded a second university in Scotland at Glasgow and introduced circuit courts of civil justice, which met twice a year at Edinburgh, Perth and Aberdeen, and although he lacked the sensitivity, the intellectual gifts and equable temper of his father, the second James Stuart did his best as a ruler. All this boded well until, in 1452, the King invited his ally, William, eighth Earl of Douglas, to dinner at Stirling Castle, under a safe-conduct. During the evening violent words were exchanged and James, having discovered the Black Douglas in a treasonable correspondence with England drew his dagger and stabbed him to death. The Douglas heirs fled for safety to England and the vast Douglas estates were confiscated by the crown.

In the following year the war between England and France ended. Rid of the Douglas menace, Scotland for the time being was at peace, but in England civil strife flared up in the Wars of the Roses. James II made a truce with the Lancastrian Henry VI and his French wife Margaret of Anjou against Edward IV of York, who was supported by the exiled Douglases. In the summer of 1460 James decided to besiege the border castle of Roxburgh, which was his by right but was held by the Yorkists. The Scottish King, born with the 'fire-mark' on his face, was curious to watch the bombardment at the closest possible range, and was killed instantly by an accidental explosion of one of his own cannons.

James III was nine years old when he became King of Scotland, and less than a year later, in 1461, Louis XI, nearing forty, succeeded Charles VII as King of France. When James was eighteen he married the Princess Margaret of Denmark, who brought him the Orkney and Shetland Islands as her dowry. Like Louis XI, with whom he renewed the military alliance, the young Scottish King, though gifted, was superstitious and morose by temperament. He relied on favourites and liked dabbling in necromancy.

He went so far as to appoint his chief astrologer Schevas as Archbishop of St Andrews. He was suspicious of his two surviving brothers, and was relieved when the Earl of Mar was found drowned in his bath, and Alexander, Duke of Albany, fled to France to marry Anne de la Tour d'Auvergne.

As Louis XI grew older, the warped and contradictory traits in his character became more pronounced. He was obsessed by imaginary plots against him and he was afraid of most of his subjects, even of his own children by his second wife, Charlotte of Savoy. He would allow no one near him in his château of Plessis-lez-Tours apart from his Scots Guards, captained by Jehan Stuart of Aubigny, a few notorious advisers and his physician, whom he paid 10,000 crowns a month, according to Philippe de Commines, the future ambassador, who acted as his secretary.

> At Plessis-lez-Tous no one was admitted but the King's domestic servants and his four hundred Scots. Round about the castle he caused a Lettice or iron gate to be set up with spikes of iron planted in the wall and crow's feet with several points placed along the Ditch. Besides which he caused four Watchhouses to be made of thick iron and full of holes out of which his Scots archers might shoot at their pleasure. These archers were very noble and cost above 200,000 francs. They were on duty night and day with orders to let fly at any man who came near[7].

During his last years Louis XI was so terrified of poison that he refused to eat, and Commines describes him as 'grown so lean and meagre that everyone who saw him pitied him. In contrast his clothes became more magnificent, and he huddled his poor, starved body in gowns of crimson lined with martens' furs and passed his time making and ruining men in order to be talked of more than his father and in order that his subjects might take notice that he was not yet dead[8]'. His Scots guarded the château in specially constructed cages, which protected every door and window, and when, after three strokes, the wretched King finally succumbed on August 1483, they buried him under the orders of their new captain, Béraud Stuart of Aubigny, in the nearby church of Notre Dame de Cléry.

Béraud Stuart was the only French Stuart grandson of the old Scottish Constable. He had grown up at his birthplace La Verrerie and, when his father died, the archives of the château record that, on 6 February 1482, Béraud Stuart was paid the sum of 1,200 livres as Captain of the King's Bodyguard[9]. Louis XI's son, Charles VIII, was a boy of twelve when he became King and he relied on the judgement and diplomacy of the Seigneur de d'Aubigny, as did his sister, the crippled Anne de Beaujeu, unloved wife of the Regent, the ambitious Duc de Bourbon. In March 1484 Béraud Stuart, then aged thirty-five, was sent to Scotland to confirm the old alliance on behalf of the French crown. Once again a Stuart played the role of father figure to a young and inexperienced French sovereign. This mission to Scotland was the first of four embassies in which Béraud was an envoy to the Scottish court. When he returned to France in September 1484, he was made Governor of the Province of Berry[10]. In the following summer Charles VIII nominated him Lieutenant-General of the 5,000 strong Franco-Scottish force that sailed to England with the Welsh usurper Henry Tudor against the Yorkist Richard III.

After the Lancastrian defeat in 1471 Henry Tudor, Earl of Richmond, had fled to seek the protection of the Duke of Brittany. On Christmas Day 1483, in the Cathedral of Rennes, he had sworn an oath to marry the Princess Elizabeth, eldest daughter of King Edward IV and so unite the red rose and the white. At the Battle of Bosworth on 27 August 1485, Henry Tudor, with his motley army of English and Welsh exiles and his French and Scottish supporters, defeated Richard of York and proclaimed himself Henry VII of England. According to Drummond of Hawthornden:

> In 1485, Henry, Earl of Richmond came with companies out of France in which that famous warrior Béraud Stuart, brother to Lord Darnley in Scotland, played a leading role and had his share in the victory of Bosworth Field which ended the bloody feud between the Houses of York and Lancaster by placing Henry VII on the throne of England. The said Earl of Richmond after he became King was ever after wonderfully attached to the Scottish nation.

Henry VII's recognition of services rendered extended to France as well as to Scotland at this period. In this unusual situation of peace with his traditional enemy the young Charles VIII turned his eyes to the growing power of Spain in Italy, but had to contend at home with the hostility of his older cousin and heir-apparent, Duc Louis d'Orléans. Béraud Stuart was ordered to suppress the incipient revolt and by 1488, after imprisoning the rebel duke in the great tower of Bourges, reconciled the cousins.

In Scotland, in this same year, a similar rebellion against James III, in which the Red Douglas, Archibald, Earl of Angus, forced the fifteen-year-old Prince James to fight against his father, ended in the King's defeat at Sauchieburn and his assasination a few hours later as he lay wounded in a nearby mill. Until he came of age three years later James IV had to submit to the will of the Red Douglas and his fellow-conspirators. James was as sensitive and intelligent as his grandfather James I, and for the rest of his life wore an iron belt as a penance for taking part in the uprising that caused his father's death. He was by far the most gifted and balanced of the early Stuart Kings. He had a flair for languages and spoke several fluently; a true man of the Renaissance, he cared deeply about literature, painting, music and architecture, and during his reign printing was introduced to Scotland. Before he visited the Western Highlands and Islands, which none of his predecessors had dared to do, he took the trouble to learn Gaelic in order to converse with the clan chiefs and the people of that wild and savage country. One of his constant companions was Pedro de Ayala, Ambassador of Ferdinand and Isabella of Spain, who commented favourably on this most civilized monarch. He liked women and had many mistresses and illegitimate children before, on Ayala's advice, he made a dynastic marriage with Margaret Tudor, the daughter of Henry VII to secure peace between England and Scotland.

Béraud Stuart was sent on a second embassy to Scotland to renew the French alliance when James IV succeeded, and when he returned to France in 1489 he brought back with him the second son of his Scottish kinsman, the Earl of Lennox. On the muster rolls of the Scots Guards for 1489 this Lennox Stuart is described as 'Guillaume Stuart, chevalier, Seigneur d'Oyzon en Berry, Capitaine de Cent Lances Ecossois'. These 100 lances represented a command of 300 men, as each lance consisted of one man-at-arms and two archers. William Stuart of Oizon, within a mile or so of La Verrerie, married a neighbouring heiress, Anne de Monypeny, whose father, Alexander de Monypeny, had bought the estates of Concressault from Béraud Stuart in 1480. William died without heirs and his brother John, who had followed him to France with the two younger Lennox Stuart brothers, Alexander and Robert, in 1493, inherited William's lands and his rank in the Scots Guards.

Unlike the Scottish Stuart Kings, Béraud Stuart seemed almost indifferent to women. Out of duty he had married twice, and by his second wife, the shrewish Anne de Maumont, he had one daughter Anne. Madame d'Aubigny was no beauty but she was well connected, descending from a natural daughter of the Duc d'Alençon, and she brought to Aubigny the rich Norman fief of Beaumont-le-Roger. To ensure the Stuart succession at Aubigny, if they produced no male heirs, Béraud got the French King's consent to betroth their daughter Anne at the age of ten to her second cousin Robert Stuart, the youngest brother of Matthew, second Earl of Lennox.

In 1493 Béraud Stuart headed an embassy to the Pope to claim the crown of the Two Sicilies for the French King, whose rival was the Spanish ruler Ferdinand of Naples. In the following year Charles invaded Italy and, after many successes in the battlefield and bedchambers in the north, made Béraud Stuart commander-in-chief of the French army for the invasion of Calabria. In the next year the French confronted the

Spaniards under their leader the Great Captain, Don Hugo Gonzalo de Cordoba. At Seminaria in June 1495 Béraud won a spectacular victory and remained to occupy the southern provinces of Italy. In spite of the fever that struck him down and resulted in long recurring bouts of malaria, 'Obegni, that Scottish man and valiant chieftain by his valour and wisdom upheld the French interest in Calabria and was renowned for governing that demi-Grecian nation with great moderation and mildness[11].' Beside his illness, Béraud had to contend with the maddening indolence of the Bourbon Duc de Montpensier, who had been appointed Viceroy of Naples by Charles VIII. Philippe de Commines, who was now French Ambassador to Venice, describes Montpensier in his memoirs as 'a good fellow but not very intelligent and so lazy that he never got up before midday'. He goes on to say that 'Aubigny, afflicted by sickness, was vexed by impatience to see that by the negligence of Montpensier, the French King's affairs became worse every day . . . . that it was a long time since the soldiers had received their pay, the money which the kingdom of Naples had yielded being already consumed[12]'.

Things grew so bad that Béraud was forced to capitulate to the Spaniards and return to France. Within three years Charles VIII had died suddenly and been succeeded by his cousin and former enemy, the Duc d'Orléans. The new King, Louis XII, an opportunist to his fingertips, promptly had his existing marriage annulled and married Charles VIII's widow, Anne de Bretagne, to keep the duchy of Brittany as part of France. By the Duchesse Anne Louis XII had two daughters, Claude and Renée de France.

Louis was even more enthusiastic than his predecessor about the war in Italy. As a grandson of Valentina Visconti, Duchess of Milan, his ambition was to annexe his maternal great-grandfather's dukedom to the French crown. As soon as Béraud had recovered from his illness, he was ordered to join Louis in an expedition to besiege Milan, which was successfully accomplished. In 1503 the Great Captain, Hugo Gonzalo de Cordoba, led a fresh army out of Sicily and Béraud Stuart was sent to Calabria again. 'The Lord Obegni had in his army the Princes of Besignone and Salerno, Malherbes with his Gascon archers and three companies of Swiss; but his principal strength consisted in his men-at-arms among whom was a wing of Scottish men who were his familiars and faithful to him.'[13] He won his first encounter with the Spaniards, but this was to be his last victory in Italy. On 21 April 1503 the reinforced Spaniards regrouped and retaliated. On the very site of his first victory at Seminaria, Béraud, with his exhausted troops, was overcome. He himself narrowly escaped with his life, the rescue of which he owed to one of his Scots Guards. But such was his reputation that the Great Captain generously allowed Béraud to return to France with his remaining troops.

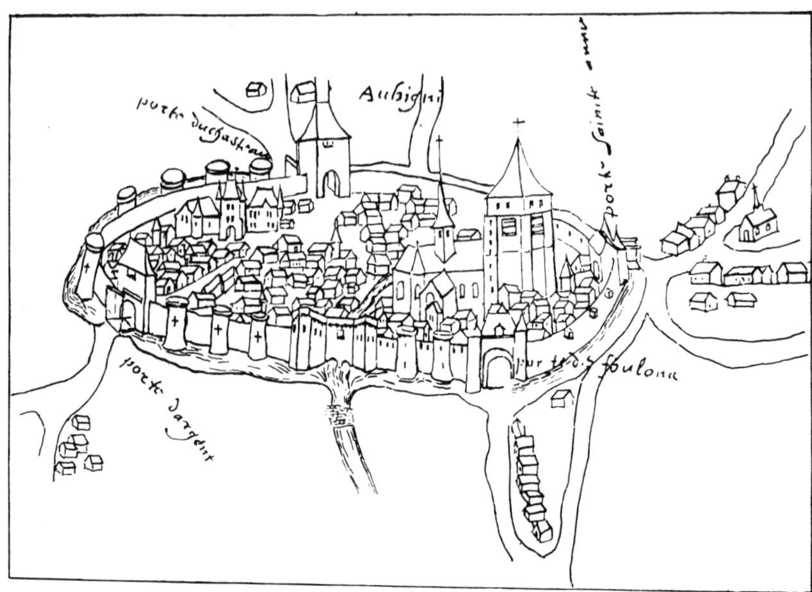

Aubigny as it appeared in the sixteenth century from a contemporary account of the town found in the Archives du Cher, Bourges.

Soon after his return he married his daughter Anne to Robert Stuart in the chapel of La Verrerie and spent the next two years writing a treatise on the conduct of war and carrying out alterations and improvements to his property at Aubigny. He was not, however, destined to enjoy his retirement for long. Ever since the marriage of James IV and the English Princess Margaret Tudor, the French King had been worried about Henry VII's political ambitions. In 1506, to counterbalance the alliance between Scotland and England resulting from this union of the thistle and the rose, Louis XII sent Béraud Stuart to renew the military alliance between France and Scotland, despite Henry VII's so-called 'treaty of perpetual peace', which was still in force. James IV was delighted to see his French kinsman again. He organized joustings and tournaments in his honour and listened avidly to his first-hand accounts of the wars in Italy and of what he had seen during his campaigns there. The Scottish King was interested in improving the buildings and gardens of his own palaces, remodelling them in the Italian style.

In his northern kingdom, James was a far-sighted European in outlook. He was in the process of building up a strong fleet captained by his two outstanding admirals, Sir Michael Wood and Sir Andrew Barton, and he was proud to tell the French King's envoy that his ship the *Great St Michael* was the mightiest warship of her day. With this fleet behind her and an able monarch, who was able to control his lowland nobles and highland chieftains, Scotland, for once, in the shifting pattern of political alliances, was not a poor relation. Béraud Stuart returned to France with satisfactory terms for Louis XII and, in the late spring of 1508 he set out once again for Scotland to ratify this treaty.

Only in his late fifties, Béraud suffered greatly from the recurrent bouts of malaria which had dogged him since the Calabrian campaign. The 600-mile journey twice in two years proved to be too much for him; he collapsed while travelling from Stirling to Edinburgh and died at the house of an old friend, Sir John Forrester, at Corstorphine before reaching the King. In his last hours on 8 June 1508 he made his will, appointing as one of his executors his son-in-law's eldest brother Matthew, second Earl of Lennox. The inventory made on the day of death describes him as Baraldi Stewart, Dominus De Albigny, Comitis de Beaumont, and shows that he died possessing £2,004 worth of plate but owing £1,850 to various creditors.[14] The Stuarts of Aubigny had so far shown no talent for amassing private fortunes, a characteristic that persisted until the last of the Stuart line.

Béraud's death before he had ratified the French alliance was a political setback for the Scottish King, who was deeply grieved by the loss of his old and valued friend. On 22 June he wrote to his cousin the French Queen informing her of Béraud Stuart's death and burial in Scotland. He recommended to her protection the two Lennox Stuart brothers then serving in France. He describes them as 'Béraud's nearest male relatives and the most worthy to succeed to his lands and offices in France'.[15]

Within six weeks Queen Anne had seen that the wishes of James IV were carried out. John Stuart of Oizon, to whom the command of the Scots Guards had been temporarily transferred during Béraud's absence in Scotland, was confirmed in his appointment. Robert Stuart, as the only son-in-law of the dead man, was declared his heir in his wife Anne's right of succession. He was named fourth Seigneur of Aubigny and, on 21 August 1508, did the customary homage for his estates to Louis XII.

Anne Stuart was now twenty and her husband thirty-three. They had been married for several years, but there was still no sign of an heir to the Aubigny estates. A papal bull granting special indulgence to the family chapel at La Verrerie is dated in the archives Christmas Day 1509,[16] but does not specify what the indulgence was for. The scant posterity left by these French fighting Stuarts, unlike their Scottish counterparts, leads one to suspect that the special relationships between them and their French benefactors had a homosexual basis. It is true that the French Kings, insecure in the midst of nobles of ambivalent loyalty, tended to trust the commanders of the Scottish mercenaries who, as foreigners, had less direct personal interest in France. This was also the case at other European courts.

But there was undoubtedly a strong attraction between the Valois and Bourbon Kings and the Aubigny Stuarts, and they continued to grant them extraordinary privileges as long as the line persisted in France.

During the year that had passed Robert Stuart had served as one of Louis XII's commanders against the Venetians. In 1510 he was storming the town of Brescia with the Chevalier de Bayard, the legendary *chevalier sans peur et sans reproche* of French history, who describes his rescue in his memoirs by his 'great companion and perfect friend, the Seigneur d'Aubigny'. In 1512 a series of military disasters for the French ended with a devastating defeat at Ravenna by the Venetians. Gaston de Foix, the French commander-in-chief, was killed, but Robert Stuart managed to retire to Brescia and hold out for the best part of a year while the Venetians besieged the city. During this time the death of his brother John brought him promotion as Captain of the Scots Guards.

By the beginning of 1513 the Venetians had forced Robert Stuart and his exhausted troops to capitulate but on honourable terms, and allowed him to return to France with his men. At this stage Louis XII's popularity had declined to zero. An English ambassador in Italy reported in February 1513 that 'the captains who have returned from Italy wish that the King were dead and that Angoulême were in his place'. Like Robert Stuart, Louis XII had no son to succeed him, and his heir was his overbearing nephew, François, Comte d'Angoulême, the husband of his elder daughter Claude de France. Angoulême was just nineteen and a devoted admirer and companion-in-arms of Robert Stuart.

During Stuart's absence in Italy a disastrous fire had swept through the town of Aubigny, destroying most of the snug well-timbered houses of the rich cloth merchants but sparing the château itself and the Priory Church of St Martin. In one way it proved a blessing in disguise, as Anne Stuart at once allowed the citizens to take all the wood they needed from the forests of Cleffy and Ivoy to rebuild the town as far as possible as a replica of the original, with the result that these well preserved, elaborately carved and decorated houses and shops give Aubigny today the aspect of the Middle Ages in microscosm.

3

THE FRENCH MARRIAGES

SINCE HIS ACCESSION IN 1509, Henry VIII, the English King, had made no secret of his hostile intentions towards France, now weakened by the failure of the Italian campaign. Within two years he had joined the Pope, Spain and Venice in what was called a Holy League, with the intention of attacking France on all sides and dismembering her. In July 1512 James IV, recalling the occupation of France a century before in the years after Agincourt and convinced that her survival was essential, finally ratified the old alliance, to show where he stood, at the same time trying to mediate between the hostile powers. By June 1513 France found herself attacked on two sides, and once again sent an urgent appeal for help to Scotland. This time James did not send troops abroad but despatched an ultimatum to Henry VIII, to which he received an insolent reply. His cousin the French Queen begged him to attack England and revenge the French defeat at the Battle of the Spurs, and sent him her ring to symbolize the French alliance. James gathered his nobles, for once united, and marched south across the border, where he met an English army at Flodden on 9 September 1513. The King fought bravely on foot, surrounded by rings of his leading nobles, but his defeat was as complete as the French defeat at Agincourt had been. Three-quarters of the Scottish nobility, 'the flowers of the Forest', fell beside their King, whose body mysteriously disappeared from the battlefield. It was the worst defeat ever suffered by the Scots fighting as allies of France, and among the dead was Matthew, second Earl of Lennox, brother of Robert Stuart of Aubigny.

Louis XII reacted to the Scottish disaster by issuing within three weeks a decree granting free naturalization to all Scots residing within his Kingdom.[1] Henceforth they were to be treated as French subjects, with the right to make wills disposing of their property as they wished, instead of it automatically reverting to the French crown (*le droit d'aubaine*). This gave them complete security in their adopted country.

The death at Flodden of one of the best and most accomplished early Stuart kings, whose reign had been characterized by the unusual loyalty of his nobles, was bad enough for Scotland, but the fact that his heir was a child less than two years old and a nephew of Henry VIII threw the country into even greater chaos. Within weeks of being proclaimed Regent the young Queen Mother, Margaret Tudor, Henry VIII's sister, had stirred up a hornet's nest and gained the distrust of the surviving Scottish nobles. She foolishly rushed into marriage with Archibald Douglas, the sixth Earl of Angus, head of the Red Douglas clan, and as such, a man hated and feared by all who were loyal to the Stuart cause.

Like his father and all the Stuart kings before him, James IV left many bastards, most of his sons receiving lands and titles and his daughters marrying powerful lords. Aside from James, Earl of Moray, a son by Janet Kennedy, there was Alexander, the dead king's favourite, who had been taught by Erasmus and afterwards made Archbishop of St Andrews, and was a son by Margaret Boyd whose daughter Katherine Stuart married James, Earl of Morton. Most notorious of all, as it was to turn out, was the red-haired Jane Stuart, whose mother was Isabel, Countess of Bothwell; as the flighty widow Lady Fleming, Jane went to France as governess to her niece Mary, Queen of Scots and upset the French court by seducing Henri II and bearing him a bastard son, Henri d'Angoulême. The only legitimate heir-presumptive to the infant King James V was John, the son of his great-uncle, Alexander, Duke of Albany, who had taken the precaution of accepting French naturalization.

These Scottish nobles of the blood royal made life impossible for Margaret Tudor and her new husband in their double role as Regent and guardian of the kingdom. The bastard Stuarts conspired with Louis XII to encourage John, Duke of Albany, to return to Scotland to oust his niece by marriage from the Regency. The plot was successful, and Albany grabbed the opportunity. He arrived just after the young King's coronation at Stirling, and with the conspirators forced the Queen Mother and Angus to flee to England to seek the protection of Henry VIII.

From this moment the politics of Scotland, France and England became more complicated than ever. With a French-speaking Regent backed by the King of France, whose interests lay in a Franco-Scottish alliance, it seemed as though the Douglas pro-English faction was doomed. Then, like a bolt from the blue, nine months after the death of his wife, Anne de Bretagne, Louis XII decided to marry again to the great annoyance of his nephew and heir-apparent François, Comte d'Angoulême. To make matters worse, the bride he chose was the Princess Mary Tudor, the youngest sister of Henry VIII. Spite rather than senility was probably the reason for this, and the whole affair had a strong element of farce about it. The reluctant bride, as silly as her elder sister, was infatuated with Charles Brandon, Duke of Suffolk, and had the bad taste to arrive in France in October 1514 escorted by her reputed lover. The wedding took place at Abbeville with Robert Stuart leading the Scots Guard of Honour at the ceremony. Less than three months later, Aubigny headed his Scots Guards once again at the bridegroom's funeral in St Denis, where Louis XII was buried in the tomb awaiting him beside Anne de Bretagne. No unwanted heir was on the way, and with scant ceremony the Tudor princess and the scandaloulsy over-attentive Suffolk were secretly married and hurriedly packed off back to England. One of the granddaughters of this marriage was the unfortunate Lady Jane Grey.

The Comte d'Angoulême to his great relief finally succeeded his father-in-law as François I on New Year's Day, 1515. He was almost the same age as Henry VIII and had the same aggressive personality. Robert Stuart of Aubigny was one of the few men he had respected and admired when they had served together in the Italian wars, and the young king celebrated his accession by making this Scottish Stuart a Maréchal de France with the privilege of being addressed as 'cousin du roi'. The King made his state entry into Paris at the end of January 1515. Before him in the procession marched twenty-four Scottish archers armed with halberds, wearing white cloth jerkins with gold borders, white hose and helmets with white plumes. According to the *Ceremonial Français* 'leading them, also on foot, was their Captain, Monseigneur d'Aubigny, accoutred in a white jewelled surcoat, adorned back and front with the new monarch's heraldic emblem, a crowned salamander of silver-gilt'. At the jousting that wound up the weeks of lavish entertainment in the capital the Venetian ambassador reported that 'the Maréchal d'Aubigny and the Duc de Bourbon were wounded by a spear and the King got a blow also'.

By the summer François I was ready to launch a new attack on Italy. At the end of August he sent an advance force under Robert Stuart and the Chevalier de Bayard to invade Lombardy. Finding all the usual Alpine passes guarded by the Swiss, d'Aubigny found some chamois-hunters to guide them over little known mountain tracks to surprise the Italian commander-in-chief, Prosper Colonna, at dinner at Villa Franca. On 13 September 1515 they joined the King and the main French army in routing the enemy at Marignano. Following this victory, the King returned to Paris for the coronation of his Queen, Claude de France, a ceremony at which the Maréchal d'Aubigny once more played a conspicuous role.

At forty-five, as one of the four Maréchaux de France, Robert Stuart of

Aubigny had reached the peak of his military career, but he had no heirs to succeed him. On Christmas Day 1516 his wife Anne Stuart died,[2] leaving no children. She was the last surviving great-grandchild of the Constable, and with her death the direct line of the first John Stuart of Darnley ended. The spectacular rise to power of the Scottish Stuarts who had linked their destiny to the royal house of France seemed to be cursed by sterility. Encouraged by his sovereign and, in the hope of refounding his own branch of the Stuarts of Aubigny, the Maréchal married again less than a year later. His second wife was a well connected young noblewoman from Auvergne, Jacqueline de la Queulle,[3] but she too failed to provide heirs.

La Verrerie in Béraud Stuart's time had been a fairly simple hunting lodge, remarkable only for its fifteenth-century chapel. But after his second marriage Robert Stuart began to live in the style he thought appropriate to his prestige as a Maréchal de France. He increased the numbers of his entourage and spent lavish sums on alterations to his property. Between 1517 and 1520, the years when François I was building his magnificent châteaux on the Loire, Robert Stuart transformed his modest *pavillon de chasse* into a noble *château de plaisance*, adding an Italianate arcaded loggia in pale rose-coloured brick, decorated with frescoes depicting the various Seigneurs of Aubigny. The loggia joins the main part of the château to a grey stone tower overlooking, on one side, the trout stream and the lake, and, on the other, the gardens. The trees and tangled briars of the surrounding forest come so close to the walls that La Verrerie seems to rise out of and blend with the green landscape like a mysterious castle in a fairytale.

Although he had defeated the Spanish Habsburgs in Italy, the growing power of Charles, the new King of Spain, made the French King anxious to strengthen his alliances across the Channel. In 1517 he considered sending Robert Stuart d'Aubigny to Scotland to further French interests there but, in the end, sent instead the French-speaking second cousin of the boy King James V—John, Duke of Albany—to renew the Franco-Scottish alliance. He then turned his attention to dealing diplomatically with his rival, Henry VIII of England, to try and obtain his support against Spain. He made the gesture of inviting his English contemporary to France to discuss the European political situation and possible mutual help against Charles, whose occupation of the Spanish Netherlands was a threat to England.

After long and elaborate preparations Henry VIII sailed across the Channel with an impressive retinue to meet the French King near Calais at the Field of the Cloth of Gold on 19 June 1520. As a pageant it was tremendous, lasting several days, each sovereign trying to outdo the other in splendour. At this ostentatiously staged encounter, Robert Stuart was ordered to muster the tallest and most imposing of his Scots Guards in their gala dress. And in the tournament, which was the highlight of the occasion, the Maréchal d'Aubigny acted as the chief judge for France. But Henry doggedly refused to be impressed and went back to England without promising François anything. The French King was furious and determined to annoy Henry through political intrigue in Scotland. In October 1520 he sent Robert Stuart[4] as a special envoy to James V, the eight-year old nephew of Henry VIII, only to recall him in 1521 when he decided the only course for France was to reopen the campaign against the Spanish Habsburgs in Italy.

When he returned to France, the Maréchal d'Aubigny brought with him his two nephews, Matthew and John Stuart, grandsons of Matthew, second Earl of Lennox, who had been killed at Flodden. These two Lennox Stuart brothers were now of age for military service and were enrolled in the Scots Guards. When their uncle the Maréchal was nominated Lieutenant-General of the French armies in Italy on 25 May 1522 they went with him to the war.[5]

Things went from bad to worse for the French after the Constable, Charles de Bourbon, a comrade-in-arms of Robert Stuart, rebelled against François I and deserted him to join the Holy Roman Emperor, Charles V. At Pavia in Lombardy in February 1525 the French were completely routed, and had the humiliation of seeing their King captured and taken as a prisoner to Madrid, where he was held until he agreed to send for his two elder sons as hostages to replace him. Henri, the younger of the two, was seven years old at this time and bitterly resented this shameful bargain. The four impressionable years he spent as a prisoner in Spain left an indelible mark on his character, which was always moody and withdrawn, and he never forgave his father, whom he eventually succeeded as Henri II.

Once back in France, François I went back on his word and broke the terms of his release. He allied himself with Pope Clement VII and once more invaded Italy, where he fought a losing campaign for the next three years. Queen Claude had died in 1524 and in 1529 after the Treaty of Cambrai was signed, François blatantly sought peace with the Emperor Charles by marrying his sister, the Spanish Princess Eleanor. This second marriage of convenience secured the release of his sons. The young Prince Henri, who returned from his captivity to find his father had remarried, was deeply unhappy but consoled himself with his passion for hunting, which, with masques and fêtes, was the main diversion of his father's court. François had decided to emulate the Italian princes and, forgetting war for the time being, become a patron of the arts. He added to the existing château at Fontainebleau and beautified it with the work of the Italian artists Primaticcio, Il Rosso and Benevenuto Cellini. He let the Florentine painters and sculptors he employed run riot in the decoration of sumptuous galleries, ballrooms and gardens at his favourite château deep in the forest. He also rebuilt, with less happy results, the old fortress château of St Germain-en-Laye.

After seven years, however, envy and hunger for power drove the restless King to look for trouble again in attacking his brother-in-law Charles. Headed by their King, the French army was forced to march once again into Savoy and Piedmont. The Spaniards in revenge invaded the southern French provinces of Languedoc and Provence, and John Stuart, as captain of the French royal archers, and his brother Matthew, fourth Earl of Lennox, were sent in January 1536 under the command of their uncle the Maréchal to deal with the Spanish invaders. At the end of that year with the Maréchal d'Aubigny they were summoned back to Paris for the marriage of their kinsman King James V of Scotland to the French King's elder daughter, the Princesse Madeleine.

The Scottish King was twenty-four when he married but he already had fathered numerous bastard children. Chief among them, by his favourite mistress Margaret Erskine, the wife of Sir Robert Douglas of Lochleven, was James, later Earl of Moray. Ever since he had taken the government of Scotland into his own hands in 1528, the King, who resembled his father in looks, with his red hair and penetrating grey eyes, but not at all in mental ability, had no lack of offers of royal or wealthy brides. Henry VIII had proposed his daughter Mary Tudor; the Emperor his sister Marie the ex-Queen of Hungary, Isabeau d'Albret of Navarre; and even the Pope his immensely rich niece Cathérine de Médicis. All these proposals were hindered by the illicit liaisons in which the King was entangled in Scotland.

However, the French alliance was the most important one for Scotland, and so, by the revised Treaty of Rouen, it was agreed that the handsome Stuart King should marry Madeleine of France. Typically, François I tried to avoid direct offence to Henry VIII by substituting the younger Princesse Marie de Bourbon for the elder. But James set out for France himself and, being very romantically inclined, fell instantly in love with the sixteen-year-old Princesse Madeleine and refused to be fobbed off. The wedding took place on New Year's Day, 1537, in Notre Dame, on the twenty-second anniversary of the French King's accession. The Maréchal d'Aubigny was resplendent at the head of his Scots Guards and the Lennox Stuart brothers, appointed to wait upon the Scottish King at his lodgings in the Hôtel de Cluny, were granted French nationality by François I. At the same time, in order to secure the Stuart succession at Aubigny, the French King allowed the childless Maréchal to adopt the younger brother John as his heir.

In February 1537 James took his frail French Queen back to the bleak climate of Scotland. He had instructed one of his male favourites, Sir James Hamilton of Finnart, a talented architect who had studied in France, to redecorate the Palace of Linlithgow in the contemporary manner to make his young bride feel more at home in that sad, grey landscape. But in spite of costly tapestries to line the walls and the great fires kept blazing in the elaborate fireplaces, the wind and rain of Scotland proved too much for the delicate princess. The dampness settled in her lungs and she died less than six months later.

James was at first inconsolable, but he had loved before and was ready to love again. Besides, the unruly behaviour of his Scottish blood relations, drawn to the side of the pro-English Reformers in order to get their hands on the rich Church lands, made it essential to maintain the alliance with Catholic France. James V lacked his father's magnetism to attract the loyalty and devotion of his nobles, so, to counter the claims of his father's and his own illegitimate offspring, a legitimate heir by a French princess was needed without delay. He sent envoys to France with instructions to find a pleasing young woman of suitable rank and known fertility, capable of bearing healthy sons.

This reduced the envoys' possibilities considerably, but by Christmas of the following year they had selected twenty-three-year old Marie de Guise-Lorraine, the tall striking auburn-haired widow of the Duc de Longueville, by whom she had had a three-year-old son, François. The young widow was of the blood royal. She was the daughter of Duc Claude de Guise and his Duchesse, Antoinette de Bourbon. Marie's eldest brother, Duc François de Guise, was married to Anne d'Este, Duchess of Ferrara,[6] granddaughter of Louis XII of France. Her pedigree and ability to produce sons made her eminently suitable to become the Scottish King's second wife. This marriage infuriated Henry VIII, a recent widower after the death of Jane Seymour, who was himself considering Marie de Guise as his next bride for the very same reasons.

James did not bother to make a second journey to France. The marriage ceremony, which was celebrated by proxy in Notre Dame in May 1539, was so disturbed by scuffles between members of the new reformed religion and the Catholics that François I was obliged to reprimand the Maréchal d'Aubigny for indiscipline in his company.[7] The new Queen was escorted to Calais by her father and her two elder brothers, the Ducs Claude and François de Guise, and Charles, Cardinal of Lorraine. She was met on arrival in Fife by James and married officially on 9 June in the cathedral at St Andrews.

In May 1540 there were rejoicings in Edinburgh and Paris when Mary of Guise gave birth to an heir, Prince James. When she was known to be pregnant the following year, it seemed as though the French alliance was firm at last. But the next boy was still-born and three weeks later the heir Prince James died of measles. By Easter 1542, however, she was again pregnant and Catholic hopes in Scotland rose once more.

At Aubigny, early in that same year, to consolidate the Stuart inheritance, John, the adopted son of the Maréchal, married the half-sister and adopted daughter of the Maréchal's wife. The Stuart fortunes were badly in need of replenishment, as their lavish expenditure at court and the vast numbers of retainers they kept in their household—at one time they had a staff of more than fifty servants at La Verrerie alone—had eaten up their revenue. Anne de la Queulle was an heiress in her own right, which was useful.[8] The Maréchal and his wife were both in their seventies and ailing, so this marriage of convenience was rushed through. It came just in time, as they both died the following year, but not before they had seen the birth of a son Esmé at La Verrerie in November 1542 and John Stuart appointed Governor of Avignon. Like his brother Matthew, Earl of Lennox, John Stuart of Aubigny was a devious character who seldom let an opportunity for self-advancement pass him by. In 1543 he made himself highly unpopular in Aubigny by denouncing Pierre Bompain, a draper's assistant who was also a Protestant lay preacher, to the royal authorities. There was an outcry when the Seigneur of Aubigny delivered the unfortunate man to be tried and burnt as a heretic in Paris. For two years John Stuart, with his sinecure as Governor of Avignon, remained out of the way in the Papal city with his wife and infant son until ironically enough, he himself became a victim of royal persecution.

In Scotland on 8 December 1542 Mary of Guise had given birth not to the hoped-for son but to a daughter, Mary Stuart. When the news was brought to James V at Falkland Palace he was in a state of nervous prostration after the humiliating defeat of the troops under his incompetent favourite Oliver Sinclair at Solway Moss. The ailing King turned his face to the wall and died six days later at the age of thirty, a weak pessimistic man, worn out by amorous excesses.

The accession of the infant Queen on 14 December plunged Scotland once again into a vicious struggle between the pro-French Catholics and the pro-English Protestants. The leading rivals for the Regency were the families of Hamilton and Lennox-Stuart, both related to the Queen and claimants to the throne if the baby girl should die. With the backing of François I, Matthew, fourth Earl of Lennox, left France at once for Scotland to put forward his claim to act as Regent for the young Queen. He was also ambitious enough to think he might marry the widowed Mary of Guise, who was only twenty-six.

His rival for the position was James Hamilton, Earl of Arran, strongly supported by Henry VIII, who saw the simplest way of annexing the crown of Scotland in the marriage of the Queen of Scots and his heir Prince Edward. This he felt he could count on Arran to arrange. Arran, with the grudging support of the constantly bickering Scots nobles, became co-Regent with the Queen Mother. In the summer of 1543 he signed the Treaty of Greenwich with Henry VIII, promising Mary, Queen of Scots to the future Edward VI of England.

François I could not contain his rage when he heard the news and immediately despatched French ships and money to Mary of Guise as well as her ecclesiastical adviser, the French-speaking Cardinal David Beaton, former principal of the Scots College in Paris. Saying they feared an abduction by the English, who had sent warships to anchor in the Firth of Forth, the Cardinal, aided and abetted by Lennox, Huntly, Argyll and Bothwell, took the seven-month-old Queen from her birthplace, the easily accessible Palace of Linlithgow, to the stronghold of Stirling Castle. Towering on its rock, dominating the highlands to the north and the lowlands to the south and the strategically important Firth of Clyde, Stirling Castle was, at this time, the most impregnable fortress in Scotland. It also happened to be part of the dowry of Mary of Guise.

The Earl of Arran, head of the Protestant party, was a vacillating irrational character whose motives were complicated by the fact that he was pathetically enamoured of the strong-minded Queen Mother. Once Mary was installed at Stirling, Arran weakly gave into the *fait accompli*, changed sides and abjured his Protestant faith. He did so on 8 September 1543 and the next day, ominously the anniversary of her grandfather's heroic death at Flodden, the nine-month-old Queen was crowned in the Chapel Royal at Stirling Castle, in the presence of the chief officers of state, who were the rivals James Hamilton, Earl of Arran, Matthew, Earl of Lennox, the Earl of Huntly, the Earl of Argyll and the Earl of Bothwell, Lord High Admiral of Scotland.

As soon as Mary had been crowned, the French King asked for a renewal of the treaty of alliance, binding Scotland firmly to France and renouncing the Treaty of Greenwich. On 24 October this new treaty was signed by Mary of Guise on behalf of her daughter, by the besotted Regent Arran, by Matthew, Earl of Lennox and by Cardinal Beaton. In December this alliance was ratified by the Scottish Parliament at Edinburgh and sealed with the royal arms of the infant Queen. On this date Mary, Queen of Scots was one year and one week old.[9]

Matthew, Earl of Lennox, was a bitterly disappointed man. In spite of all he had done to bring about the vital French alliance, he seemed no nearer ousting Arran, the rival he disliked and despised, from the co-Regency. This filled him with so much rancour that, with no apparent scruples, he decided to change his allegiance and enter into secret correspondence with

Henry VIII. He had not long to wait for an encouraging response. The English King was obsessed with the business of profitable marriages and getting heirs. He went straight to the point by making the bachelor Earl the offer of a semi-royal marriage that would bring him within the English, as well as the Scottish, succession. The bride Henry offered Lennox was his own niece, Lady Margaret Douglas, daughter of Queen Margaret Tudor by her second husband, the Red Douglas, Archibald, Earl of Angus. France was a long way off, England was conveniently close. The bait was too tempting for anyone as ambitious as Lennox not to swallow. He accepted, and when the formalities of the marriage contract had been completed, he found himself irrevocably on the English payroll, committed to do all he could to hand over Mary Stuart to Henry VIII. In return, Henry promised him the Regency of Scotland once the English had successfully subjugated that country with Lennox's help. Lennox's *volte-face* caused consternation in Scotland and outraged fury on the part of his former patron François I.

When the traitor Earl left for his English marriage in June 1544, he was formally banished and his estates in Scotland confiscated. In France, frustrated by being unable to lay hands on Lennox himself, the King seized his unfortunate brother, John Stuart of Aubigny, and on 8 August 1544 had him imprisoned in the Bastille and ordered his property to be sequestrated.[10] John Stuart remained a prisoner for nearly three years until the death of François I, but his estates were not, after all,confiscated. The King, however, ordered inventories to be drawn up of the contents of the châteaux of Aubigny and La Verrerie by François de l'Aubespine, the Governor of Berry, 'the Sieur of Aubigny having been arrested and imprisoned in the Bastille'.[11] His wife and their only son Esmé, who was only a few weeks older than Mary, Queen of Scots, were allowed to stay on unmolested at La Verrerie. For the next three years, until the deaths of the French and English Kings in 1547, there was no communication between the Lennox Stuart brothers.

While John Stuart of Aubigny languished in the Bastille, his elder brother Matthew enjoyed enviable popularity at the English court. In 1546 his wife Margaret, Countess of Lennox, gave birth to Henry Stuart, Lord Darnley, and a few years later to a second son, Charles. Nineteen years later, by contriving the marriage of his son Lord Darnley to the widowed Mary, Queen of Scots, Matthew, Earl of Lennox became grandfather of James VI of Scotland, who, at the beginning of the seventeenth century would become the first sovereign of England, Scotland and Ireland. During his grandson's minority, while his unhappy daughter-in-law dragged out her life as a prisoner in England, Lennox at last achieved his own ambition of becoming for a brief period Regent of Scotland.

April 1547 saw the end of John Stuart of Aubigny's captivity. The new

King of France, Henri II, who had despised his father ever since he had been sent as a hostage in his place to Spain twenty years before, released the Seigneur of Aubigny from the Bastille, restored him to favour at the French court and reinstated him as captain of the royal bodyguard. The grateful favourite, no less ambitious than his brother, responded by doing all he could to arrange the betrothal of the five-year-old Scottish Queen to Henri's three-year-old son, the Dauphin François.

After the preliminaries had been set in motion between the French King and the Scottish Regents, Mary of Guise and Arran (Cardinal Beaton had met a grisly death at the hands of the Protestants the year before), a mission was despatched to France to conclude the match. In England the Protector Somerset, uncle of the nine-year-old Edward VI, reacted to the proposed French marriage by invading Scotland in September 1547 and routing the Scots at the Battle of Pinkie Cleugh. The English troops followed up their victory by putting the countryside to the south of Edinburgh to fire and sword.

Arran in a typical fit of panic appealed for help to Henri II. For safety he sent the young Queen first to the island of Inchmahone in the Lake of Menteith, then to Stirling and finally to Dumbarton. By the New Year the first French troops had landed in Scotland, and in January 1548 Arran signed a formal promise to the French King to obtain the Scottish Parliament's immediate consent to the Queen's marriage to the Dauphin and to send her to France as soon as possible. He also agreed that all the Scottish key fortresses should be garrisoned by French troops. For this Arran was awarded the duchy of Châtellerault in Touraine in February 1548.

By June 1548 the main body of 6,000 French troops under the command of Montalembert, the Sieur d'Essé, had landed in Scotland and occupied the specified strongholds, and preparations began for the Queen's voyage to France. The French ambassador, Louis de Brezé, stepson of Henri II's glamorous mistress Diane de Poitiers, and others, wrote glowing description of the future Dauphine. Henri II was so impressed that he sent his own royal galley to fetch the young Queen. The escorting French fleet sailed up the Firth of Clyde to Dumbarton Rock in July.

To part with her only child and to stay behind in a hostile land was a cruel wrench for the Queen Dowager. At the beginning of August she watched her five-and-a-half-year-old daughter board the French royal galley, followed by her nearest relatives, a troop of illegitimate Stuarts. These were headed by her half-brother, the dour Lord James Stuart, and by the Lords Robert and John Stuart, illegitimate sons of her grandfather James IV. Mary's governess was another of them, the middle-aged widow Lady Fleming, whose husband had been killed at Pinkie, who was born Jane

Stuart, the daughter of King James IV by the Countess of Bothwell. We have already mentioned Jane, who was no beauty by conventional standards, being small and red-haired with coarse features, but she was so vivacious and amusing that she nearly always succeeded in getting her own way. She was the mother of Mary Fleming, one of the four girls, all named Mary, who were the Queen's inseparable companions from her earliest childhood.

The stormy voyage through the Irish Sea lasted just over a week, and on 13 August 1548 the royal party disembarked at the little port of Roscoff, near Morlaix, on the northern tip of the Breton coast.

4

MARY STUART, QUEEN OF FRANCE AND SCOTLAND

MARY STUART, anointed Queen of Scotland and future Queen of France, had scarcely been a day on French soil when her official escort, Louis de Brezé, was recalled to join the King in Flanders. He handed his royal charge over to the Duchesse Antoinette de Guise, who had travelled to Brittany to welcome her Scottish granddaughter, whom she was meeting for the first time. The two took to one another at once.

The Vicomte de Rohan, representing the noblest family in Brittany and related by blood to the Stuarts,[1] was there to greet Mary and to arrange for her to spend some time at the Dominican convent at Morlaix to recover from the strain of the voyage. Towards the end of the month the little Queen of Scots, the Duchesse de Guise and their retainers set off slowly through Brittany, Anjou and Touraine to join the French court.

The French royal family, as passionate about hunting as the Stuarts, always spent the autumn either at Fontainebleau or St Germain-en-Laye. This year King Henri had decided on St Germain, where the forest still comes almost up to the castle walls. In those days it was vast, with magnificent oaks and chestnuts, lakes and mossy rides where game of every sort abounded. The royal forest stretched for miles as far as the outskirts of Paris.

The château itself was, as now, an ugly top-heavy octagonal building in red brick which François I had remodelled on Renaissance lines over the foundations of the medieval donjon, with its moat, drawbridge and chapel which dated from the time of Saint Louis. He had made a feature of the roof, whose terraces were reminiscent of his château of Chambord on the Loire, and whose elaborate chimneys were ornamented with the King's monogram in the Italian style. From these roof-top terraces the courtier had a splendid choice of views at all times of the day: the surrounding forest, the gardens of the château sloping down to the River Seine, and in the distance the roofs and spires of Paris. The château of St

Germain-en-Laye is associated more than any other with the royal Stuarts in France. It was to be Mary's home for the next thirteen years, the only happy years of her life.

When Mary reached St Germain at the end of October, she was received by her intimidating future mother-in-law, Cathérine de Médicis. Henri II's rich Florentine wife, niece of the Pope, was a complex figure, very conscious of her lack of charm and physical attraction. Fifteen years after her marriage, she was as squat as a toad with thick lips and dark protruding eyes in a pasty face. There was nothing lack-lustre about those eyes, and although she had accepted the humiliation of acting, at this stage, a secondary role to her husband's recognized mistress, the beautiful and accomplished Diane de Poitiers, Cathérine knew time was on her side and played a waiting game.

Diane de Poitiers was nearly fifty when Mary Stuart arrived in France, and although nearly twenty years older than her royal lover, she was everything the neglected Queen was not. She was tall and slender with the energy and grace of a young girl. This, and her fabulously fair complexion and unlined face, she owed to her spartan regime of daily cold baths and her passion for an outdoor life. Henri II commissioned the Italian painters and sculptors who had come to Fontainebleau during his father's reign to immortalize his adored mistress as Diana of the chase, and her shapely red-gold head set on a slender neck and tall longlimbed figure appears in countless paintings of the period. Diane, known officially as the Duchesse de Valentinois, had become Henri II's mistress after the death of her elderly husband, the Sieur de Brezé, Sénéchal of Normandy, for whom she continued to wear black and white mourning—colours most becoming to her—for the rest of her life. She had been Henri's mistress for twelve years but, although she had two grown-up daughters by de Brezé, she had never had any children by the King. During the summer of 1548 Diane's daughters had both made advantageous marriages: Françoise de Brezé to the Duc de Bouillon, and Louise to Mary Stuart's cousin, the youngest son of the Duc de Guise.

Diane de Poitiers was born at the turn of the century, and her whole personality embodied the spirit of the Renaissance, with its liberation of thought and taste and its glorification of the naked human body. Her approach to life was open and joyous, and complemented that of the sombre introspective Henri II, who was shy with women and felt ill at ease in the company of the brittle court beauties who blossomed and faded while the seemingly immortal Diana reigned supreme, untouched by time.

At the beginning of November the King came back from the campaign in Flanders to spend the winter at St Germain with his family.

His eldest son, the Dauphin François, was five years old, delicate, backward for his age and deliberately spoilt by his doting mother.

An instant warmth sprang up between the undemonstrative Henri II and the little Scottish Queen. He liked her dignity and sureness of expressing herself, although her French still had the trace of a foreign accent. Mary had never known her own father, but she had seen portraits of James V at thirty which showed him to have the same melancholy look in his dark eyes as Henri, who in no way resembled the sly and arrogant François I.

Henri found her extremely well educated for her age, and the gravity of her conversation and demeanour delighted him. He ordered Diane de Poitiers to take charge of her from now on. As her protegée Mary modelled herself on Diane. She had the same quickness of mind and absorbed her taste in art, music and literature besides sharing her love of outdoor sports. Within a very short space of time Diane had packed off the four Scottish Marys to a convent at Poissy, ostensibly for them to learn French, but rather to ensure that Mary, as future Queen of France, should speak nothing but the purest French of the court. Soon the friendship between Mary Stuart and the King, fostered by Diane, to Cathérine de Médicis's great chagrin, had developed into a touching *amitié amoureuse* between the two sovereigns of such disparate ages. Mary charmed Henri II much as another Princess with Stuart blood—Marie-Adelaïde of Savoy—enchanted the blasé Louis XIV a century and a half later in the stiff atmosphere of Versailles.

The King was a strict observer of protocol and never forgot Mary Stuart was an anointed Queen in her own right, and ordered that the future Dauphine should always be given precedence over his own children. This sense of being set apart even from her closest friends left its mark on Mary. On the positive side it helped to give her an unusually happy childhood. As an outsider of royal birth she asserted her natural independence of spirit to withstand the domineering coddling of Cathérine de Médicis, which wrought so much havoc in the personalities of the Valois family. Diane de Poitiers' energy and good sense supported her in this, though, unfortunately for Mary in later life, she could not let her head rule her heart as Diane had always done so successfully.

For the seven years after Mary's arrival at the French court Henri II was occupied with war and Cathérine de Médicis with an almost non-stop succession of pregnancies. Diane de Poitiers and Mary's Guise uncles, Duc François de Guise and Charles de Guise, the Cardinal of Lorraine, supervised her education. The tutors they selected were all distinguished scholars, philosophers, mathematicians and poets, who found the Scottish Queen an apt and precocious pupil. She had a facility for languages and music, and wrote verse in French and Latin.

By 1550 France was suffering not only from the long drawn out war against Charles V but from the first violent outbreaks of the wars of religion, which were to tear the country apart for the remainder of the century. Protestant fanatics plotted the assassination of leading Catholics, and among the intended victims was the young Queen of Scots. A Scots guardsman, ironically enough named Stuart, planned to poison her, but the plot was discovered and Stuart fled to England. From there he was sent back to be tried and executed at Angers.

During that spring, when she was eight years old, Mary went from St Germain to the exquisite château of Anet on the river Euse south-west of Paris, which Diane de Poitiers had been building during the last three years. No expense had been spared by the King to make this château as elegant and beautiful as the mistress for whom it was designed. Philibert Delorme was the architect. The light and lofty rooms looked out over the river, with its dream-like willow trees, and Diane's emblem of the crescent moon decorated the house, the courtyard and the entrance gateway. A three-quarter length portrait of Henri II hung over the chimney-piece in the *salle des gardes*. The whole atmosphere was gay and intimate, in contrast to the gloomy formality of the official palaces where Cathérine de Médicis held sway.

Diane loved being in the open air, and at Anet Mary Stuart and the other royal children were allowed to run wild and play as they pleased while the adored mistress entertained her grave and adoring lover. It was an idyllic existence, but one that was nearly wrecked for a few tempestuous months when the usually diffident and loyal Henri was swept off his feet by the flirtatious Lady Fleming, Mary's Scottish governess. Diane was past fifty but was still as slender as a girl, with a cool grace that up till then had frozen out any younger rivals. Lady Fleming, or Flamin as she is identified on Clouet's crayon portrait, was small and coarse featured, and never stopped talking loudly in almost incomprehensible French. Why she should ever have been chosen as the Queen's governess is a mystery, apart from the fact that she was a bastard daughter of James IV.

She did, however, succeed in captivating the French King by her outrageous self-assurance and for a time he had eyes for no one else. The widowed Lady Fleming was in her late forties, so it was to everyone's astonishment when in her bold manner she announced: 'Dieu merci! Je suis enceinte du Roy, dont je me sens honorée et heureuse!' She was only too visibly pregnant, which infuriated both the French Queen, who was in the same state, and Diane de Poitiers, who had never borne her royal lover a child. During these painful months the recognized mistress kept a sense of proportion about the whole affair, although it was obvious she was deeply hurt and shocked. Once Lady Fleming had been delivered of a bouncing red-haired son, Diane and Cathérine de Médicis, for once united, saw to it that the insufferable governess was sent back to Scotland immediately.

The half-Scottish royal bastard, grandson of James IV and of François I, was christened Henri d'Angoulême and was brought up with the other members of the Valois brood. From his earliest days this cuckoo in the nest of Cathérine de Médicis weaklings was an irresistible *force de la nature*. He grew as tall as his mother had been tiny and as energetic as his father was reserved. His portrait at Versailles[2] shows him as a wild handsome young man, who became the boon companion of Mary Stuart's dashing red-haired cousin Duc Henri de Guise. Henri d'Angoulême became Governor of Provence, Grand Prior of the Chevaliers de Malte and Admiral of the French fleet in the Levant. His agility as a dancer made him popular at the frivolous court of his half-brother, the last Valois King, Henri III, and his accomplishment in this art he no doubt inherited from his maternal ancestors.

The scandal of the Scottish countess soon died down as Cathérine de Médicis kept on producing more and more Valois sons—the future Charles IX and later Henri III and, finally, in 1554, François, Duc d'Alençon, who was later to be considered as a possible bridegroom for the elderly Elizabeth I of England.

After his lapse from grace with Lady Fleming, the chastened King went back to the less traumatic business of fighting the Emperor, accompanied by Duc François de Guise and by the Captain of the Scots Guards. During the Seigneur d'Aubigny's absence at the wars, his only child, the beautiful capricious Esmé, narrowly escaped drowning in the lake at La Verrerie. The gardener who found him struggling in the water with a broken arm was generously provided for by the grateful mother, who also gave a window to the church at Aubigny to commemorate her son's rescue.

In 1552 Charles V massed all his troops for an all-out attack on the key fortress town of Metz, in Lorraine, the Guise home territory. The heroic resistance of Duc François de Guise finally forced the Spaniards to withdraw. This defeat deeply affected the ageing emperor, who remarked: 'I see now that fortune, like all women, prefers a young King to an old Emperor'. He vowed that within three years he would become a monk. In that time he devolved his responsibilities on others and in 1556 formally abdicated as Emperor. François de Guise was acclaimed as the saviour of France, and the power and prestige of his family soared even higher. After their greatest rival for the power behind the throne, the

Mary Stuart, Queen of Scots, Dauphine de France in 1557 as portrayed by one of the Clouet brothers.

Constable Anne de Montmorency, was defeated and taken prisoner by the Spaniards at St Quentin in 1557, François de Guise was sent to recapture Calais from the English. He succeeded, ending a foreign occupation that had lasted for 210 years, and was acclaimed once again as a national hero.

His niece Mary Stuart was now fifteen, and the charmed years of her childhood and adolescence were passing. The sense of uniqueness with which she had grown up now had its darker side. She became aware of the personal isolation of her position, because of her birth and destiny, which was to remain with her for the rest of her life. By her mid-teens she had outgrown in a physical as well as a spiritual sense the other beauties of the Valois court. She had the unusual height of the Guise family, the reddish-gold hair, amber eyes and creamy delicate skin. She had the fashionable small head poised on a long graceful neck, and the long slender limbs made so desirable by Diane de Poitiers. Like Diane, she too excelled in dancing and was a marvel of lightness, eclipsing all the other ladies of the court. She was Queen already of her distant homeland, and the promised bride of the heir to the throne of France. The only shadows on this brilliant future were the character and appearance of her husband to-be and the jealousy of her future mother-in-law. The Dauphin François was only a little more than a year younger than Mary but he was a poor sickly creature, a child in comparison with this accomplished, sophisticated, very much admired and beautiful young woman.

However, for reasons of state she had no choice in the matter. To forestall English revenge for the loss of Calais, Henri II needed to ensure the backing of his Scottish allies, so, as far as he was concerned, the sooner Mary and his son were married the better. He lost no time in asking for Scottish Commissioners to be sent to France to formalize the marriage contract between their Queen and the Dauphin. In February 1557 Mary of Guise authorized her mother, the Duchesse Antoinette de Guise, to act as her proxy.

At Fontainebleau, on 16 March 1557, Mary Stuart then aged fifteen years and three months old signed her assent to her marriage.[3] In April, still at Fontainebleau, she signed an additional clause agreeing to hand over Scotland to her husband, the King of France, should she die without heirs.[4] This secret agreement to hand over her kingdom to a foreigner, even though he was an ally, caused an outcry in Scotland. The Protestant nobles and clergy found these terms humiliating and unacceptable. The negotiations dragged on until December, when finally, on the anniversary of Mary's accession, the Scottish Parliament reluctantly gave its consent to the marriage. A mixed Commission of Catholic and Protestant nobles and prelates was set up and sailed to France while waiting for the dispensation from Rome to allow the marriage of fourth cousins.

The dispensation was received at Moret-sur-Loing on 9 April 1558,[5] and the formal marriage contract signed in Paris on 19 April at the Palace of the Louvre. Two separate contracts were in fact signed, and they can still be seen in the French National Archives. The first official contract contains terms satisfactory to all the Scottish witnesses, Catholic and Protestant alike. In large bold handwriting the autograph signatures of Henri and Cathérine of France head the list, followed by those of François and Mary, Antoinette de Bourbon, James Beaton (Archbishop of Glasgow and official Scottish ambassador to France), Lords Seton and Fleming (the legitimate son of Henri's Scottish mistress Lady Fleming), and the Bishop of Orkney, all of whom were Catholics. Signing for the Protestant lords were Lord James Stuart the Queen's elder illegitimate brother, the Earl of Cassilis and John Erskine of Dun. As part of her marriage jointure Mary was to receive the duchy of Touraine.

This contract stipulated that as Mary's consort, the Dauphin should assume the title of King of Scotland and that, on his accession to the French throne, the two kingdoms should be united under one crown. Dual nationality was to be granted to the inhabitants of both countries. Henri II further requested that the crown of Scotland should be sent to France for the coronation of his son. The Scottish Parliament deliberated for some time before agreeing to these last two clauses.

At the same time the second secret treaty customary in Renaissance diplomacy was signed, and to this treaty members of the Guise family and the Catholic Scottish Commissioners only were party. Three secret deeds were signed by Mary promising that, in the case of her death without children, her rights to the throne of England were to pass to the French King. The second deed stated that Scotland was to become a province of France until such time as all the money spent by France in her defence was paid off. Thirdly, Mary pledged herself to renounce any agreement her Scottish Parliament might try to force upon her at variance with the two preceding clauses.

Once all these formalities were completed, the betrothal took place at the Louvre and, less than a week later, on Sunday 24 April, the royal marriage took place at Notre Dame. The preliminaries, which were enacted in front of the cathedral, were dominated by the presence of François, Duc de Guise, at the head of the vast procession. He was followed on to the porch and into the nave of the cathedral by the Bishop of Paris, red and yellow clad musicians heralding the ranks of the hundred King's men of honour, the princes of the blood, abbots, bishops and cardinals. The Cardinal-legate from Rome solemnly followed a vast gold cross held high by a sombrely robed priest. The Dauphin, clothed in purple, was led in by Antoine, King of Navarre. But the central glory of this vast tapestry of colour, and at the core of the humming chants and sounding horns, was the bride. Held by the hand of the melancholy yet affectionate King, Mary Stuart proceeded along the nave like a shaft of light, dressed all in white, a beautiful crown of gold embedded with pearls, sapphires and rubies, surmounted by an enormous carbuncle, on her head, her neck and shoulders covered by a diamond necklace, and the ground swept by the long train of her bridal dress.

As Reine-Dauphine, Mary Stuart, wearing the seven magnificent pearl ornaments, the gift of her mother-in-law, was the cynosure of all eyes at the magnificent ball that followed at the Louvre, outshining for this brief period of splendour the light cast upon the court by Diane de Poitiers. The dark days of the power of Cathérine de Médicis were still to come. The Scots Guards were much in evidence on this occasion, led by the Seigneur d'Aubigny, whose son Esmé, almost the same age as the bride, had just been granted his commission in his father's company.

Because of his relationship to the new Dauphine, John Stuart about this time bought a town house in Paris in what is now the rue Malebranche, a steep cobbled street leading down to the Luxembourg Gardens. Now that Mary Stuart was Reine-Dauphine of France, the importance of the French Stuarts and their closeness to the Guise family increased at court, where the effeminate good looks of Esmé Stuart did not pass unnoticed. But Philip II of Spain was stepping up the war in Flanders, and the Stuart father and son had to return to active service.

In November, Mary Tudor died childless. But by the terms of Henry VIII's will and the consent of the English Parliament, Mary's Protestant half-sister Elizabethe succeeded to the throne. In Catholic eyes Elizabeth was a bastard, and the legitimate heir to the crown of England was Mary Stuart. The war was draining the resources of both France and Spain, however, and Henri II put out peace feelers to his enemy England while negotiating at the same time a Spanish marriage for his daughter the Princesse Elisabeth de Valois. Duc François de Guise was sent to discuss peace terms with the new English Queen in London. In April 1559 Henri II signed the Treaty of Cateau-Cambresis with Philip II of Spain and Elizabeth I of England.

As a result of this peace, the Constable Anne de Montmorency was released but the Captain of the Scots Guards, Monseigneur d'Aubigny who had been captured earlier in the year was still kept prisoner. The citizens of Aubigny-sur-Nère were asked to contribute 3,000 écus d'or towards the ransom of their Seigneur. They demanded in return exemption from all taxes for the next seven years. This demand was rejected, but the Constable de Montmorency and others finally paid 5,000 écus d'or for 'the ransom of Jehan Stuart, prisonnier du Comte de Mansfeld'.[6]

It was a summer of court festivities to celebrate the peace and two important royal marriages. On 21 June Mary Stuart's closest friend, Elisabeth de Valois, was married by proxy and became the gloomy Philip II's third wife, a prospect from which the liveliest and most talented of the Valois children shrank. On 27 June a marriage contract was signed between Henri II's sister Marguerite and the ruler of the mountainous duchy of Savoy. To celebrate these weddings a tournament on the most extravagant scale was arranged to take place on 29 June 1559.

The King, whose love of jousting amounted to a mania, was determined to be the star of the tournament. To oppose him he chose the Dukes of Savoy and Ferrara, the Duc François de Guise and the new Captain of the Scots Guards, Gabriel de Lorgues, Comte de Montgomery. As guests of honour the Dauphin and his wife sat under a magnificently embroidered canopy in which the arms of England had blatantly been incorporated with those of France and Scotland. To emphasise what was obvious, just before the tournament began two heralds entered the lists wearing the arms of Scotland, France and England embroidered on their tunics. The English Ambassador Throckmorton could hardly believe his eyes when he saw this double insult. Henri II had in fact proclaimed his daughter-in-law Queen of England, and had had a great seal struck bearing the profiles of the Dauphin and Dauphine and the arms of England, France and Scotland.

Henri II, gallantly displaying Diane de Poitier's colours of black and white, entered the lists with great élan. Bout followed bout, with the middle-aged King obviously growing more and more excited until, against all advice, he insisted on the Captain of the Scots Guards breaking a last lance with him. Montgomery refused, saying he was too exhausted, but the King forced him to accept his challenge. The two rode at one another. Both lances were shattered. Montgomery's snapped in two, one splinter lodging in the King's throat and the other in his eye. He was carried to the nearby Hôtel de Tournelles, where he lingered on in agony for nine days while surgeons tried in vain to remove the festering splinters. Gangrene soon infected his whole body, and on 10 July 1559 Henri II died, surrounded by all the members of the royal family.

Montgomery was banished from court and John Stuart of Aubigny reinstated in his place as Captain of the Scots Guards. Mary Stuart was now Queen of France as well as of Scotland and, by the terms of her marriage contract, the feeble François II was monarch of both kingdoms.

From now onwards John Stuart's role at court grew in importance. His brother Matthew, Earl of Lennox, after an estrangement of over fifteen years, hastened to make up for lost time. He sent his elder son, Henry, Lord Darnley, a tall blond youth of thirteen, to offer his congratulations to his cousin, the new Queen of France, who invited Darnley to stay and attend the coronation in Reims on 18 September 1559. The Earl and Countess of Lennox made use of the occasion to petition Mary Stuart for the return of the confiscated Lennox estates in Scotland. At this stage Mary had sense enough to refuse. The handsome Lord Darnley made the acquaintance of his other cousin, the equally foppish Esmé Stuart, and spent some time hunting with him at Aubigny before returning to England.

The Guise brothers—the soldier hero and the wily Cardinal of Lorraine—now made it their business to manipulate the young and inexperienced rulers of France to further their own ends. It was important for the Guise family that their niece Mary Stuart produce an heir as soon as possible, but by Christmas 1559 there was no likelihood of such an event. The retarded sexual development of the young King made the fathering of a child in the near future improbable. Accompanying his physical defects was the intellectual one that he had no idea of government and that it was a subject in which he seemed entirely uninterested. He was spoilt and undisciplined, and abnormally interested in hunting, which was the only thing he and his wife had in common. Upon her husband's death Cathérine de Médicis had been quick to assert herself, and revealed her astute Machiavellian sense of cunning in politics. She allied herself to the young Queen and together they took control of affairs of state. In spite of Mary's adoration for Diane de Poitiers, the dowager Queen succeeded in having the late King's mistress dismissed from court, took possession of the Loire château of Chenonceaux, and promptly moved in. The Duchesse de Valentinois was given the château de Chaumont in exchange, but she detested it in spite of its fine view over the river. Still magnificent at sixty, Diane accepted her dismissal, and, with her incomparable sense of style, retired to end her days at her own elegant château of Anet.

When it became evident that François II was no more than a cipher in the hands of the fanatically Catholic Guise brothers, the Protestant nobles decided to take action. In the spring of 1560 the Prince de Condé secretly headed a plot to attack Amboise and seize the person of the King. The conspiracy was betrayed and the Cardinal of Lorraine tricked the Protestant leaders into attending a conference at the château. When they arrived, they were seized and publicly tortured and executed; the nobles were hanged from the windows and the commoners thrown in sacks to drown in the Loire. This unedifying spectacle was watched by the whole court.

The Conjuration of Amboise branded the Scottish Queen as the 'whore of Rome' in the eyes of the Protestants and proved to be a turning point in the French wars of religion. In Scotland many of the most influential nobles had become militant Protestants. Among the leaders was the Queen's hard-headed bastard brother, Lord James Stuart. Along with the coarse outspoken Earl of Morton, he headed the Protestant Lords of the Congregation who, in July 1560, signed the Treaty of Edinburgh, recognizing their fellow Protestant Elizabeth as lawful Queen of England. They took it upon themselves to guarantee the withdrawal of all foreign troops from Scotland. This looked to the French as if the traditional alliance between Scotland and France was shattered, contravening the terms of the Scottish Queen's marriage contract.

In France John Stuart of Aubigny did homage for his estates to François II. He and his son Esmé were sworn King's men, upholding the Catholic faith in their province of Berry and enforcing repressive measures whenever they could against the Protestant cloth merchants of Aubigny. The rising tide of Protestantism was not checked even by the savage exemplary punishment meted out to its leaders at Amboise. The neurotic King could not forget the horrors he had authorized and went in fear of his life. Mary, directed by her Guise uncles and by her mother-in-law, tried to keep some control over state policy, but her time as Queen of France was fast running out. With her husband she spent the early autumn hunting season at Fontainebleau until, at the end of October she agreed that the court should move south to Orléans.

The damp climate of this region affected the King's chest. He had been ailing for some time, suffering from crippling headaches and an earache which in November developed into an agonising infection of the middle ear. The pain grew more excruciating each day, but the doctors were unable to relieve his sufferings. Mary was constantly at his bedside during the three weeks he lay in agony. He died at the beginning of December, a day or so before her eighteenth birthday. Dressed in the white mourning of the Clouet *deuil blanc* portrait, and stunned by the change in her fortune, she remained at Orléans in her apartments, which were draped in black velvet in accordance with the etiquette of royal mourning. Not only was her brief married life over but also her reign as Queen of France, the country she had known and loved for the last twelve years. She was childless and so of no importance in the French royal scene, unless she were to marry her brother-in-law the new King, Charles IX, who was only ten years old.

During the traditional forty days of mourning her desolation and boredom were relieved by the unexpected visit of her English cousin Lord Darnley, who had been sent privately by the Lennox family to offer their condolences to Mary. The official English diplomatic visit of condolence did not take place until February 1561, after Queen Elizabeth had viewed the new situation in France from those aspects that affected her own interests.

During the months following the death of François II, speculations had been rife about a suitable second husband for the Queen of Scots. The deformed, mentally retarded Don Carlos of Spain, stepson of Mary's childhood friend Elisabeth de Valois, was suggested as a possible husband. But this prospect was dashed by the fears of a Scottish-Spanish alliance on the part of Elizabeth of England and by Cathérine de Médicis, who foresaw the death of Philip II and wanted Don Carlos for her daughter. The Guise family pressed for a Papal dispensation to enable their niece to marry the child King Charles IX, but Cathérine de Médicis would not have that either. In Scotland the Protestant nobles, who had been uneasy about their Queen's marriage in the first place, were anxious to have her back and married in their own country. The Seigneur d'Aubigny was well aware that his nephew Henry, Lord Darnley, had pleased the Queen on the two occasions he had visited her in France. Darnley had blood ties with both the English and Scottish royal houses as well as being a Stuart and a Catholic. Encouraged by the Cardinal of Lorraine and by Matthew, Earl of Lennox, John Stuart during the three months before Mary sailed back to Scotland saw to it that young Darnley's name was frequently mentioned in her presence.

By this time the Queen Mother Cathérine de Médicis had shown her hand and had emerged as the guiding political spirit in France. As Regent for her son she increased repressive measures against all members of the Protestant religion throughout France. One of the special orders she issued in the name of Charles IX was to instruct John Stuart of Aubigny to use all his power against those known to practise the reformed religion at Aubigny.[7] Stuart acted with zeal and the following year was honoured by a visit from the young king whom he entertained at the château of Aubigny.[8]

Cathérine de Médicis now made up for her years as a neglected and powerless wife during the reign of her husband, and began to use the Guise brothers as her champions as leaders of the Catholic League in the Wars of Religion. On 1 March 1562, by ordering the massacre of Huguenots at a prayer meeting at Wassy in Champagne near the Guise castle of Joinville, Duc François de Guise began the series of terrible wars which ravaged France for the next thirty years. François de Guise, Mary Stuart's uncle, was assassinated less than twelve months later by a Protestant named Poltrot, but his sons Duc Henri de Guise, scarred on the left cheek like his father and also known as 'le Balafré' (the scarred one) and his brother the Cardinal Louis de Lorraine carried on the family tradition as leaders of the militant Catholic League. The Seigneur d'Aubigny was one of their chief supporters, remorselessly hunting down Protestants in his province of Berry while continuing to further his private interests at court.

On 14 August 1561 Mary Stuart left the country that had been her home, never to see it again. Back in Scotland, in spite of her youth and beauty and her romantic appeal as a young widow, she was faced with a role she was not equipped to play. Her French speech and manners were suspect from the start. For the first time in her life she had to cope without the support and promptings of her clever Guise relations. The Queen was well educated and had many accomplishments, but what she lacked was any political skill or indeed, left to her own devices, any common sense. She found herself facing the hostility and open criticism of the Scottish lords, the majority of whom were her enemies in matters of religion. Mary had wits enough not to attempt to impose her faith upon them or upon her subjects, but she also made it quite clear that she herself had no intention of adopting the reformed religion nor indeed of adapting her style of life in any way. She found the manners and customs of her squabbling Scottish courtiers remote in every way from the sophisticated ceremonial of the Valois court in France. From the moment she took up residence in Holyrood House, modest in comparison with the Louvre, she was a pawn, not a Queen, in a relentless game from which she was destined never to escape.

Except for the French followers who had accompanied her on the voyage to Scotland, Mary was isolated in the midst of an alien people. She was hemmed in by the jealousy of the Protestant nobles and the vituperation of the Protestant clergy, who, by denouncing the doctrine of the divine right of kings, reduced their sovereign to the common level where she could be held culpable of any crime with which they chose to accuse her. The mouthpiece of their God-Judge, Calvin, was John Knox, who harangued and insulted the Queen and, in spite of her spirited defence, convinced her subjects by sheer weight of words that she was a weak, silly and worthless woman.

Mary lost her nerve during those first testing years in Scotland. She was brave like all the Stuarts, and undertook long and exhausting dialogues with Knox, replying with dignity and scorn to his diatribes. But she emerged the loser. The guile and ruthlessness of her Guise relations was no longer there to support her, and she had no one to lean upon. Her half-brother, Lord James Stuart, was a Protestant. In other words, he was an enemy. Mary Tudor's bloody persecution of Protestants in England remained a grim and all too recent memory for the members of the Scottish Kirk, and although Mary Stuart showed herself unfailingly tolerant towards them and made no attempt to impose her own religion on her subjects, the Scottish lords made it their business to keep on good terms with Mary's rival Elizabeth.

After four years as Queen in the country of her birth, Mary at twenty-two was still a widow, vulnerable in a sullen hostile land, and homesick for France where she knew she no longer had any place. Distraught in spite of the frivolous distractions she allowed herself among her intimate circle, Mary was losing her grip on the situation. In England her rival queen, nine years her elder, was also unmarried. Much more controlled by temperament than Mary, Elizabeth was a politician to her fingertips, and used her independence to offset the intrigues of her favourites. When they displeased her, she treated them with the same ruthlessness as Cathérine de Médicis. But Mary Stuart was incapable of acting in this way. She was headstrong and weak at the same time; unable to take the long view, she became a victim of her whims and passions instead of governing them. In Scotland she was still regarded as a foreigner and resented as such. It was a boring, frustrating life for a beautiful lively young woman, over-feminine in her feelings and susceptibilities and ready to fall in love with any man capable of arousing her romantic desires. Up till now no one with these qualities had emerged from her tightly knit circle of French courtiers, apart from whom Mary Stuart found herself almost completely alone.

The problem of Mary's marriage, however, was uppermost in the minds of Mary's Guise cousins in France. To further the Guise family ambitions, Duc Henri and his brother the Cardinal were encouraging John Stuart of Aubigny to push the marriage of his nephew Henry, Lord Darnley, to their cousin the Scottish Queen. And in England Queen Elizabeth saw in this same marriage a means of fomenting religious troubles advantageous to English interests in her rival's kingdom. In February 1565 Elizabeth provided passports for the banished Earl of Lennox and his elder son Henry to visit Scotland. Mary responded as Elizabeth had hoped. She greeted the pair with delight. After the rude disrespectful manners of most of the Scottish nobles, the Earl of Lennox and his son, who both spoke French and knew the French court, were welcome guests. In the years that had passed since young Darnley had visited her in France he had grown into an extremely elegant courtier. He was only eighteen but was at least a head taller than she was and, in this, he reminded her of her adored Guise cousins. Once again she lost her head. In spite of the difference in their ages, she fell, for the first time in her life, hopelessly in love.

Less than five months later she married the object of her passion in the chapel of Holyrood. She wore black velvet and was escorted to the altar by the Seigneur d'Aubigny's brother, Matthew, Earl of Lennox. His ambition had at last been satisfied. His son would wear the crown matrimonial of Scotland and all the confiscated Lennox lands were restored to him.

In France the news of the marriage was received with mixed feeling. But for John Stuart of Aubigny it was an unqualified triumph. His prestige and that of his son Esmé at the Valois court rose immediately, and he became on even more intimate terms with the Guise brothers.

Mary's married happiness was short-lived. She found out all too soon that the husband she adored was weak and dissolute under the veneer of his fine court manners. He showed all the inhuman brutality in his nature by letting her know he had married her out of personal ambition. At nineteen he revealed himself for what he was, a cynical roué of the Elizabethan court, a man who continued after his marriage to give himself over to debauchery and cold lechery, which he had neither the depth of character nor the intelligence to bother to conceal from his wife. Within a few months of her marriage Mary was pregnant and appalled at the ravages wrought on the once handsome face of the father of her unborn child. Nothing she could do could arouse a streak of chivalry in her husband. As she suffered more and more from physical nausea and sickness of heart, Darnley was absent, whoremongering in the streets of Edinburgh. When he was in her company, he was invariably drunk. There was no more talk of a coronation for her consort. Mary now relied for advice and sympathy from her own small group of faithful attendants. Her closest confidant was an Italian who had come to Scotland with the Ambassador from Piedmont. His name was David Rizzio and he became the Queen's secretary, dealing with all her diplomatic correspondence in Italian, French and Spanish. He was an odd-looking little man but very intelligent and trustworthy, and an excellent musician. So it happened that he was scarcely ever out of the Queen's company for business or pleasure, but there is no evidence that he ever aspired to become her lover, or that she thought of him in terms other than friendship. He was a *cavaliere servante* in every sense of the word, and it became the custom for Rizzio to join the Queen and her ladies at supper and to entertain them with his playing and singing.

Darnley was pathologically jealous of this intimate little circle, from which he was excluded, and determined to get rid of 'Master Davie', as he sneeringly called Rizzio. He began plotting with some Protestant lords to engineer a murder as cold-blooded and macabre as any Renaissance tragedy. On the evening of 10 March 1566 the conspirators, headed by Patrick, Lord Ruthven, a 'reputed dealer in witchcraft' and pale as death in armour, entered the Queen's apartments by Darnley's private staircase, followed by the tall figure of the drunken Darnley. They seized Rizzio and stabbed him to death in front of the Queen. The alarm was given, but the Earl of Morton, who was one of the conspirators, with 200 armed men guarded all the entrances to the palace, and the murderers escaped, leaving the bleeding corpse of Rizzio in the doorway of the Queen's bedroom.

Three months after this traumatic experience, on 19 June 1566, Mary gave birth to a son in a tiny room in Edinburgh Castle. There was no reconciliation between the Queen and her husband. She named her child James, the sixth of his name among the Stuart Kings. As the infant Prince James was next in succession to both the Scottish and English thrones, Mary asked Elizabeth to be his godmother. She accepted and sent the golden font for the christening. When he was officially baptised in December at Stirling Castle, there was no sign of his father at the ceremony. At twenty Darnley, now permanently disfigured by his vices, was talking wildly of leaving Scotland for France.

The year which had begun with the murder of Rizzio and ended with the baptism of the heir-presumptive to the crowns of Scotland and England also saw the death of Diane de Poitiers, the woman who had most influenced Mary Stuart's life. She died at her château of Anet and was buried in the elegant black and white marble chapel she had designed to house her tomb.

Less than two months after James's christening his father Darnley was found dead after a mysterious explosion at Kirko' Field, a country house just outside Edinburgh, where Mary had arranged for her estranged husband to convalesce after an attack of so-called measles. The disappearance of Darnley from the scene was no cause for mourning but the circumstances of his death were highly suspect. Mary's reputation, already tarnished by the affair, was further blackened by the discovery of incriminating love letters to the notorious womanizer and unprincipled adventurer the Earl of Bothwell, generally believed to be the instigator of the crime. It was irretrievably lost when she allowed herself to be carried off by him to Dunbar Castle and then married him by Protestant rites a few weeks later on 15 May in the great hall of Holyrood, only twelve days after Bothwell had obtained a divorce from his wife Lady Jean Gordon. Mary had met James Bothwell, as she had Darnley, in France when he visited her father-in-law's court as Lord High Admiral of Scotland. He was as dark and wild in appearance, as the much younger Darnley had been blond and foppish, and was irresistible to women.

The result of this disastrous third marriage was a confrontation at Carberry Hill near Musselburgh between the Queen and her new husband Bothwell and the rebel lords with banners depicting Darnley's murder, ending with the Queen's humiliating defeat and her desertion by

Bothwell, who rode off to save his own skin, eventually escaping to Norway. That was the last she ever saw of the man for whom she had risked so much. Mary was forcibly escorted back to Edinburgh and lodged in the house of the Provost of the city, while the citizens shouted 'Whore' and 'Adultress' at her when she appeared at the window with dishevelled hair and tears streaming down her face. This was exactly a month after the fatal wedding day. From Edinburgh she was transferred to the Douglas stronghold in the middle of Lochleven, whose owner was half-brother of her own half-brother, now Earl of Moray. There she was forced to sign her abdication, and on 29 July 1567 her thirteen-month-old son was crowned King James VI of Scotland in the Protestant church at Stirling. Less than four weeks later James, Earl of Moray, was proclaimed Regent. He remained in close and constant communication with Queen Elizabeth, and further insinuated himself into the English Queen's good graces by taking possession of most of his half-sisters jewels and selling some of the most splendid ornaments, including the magnificent set of seven large pearls that had been a wedding present to Mary from Cathérine de Médicis.

In May 1568, with the help of one of the Douglas sons, Mary escaped from Lochleven to join the Hamiltons, who hoped to restore her and use her for their own ends, but once more the Queen was defeated by Moray at Langside near Glasgow and, as there was no French ship available in the Firth of Clyde, she fled in desperation to England to throw herself on the mercy of her rival, Queen Elizabeth. If only she had had the sense to wait for a ship to France she might, in the long run, have had a happier life. There she had her Guise relatives and her estates in Touraine; instead at twenty-four, she committed a fatal act of folly by choosing captivity, which ended in her death twenty years later.

5

THE FASCINATING ADVENTURER

SOON AFTER THE INFANT JAMES VI had been proclaimed King of Scotland, his father Darnley's French cousin, Esmé Stuart, at twenty-five, became the seventh Seigneur d'Aubigny and Captain of the Scots Guards in France. Esmé was tall and slender with auburn hair and, although somewhat effeminate, was unusually good-looking in the fashion of his time. He was dismayed to find, however, that not only had he inherited the debts of his father, John Stuart, but those of his predecessor, the extravagant Maréchal d'Aubigny, as well. Esmé was practical and ambitious. He left it to his mother to manage the estates in Berry as best she could while he proceeded to advance his military career under Guise patronage on the side of the Catholic League in the Wars of Religion. In 1570 in Scotland the Protestant Regent Moray was murdered, and Esmé's prestige in France rose when his uncle Matthew, Earl of Lennox, the Scottish King's paternal grandfather, became Regent in his place.

In August 1572 Esmé Stuart took part in the St Bartholomew's Day massacre of leading Protestants in Paris, instigated by the Guise brothers and the Queen Mother. He was by now a well known figure at the Valois court, though still embarrassingly short of money. He remedied this by marrying, later in 1572, his fourth cousin, Cathérine de Balsac d'Entraigues,[1] a strong-minded and wealthy widow of untiring energy and masculine personality. She seemed content with the arrangement that she should stay at La Verrerie to run the Aubigny estates and bring up the children Esmé fathered on the rare occasions he visited her. Five healthy children survived among several others born of this strange marriage—two sons, Ludovic and Esmé, and three daughters, Henriette, Marie and Gabrielle.

When Charles IX was succeeded by the last and most decadent of the Valois Kings, Henri III, in 1574, Esmé Stuart's blanched pierrot-like beauty assured him a place in the new King's circle of mignons, who, perfumed, fantastically dressed and chattering like magpies, distracted the sovereign from the troubles of his strife-ridden kingdom. But in spite of royal favours, the Seigneur d'Aubigny was living well beyond his means.

In Scotland his relative, the young Scottish King, cooped up in Stirling Castle, was forced to lead a lonely and unnatural childhood. James could remember neither of his parents, for his Darnley Stuart father had died mysteriously when he was nine months old and his mother was a remote figure imprisoned in an English castle, where she had been weaving Catholic plots for years. Until he was five his guardians, both of whom hated his mother, had been the Earl and Countess of Mar, and, at that tender age, he had had the traumatic experience of seeing the murdered corpse of his grandfather, the Regent Lennox, carried past his windows.

In this year the forlorn little boy was handed over to the stern grammarian George Buchanan to be educated. Buchanan was the choice of the Protestant Lords of the Congregation who had forced his mother's abdication. He was a learned man who had studied at the Scots College in Paris and then at the University of Bordeaux, where he had met and admired the humanist philosopher Montaigne. He stuffed his pupil's head to bursting point with continental treatises on the education of princes, at the same time perplexing him with strong doses of stern democratic Scottish Presbyterianism, which maintained that a monarch was no more than 'God's silly vassal'. Buchanan made James an excellent classical scholar and gave him an insatiable thirst for knowledge; he also taught him to speak and write correct French, but he never spared the rod, bullying James unmercifully and keeping him as far as possible from the influence of women, all of whom he genuinely detested. His tutor made it quite plain to the King that if his Catholic mother had not been directly involved in the murder of his father, she had at least condoned it in order to marry the suspected murderer, Bothwell.

Thus James grew up possessing a remarkably retentive memory and a precocious mind. His mental ability belied his unprepossessing appearance. His head was disproportionately large for his ungainly body, his pale eyes lolled about, and his tongue was too big for his mouth, which slurred his speech and made his eating and drinking habits disgusting to watch. Buchanan had neglected to instil into him any courtly graces, so, to compensate for his unfortunate appearance, James developed an uncouth and bumptious personality. Over-educated, conceited, starved of affection, forbidden all pleasure except hunting and hawking, the young King at thirteen rebelled against the domination of the ageing Buchanan and, when preparations were being made for his state entry into Edinburgh, he took the bold step of writing to his nearest relative on his father's side, Esmé Stuart of Aubigny, inviting him to come to Scotland for the occasion. His only other Darnley relation, his father's younger brother, Charles, fifth Earl of Lennox, had lived in England and had died three years before, leaving a baby daughter, Arabella Stuart, who was brought up by her Cavendish grandmother at Chatsworth. The Lennox property in Scotland reverted to James, who gave it to one of his bastard great-uncles, Robert Stewart, whom he created sixth Earl of Lennox.

The Guise family urged Esmé Stuart to accept the Scottish King's invitation when it arrived in May 1579. Duc Henri de Guise, who bore the same relationship to James VI as Esmé did, but on the maternal side, saw in it an opportunity to further Catholic interests in Scotland, and perhaps, on certain conditions, to obtain the release of Mary Stuart. From what the Duc de Guise had heard about James from the French envoys to Scotland he was sure the boy would respond to Esmé's charm. He urged his protegé to accept the invitation without delay. The King's state entry was fixed for October 1579, so the Guise brothers immediately started fitting Esmé out with an impressive wardrobe of the latest French fashions and jewellery. They advised him to be careful not to shock the unsophisticated Scottish lords. By the time he had said goodbye to his wife and young family at La Verrerie, the Seigneur d'Aubigny was described as being 'a man of comelie proportions, civile behaviour, red beardit and honest in conversation'. From the Guise private funds he was provided with 40,000 gold pieces to spend at the Scottish court to bribe influential noblemen and gain their support for the Guise interests. Duc Henri de Guise accompanied him to Calais and spent six hours closeted with him in private conversation in the cabin of his galley. During this farewell interview his patron handed over considerable sums of money from the French King, telling him more subsidies would be forthcoming from the Pope and the King of Spain if he played his cards well. As he set off on his voyage of adventure, in his high-crowned feathered hat, his starched ruff, pearl ornaments and earrings, the Seigneur d'Aubigny was a figure to dazzle any lonely, impressionable boy.

Esmé Stuart sailed at the beginning of September 1579 and landed at Leith on the 8th of that month. As Guise had foreseen, the adolescent King was ripe for seduction and initiation into the pleasures of homosexual love. James fell completely under his French cousin's spell, and his infatuation for Esmé formed his sexual tastes for the rest of his life, in which a series of beautiful young men managed to guide his policies and to influence his judgement as a ruler. Esmé taught him the subtle art of political manoeuvring, learned from the Guise family, to combat the disrespectful unruliness of his rough and often brutal nobles, many of them his own bastard relations. He sharpened James's already quick wit and encouraged him in his revolt from the drab, over-strict teachings of George Buchanan. Most important of all, Esmé made him see that in the Presbyterian religion his power as an absolute monarch was threatened.

That James's passion was immediate and overwhelming is shown in the report received at the French court as early as 29 October 1579, barely seven weeks after Esmé's arrival. The despatch was sent by Castelnau, Henri III's ambassador in London and says: 'The success of the Lord of Aubigny is such that it seems certain that he will be made Earl of Lennox and it is thought by many that he will be named successor to the crown of Scotland should the King die without children. But this would be dependent on a clause by which he would guarantee to embrace their religion.' He adds cynically: 'Those who would rule must learn to dissimulate.'

The power the persuasive Esmé exercised over the highly intelligent boy was remarkable. After the dreary harangues of the ministers of the Scottish Kirk and his preceptor, Esmé's view of life was a liberating breath of air, perfumed with delightful vice, which James found irresistible: his hero-worship verged on the maudlin. One year after Esmé's arrival, James, without any scruples, forced his great-uncle Robert, sixth Earl of Lennox, to hand over to Esmé the Lennox estates given to him only three years before. Robert's wife, Elizabeth, was peremptorily summoned to Holyrood to hand over the Lennox title deeds and documents to the Seigneur d'Aubigny, who wrote out a receipt in French for the Countess in exchange for the vacant earldom of Mar for her husband.

On 29 October 1581 Esmé's title was upgraded to a dukedom and he was granted precedence over all the other Scottish peers, however noble their blood. The King appointed him Regent of Scotland and, on this date, ordered his styles and titles to be proclaimed at the Mercat Cross of Edinburgh. They made an impressive list: 'Lord of Aubigny in France, Earl of Darnley, Lord of Tarbolton, Lord of Dalkeith, Duke of Lennox, Baron Banneret, Knight of Creuxstone, Lord of our Sovereign Lord's Parliament and Great Chamberlain of Scotland.'

There were sour looks and hostile murmurings from the affronted Scottish nobles, but Esmé was more than a match for their unsubtle machinations against him. Secure in his wealth and titles and confident of the sexual power he wielded over the fifteen-year-old King, Lennox, once Regent, began a systematic suppression of his opponents. At the end of that year he brought off his masterstroke by having the former Regent Morton put on trial and beheaded for his alleged part in Darnley's murder fourteen years before.

James was born a physical coward and his admiration for Esmé's daring and ruthlessness knew no bounds. The pair, conversing in French, were inseparable and as the king heaped more wealth, land and titles on his favourite, there was an uneasy feeling in the country that this upstart French Stuart might well find a way to achieve his crowning ambition.

The French secretly continued to subsidize Lennox but outwardly pretended to remain neutral in the domestic affairs of Scotland. They made no protest when the Duke of Lennox, hitherto a devout Catholic, publicly abjured his faith and professed himself a convert to the Presbyterian religion. Esmé did this all the while maintaining secret correspondence with the Spanish ambassador in Paris who sent disguised Jesuit priests to Scotland with letters from Philip of Spain and the Pope. This was in 1582, the year George Buchanan died. These priests brought the sums of money the Guise brothers had promised, as well as letters urging Lennox to raise an army to restore the Catholic religion in Scotland and to free Mary, Queen of Scots.

Privately Lennox remained a Catholic all his life yet advised that the orders contained in these secret letters be treated cautiously. He wrote that he was willing to attempt what was asked only on condition that James continued to rule as King after his mother's release. He went so far as to tell the Pope and the King of Spain that he was confident of gaining the consent of the young King, not only to the suggested enterprise, but to the idea of changing his religion if it were successful. He knew that the austerity of the Scottish Kirk had no appeal for James, and that he bitterly resented its interference in his rights as a monarch. In James's view the Pope at least treated other sovereigns as equals in political affairs. Lennox said, however, that he did not consider it prudent to tell James of the plan until an army of at least 15,000 men had been raised.

Elizabeth's secret service kept her informed of most of these proposals. She did not like the way things were shaping in Scotland and decided that the sooner the French-born Scottish Regent disappeared from the scene the better. She bribed the most disgruntled Protestant lords, including the Earl of Gowrie, nephew of the Earl of Morton on whom Lennox had wreaked his barbarous revenge.

Gowrie was a man of some imagination. He formed a conspiracy of Protestant nobles, among them Morton's nephew Angus, to kidnap the King when he was hunting in Perthshire in August 1582. James was held a closely guarded prisoner in Ruthven Castle, Gowrie's stronghold, for several months while the hated Lennox was seized and deposed. He was imprisoned in the fortress castle of Dumbarton and the Ruthven raiders, with the approval of the Scottish General Assembly and English backing, took over the government.

A contemporary portrait sketch of Esmé Stuart, seigneur d'Aubigny and newly created Duke of Lennox shortly after his expulsion from Scotland. *Rés. Bib. Nat. Cabinet des Etampes.*

Esmé Stuart was cornered. He was stripped of all his titles and the Lennox lands were once more confiscated. He and James were never allowed to meet again, and arrangements were made to send the Lord of Aubigny back to France. Elizabeth could not resist seeing this notoriously attractive French Stuart for herself and, on her orders, the Scottish lords who had forced the captive King to sign a deed expelling his dearest love from Scotland sent him via London instead of by ship from Dumbarton.

As he left on his homeward journey through England, Lennox managed to have a last touching letter smuggled in to James. In this note, dated 16 December 1582, Esmé says that 'a piteous addition to my departure is that, having suffered pains, torments and *ennuis* for three years in my devotion to the King's service, I should have to leave seeing his Majesty turned against me'.[2]

The French ambassador in London had in the meantime written to Cathérine de Médicis warning her that Lennox's life was in great danger. Henri III at once sent La Mothe Fénélon as his special envoy to Scotland to intercede for the Seigneur d'Aubigny's life. Elizabeth astutely managed to delay the French envoy until after Esmé was known to have set out for London.

The charmer she was so curious to see was forty-one, nine years younger than herself. She did not mince her words, but charged him roundly with such matters as she thought culpable. But even the experienced politician could not resist James's ambitious favourite. He answered her accusations and upbraidings with such honeyed gentleness and good sense that the wily Queen was quite softened by the end of the interview, and even reluctant to send him away.

He kept up the front of the fascinating adventurer until the moment of his departure for France, but the separation from James for whom he seems to have felt a genuine affection and the brutal manner of his dismissal left him a broken man. He reached Paris at the beginning of 1583 and in early February suffered a first stroke. In spite of the care of the royal doctors, he only partially recovered and remained in the Stuart town house in the rue Malebranche growing steadily weaker. He never saw Aubigny or La Verrerie again. A second stroke was followed by a third and he died at his home in the Latin Quarter of Paris on 26 May 1583.

On his death bed he reaffirmed his love and devotion for King James and recommended his children to his care. He asked for his body to be buried at Aubigny, but requested that his heart should be sent back to the King in Scotland. So ended the meteoric rise and fall of the French Stuart who became the Duke of Lennox. His fame persisted but his fortune vanished overnight.

At the end of May James, unaware of his favourite's death, managed to escape from his captors and, on his seventeenth birthday, 19 June 1583, declared himself of age. With the aid of the nobles who had helped him to freedom, he had Gowrie seized and executed, while the other conspirators fled to England.

His triumph was blighted when the news was finally broken to him of

Esmé Stuart's death. Utterly desolate at the loss of the first love of his life, whom he had hoped would now be able to rejoin him in Scotland, James sank into a typical Stuart state of introspective melancholy. A contemporary Scottish writer describes how James reacted to this blow:

> 'The King, sore in mynd and without all quietness in sperit till he should see some of his [Esmé's] posteritie, to possess him in his father's house and rents, with all diligence he directit Patrick, the Master of Gray, to go to France for the Duke of Lennox his eldest son called Ludovic, who convoyit him saiflie in Scotland about the thirteenth day of November 1583. He was honorablie convoyit from Leyth to Kinneill by the Earls of Huntlie, Crawford and Montrose and the King ressavit him and embracit him very thankfully. Next the King sent for twa of this young Duke of Lennox's sisters and the eldest he causit to be marrit to the Earl of Huntlie and the second to the Earl of Mar: and all this was done in commemoration of the singular gude will and favour the King bore to their father.[3]

Patrick, the Master of Gray, like James and the late Duke of Lennox, was a known homosexual. He was a descendant of the suspected murderer of James III after Sauchieburn, and his family had always been intriguers. He had first met Esmé Stuart when he had visited Paris as a young man with Queen Mary's ambassador James Beaton. He spoke fluent French, and soon struck up an intimate friendship with the Captain of the Scots Guards, whose pale skin and hair was in striking contrast to Gray's dark androgynous good looks. Like Esmé Stuart, Gray was used by the Guise brothers to act as their agent in Scotland. He was a much more unscrupulous character than they guessed; a complete opportunist, he succeeded in insinuating himself into Elizabeth's favour and furthered his own interests by acting as agent for the English Queen as well.

When Gray arrived in France in November 1583, Ludovic Stuart of Aubigny was nine years old, a sturdy boy of independent spirit like his mother, an expert in all forms of hunting and the possessor of a strong sense of humour. The twice-widowed Duchess of Lennox was an outspoken woman who had accepted her husband for what he was and made the best of it. She had already acted in her children's interests three months after husband's death by appointing a wealthy neighbour, the Seigneur de Culan in Berry, as guardian to her young family.[4] When the Master of Gray appeared at Aubigny, she carefully considered the proposals he brought from the Scottish King. James wanted to adopt the boy as his godson and restore the Lennox lands and titles to him. It was just as much her decision as Gray's persuasion that young Ludovic Stuart returned with him to what proved to be a brilliant future.

During the voyage the young Duke was no doubt initiated by Gray into the kind of life he could expect to lead at James's court, but, along with his father's volatile, pleasure-loving tastes, Ludovic had inherited his mother's toughness and resilience of character, and from the first showed that he was well able to look after himself. Free at last from the censorious George Buchanan, James, after greeting the boy with extravagant marks of affection, took it upon himself to act as his tutor. Ludovic proved an apt pupil, sharing the King's love of the classics and his passion for hawking and hunting. They spoke French together at first, until Ludovic learned to speak English with James's broad Scots accent.

True to his promise to his dead favourite, James kept in constant touch with Ludovic's family at Aubigny through the frequent visits of the Master of Gray to France. It was he who arranged with the French King that on Ludovic's becoming second Duke of Lennox in Scotland, his younger brother Esmé should inherit the lands and title of Aubigny in his place. James, with all his dislike of Presbyterianism, which did not suit him in the least, was shrewd enough to see that if he wanted to achieve his life's ambition of becoming sovereign of England as well as Scotland when Elizabeth died, he must remain a Protestant and keep on as good terms as possible with her. So in 1585, although his mother was still Elizabeth's prisoner, he made an alliance with England and saw to it that he continued in regular secret correspondence with Elizabeth's powerful secretary, Sir Robert Cecil.

Patrick, the Master of Gray, was sent by James to make a show of interceding for his mother's life when Elizabeth ordered her trial and execution for complicity in Babington's alleged plot to murder the English Queen, and Gray coolly continued with the duplicity that was second nature to him throughout the affair, making no real effort to dissuade Elizabeth from doing away with her rival. No diplomatic protest came from Henri III on behalf of his sister-in-law. Both he and his mother, Cathérine de Médicis, were sick and tired of the ambitions of her Guise cousins in France. James's own attitude to the mother who had abandoned him as an infant, and had possibly murdered his father, was distant and ambivalent. Obsessed with conflicting feelings of guilt and a desire to have his problems solved once and for all, he remained passive.

Deserted by all, the former Queen of Scotland and of France went to her doom in February 1587. She died superbly, in her own eyes a martyr to her Catholic faith, while her son James and her cousin Elizabeth conveniently looked the other way.

The French King had been harassed for more than a year by Henri de Guise and Henri de Navarre, and it was ten months before he was able to celebrate a solemn requiem for Mary Stuart in Notre Dame. The funeral oration was preached by the Archbishop of Bourges in the presence of many of those who had witnessed her marriage to the French Dauphin nearly thirty years before. In 1588, just before Christmas, Henri III decided to get rid of the troublesome Guise brothers once and for all. He summoned Henri de Guise and his brother the Cardinal Louis to a meeting of the States-General at Blois. On the day before Christmas Eve, the King sent for the Duke, saying he had important matters to discuss with him in his private quarters before the meeting. When Le Balafré reached the King's private apartments, he was set upon by the King's guards and stabbed repeatedly. The magnificent swaggering six-foot Duke fought back desperately, but in the end was overcome and fell dead. The King kicked the huge bleeding corpse with his elegantly shod foot, saying 'look how he seems even taller dead than alive'. The next day the Cardinal of Lorraine was done to death in the same way in another part of the château; the two bodies were thrown out of the windows to be burned in the courtyard below and their ashes scattered in the Loire.

By twelfth night in the New Year Cathérine de Médicis was dead. Her darling Henri, mistrusted by enemies and former allies, became a fugitive in his own land until he joined forces with the King of Navarre. This flimsy alliance was destroyed in August, when Henri III was stabbed and died. With him died the Valois dynasty.

His heir was his swashbuckling Protestant brother-in-law, the Bourbon Henri of Navarre, who had escaped the Guise-instigated massacre of St Bartholomew soon after his marriage to the Princess Marguerite de Valois. Henri of Navarre and the Reine Margot were completely incompatible, and since their marriage had lived apart and had produced no heirs. Navarre had led the Protestants in the Wars of Religion against the Duc de Guise, who headed the Catholic League. His right to the succession was at first disputed by the citizens of Paris, who raised the barricades to prevent the Béarnais King from entering his capital. Henri mustered an army of about 8,000 men and appealed for help to his fellow-Protestants James VI of Scotland and Elizabeth of England. He marched to Dieppe to meet the expected Scottish reinforcements, which were commanded by Sir James Colville of Easter Wemyss, who had successfully fought as a mercenary with him only two years before at Coutras. Colville with his force of Scots helped Henri IV to win the first victory of his reign at Arques-la-Bataille on the Normandy cliffs on 2 September 1589.

A few weeks later James, accompanied by Ludovic Stuart as Lord High Admiral, sailed to Norway intending to bring back to Scotland his bride, Anne of Denmark. The wedding had taken place by proxy earlier but the bride's ship had been driven by storms into the harbour of Oslo. Anne of Denmark was nominally a Protestant when she married, which pleased

Voicy l'Amour du peuple, & la paix de l'Eglise
La gloire des françoys la peur des estrangers
Voicy ce Mars hardy qui soubs le nom de Guyse
A faict armer la terre et trembler l'univers.

Henri Duc de Guise at the height of his popularity when he was acclaimed as the pride of France and the terror of foreigners.

the Scottish Kirk. James knew he had to marry someone, and at first found his handsome fair-haired wife quite agreeable for a woman.

Anne of Denmark was a good wife for a homosexual. She was extravagant and frivolous, and liked eating, drinking and dressing up.

The weeks of the honeymoon stretched into months, the couple carousing with Anne's brother Christian in Oslo. The ship bringing the pair back to Scotland ran into storms off North Berwick, for which James was convinced a coven of Scottish witches was responsible. His obsession with witchcraft was just about the only point he had in common with the ministers of the Scottish Kirk. Fancying himself as a writer, he published his own views on Daemonology in 1597.

In the year of his marriage he made Ludovic Stuart his Lord Great Chamberlain as well as Lord High Admiral, and sent for the two elder Aubigny girls to marry the Scottish Catholic Earls of Huntly and Mar. In 1590 the young Duke of Lennox made the first of his three marriages when he took as his bride Sophia, daughter of the Earl of Gowrie who had kidnapped the King and dismissed Ludovic's father from office. In Aubigny the Dowager Duchess of Lennox, although a Catholic herself, was strongly in favour of Henri IV and sent her second son Esmé to fight for France's Protestant King. In 1593 Henri IV, for the sake of uniting his kingdom, abjured his Protestantism and succeeded in pacifying France after forty years of bitter civil war. He made up for his seeming betrayal in the Edict of Nantes in 1598 by giving Protestants freedom of conscience and civil liberty. James fully approved of the French King's action. In his treatise *The True Law of Free Monarchies* and his *Basilikon Doron*, written for the edification of his heir, Prince Henry, James condemned Presbyterianism and asserted the divine right of kings. Through his secret correspondence with the English secretary of state, he was confident enough to establish Episcopacy in Scotland on English lines (he learned, for example, that Elizabeth continued to burn candles in her private chapel) and to appoint three bishops in 1600.

The second Duke of Lennox was sent to Paris by James as his special envoy to the French King in 1601, the year after his brother Esmé had done his homage to Henri IV for the Seigneurie of Aubigny.[5] By this time Ludovic Stuart was already a widower without children. During his two-year absence in France his brothers-in-law, sons of the Earl of Gowrie who had been beheaded seventeen years before, formed a mysterious new Gowrie Conspiracy for the abduction of James.[6] The King was able to forestall this, and had the Earl of Gowrie and the Master of Ruthven executed and the Ruthven estates confiscated.

Part Two

The Century of the Stuarts, 1603–1688

6

THE STUART COURT AT WHITEHALL

AFTER RIDING 397 miles from London to Edinburgh in sixty hours, Sir Robert Carey, Cecil's messenger, reached Holyrood House just before midnight on 26 March 1603 to tell James VI that Queen Elizabeth was dead and that he had been proclaimed James I of England, France and Ireland. At thirty-six, after more than twenty years' apprenticeship for the role of first sovereign of Great Britain, James had achieved his own and his family's ambition. This culminating point in the rise of the House of Stuart marked the beginning of a century of drama in which the Stuart court held the stage to play out the concept of the divine right of kings. The century began with triumph, descended into chaos, was transformed into a brief blaze of splendour at the Restoration, and ended like a Jacobean tragedy with the leading players chased from the scene to France, to wait for the recall that never came.

But on this dark night at Holyrood House James could only imagine the first exciting act. His handsome, intelligent son Prince Henry was ten, he had a lively daughter Elizabeth aged seven, and another son Charles who was nearly three, so that in spite of his personal distaste for women, the dynasty was assured. James had learned well the lessons of political manoeuvring taught him by the first Duke of Lennox, to curb the power of his tiresome illegitimate relations and of the ministers and laymen of the Scottish Kirk. By the time he succeeded as monarch of the two kingdoms he had managed to impose his will but he was exhausted. The squabblings of the clergy and the infighting of the nobles he despised and feared made him only too thankful to leave Scotland. After all, out of the five Kings called James who had preceded him, only one had died in his bed.

Preparations for his journey to London were made in record time. Without bothering even to summon the Scottish Parliament, he abruptly took leave of his people at the close of divine service in St Giles' Cathedral, Edinburgh, on Sunday 3 April and left two days later, ahead of the Queen and his family, and attended by his favourites, who had all been assured of high places at the English court. Ludovic Stuart was naturally among them, along with his Scottish brothers-in-law, the Earls of Mar and Huntly.

James's progress south was slow and spectacular. Curious to see their new King, crowds turned out on the way as the royal party proceeded from one great country house to another en route to the capital. He astonished many by his over-familiarity, so far removed from the theatrical formality of Elizabethan progresses. Because of his speech difficulty he had a tendency to shout in his loud unattractive voice, another reason was to try to make his broad Scots intelligible to his English subjects. He also frequently punctuated his conversation with blasphemous oaths, for James was an intellectual who liked to shock.

He was joined by the Queen and his two elder children in the summer, and crowned on St James's day, 25 July 1603. All boded well, in spite of a minor outbreak of the plague to mar the occasion. James had a strong ally in Henri IV, and like him had a wider view of kingship. After his coronation he proclaimed peace with Europe and granted toleration to Roman Catholics. In January 1604, elated by the first impact he had made in his capital, James called the Hampton Court Conference at which he made his famous pronouncement 'No Bishop, no King', in favour of Episcopacy as against the various forms of austere Puritanism, which he loathed. The most important result of this controversial conference of churchmen was the King's ordering a new translation of the scriptures. The Authorized Version of the Bible took five years to complete, but made as outstanding a contribution to English literature as the plays of Shakespeare. As light relief to the weighty questions of religion James wrote his *Counterblast to Tobacco*, in which he elaborates with his fantastic wit his dislike of the 'noxious weed' brought by Sir Walter Raleigh from America.

He had a low opinion of the intelligence of women, and refused to share a house with either his wife or daughter, both of whom had strong and attractive personalities. The Queen was given her own establishment at Somerset House in the Strand and later at the Queen's lodging at Greenwich. Prince Henry and his sister first lived at Oatlands Palace in Surrey, and later the Prince moved to Hampton Court, St James's Palace and Richmond.

When Henri IV sent his intimate friend Sully as special envoy to congratulate King James on his accession, the great French finance minister was astonished when he was invited to dine at Greenwich Palace to find ceremonial far exceeding that of the French court. The monarch, whose table manners were abominable, was served, seated on a dais alone,

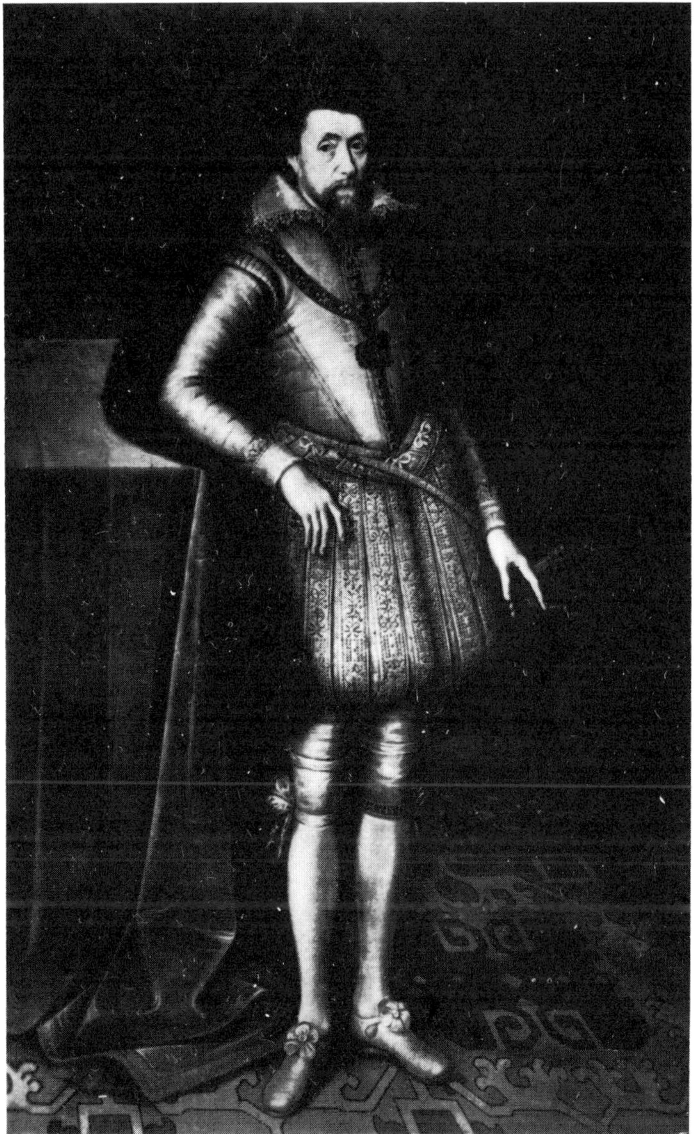

The famous Ghaeraedts portrait of James VI and I as the first King of Great Britain, wearing the Order of the Garter, painted about 1608.

by noblemen on bended knee. Sully noted with some interest that 'those chosen for this honour were invariably young and exceptionally good-looking'.[1] In fact, cup-bearer invariably was the first step to the King's bed-chamber.

James was enjoying to the full the luxury and ceremony he had been

One of the last portraits, in miniature, of James VI and I's Queen, Anne of Denmark, towards the end of her life.

deprived of during his repressed childhood. Esmé Stuart had aroused in him a passionate love for beautiful things as well as beautiful young men, and from him he had acquired a taste for richly ornamented clothes, play-acting and court festivities, the only pleasures he had in common with his Queen. He also had a genuine love of literature, and during his reign Shakespeare and the Jacobean dramatists were writing their greatest plays. *Hamlet* was first performed in 1604. At the end of this year a remarkable genius in architecture and stage design, Inigo Jones, arrived back in England from a visit to Denmark with a recommendation to Queen Anne from her brother Christian. For the next thirty-five years, twenty-five of which were spent in close partnership with Ben Jonson glorifying the Stuart image of Kingship in the allegories and masques he devised for the court, Jones also designed some of the most splendid public buildings and great houses in England. In 1604 James sent his friend Ludovic Stuart back to France with Sully as his envoy-extraordinary to Henri IV. This appointment bore out Sully's report that the Duke of Lennox was among the most pro-French of the Scottish faction surrounding James, unlike many of the English nobles, who were being suborned by the King of Spain to act against France. Many of these nobles were angered by the offices handed out by James to his Scottish favourites.

The Gunpowder Plot of 1605 gave the King second thoughts about his granting liberty of conscience to Roman Catholics, and laws against the public practice of their religion were imposed. With remarkable *sang-froid*, however, and ignoring the terror inspired by the discovery of the plot to blow him up at the opening of Parliament, James insisted that the ceremony of creating his younger son Duke of York should take place as planned on St Andrew's Day (30 November) at Whitehall.

This glittering piece of pageantry, in which the chief actor was a timid child of five whose legs were so weak he could scarcely walk unaided and who could only stammer out a few words in his strange Scottish accent, was the future Charles I's earliest memory. Dressed in a white satin suit covered with diamonds, he was carried by his lords and attendants to the royal dais to preside over a great feast in the old banqueting hall of the Palace of Whitehall. His first impression of his father's court was that of an enchanted theatrical world, a dazzling world of light and gaiety after the gloom of Holyrood House, the forbidding Scottish palace where until then he had spent his childhood. Alone with his tutors, he had struggled against physical disabilities and personality problems. Like James, he could not articulate clearly, and his father at one point had wanted the string of his tongue to be cut. His guardians resisted this, but he spoke with a stutter until the end of his life.

Before Charles arrived in London, Inigo Jones and Ben Jonson's first spectacular production, *The Masque of Blackness*, based on an original idea of the Queen's, was presented at court. In this the Queen and her ladies appeared as Ethiopians who were blanched by the light emanating from the wise and generous monarch of the white realm of Albion. This masque was the first to employ complicated stage machinery and lighting effects to create transformation scenes in the best pantomime tradition. The foreign diplomats who saw it were impressed by the imagination and strangeness of Anne of Denmark's choice of subject, and one of them, the Venetian Ambassador, reported that they were all astounded by its beauty. From 1606 onwards the young Prince Charles was either a spectator or an actor in the yearly Twelfth Night and Accession Day masques. They made a deep impression, forming in him, unconsciously, the role he was destined to play as the supreme actor in his kingdom.

In the real world James pursued a policy of colonization by founding the first English settlement in Virginia, with Jamestown as its capital, and, seeing himself as a European statesman, placated Spain and the Netherlands with treaties of mutual interest. In 1610 he signed a new alliance with France, promising a truce between their two countries for the next twelve years. His elder son Henry, named after James's own father Henry, Lord Darnley, as well as after his ally Henri IV of France, was made Prince of Wales, and to celebrate his investiture Inigo Jones designed the masque *Barriers,* which was presented on Twelfth Night 1610. In this the handsome hero-prince is summoned by King Arthur and Merlin to restore the fallen house of chivalry. For this highly allegorical entertainment, and for the Christmas Masque of 1611, Ben Jonson wrote the texts, with the Prince of Wales in the role of Oberon, the Faery Prince—romantic and scholarly, a perfect horseman, and the son of King Arthur. Sketches by Inigo Jones for Henry's costumes show him as a medieval knight and as a young Roman emperor.

The popularity and ability of the Stuart heir seemed to herald the continuance of a golden age of peace and prosperity, with the Stuarts as patrons of Shakespeare, Inigo Jones, Ben Jonson and others. Encouraged by the Spanish Ambassador Sarmiento, who had become the confidant of the Queen, James had the grandiose idea of a Spanish marriage for his elder son. But all these dreams vanished when Henry, after playing tennis, died suddenly of fever on 6 November 1612, a fortnight before his nineteenth birthday. In 1653 Arthur Wilson wrote in his *Life of James I*: 'Some say he was poysoned with a bunch of grapes, others by the venomous scent of a pair of gloves presented to him by an ill-wisher but his physicians gave out that he died of a strong, malignant fever'. James still did not give up the dream of a Spanish alliance, hoping that Charles might marry a Spanish Infanta. In that way he might preserve the balance between Protestant and Catholic powers.

The death of the Prince of Wales, coming eighteen months after the assassination of his most important European ally, Henri IV of France, made it more urgent than ever for James to establish his position as Christian non-papal mediator between nations on the continent. He therefore hurried on the preparations for the marriage of his daughter Elizabeth to Frederick, the Elector Palatine, head of the German Protestant princes.

As James's Master of the Household, one of the many Scottish-held appointments that angered the English nobles, Ludovic, Duke of Lennox, had charge of the wedding arrangements. The ceremony took place on St Valentine's Day, 1613, in the Chapel Royal at Whitehall. The radiant bride, her hair flowing loose, was escorted to the altar by a pair of bachelors, her brother Charles and the Earl of Northampton, and returned from the chapel between two married men, the imposing Duke of Lennox and the Lord High Admiral of England, the Earl of Nottingham.

At this time Ludovic was once again a childless widower, his second wife Jean Campbell having died in childbed. Shortly afterwards he married his third wife, the twice-married but also childless Frances Howard, Countess of Hertford. The pair turned out to be very well suited, and became one of the most amusing couples at the Jacobean court. They were leading lights in the court entertainments devised at Whitehall by Inigo Jones and Ben Jonson. They acted with the professional players in the masques, as well as taking part in the exuberant extravaganzas devised for the King and his foppish young men and the Queen and her ladies, which more often than not ended up in drunken romps and revels.

Two months after Princess Elizabeth's marriage, while the Duke of Lennox was absent in Heidelberg with the young couple, Robert Cecil, Earl of Salisbury, died and James appointed as his successor his handsome French-educated favourite Robert Carr. Carr had risen to the position of private secretary through the usual channels of cup-bearer and gentleman-in-waiting.

Lennox had not long been married to the irrepressible Lady Hertford when James sounded him out about his brother Esmé, the Seigneur d'Aubigny. He asked about the possibility of his changing his religion and coming to settle in London. Esmé agreed, went to Whitehall, and married the rich Anglican bride James had found for him, Lady Katherine Clifton, who in the next ten years produced seven sons and three daughters. When the second Esmé Stuart left Aubigny for England in 1614, Ludovic had to resign his nominal captaincy of the Hundred Scottish Men-at-Arms in the service of Louis XIII of France. To make his government position in England legal, James created Ludovic Earl of Richmond in the peerage of England, as well as Knight of the Garter.

By 1614 the outrage caused by the scandalous marriage the previous September of Carr, ennobled as the Earl of Somerset, and the notorious Countess of Essex had died down. The King in his late middle age was now newly besotted by another beautiful young man, the much cleverer George Villiers, younger son of an obscure Leicestershire squire. He had risen in the usual way in the King's favour, then became first of all Earl, then Marquess, of Buckingham. Vain and unscrupulous, he soon became the most influential figure at court. James doted on this slim youth with deep blue eyes and dark curling hair, calling him affectionately 'Steenie', because to James he resembled St Stephen, and himself his 'dear old Dad'. The reserved and morally upright Charles, Prince of Wales, at first resented this new rival for his father's affections, but soon he too fell under Buckingham's spell.

The second Esmé Stuart had his numerous offspring baptised as Anglicans in the chapel royal at Whitehall. His eldest sons Henry and James, born in 1616 and 1617 respectively, had Charles, Prince of Wales, as their godfather. Five other sons were born to Esmé Stuart in London—George, John, Bernard, Francis and Ludovic. The seventh, who outlived them, returned to France to enter holy orders and to claim the Aubigny estates. He turned out to be the most wordly of them all.

The affairs of Elizabeth and her husband the Elector Palatine went well until 1619, when he accepted the crown of Bohemia in defiance of the Catholic Habsburgs. Within months he was defeated in battle and deprived of all power and possessions. It was the beginning of the bitter religious wars that ranged over central Europe for decades. So it was that Elizabeth, known as the Queen of Hearts, became, as the wife of the Winter King, the Winter Queen.

In the New Years' Honours of 1623, Ludovic Stuart's earldom of Richmond was upgraded to a dukedom in the peerage of England, which took precedence over his Scottish title of Duke of Lennox. On the eve of the opening of Parliament in February of that year he died at the age of fifty, in a manner as singular as it was sudden. In the morning Ludovic, as Master of the Household, was due to attend the King but failed to appear. James, wondering where he was, sent a messenger to his house. The Duchess, who had left her husband asleep, opened the curtains of his bed and was horror-stricken to find him a corpse. She told friends privately that no one was more astonished than she was, as he had given her ample proofs of his virility only a few hours before. The King was so affected by the death of his friend of forty years' standing that he ordered Parliament to be prorogued for a week, during which time Ludovic Stuart was given a magnificent funeral and buried near Mary, Queen of Scots, in Westminster Abbey.

His widow, after a decent period of morning, turned her roving eye on the King, who had been a widower since Anne of Denmark's death four years earlier in 1619. She said that after her husband no other man was in the kingdom worthy to be her fourth husband. But James was old and ailing and still hopelessly infatuated with his beloved Buckingham. Women, even though they were as amusing and attractive as Frances

Stuart, had very little appeal for James, so that her hopes of ending her life as Queen of England were dashed.

Esmé, third Duke of Lennox and Richmond, only survived his brother by one year. He died in 1624 shortly after being invested with his brother's Order of the Garter at Windsor. The deaths of the Lennox Stuart brothers affected the ageing King deeply, but once again he showed unfailing generosity in providing for the orphaned children. The eldest son Henry went back to France to become eighth Seigneur d'Aubigny, taking with him his four younger brothers to be brought up by their grandmother, the formidable old Duchesse Cathérine.

Esmé's second son James, who was seven years old when his father died, stayed behind in England to become fourth Duke of Lennox and Richmond. Charles, as Prince of Wales and afterwards as King, continued, as his godfather, to look after him, sending him to Cambridge and afterwards on the Grand Tour. James became a Privy Counsellor, a Warden of the Cinque Ports and Knight of the Garter, and remained close to the King during the Civil War, his imprisonment, trial and death. He married Buckingham's beautiful daughter, Lady Mary Villiers, but they had no surviving children.

Following the outbreak of what was to be called the Thirty-years War, James had hoped to redress his misguided policy by seeking an alliance with Spain. With his secret connivance early in 1623 Charles embarked on a romantic adventure. The Prince of Wales and Buckingham, who was the instigator of the enterprise, went to the continent disguised as merchants, travelling under the nondescript names of Tom and John Smith. On their way to Spain they are known to have lodged in the rue St Jacques, most probably at the Aubigny Stuarts' town house. From there they paid an incognito visit to the Louvre and from a gallery watched a ballet in which the thirteen-year-old Princesse Henriette Marie performed with her sister-in-law, the Queen of France. Buckingham, from that distant glimpse, nevertheless lost his heart to Anne of Austria, the French Queen and sister of the desired Infanta. In March the two 'merchants' were in Madrid. Charles, a heretic in the eyes of Philip IV, had little chance as a brother-in-law, even if the behaviour of Buckingham, newly created Duke, had not antagonized their host. By October the pair were back in England with nothing achieved.

Buckingham's thoughts then turned to a French marriage for Charles, to spite the Spanish King. He suggested an alliance with the Princesse Henriette Marie and a marriage contract was negotiated. It was the secret clauses agreed to by James in the contract that contained the first seeds of the downfall of the Stuarts; they granted full liberty of conscience and of worship for the princess's suite and laid down that the persecution of

Catholics in England, which had gone on since the Gunpowder Plot, was to cease at once. In letters between the bride-to-be and the Pope it was laid down that she would decide the religious up-bringing of any children born of the marriage. The preliminary articles, to ensure English neutrality in any French war with Spain, were drafted by Richelieu, and signed on behalf of King James by Lord Kensington on 10 November 1624. But the final terms of the marriage treaty were not completed until after James's death on 27 March 1625, and were between 'Madame Henriette, soeur du Roy de France et Charles premier Roy de la Grande Bretagne'.

When the papal dispensation permitting the Princess to marry a Protestant finally reached Paris, the wedding took place on a dais outside Notre Dame, with the Duc de Chevreuse acting as proxy for Charles I. Two weeks later Buckingham at his most flamboyant arived in France to escort Henrietta Maria (as we shall now call her) back to England. Queen Anne of Austria as well as the Dowager Queen Marie de Médicis travelled with her as far as Amiens, where Buckingham made a final bid to press his attentions on the Queen of France and nearly succeeded in compromising her honour.

Charles was waiting somewhat nervously at Dover, and the young couple journeyed as far as Canterbury, where they spent their first night in England. Henrietta Maria found Charles as handsome as the portrait Lord Kensington had brought her at the time of her betrothal. She was just fifteen, nine years younger than her husband, and eager to be a loyal and loving wife. The small, dark, voluble daughter of the amorous Henri IV and the Florentine Marie de Médicis was passionate by nature and given to violent outbursts of temper if she did not get her own way. Charles was patient, reserved and stubborn, and at first she found him disappointingly undemonstrative. The only time he gave in to her she made one of the most serious blunders of her life, when she flatly refused to take part in the Anglican coronation service. His subjects were outraged and the Queen paid for this tactical mistake for the rest of Charles's reign and in her exile.

In France she had adored acting and dancing in ballets at the Luxembourg, and to win her husband's admiration in the first year in England she caused another scandal by appearing in a French masque *Artenice*, designed by Inigo Jones, in which she played a speaking part. The uproar died down and she and Jones continued their collaboration, the Queen appearing in most of the court masques throughout the 1630s. Jones had redesigned her chapel at St James's Palace, where she and her French attendants regularly heard mass.

In spite of their clashes, the new King and Queen later became a devoted couple, setting quite a different tone at court to that of the preceding reign. The age of James, with his fondness for handsome young men and disreputable drunken romps and revels was past. The murder of Buckingham in 1628 struck a death blow to the tradition of the King being manipulated by a male favourite. After Buckingham's assassination Henrietta Maria became and remained until the Civil War her husband's chief adviser. The first two children born to the royal couple died in infancy. By the time an heir, Charles, was born on 29 May 1630, the King had sufficiently asserted himself as a husband to dismiss the Queen's trouble-making French retinue. Ludovic Stuart's still fascinating widow, the Duchess of Lennox and Richmond, was invited to be godmother to the future Charles II. She caused a great stir at the christening by the lavishness of her presents and the magnificence of her clothes and jewels, which quite outshone those of Henrietta Maria. Charles and all the other Stuart children were baptized members of the Church of England, which the Catholic Queen found hard to accept, though she had nothing else with which to reproach her husband. He was a model husband and father, and they both loved their children dearly. Putting his troubles with Parliament aside Charles emerged as a serious patron of the arts. At the age of twenty-three, as Prince of Wales, he had bought the Raphael cartoons. Before then, through his ambassadors on the continent, particularly Sir Henry Wotton at Venice, he had added priceless works of art to the royal collection. In 1630 Rubens, who had worked for Henrietta Maria's mother at the Luxembourg, came to England and began the decorations for Inigo Jones's magnificent new banqueting hall at Whitehall, for which he was knighted. Van Dyck, the portraitist, arrived from the Low Countries, and in the realm of the theatre the court masques of Ben Jonson and Inigo Jones, and, after their quarrel in 1633, of Inigo Jones and Carew and Davenant, glorified the ideal state and the Stuart conception of divine and harmonious monarchy.

During the 1630s Charles sent James, Duke of Richmond, to ask his other godson, Henry Stuart, Seigneur d'Aubigny to join him at the English court. Henry at first refused, saying he did not want to leave his grandmother, the formidable old Duchess of Lennox, and his friends in France. When she died, he changed his mind and joined his brother James on a diplomatic mission to Savoy. Afterwards Charles paid for him to go on the Grand Tour with his French tutor. Henry unfortunately caught a fever and died in Venice and was buried in the Church of SS Giovanni and Paolo.

His brother George was still studying at the College de Navarre in Paris, and King Charles sent him on the Grand Tour. After visiting Aubigny George went to England. In the next year, 1638, he married

Henrietta Maria stands in the forecourt of one of Inigo Jones's most beautiful architectural creations, the Queen's House in Greenwich.

Lady Katherine Howard, daughter of the Duke of Suffolk.

The Ship-money case of Rex *v* John Hampden brought the first rumblings of discontent in the late 1630s. Charles had taken the leading role in the Twelfth Night masque *Britannia Triumphans*, in which the King justified the levying of ship-money as a legitimate means of keeping the seas free from the pirates who menaced British shipping. The last of the Court masques, *Salmacida Spolia*, performed in 1640, was an evocation of royal power threatened by adversity. The King and Queen both appeared in it as the god and goddess dispelling the evil forces menacing the State, but already Inigo Jones' dream world was fading into

Charles I commissioned Van Dyck to paint this portrait of himself to commemorate the white stallion which was the gift of his brother-in-law Louis XIII. (Reproduced by gracious permission of Her Majesty The Queen.)

cold reality. With the abolition of the Courts of High Commission and the Star Chamber, and Charles forced to sign the death warrant of his old friend and wisest counsellor Strafford, the stage darkened to be reset for the real drama of the Civil War.

The Aubigny Stuarts, with the exception of the crippled Abbé Ludovic, all rallied to the Royalist cause. When the King raised his standard at Nottingham in August 1642, George Stuart immediately raised his own troop of horse in support of his godfather. He was killed at Edgehill in the first battle of the war, watched from a nearby knoll by the two elder Stuart princes, Charles aged twelve as swarthy as his nine-year-old brother James was fair. George, the ninth Seigneur d'Aubigny, was buried in the Cathedral of Christ Church College in Oxford, which had become the Royalist headquarters. He left two children, a son Charles born in 1639 and a daughter Katherine born in 1640. His young widow acted as a courier for the King between Oxford and London. This was a dangerous mission as the capital was in the hands of the King's opponents throughout the war and she was in fact captured by the Parliamentary forces and imprisoned. After her release from the Tower of London she married Lord Newburgh, owner of the best racehorses in England. When the Royalist cause collapsed, they were forced to flee to Holland, and she died at The Hague in 1650. Her son and daughter were cared for by relatives in England, where they remained safely in obscurity until the end of the Commonwealth.

Lords John and Francis Stuart were killed at Alresford in 1644. Their brother Bernard (the English form of Béraud), after the third battle of Newbury in November of that year, was made Colonel of the King's Life Guards, an appointment coveted by Prince Rupert, who was already Master of the Horse and General of all the King's forces in England. Bernard was a first-class cavalry commander, and was created Earl of Lichfield shortly before the decisive Royalist defeat at Naseby in June 1645. His eldest brother James, Duke of Richmond, fought beside and had an enduring friendship with Rupert and the Prince's love affair with James's wife Mary, daughter of George Villiers, first Duke of Buckingham, did nothing to disrupt the friendship. Richmond was one of the King's most faithful friends. He was with Charles during his imprisonment at Holdemby House in Northamptonshire and at Carisbrooke Castle in the Isle of Wight. He shared the King's last Christmas at Windor and attended him at his trial and execution. He was at St James's Palace the night before Charles's death, when the royal children, the Princess Elizabeth who was fourteen and the eight-year old Harry, Duke of Gloucester, were brought from Syon House to take leave of their father. The Princess was in floods of tears but Harry, when the King took him on his lap, assured him staunchly that 'he would be torn to pieces first' if the Roundheads tried to make him King instead of his elder brothers.

The morning of 30 January was bitterly cold. Charles, resigned to his fate and feeling that he was dying in a just cause, dressed carefully for the final role he had been called upon to play. He put on an extra shirt in case he should shiver on the scaffold and the spectators might think he was

Charles I's godsons, Lords John and Bernard Stuart, sons of the third Duke of Lennox, were both killed in the Civil War, Lord John at Alresford and Lord Bernard at Naseby.

afraid, then fixed his pearl earrings, which had, along with his Van Dyck collar, become part of his image, and the Garter jewel he would wear on the journey to his death. He took communion from Bishop Juxon and then waited until the guards knocked on the door of his room at ten o'clock to tell him the time had come to leave St James's Palace. He walked briskly through the park with his dog Rogue at his heels. The winter sunshine shone bleak and cold, and he quickened his pace between the double line of guards to reach Whitehall in twenty minutes. There he had to wait another four hours before being summoned to step out through the window of Inigo Jones's banqueting hall on to the small, closely guarded scaffold draped in black. James, Duke of Richmond, was among the group of friends who waited with him and persuaded him to eat a bite of bread and drink a glass of claret to sustain him in his ordeal.

When he came to enact the part, he played it perfectly as the martyr king going from a 'corruptible to an incorruptible crown'. He died having acknowledged his fault in sending his trusted servant Stafford to the same death, but he did not grant the customary pardon to the masked executioner and his assistant. In Charles's eyes he was the divinely appointed lawgiver facing a ritual murder. He lay down and stretched out his hands as a sign to the headsman that he was ready for the fatal blow. One stroke severed the King's neck, then the masked man held up the resigned countenance by the long hair saying 'Behold the head of a traitor!'

There were no acclamations when this supreme royal spectacle was over, only a prolonged horror-stricken groan, which subsided into a numbed silence. The crowds dispersed aimlessly. There was a feeling of anticlimax. Tyranny they were told was ended; before them stretched the prospect of a Puritan republic, sober and respectable, from which the colour, pleasures and entertainments of the monarchy were banished. The Stuarts had lived in a privileged dream world, as insubstantial as the 'cloud-capped towers' of Shakespeare's *Tempest*, now dissolved by Cromwell's cruel necessity into stern reality. The English quality of adaptability accepted the change as inevitable. Those who could not accept it, and had the means to do so, went abroad to France or Holland, to a Europe emerging from the ravages of the Thirty Years War. The Peace of Westphalia, which ended that war, had been signed in 1648, the year before Charle's execution, and for the next 200 years the quarrels were to be about politics, trade and colonial expansion.

7

THE FIRST EXILE

THE FIRST OF THE EXILES that were to befall the royal Stuarts in the seventeenth century took place in 1644. Henrietta Maria was in a highly nervous state, seven months pregnant with her ninth child and convinced that she would die and never see her husband again. The King was as distressed and anxious as she was, and sent her under the escort of Henry Jermyn to the comparative safety of the West Country. After saying goodbye to her at Abingdon, he scribbled a frantic note to his own and his late father's elderly French physician: 'Mayerne. For the love of me go to the Queen.' Anne of Austria, the widow of Louis XIII, sent Madame Peronne, the midwife who had delivered Louis XIV and his brother Philippe, to help Mayerne during the confinement. On 16 June 1644, at Bedford House, Exeter, Henrietta Maria after a long and difficult labour, gave birth to a small but healthy daughter. She then contracted puerperal fever and was so ill that there were fears for her recovery. As soon as she was well enough, Charles urged her to go to France with Madame Peronne, and to leave the child for the time being in the care of Anne Villiers, Lady Dalkeith, daughter-in-law of the Scottish Earl of Morton. The Queen had already sailed from Falmouth when, on 21 July in Exeter Cathedral, the princess was christened Henrietta after her mother. The Royalist city of Exeter was besieged and taken by the Parliamentary forces the following spring, but their commander, Fairfax, allowed Lady Dalkeith to take the baby to Oatlands in Surrey. They stayed there until July 1646, when things were going so badly for the Royalists that the King instructed Lady Dalkeith, now the Countess of Morton, to take his youngest child to join her mother and brother Charles in Paris.

Back in France, after an absence of twenty years, Henrietta Maria found herself in an unenviable position. For the past three years the government had been in the hands of her Spanish sister-in-law, Anne of Austria, and Richelieu's successor, the Italian Cardinal Mazarin. Both were unpopular, not only with the dead King's jealous brother Gaston d'Orléans, his daughter La Grande Mademoiselle, and the Bourbon princes of the blood Condé and Conti, but with the Parlement and people of Paris as well. The French Queen Mother gave Henrietta Maria a sparsely furnished suite of rooms in the Louvre, and made her a modest allowance, which was the best she could do in her own difficult circumstances. In the summer of 1648 the hostility of the people of Paris broke out into the open rebellion known as the Fronde of the Parlement. Anne of Austria and Mazarin took the ten-year-old Louis XIV and his brother to the safety of St Germain-en-Laye, but Henrietta Maria and her daughter were left behind to spend a cheerless Christmas and New Year in the almost deserted Louvre.

It was in that cold empty palace in the middle of February 1649 that Lord Jermyn broke the traumatic news that Charles had been beheaded on 30 January. She had known that he had spent Christmas at Windsor, and though the silence of the past weeks had been frightening, she was convinced the English people would never dare kill her husband in cold blood. When she had recovered from the first numbing shock, she asked Henry Jermyn to tell her the harrowing details of the execution and its aftermath. He told her that he with some others had kept vigil during the week that the King's embalmed body had lain in St James's Palace; that James Stuart of Aubigny, Duke of Richmond, had scratched the name King Charles and the date of his death on the coffin before he and four others—the Marquess of Hertford, the Earls of Southampton and Lindsay and Bishop Juxon—conveyed it to Windsor for burial in St George's Chapel. The Marquess of Montrose had gone to Holland to break the news to the Prince of Wales and the Duke of York, who were living with their eldest sister, Princess Mary of Orange, but the two younger Stuart children were still prisoners in St James's Palace, where they had said farewell to their father.

Charles I had made his tragic exit from the scene, but it was Henrietta Maria who was left, at thirty-nine, to face the desolate reality of being widowed, penniless and regarded as a foreigner in the country of her birth, where she had been brought up in luxury as a princess of France. During the last five years she had sold most of her jewels to send money to her husband, and now she knew she had to depend on the charity of her sister-in-law. The emotional shock was eased by the devotion of Henry Jermyn, but it could not make the loss of her husband and her predicament as an impoverished Queen in exile any easier to bear. She turned for comfort in these depressing circumstances to her daughter Henrietta, who had never known her father. The young princess knew what he looked like from the many portraits and paintings of the King.

The double portrait now to be seen in London in St Mary's Church in the Strand gives an idea of the King and Queen as a young married couple. In this Henrietta Maria stands looking up at her grave handsome husband. She wears a long-sleeved low-bodiced dress of white silk and lace. On the fourth finger of her left hand she wears a broad gold wedding ring and a pearl ring. There are pearls at her throat, pearl drops in her ears, and the dark tendrils on her forehead and at the nape of her neck are encircled with pearls. Charles, for once, is not dressed in sombre colours, but wears a jacket of crimson satin with white satin sleeves slashed with crimson velvet over red satin knee-breeches, white silk stockings and white satin shoes ornamented with white rosettes. His own dark brown hair is worn long and his pale face has an elegant Vandyck beard; like his wife, he wears the pearl drop earrings he never relinquished, even on the morning of his death. On the King's right are the royal arms of England, Scotland and Ireland, and on the Queen's right the royal arms of France and Navarre.

With her husband dead and five children either in exile or under guard, Henrietta Maria, though very conscious of her status as a Daughter of France, swallowed her pride and asked Cromwell for a pension as the widow of King Charles I. He replied brutally, without hesitation, that as she had refused to be crowned Queen Consort of England in 1625, she had absolutely no claim to a pension as Queen Dowager. She accepted this refusal with dignity, and resigned herself to remaining a poor relation at the court of her young nephew, Louis XIV, while she hoped against hope that the royalists in England might rally to support her eldest son Charles. At nineteen Charles was already a man of the world and the father of a son, James, born in Brussels the previous year to his Welsh mistress Lucy Walter. When the Marquess of Montrose, James Graham, brought the news of his father's execution to the Prince of Wales, he had already left Lucy Walter and the boy, who later became James, Duke of Monmouth, in Brussels and was living in the Hague. James Graham, the 'Great Marquess' of the year of victories, 1645, stayed for a time at the Wassenaer Hof, which had been for twenty-five years the shabby but friendly home of Charles I's sister Elizabeth, the exiled Queen of Bohemia. The Winter Queen, despite her debts and the cares of her large family, was as energetic and sympathetic as ever. In her house Montrose discussed his plans to regroup the royalist exiles in the Low Countries for a counter-attack on Cromwell in the north of Scotland. He fell under the spell of this indomitable woman, who had been the Elector Palatine's dazzling bride almost forty years ago, and he fell in love with her favourite daughter, the intelligent and talented artist Louise. In the spring of 1649 Montrose left the Hague to raise a mercenary force in Denmark and Sweden for the rising in Scotland, advising Charles and James not to set out for Scotland until they had received good news of the attempt. With Elizabeth of Bohemia, who was an inveterate letter-writer, Montrose kept in constant touch until his expedition sailed in March 1650. Charles and James were in Paris visiting their mother and their youngest sister, and it was to Paris that messengers brought the news that dashed their hopes; the invasion from the Orkneys had proved abortive, and they waited in vain to hear of Montrose's escape to the continent. Instead he was betrayed at Loch Assynt in Sutherland and brought to Edinburgh to be executed by the Covenanters under Argyll. Montrose was dragged on a hurdle with a hempen rope round his neck to be hanged, drawn and quartered in the Grassmarket of Edinburgh, but the Great Marquess, who had written as a young cavalier:

> He either fears his fate too much,
> Or his deserts are small,
> Who dares not to put it to the touch,
> To win or lose it all.

faced the common hangman with a composure that no one present could ever forget.

In 1648 James, Duke of York, the heir-apparent, went to France to be with his mother during this anxious time. At eighteen James was tall, fair and very handsome, with a haughty expression. He spoke French fairly well but was handicapped by the slight stutter he had inherited from his father. At court he chafed against his enforced inactivity; his ambition was to serve in the French army under the man he most admired—Henri de la Tour d'Auvergne, the Protestant Maréchal Turenne.

In the summer of 1650 Charles received an offer of the crown of Scotland from the very Argyll and Covenanters who had put Montrose to death. He had enough Bourbon-Médici opportunism in his blood to accept their terms unconditionally and went to Scotland. Cromwell opposed this move and marched to Dunbar to defeat his former ally, the Scottish General Leslie ('Crooked Davie'). This did not deter the Scots, who were not prepared to swallow Cromwell's rule, and in defiance they crowned the Stuart heir King Charles II of Scotland at Scone on New Year's Day, 1651. It was only after he had been crowned by Argyll that Charles realized what this meant: he was forced to sign the Covenant, to accept the narrowest form of Presbyterianism as his religion and to promise to impose it upon England. He was also made to renounce his own parents publicly as being the most infamous of creatures. All the usual amusements were forbidden him during the humiliating months he spent as the nominal head of the Covenanting army, which, led by Leslie, invaded England on August 1651. On 3 September 1651 the Scots faced Cromwell at Worcester, a battle that resulted in total defeat for the

Covenanters. Charles was one of the lucky few to escape. He was rescued and saved from the same fate as his father by a Jesuit priest named Father Huddleston, a debt he never forgot, and for two months lived as a penniless fugitive in the West of England, unable to get word to his family that he was still alive. His unusual height and strongly marked features—'a tall, black man about six feet high' the description circulated—would have made his recognition and denunciation to the searching Roundheads almost certain if it had not been for the loyalty of the royalist sympathizers among the country people, gentry and commoners alike.

At the end of November 1651 Charles arrived in France, having escaped in a fishing boat. His hair was cropped short like a Roundhead and his skin was so coarse and weather-beaten that he was almost unrecognisable. He turned up in Paris a hardened adventurer who had survived his ordeal and had only one idea in his head—to enjoy life to the full and to treat the world from now onwards with cynical detachment.

There had been talk that Charles might marry a Palatine princess, but that came to nothing. Then a match was proposed to Gaston d'Orléans's daughter, Anne Marie, Duchesse de Montpensier, the richest heiress in France. At first the King's niece seemed to welcome the prospect with some pleasure. But as Charles's fortunes sank in the two years after the abortive Scottish attempt, la Grande Mademoiselle, although already twenty-five and still unmarried, grew more haughty and distant, until at last she dismissed the idea as beneath her notice. Never wanting for women, Charles shrugged off this refusal and openly sought his pleasures in Paris. He quickly discarded a member of his mother's household in favour of a warm-hearted and dazzlingly beautiful widow, the Duchesse de Châtillon. Charles had pet names for everyone he liked, and as he was charmed by the Duchesse and her chattering ways, he gave her the famous nickname Bablon. Older than he, she captivated all who met her, and together they maintained a life-enduring friendship. But in the main the exiled King without a crown dallied in Paris for the next two years until the Anglo-French alliance drove him into Germany in 1654.

Meanwhile Cardinal Mazarin and the Queen Regent Anne dealt with yet another rebellion, the Fronde of the Princes. In December 1651, only a month after Charles' return to France, the rebellious princes, Gaston d'Orléans, Beaufort, Conti and Condé, were brought down by Turenne's defection to the Government. Mazarin was briefly recalled to his post as premier. In the following months the renegade Protestant Turenne defeated his former cohorts at several encounters, at one of which la Grande Mademoiselle herself went into battle at Orléans on her father's behalf. After her spectacular victory she helped the Bourbon Condé enter Paris by seizing the cannons in the Bastille, but was betrayed by Condé's insufferable arrogance which soon enraged the Parisians. The Fronde rebels began to bicker among themselves, and as they disintegrated, Mazarin wisely removed himself from the scene. This created a false atmosphere of reconciliation between the rebels and their King and government. In 1652 the King's government prevailed and Gaston d'Orléans and his daughter were banished to their private country estates.

When order had been temporarily restored, James, Duke of York reappeared on the scene to ask his cousin's permission to serve as a volunteer under his idol Turenne. Louis XIV accepted the young Duke's offer and, during the next three years, James proved himself an excellent soldier, fighting five campaigns with the French army. He distinguished himself as a reliable and enterprising company commander, and at the Battle of the Dunes in June 1658, when he found himself fighting alongside the English Commonwealth forces against the Spaniards commanded by the rebel Condé, he was personally cited for bravery by Turenne. The result of this victory was the capture of Dunkirk by the English. Also mentioned in despatches by Turenne in this engagement was an eccentric Gascon minor nobleman, the Comte de Lauzun, who was to play a key role in James's life in the future. Turenne became James's substitute father-figure and there is little doubt that the Protestant Marshal's conversion to Catholicism by Bossuet in 1668 had a decisive influence on the Duke of York's change of religion in the same year.

As an ex-Queen, Henrietta Maria found time hanging heavily on her hands; she also found it boring to live in the shadow of her Spanish sister-in-law at court. Ever since one of the great ladies of France (later canonized as St Jeanne de Chantal), with the encouragement of St François de Sales, had founded the Order of the Visitation of St Marie in 1610, the fashion for founding these very special convents had swept through France and Italy. Henrietta Maria was devout but she was also worldly, and this order appealed to her as being religion in its most attractive form – no gloom, no excessive penances but intelligent conversation, good manners, tranquillity, visits from friends of either sex, good but simple living, and the nuns and their guests alike all ladies of quality. These Convents of the Visitation were designed as agreeable retreats for well born widows and discarded royal mistresses, where a first-class education in the most exclusive sort of boarding-school was provided for their daughters.

With all the determination she had inherited from her parents, and her own force of character, the exiled Queen of England searched until she found what she wanted. It was a small elegant château at Chaillot on the outskirts of Paris, which had been built about 1600 by her father's old friend and companion in gallantries, the Maréchal de Bassompierre, to house his mistresses. It stood in the midst of gardens and orchards high above the Seine on the site of the present Trocadéro, overlooking the busy road to St Germain-en-Laye. There was a farm attached to it, vineyards on the slopes behind the house and a woodland path leading to the pretty village of Passy nearby. The Maréchal de Bassompierre had been Ambassador in England when she was first married, and had helped to smooth out the difficulties she had encountered as a young and inexperienced Queen. She made out such a convincing case for buying this property and establishing it as a convent that Louis XIV and his mother both contributed towards the purchase.

The King allowed her to choose furniture from the royal palaces for her private apartments on the first floor, overlooking the river. He and his mother gave her money to build a chapel with the characteristic baroque domes that were beginning to change the Paris skyline, and, to please the foundress, no expense was spared in incorporating a royal tribune. By 1654 nuns and pupils had been chosen and installed, and Henrietta Maria celebrated the completion of the chapel by having her daughter received into the Catholic faith and rebaptized with the additional name of Anne, after her godmother Anne of Austria. In February 1654, soon after this, Henriette Anne made her debut as the Muse of Poetry at a ball in the Palais Royal to celebrate the marriage of one of Cardinal Mazarin's nieces, Anna-Maria Martinozzi, to the Prince de Conti. The Princess danced the leading role opposite her cousin Louis XIV, who was dressed as Apollo. Henrietta Maria was recovering from the blow of hearing that Mazarin had made, in her eyes, the unforgivable gesture of recognizing Cromwell as Lord Protector of England. But this shrewd political move paid off shortly afterwards, unexpectedly in her favour, when Cromwell released her youngest son Henry and sent him to join his mother in France, giving him £500 for his travelling expenses.

The young Duke of Gloucester had been apprenticed to a shoemaker that he might earn his bread honestly, and had been called for the last four years simply Master Harry Stuart. His elder sister, the Princess Elizabeth, had been imprisoned on the Isle of Wight with him, but she had never recovered from that last terrible leave-taking they had had with their father at St James's Palace the night before his execution. She had pined away with grief and died a year later.

Harry, Duke of Gloucester, was just fourteen when he arrived in Paris to meet the mother he scarcely remembered and the sister he had never seen. He was tall for his age, robust and fair-haired like James, and spoke no French. After a few months with a French tutor he became quite fluent and enjoyed learning the aristocratic sports of riding, fencing and tennis.

Charles paid a fleeting visit from the Hague when he heard of Harry's

L'Abbé Ludovic Stuart d'Aubigny, confidant of Henrietta Maria during her exile, was the surviving son of the third Duke of Lennox.

arrival at the Palais Royal. He had taken his sister's conversion to Catholicism philosophically, knowing she would probably marry and settle in France, but he spoke very seriously to his impressionable young brother on the subject. Charles knew that if Henry was also converted by his mother, his own chances of being restored to the throne of England would suffer.

Henry's conversion was exactly what his mother was planning, with the support of the Abbé Ludovic Stuart of Aubigny and her almoner, the ex-playwright the Abbé Walter Montagu, who had written the masque *The Shepherds' Paradise,* with settings designed by Inigo Jones, in which she had played Belezza, the Princess of Navarre, in 1633. Walter Montagu was himself a recent convert. With France's recognition of the Commonwealth in England, Henrietta Maria saw no future for her sons other than as mercenaries in the service of some European power. So, in spite of Charles, she decided that the best career for her youngest son was to become a prince of her own church.

In November 1654 Charles was in Cologne with his friend the Marquis of Ormonde, when he received a disquieting letter from the Duke of Gloucester telling him of his mother's plans. Charles was furious and replied at once in no uncertain terms. He was a born letter-writer, as the hundreds which survive in his own hand testify. He wrote:

> Dear Brother, I have received yours without a date in which you tell me that Mr Montagu has endeavoured to pervert you from your religion. I do not doubt but you remember very well the commands I left with you at my going away concerning that point.
>
> I am confident that you will observe them, yet your letters that come from Paris say that it is the Queen's purpose to do all she can to change your religion, in which, if you do hearken to her, you must never think to see England again: and whatsoever mischief shall fall upon me or my affairs from this time, I must lay all upon you as being the only cause of it. Therefore, consider well what it is to be the cause of ruining a brother that loves you well, but also your King and your country. Do not let them persuade you either by force or by fair promises; for the first they neither dare nor will use; and for the second, as soon as they have perverted you, they will have their end, and they will care no more for you. I am also informed that there is a purpose to put you into the Jesuit's college, which I command you, never to consent to. And whensoever, anyone shall go to dispute with you in religion, do not answer them at all; for though you have reason on your side, yet they, being prepared, will have the advantage of anybody who is not upon the same security as they are. If you do not consider what I say unto you, remember the last words of your dead father, which were to be constant to your religion and never to be shaken in it. Which, if you do not observe, will be the last time you will hear from me. Dear brother, Your most affectionate brother, Charles R.[1]

To lend weight to his words Charles signed the letter with the official royal signature he normally only used in formal communications. In the many family letters he wrote he used a scribbled monogram of an entwined C and S for Charles Stuart. To follow up his instructions he despatched Ormonde without delay to bring Henry back with him from Paris, well out of reach of his mother. Though he loved her dearly, calling her familiarly Mam, short for Maman, when not addressing her respectfully as the Queen, he knew her character only too well. Henrietta Maria made the expected hysterical scene, but Ormonde remained unmoved and forced the young Duke to pack and leave with him for Germany.

When they had gone, she accepted the situation, decided that perhaps after all Charles was right and returned to Chaillot to make plans for Henriette Anne's future. James, fourth Duke of Lennox and Richmond, died in Holland in 1655 leaving no son by his wife, the beautiful Lady Mary Villiers. Nothing had been heard of the heir to the dukedom and to the Aubigny estates since George Stuart's young children, Charles and Katherine, had been taken away by English relatives after their father's death at Edgehill. When Louis XIV came officially of age in 1656, therefore, Henrietta Maria's adviser, the Abbé Ludovic Stuart, now a canon of Notre Dame, claimed the Aubigny estates and did homage for them on 5 August 1656. The Abbé Ludovic was decidedly effeminate in manner, with a highly cultivated, malicious turn of mind. In the reaffirmation of the original donation by Charles VII of France of the *seigneurie* he had himself described grandly as 'Messire Ludovic Stuart, Prince of the Blood Royal of Scotland, tenth Lord of Aubigny and La Verrerie'.

Louis XIV was always kind to his aunt, and, to try and console her for the loss of the Duke of Gloucester, gave Henrietta Maria a pretty country house at Colombes on the river just outside Paris, as a change from her apartment at Chaillot. Two years later, when the Lord Protector died, her hopes were raised that there might be a royalist rising in favour of Charles, but Parliament continued to support Cromwell's son Richard and the Commonwealth continued.

Cardinal Mazarin was engaged in negotiating peace with Spain, the first condition being that Louis XIV should marry the Infanta Marie Thérèse. This was depressing news for the Stuarts, as it meant that James, who was reduced to fighting as a mercenary against the Spaniards, would be once more without means. The Stuarts had never been more embarrassing poor relations in France as they were now to Mazarin, completing the formalities of the Treaty of the Pyrenees. But, unknown to the Cardinal and the exiled royal family, political feeling across the Channel was undergoing a dramatic change. Richard Cromwell was proving himself totally inadequate as a ruler and causing general dissatisfaction in a country weary of years of restrictive Puritan rule. The Governor of Scotland, honest George Monk from Devon, had the imagination to sense that the time was ripe for a change. The General's brother was a doctor then living in France, and through him he got in touch with Charles's agent, the Chevalier Granville. Dr Monk and

Granville went secretly to Scotland to discuss restoring the monarchy on terms acceptable to the people of Britain.

As a result of these discussions, on 3 February 1660 General Monk marched into London with his troops and dissolved the Long Parliament. His intuition had been right. His military coup was accepted with relief by all classes of society. A month later the Rump Parliament voted its own dissolution. The new assembly drew up proposals to be forwarded to the King, in which he was to agree to a general amnesty and religious toleration.

Charles received a message to leave Spanish territory without delay and return to Holland. He obeyed and left Brussels just in time to avoid arrest by the Spanish authorities. He joined the Duke of York at Breda, where together they received the astonishing offer of the restoration of the Stuarts from the new free Parliament in London. Charles sent the Chevalier Granville back with a declaration to both Houses of Parliament accepting their terms. On 1 May Parliament invited the King formally to return, and sent him a very acceptable £30,000 in gold for his present needs. A week later he was proclaimed King.

Towards the middle of the month the English fleet sailed to Holland to take the Stuart brothers home. Charles's first act, even before the fleet arrived, was to appoint his brother James Lord High Admiral, an office which was to bring out his best qualities of bravery and a conscientious sense of duty. On 23 May the King, with the Duke of York and Harry, Duke of Gloucester, went aboard the finest ship of the English navy, whose name was tactfully changed for the occasion from *Naseby* to *Charles*. They sailed from Scheveningen to Dover, where Monk and enthusiastic crowds were waiting to greet them. From Rochester, where they spent their first night once again in England, Charles scribbled off a note to Henriette Anne at Colombes: 'My head is so prodigiously dazed by the acclamations of the people and by quantities of business that I know not whether I am writing sense or no . . .' This was addressed and sealed, as were most of his subsequent letters to her, 'For my deare, deare sister'. On the following day, 29 May and Charles's thirtieth birthday, the King entered his capital in triumph.

The majority of his subjects were more than ready to enjoy the relaxation of restrictions on normal human pleasures. As for Charles, he was determined to settle down to the comfortable existence he had been denied so long. Indolent and easy-going by nature, he meant to use every ounce of his energies to avoid ever having to go on his travels again. He was pleasure-loving and mercurial by temperament, disconcertingly shrewd and nearly always kind. Live and let live was his motto, and within months of his restoration his bachelor court had become a byword

Charles II soon after the Restoration.

in Europe for gaiety and licentiousness. The theatres in England, closed by law for eighteen years, now reopened. Sir William Davenant, who had written some of the most spectacular masques for the King, including *Britannia Triumphans* in 1638, reappeared on the scene. Soon after the Restoration he joined forces with Sir Thomas Killigrew, Charles's Master of the Revels in exile, and set up two companies in London in which professional actresses appeared for the first time.

There was soon keen but friendly rivalry in the pleasures and entertainments provided at their respective courts between the strictly brought up Louis XIV and his cousin Charles II. French aristocrats who had offended in some point of etiquette at the stiffer court of Louis XIV, and French beauties who felt their charms were not sufficiently appreciated, crossed the Channel to seek the freedom of manners for which the English court was already renowned.

Unfortunately the Stuart restoration had come too late for the Dowager Queen of England and her youngest daughter, as members of a reigning family, to receive last-minute invitations to the wedding of Louis XIV and the daughter of Philip IV of Spain. The French court had been moving south in slow and stately stages towards St Jean-de-Luz on the Spanish frontier, where the ceremony was to take place. Henrietta Maria and the Princess were at Colombes when they received Charles's first letter from England. The Queen Mother's first reaction was one of royal disappointment. They had missed the French royal wedding and now they had missed the Restoration. Practical as ever, she soon recovered her sense of proportion and began to look forward to the family reunion Charles said he was planning for September. In the meantime there was one consolation, for during the state entry of Louis XIV and his bride into Paris in August, the mother of the King of England and the Princess Henriette Anne were given places of honour at the Hôtel de Beauvais in the rue St Antoine.

Charles's elder sister, the widowed Princess Mary of Orange, was invited to London from the Hague, accompanied by her aunt, Elizabeth of Bohemia, with whom the Stuart brothers had often stayed, and whose sons, Rupert and Maurice of the Rhine, had fought for Charles I in the Civil War. Since her husband had been defeated as King of Bohemia almost forty years before, she had cheerfully brought up her thirteen children in exile with very little money. With age the Winter Queen had lost much of her beauty but none of her spirit during her 'long journey uphill'. She found Princess Mary of Orange patronisingly dull and deadly lazy, but James, Duke of York, was her favourite godson. She teased him out of his stiffness and moodiness. At the Hague also she saw him become entangled with Edward Hyde's daughter, plain 'Nan Hide', one of the Princess Mary's ladies-in-waiting.

Just before Henrietta Maria and Henriette Anne were due to set out for England, they received the heartrending news that Harry, Duke of Gloucester, had died of smallpox on 13 September. Neither his mother nor sister had seen him since their angry parting six years ago. The court went into mourning and the visit was delayed slightly. When the Queen and the Princess, with the Abbé Walter Montagu and Henriette Anne's school friend, the beautiful blonde Frances Stewart, reached Calais towards the end of the month, the Duke of York as Admiral of the Fleet was waiting to escort them in his private yacht. The meeting between mother and son was tense as James, against his strong-willed mother's wishes, had secretly married the eight-months pregnant Anne Hyde, about whom there was a lot of unpleasant gossip at court.

Charles had specially asked his mother to bring some pretty maids-of-honour with her, but he was not prepared for the effect the ravishing Frances Teresa Stewart had on him. The granddaughter of a Scottish cavalier, Walter Stewart, Lord Blantyre, she had been born in France and, like Henriette Anne, spoke and wrote French better than English. She caused a sensation at court, where Charles was instantly enamoured of her and called her 'La Belle Stuart', but her only response was to tease him unmercifully. Her intelligence did not appear to match her looks. She had an ice-cold temperament, flirted outrageously and affected to have a very

Frances Stewart, the daughter of the first Earl of Blantyre, 'La Belle Stuart', was Charles II's favourite and later married Charles Stuart Duke of Richmond, seigneur d'Aubigny. (Reproduced by gracious permission of Her Majesty The Queen.)

childish turn of mind. While the rest of the court gambled for the highest stakes around her, La Belle Stuart amused herself by building card-houses or persuading her admirers to play her favourite game of Blind Man's Bluff. She appeared to be oblivious to the jealousy her classical beauty aroused. Indeed she outshone even the showiest of Cardinal Mazarin's nieces, Olympe Mancini, wife of the French Ambassador to England, the Comte de Soissons.

Both Soissons and his wife reported favourably on the younger Stuart Princess, describing their first informal glimpse of her on 3 November, the morning after her arrival. They saw her in her bedroom at Whitehall wearing a loose gown of brightly printed Indian cotton, with her chestnut hair gathered into a muslin mob cap. The Princess was playing cards with her brother and sister, the Duke of York and the Princess of Orange. 'She had small, perfectly shaped white teeth (unlike her mother's protruding ones) which made her smile irresistible.'

At sixteen Henriette Anne was not and never would be a conventional beauty. She was small and slightly built, with a long bony face and deep-set sharp blue eyes. She had the slight deformity of one shoulder being slightly higher than the other, but she danced with an astonishing lightness and grace. She had her mother's spikiness of personality but it was mellowed by a relaxed and mocking sense of humour and witty turn of phrase she shared with her brother Charles. Her quick intelligence and her distinction made her stand out among the overblown beauties who thronged her brother's court. She and Charles delighted in each other's company, and she remained his 'deareste sister', who meant more to him than any other woman in his life.

The first winter of his reign, in spite of the apparently heedless round of pleasure, had serious undertones. First and foremost for Charles was the urgent necessity to establish not only good relations with France but a 'strict alliance'. The most satisfactory way, of course, was to have an alliance by marriage. As Louis XIV was already married, the next best thing was for the Stuart Princess to marry the French King's only brother, Monsieur. Philippe d'Orléans was only too well known for his fondness of his own sex, his hysterical spiteful nature and his pathological jealousy of his elder brother, and Charles regretted such a husband for his sister, but he felt sure she would find compensations to offset Monsieur's vices and failings.

The chief attraction in the marriage for Henriette Anne was the prospect of being able to spend the rest of her life in France. Though she was English by birth, she knew no other country than the one in which she had been brought up, whose language she spoke as her mother tongue, and in whose Catholic religion she had been re-baptized and

The beloved Henriette Anne, the last child of Charles I and Henrietta Maria portrayed as the Duchesse d'Orleans holding in her hand a compass to indicate the charm that drew people towards her.

confirmed at an early age. From Henrietta Maria's point of view her daughter's marriage to the Duc d'Orléans, if Louis XIV's Infanta wife did not produce children, gave her the chance one day of becoming Queen of France. Louis XIV was also anxious to keep England on his side, and when he heard that his enemy the Duke of Savoy had sent an envoy to England with an offer for the hand of Charles's younger sister, he did all he could to encourage Monsieur's marriage.

The English court moved from Hampton Court to Whitehall for

Christmas. The Princess of Orange was already sickening when they arrived, and died of smallpox on Christmas Eve. Before the New Year her godson, the infant son of the Duke and Duchess of York, who had been born scarcely a month after his parent's private marriage, died too. Three deaths in the family within four months was an ominous start to the reign. Charles was more anxious than ever to hurry Henriette's marriage to the French heir-apparent in case she too fell a victim to the same disease. At the end of January he sent his mother and sister, the Abbé Montagu and La Belle Stuart back to France, with the Earl of St Albans to represent the English King at the signing of the marriage contract.

Monsieur was now looking forward to his role as the next royal bridegroom. With his love for dressing up and pageantry he was determined that his wedding in Notre Dame would put his brother's in the small dark whitewashed church at St Jean-de-Luz in the shade. At the beginning of March, while they were still waiting for the papal dispensation to allow the marriage of first cousins to arrive, Cardinal Mazarin became mortally ill. On 9 March 1661, the day the Cardinal died, the dispensation arrived. Anne of Austria was deeply distressed by the death of her chief adviser and supposed lover. Plans for the wedding were postponed, although the marriage settlement was agreed and the contract finally signed on 24 March by Seguier, Fouquet and Le Tellier on behalf of the French King and by the Earl of St Albans on behalf of Charles II.[2]

Instead of the splendid wedding in Notre Dame, the couple were married quietly on 31 March in the Queen's private chapel at the Palais Royal. The ceremony was performed by Monsieur's friend the Bishop of Valence, assisted by the Abbé Walter Montagu, and only the French royal family and the Princes of the blood were present. Lord St Albans represented Charles II. It was all very disappointing for Henrietta Maria, but at least, for good or ill, her daughter, the Stuart Princess, was now Madame, sister-in-law of Louis XIV and second lady in France.

8

HENRIETTE ANNE STUART AND THE TREATY OF DOVER

THE DUC D'ORLÉANS AND HIS YOUNG WIFE went to live at Monsieur's new palace at St Cloud, but the importance of having her own establishment in its beautiful setting of gardens and fountains could not disguise the fact for Henriette Anne that, more than most royal marriages, hers was a hollow sham. Within a few weeks Monsieur had began openly to neglect her, and he soon drifted back to his young men. Even the friendship they had enjoyed as children vanished with their enforced intimacy and, before her seventeenth birthday, the Duchesse d'Orléans was thoroughly disillusioned.

By the autumn things had improved for her. The King too was disenchanted with his marriage, and bored to death with his desperately dull Queen. The more she tried to please him, the more she irritated him. Louis invited his brother and his wife to join him at Fontainebleau for the hunting season. Henriette Anne had all the qualities the Spanish Infanta lacked. She amused the King with her lively wit; she had style, she was cultivated, and adored music, the ballet and, above all, Molière's comedies, which would have shocked the pious little Marie-Thérèse if she had been able to follow them, which she could not. The King's face began to light up whenever Madame joined the circle, and she soon became his acknowledged favourite and the most influential figure at court. This was exactly what Charles II had hoped would happen, and the Duchesse d'Orléans, who had a great deal of his and her mother's opportunism, decided to take advantage of everything her favoured position could give her. The awareness of her power over the King, for whom she was now his 'délicieuse Henriette Anne', and her brother Charles's weekly letters reminding her of the political importance to him of her marriage, helped to sustain her spirits in spite of her husband's abominable behaviour to her.

To everyone's surprise Monsieur fulfilled his conjugal obligations, and when Charles II sent over Lord Crofts of Saxham, Sir Charles Berkeley and Laurence Hyde to congratulate Louis XIV on the birth of the Dauphin in November 1661, these members of Charles's intimate circle found Madame very ill, with a racking cough and unable to sleep without drugs. To prevent a miscarriage, the doctors insisted on her staying in bed. During these months of confinement her Spanish mother-in-law, Anne of Austria, was working behind the scenes to find a more suitable favourite for the King than his English sister-in-law. A year after the marriage Madame presented her husband with a daughter, Marie-Louise. When Henriette Anne appeared back at court, she found to her dismay that Louis was apparently infatuated with one of her own ladies-in-waiting, the self-effacing ash-blonde Louise de la Vallière. Anne of Austria felt she owed it to her brother Philip IV of Spain to protect the interests of his daughter.

The political and artistic influence of Madame was, however, in no way affected, as Charles noted with satisfaction: 'I am very glad to find the K. of France does still continue his confidence and kindnesse to you.' This was just before Henrietta Maria, accompanied by the Abbé Ludovic Stuart as her chaplain and Frances Stewart as a maid-of-honour, left for Portsmouth for her son's marriage to the Portuguese Infanta Catherine of Braganza. Like the French King's Spanish marriage, this diplomatic union was for reasons of state and to replenish a depleted exchequer. Charles had chosen the Portuguese Princess because he had 'an unconquerable aversion to northern women', so that all German or Scandinavian princesses were ineligible, and because, as part of her rich dowry, she brought him the cities of Bombay and Tangier.

He went to Portsmouth to meet his shy, only moderately attractive, bride who was suffering so much from seasickness that the ceremony had to be postponed for a day and then took place quietly in her temporary lodgings. The Bishop of London performed the Anglican ceremony, while the Abbé Ludovic Stuart, at the request of the Queen Mother and the bride, remarried the pair privately according to Roman Catholic rites.

On 23 May the bridal party was still at Portsmouth, and Charles dashed off a letter to his sister telling her of the event. 'My Lord St Albans will give you so full a description of my wife as I shall not go about to do it, only I must tell you I thinke myself very happy. I was married the day before yesterday . . . and I hope I shall intertaine her at least better the first nights than Monsieur did you. I shall go on Monday next to Hampton Court and shall staye till the Queene [his mother] comes.' Charles always refers in his letters to his mother as the Queen, but Catherine of Braganza as his wife.

But this flippant beginning did not augur well for the sexual compatibility of two entirely different personalities. The King was deeply sensual but superficial in his many amorous relationships, and was used to all the tricks of love practised by Lady Castlemaine and his other mistresses. His strictly brought up, innocent little Queen fell hopelessly in love with the stranger who became her husband, and was sensible enough to realize that it could never be reciprocated. He wounded her deeply during the first months of their marriage by flaunting his mistresses in her presence. Her failure to produce children was the final humiliation, although he dutifully slept with her from time to time. At last she showed enough spirit to try, if she could not win his love, to gain his respect and affection, and in this she succeeded. Charles was, above all, loyal to his family, and it was as a member of his family that he treated her, refusing to divorce her for barrenness, until the end of his life.

He was an excellent host to his mother, and entertained her so well in London that Henrietta Maria decided to stay on, moving from Hampton Court to Greenwich, then back to Somerset House, where she had spent so many happy days more than thirty years before. Charles kept Madame up to date with all her doings. Writing from Whitehall on 8 September 1662 he says:

> I assure you there is nothing I love so well as my dearest Minette, and if I ever fail you in the least, say I am unworthy to have such a sister as you. The Queene has toulde you I hope that she is not displeased with her being here. I am sure I have done all that lies in my power to let her see the duty and kindness that I have for her. The truth is, never any children had so good a mother as we have, and you and I shall never have any dispute but only who loves her best . . . The Chevalier de Gramont begins his journey tomorrow or the next day, by him I will write more at large to you. I am doing all I can to get him a rich wife here . . . so farewell my dearest Minette, for I am intierly yours.
>
> C.S.

The Chevalier de Gramont was a dashing young wit who had been banished from the French court for thrusting his attentions on one of the King's mistresses. He was a grandson of La Belle Corisande, with whom Henri of Navarre had once been madly in love, and was quite possibly, like Louis XIV and Charles II, a grandson of Henri IV. He soon became the constant companion of the waspish Abbé Ludovic Stuart, the latter propelling himself swiftly along the corridors of Whitehall in his elegant wheelchair, noting with his keen eyes all the scandals of the court, where parties of pleasure and gambling for enormously high stakes were to be found everywhere. 'One plays from morning till night, or rather from night till morning at this gay, delicious court and the King misses none of it', reported Philibert de Gramont. In fact King Charles was by nature a gambler, like all the Stuarts, but the only one of them who gambled with good-natured cynicism for material profit. Like all gamblers he was always short of cash; however much his Parliament voted him, it was never enough to cover his vast expenses, both public and private.

In October 1662, in spite of his Portuguese bride's handsome dowry, Charles was extremely hard up. Without any apparent scruples or making any fuss he calmly returned Dunkirk, the port he could not afford to garrison, to the French King, for the large sum Louis was prepared to pay. So much for the trophy which Cromwell's Ironsides, not to mention his brother, the Duke of York, had won at the Battle of the Dunes four years before. At the end of the year the missing heir to the Aubigny estates appeared at the English court; he was Charles Stuart, aged twenty-three, had succeeded his uncle James as third Duke of Richmond and Lennox in 1655 but had never bothered to do anything about it. He was an affable young man, quite good-looking and easy-going, and raised no objections to his other uncle, the Abbé Ludovic, retaining possession of Aubigny in the meantime. Philibert de Gramont was not, however, impressed by him, thought he drank too much and 'was a pretty dull sort of fellow'. But the King took to him at once, to his regret as it later turned out, and introduced him to the pleasures of his Whitehall seraglio, over which he ruled like an Oriental sultan. Charles conferred titles on recognized mistresses with the same careless abandon with which he fathered bastards, and was constantly adding to his harem specially selected maids-of-honour summoned to attend upon the long-suffering Queen Catherine.

The King's relations with his mistresses followed the pattern set by his French grandfather, Henri IV. He needed change and variety, liked to avoid scenes and good-naturedly recognized his many bastards, providing them with titles and seeing to it that they made advantageous marriages. The first of these took place when the Duke of Monmouth married Anne, Countess of Buccleuch, in April 1663. He was very fond of James, who was just fourteen; the bride, one of the richest heiresses in Britain, was twelve. The reigning mistress since just before the Restoration had been Barbara Palmer, who had shared the triumph of his return. She had a complaisant husband, ennobled by the King as Lord Castlemaine in 1661, and was as bold and greedy for money as Louis XIV's Madame de Montespan; and, like her, she gave her sovereign many children. Lady Barbara's position was unchallenged until the arrival from France of La Belle Stuart. Frances Stewart was far more beautiful than her portraits suggest. She was tall and slender, with a swan-like neck, and looked equally ravishing in the immodestly low-necked gowns of the

Restoration court or dressed as a swaggering boy. She made the most of her looks and used her maddeningly cool offhand manner to tantalize the King, who became incurably, almost comically, infatuated with her, to the fury of Lady Castlemaine and the despair of the neglected little Queen. To keep her place in the King's affections the Castlemaine cleverly pretended to take the young newcomer under her wing. She was her constant supper-companion, where the King was certain to drop in, and she even went so far as to persuade Frances Stewart to share her bed. The two were inseparable, the classical blonde beauty of La Belle Stuart a striking foil for the insolent brunette good looks of Lady Castlemaine.

Charles's infatuation for his sister's school friend lasted to everyone's amazement for six years, during which time the offended Castlemaine stormed out of Whitehall periodically, taking her brood of children with her. But she always returned to flaunt a series of affairs with innumerable lovers, ranging from court rakes like the Comte de St Germain, Buckingham, Sir Charles Berkeley and John Churchill to the dramatist Wycherley, the strong-man rope-dancer Jacob Hall and a disreputable actor and scroundrel named Cardell Goodman.

All Castlemaine's flamboyant attempts to distract the King from the pursuit of her rival were vain. His passion was so genuine that, according to one despatch from the French Ambassador in London, when Queen Catherine was so ill that her life was despaired of, the talk of the English court was that Charles would certainly marry Frances Stewart should his wife die. A subsequent French envoy, Courtin, tried his best to make use of 'the most beautiful girl at the English court' to gain advantages for King Louis from King Charles.

In spite of his spaniel-like attachment to the cold-hearted Miss Stewart, the most important woman in Charles's life at this time was his sister Henriette Anne, whom he loved and respected and was, besides, the essential link between him and his cousin the King of France. By 1664 the growing power of the Dutch at sea made them England's greatest enemies in trade and commerce. Charles had to build up a strong navy and to reinforce his ports and dockyards. For this he needed far more money than he could ever hope to get from his Parliament in order to control the Channel, which in Charles's eyes was an essentially English sea.

Since the end of the Thirty Years War in 1648, seapower and the development of overseas colonies had replaced religious differences as the main factors in European politics. Britain's rivals in the struggle for trade were Protestant Holland and Catholic France. Of these two powers, Charles was inclined by temperament to an alliance with France. Not only was the alliance traditional, stretching far back in the Stuarts' history, but the practical Charles knew that his cousin Louis was five times as rich as he was, and did not have to answer to a parliament. Charles reckoned shrewdly enough that Louis, with his hands full maintaining French military supremacy in the Low Countries, would be glad to make a bargain with him for the help of the British Navy against the Dutch at sea. Charles wanted regular subsidies from Louis to help him build his navy. He also needed extra money for his own extravagances, and saw in his sister the Duchesse d'Orléans a reliable go-between to circumvent normal diplomatic channels, so that neither his Parliament nor Louis's ministers need know how large an amount he would receive.

As early as October 1662, the same month as the sale of Dunkirk, which had been accepted but not well received by the English public, Charles sent the first of many special envoys, a young man named Ralph Montagu, to sound out Louis through Henriette Anne about the idea of a 'strict alliance' between the two Kings. During the next eight years letters too incriminating to be entrusted to the ordinary weekly post were sent to the Duchesse d'Orléans, at first in clear and in the later stages in cipher, to negotiate the Treaty of Dover, which was finally to be signed in the early summer of 1670.

On 26 October 1662 Ralph Montagu arrived in France with two letters, one in English for Madame and a formal letter of credence in French to introduce himself to Louis XIV, both in the handwriting of the English King. In the highly confidential correspondence thus initiated Madame showed herself to be an astute and efficient diplomatist. Charles wrote in English and Madame in French and the translations were made by the bilingual Abbé Walter Montagu, Queen Henrietta Maria's almoner and Ralph Montagu's elder brother. Ralph Montagu was twenty-four when he made his first journey to France, and Madame was eighteen. He fell in love with her and remained devoted to her for the rest of her short life, being appointed official English Ambassador to France a year or so before her death. These first dispatches carried by him were the official letters of credence in French signed 'Charles R.'; the other, more important informal note in English to his sister reveals the low state of the British Exchequer and excuses himself for the delay in paying the £10,000 due to her as her dowry. This is signed with the monogram of the entwined initials C and S.

Ralph Montagu was popular at the French court and was invited to stay on for the Twelfth Night festivities at the Palais Royal, when Molière's comedy *Ecole des Femmes,* dedicated by its author to Madame, was given its first performance, followed by a banquet and a concert of string music. Two days later Montagu watched enraptured as Madame danced the role of Chief Shepherdess, partnered by Louis XIV as the

Chief Shepherd, in a ballet composed for the occasion by Lully. When the special envoy returned to Whitehall with glowing accounts of his sister's success, Charles wrote back to her, teasing her: 'I wonder that Monsieur let Mr Montagu stay so long, for he is undoubtedly in love with you.' Then he goes on to complain ruefully of the impossibility of staging such entertainments at Whitehall, as 'there is not one man here who can dance tolerably'. Times had indeed changed since the accomplished dancing of royal and aristocratic masquers and spectators in Inigo Jones's day.

By 1664 things were so advanced, and relations between the English and Dutch so strained, that Charles was writing to his sister to see if she could lay her hands on a copy of the treaty signed between their grandfathers James I and Henri IV of France in 1610, and 'the renewal of it when I was P. of Wales which I never saw being at a great distance from the King my father in 1644. I fear I shall not be able to find a copy of this treaty between England and France here, it being made at such a disorderly time. Pray gett a copy of it and send it immediately hither'. Madame procured copies but Charles, having perused them, found that the circumstances had changed so much that it was better to start from scratch. 'Pray assure the K. my brother that nothing can be more welcome than a strict friendship between us.'

Henriette Anne was once more pregnant and her brother, ever solicitous for her welfare, wrote on 29 February—1664 was a Leap Year—'I was in greate paine to heare of the fall you had lest it might have done you prejudice in the condition you are in but I was glad to find from your letter that it had done you no harme.'

On the day after the opening of Parliament on 16 March 1664 he wrote to tell her about the speech from the throne recommending the repeal of the Triennial Act. By 24 March he was writing to his sister:

> The House of Commons are now upon breaking that vital act of the Triennial Bill, which was made at the beginning of our troubles, and have voted on it, so that it now wants nothing but putting it into forme, the truth is that both Houses are in so good humour as I do not doubte but to end this session very well. By the letters I received from Ld. Hollis he has by this time demanded commissioners to treate with him and I hope that the treaty will go on to our satisfaction. My Lord Hollis writes such letters of you, as I am afraid he is in love with you and they say his wife already begins to be jealous of you. You must excuse me as long as this parliament sits if I miss now and then a post for I have so much businesse as I am very often quite tired.

On 6 July Madame gave birth to a son nearly three weeks overdue. Monsieur immediately sent his premier maître d'hôtel, a M. de Boyer, to announce the arrival of 'un gros garçon' to his English uncle. Charles was ill when he got the news, having caught a chill by imprudently removing his waistcoat and his wig because of the heat on a visit to the fleet at Chatham. Nevertheless he wrote at once to tell his sister how pleased he was. 'My fever has so newly left me and my head was so giddy I could not write to you on Monday last to tell you the extreme joy I have at your being safely brought to bed of a son.' He then goes on significantly: 'I am now sending Sir George Downing into Holland to make my demands there. They have not given me any satisfaction for all the injuries their subjects have done myne [in the East Indies].' The attitude of the East India Company at Amsterdam he describes as being 'very impertinent.'

The much-hoped for Orléans heir, named Philippe-Charles after his father and uncle, was unfortunately not destined to survive childhood. Replying to her brother's congratulations, Henriette Anne told Charles how much her elder daughter Marie-Louise resembled him in looks.

By the autumn of 1664 the first skirmishes between the English and Dutch were already taking place. Charles in his letters to Madame kept stressing that she must at all costs persuade Louis XIV that the English were not the aggressors but had suffered intolerable provocation in Guinea and other colonies. On 24 October 1644 he wrote jubilantly to her about the English capture of New Amsterdam: 'You will have heard of our taking New Amsterdam which lies just by New England. Tis a place of great importance to trade and a very goode towne. It did belong to England heretofore but the Dutch by degrees drove our people out of it and built a very good towne. But we have got the better of it and tis now called New York. He that took it and is now there is Nichols [the Governor of Massachusetts] my brother's servant, whom you know very well.'

In February 1665 he got Parliament to pass a Bill for £2,500,000, and on 4 March Charles officially declared war on Holland. On his thirty-fifth birthday, 29 May 1665, Charles was writing cheerfully from Whitehall to Madame at St Cloud: 'I hope in a few days my brother will meete with their [the Dutch] fleete and make them much more reasonable than they are at present. I have had no letters from my brother this day, but I beleeve a Battle will follow very quickly.' It did.

On 3 June James, Duke of York, as Lord High Admiral, with Prince Rupert as Admiral of the White and the Earl of Sandwich as Admiral of the Blue, won a victory off Lowestoft, sinking or capturing between twenty and thirty Dutch ships and blowing up the Dutch admiral in his flagship. Charles never lost the human touch, and in announcing the good news to Henriette Anne he also tells her how distressed he was to lose one of his closest friends, Charles Berkeley, Earl of Falmouth, in this sea battle. Berkeley was a notorious Restoration rake and one of Barbara

Castlemaine's innumerable lovers. Clarendon describes him as 'a young man of dissolute life, prone to all wickedness', Navy Secretary Samuel Pepys dismisses him in his diary as a pimp, but Charles mourned him deeply.

The Duchesse d'Orléans at the French court was worried that her brother's actions would alienate Louis XIV and make her position very difficult with regard to negotiating the treaty Charles so earnestly desired. She urged him to call off the war and make peace with Holland. Charles, however, did not. The outbreak of the plague that summer in England made the Queen Mother decide to return to France, while Charles and his courtiers moved out from London to Hampton Court. The death roll was mounting daily, and when cases were reported at Kingston-on-Thames, the court moved again to Salisbury, where Charles, 'between violent bouts of colic', visited the fortifications at Portsmouth and the Isle of Wight, as well as taking 'a little turn into Dorsetsheere' to stay with his friend Lord Ashley at Shaftesbury.

When Philip IV of Spain died at the end of 1665, Louis XIV, although he had renounced any claims to the Spanish Netherlands on his marriage to the Infanta Marie-Thérèse, changed his mind, invoking the Law of Devolution, a custom in the Spanish Netherlands that gave the children of a first marriage, even if female, the right to inherit over the son of a second marriage. The French Queen Mother, Anne of Austria, was dying of cancer, so, to avoid distressing her, Louis postponed declaring war until after her death on 20 January 1666. A week later, however, he declared war on England. Outwardly Charles appeared unruffled and wrote to Madame on 29 January from Hampton Court: 'We had some kind of an alarum that the troops which Monsieur de Turenne went to review were intended to make us a visit here, but we shall be very ready to bid them welcome by sea or land . . . I cannot tell what kind of correspondence we must keep with letters now that France declares war with us.'

Turenne and Louis XIV campaigned instead in Flanders so successfully that England was left undisturbed. Charles was able to spend much of his time hunting until, in May 1667, the Dutch pounced and took a terrible revenge for the defeat at Lowestoft.

The Dutch Admiral de Ruyter attacked Sheerness and Chatham, broke the boom across the Medway, and sailed up the Thames burning more than sixteen ships, including the *Royal James*, and taking the *Royal Charles* as a prize. The Dutch remained for over a week in the Thames estuary, a disgrace Charles never forgave nor forgot. He made peace with Holland in July and cleverly managed to insist that New Amsterdam remained English and kept the name New York. From this moment onwards the urgency of concluding an alliance with France, with whom

Charles was once again at peace, became his greatest preoccupation.

During this time both Charles and his sister were suffering from problems in their sentimental lives. Henriette Anne's matrimonial life had become even more unbearable by her husband's infatuation for the beautiful but penniless Chevalier de Lorraine, a member of the Guise family. Monsieur was spending all his money and lavishing jewels on this spiteful young man, who treated Madame with studied insolence while openly making Monsieur the laughing stock of the court.

Charles, for the first time in his life, had received a mortal blow to his sexual pride. On discovering the object of his adoration, La Belle Stuart, in bed with his friend Charles Stuart the Duke of Richmond in the apartments he had given her at Whitehall, he forbade the pair to see each other again; but in March 1667 the unrepentant couple eloped to Richmond's country house, Cobham Hall near Gravesend. Charles was so wounded that he refused to allow them back at court. Henriette Anne wrote several times pleading with her brother to forgive them, but for more than a year they were in disgrace. To Madame the King wrote: 'I wish I could give you satisfaction in the business of the Duchess of Richmond wherein you may think me ill-natured, but if you consider how hard a thing it is to swallow an injury done by a person I had so much tenderness [the word love is crossed out] for, you will, in some degree excuse the resentment I use towards her. You know my good nature enough to believe that I could not be so severe if I had not great provocation and I assure you her carriage towards me has been as bad as a breach of friendship and faith can make it, therefore I hope you will pardon me if I cannott so soon forget an injury so near my hart.' However, when he heard in April the following year that Frances Stuart was stricken by smallpox, the King's chivalrous feelings once more reasserted themselves. In no time she was forgiven and, as soon as the danger of infection was past, he went to see her and was once again completely captivated by her beauty and teasing wit. He wrote to his sister how relieved he was that she was not too much marked but, alluding to Charles Stuart, Duke of Richmond, he says, 'as for her husband, he cannot alter from what he is, let her be never so much changed'. Richmond was commonly regarded as an incurable drunkard.

The King's life was extremely complicated at this moment. Hearing that he had rushed off to see Frances Stuart, Lady Castlemaine, who had been back in favour, flounced off again in a huff, while at Whitehall the poor Queen was desperately ill again, this time the result of a genuine miscarriage. 'Which though I am troubled at it yet I am glad that tis evident that she was with child which I will not deny, up till now, I feared she was not capable of.' Henriette Anne, who was also pregnant again, sent over some special pills 'to make the Queen hold faster next time'. Charles, as we have said, never once considered divorcing his wife because she could not bear live children. As it turned out, even if he had married Frances Stuart, the result would have been the same, for she too never had any children.

After Louis XIV had established his claim to the Spanish Netherlands, Charles directed all his energies towards concluding the French alliance. From 1668 onwards letters to his sister were carried by trusted friends like the Comte de Gramont, Sir John Trevor, Ralph Montagu and James Hamilton, and in January 1669 Charles sent a set of ciphers to be used to interpret them. The first of these letters, dated 20 January of that year, stresses the need to unite the interests of England and France: 'the only thing which can give any impediment to what we both desire is the matter of the sea, which is so essential a point to us here, as a union upon any other security can never be lasting, nor can I be answerable to my kingdoms if I should enter into an alliance wherein their future security were not provided for'. Charles found his sister's next pregnancy devilishly inconvenient, as at this stage he thought a personal visit by Madame to England preferable to letter-writing. All during this difficult pregnancy, which ended disappointingly in the birth of another daughter—her son, the little Duc de Valois, had died the previous year—Madame was kept ciphering and deciphering top secret letters and preparing a draft treaty with Louis XIV. Two weeks after the birth of this daughter, Anne Marie, Queen Henrietta Maria died at Colombes after twenty years of widowhood. She was buried in the chapel of Chaillot where the entire French court assembled to hear the most celebrated preacher of his day, Bossuet, pronounce her funeral oration.

In November 1669 Charles asked for an inventory of his mother's property to be made, including her furniture and effects at Chaillot. Monsieur was furious, claiming all his mother-in-law's possessions in France for himself, in his wife's name. Charles addressed his request to the Archbishop of Paris, Péréfixe Hardouin. The Archbishop granted written[1] permission to visit the convent to the Montagu brothers on 6 November. Ralph was now the English Ambassador to France, and the Abbé Walter Montagu was the late Queen's almoner. On 13 November the Abbé Montagu wrote out a receipt to the Mother Superior for a casket of silver that Charles had asked to be brought back to him in England[2]. The nuns were then instructed to keep what they wanted in the way of furniture, linen, and china after the Duchesse d'Orléans had made her choice.

Just before the Treaty moved towards its final stages, Henriette Anne had a short respite from her secret diplomatic activities when the young

Duke and Duchess of Richmond and Lennox at last paid a visit to France to claim their Aubigny estates. The Abbé Ludovic Stuart of Aubigny had died in 1665, ironically enough on the very day the envoy from Rome arrived in Paris with his Cardinal's scarlet *calotte*, and the estates had reverted to his nephew, the rightful heir. With all the trouble about the elopement and falling out of favour with King Charles, the Richmonds had never bothered to go to France. However, on 11 May 1670, the charming drunkard Charles Lennox Stuart did homage as the eleventh and, as it turned out, last Stuart Seigneur d'Aubigny.

During their visit Madame had received instructions that the time had come for the treaty to be signed at Dover. Louis XIV was agreeable that she should travel to England for this purpose, but Monsieur raised endless objections to his wife's going without him. In the end Louis arranged a visit of the whole French court to inspect his new possessions in Flanders, during which time it was arranged that Madame and her suite would spend a few days visiting her brother for his birthday.

The treaty that was to be signed at Dover had two parts. The official part stated that England and France agreed to be firm allies against Holland, for which Charles was to be responsible for the naval side in case of war and for this receive certain subsidies from France. The secret clause was kept from all but three Catholic members of Charles's inner council, and laid down that, in return for more money to be paid as a regular pension, Charles at a convenient time would declare himself a Catholic. At the very last moment there was a hitch arising out of the styles of the monarchs of England and France. Colbert de Croissy, the French Ambassador in London, tactfully got over this difficulty by referring to Charles in his version as King of England, Scotland, France and Ireland, while the French version referred to Louis XIV by his customary title 'Sa Majesté Très Chrétienne'. The treaty was of course written in French. It was signed by Colbert de Croissy on behalf of Louis XIV (who was horrified at the vast sums of money demanded by Charles), and by Charles R., Arlington, Arundel, Clifford and Bellings for England. The Duke of York had been tactfully called away before the actual signing, so his name does not appear, nor does Madame's. Even Buckingham, who had been one of the instigators of the treaty, was kept in ignorance of the secret clause.

Charles's cynicism could go no further, though, after he had paid his debts, he did use the subsidies for strengthening the navy, of which he and his brother were so proud. But to gain them he had to put aside the principles that had made him detach his brother Harry from his mother when she had tried to convert him. Charles, the most astute politician the Stuarts ever produced, signed a death warrant for his family. The signing of the public treaty and the secret clause took place on his fortieth birthday, the tenth anniversary of his Restoration.

For the next ten days the town of Dover was *en fête* to celebrate this triple occasion. Madame and her suite were lodged in the specially refurbished old castle, while lesser members of the French party had to be accommodated in cottages. Queen Catherine and the Duchess of York both came to meet their sister-in-law, and Charles organized steeplechasing and horseracing on the downs, on which there was heavy betting, followed by gambling and other entertainments at night. Henriette Anne blossomed in her brother's company. His admiration for the able part she had played throughout the difficult negotiations made up for all the coldness and unpleasantness she had had to suffer from Monsieur. She genuinely felt that what she had achieved was in the best interests of both England and France, and could not see anything shocking in the secret clause to which she was party. Her brother desperately needed the money; her brother-in-law needed the naval support of Britain and could pay for it. In the long term it meant that the Catholic Stuarts were irrevocably ranged on the side of France and vice versa.

Reluctantly the time came for Henriette Anne d'Angleterre to return to her wretched married life in France. When Charles came to say goodbye, needless to say his roving eye fell upon one of her newest maids-of-honour, a small kitten-faced brunette with a bold look and a pouting sensual mouth. He asked her name and was told it was Louise-Renée de Pencoët, Mademoiselle de Kéroualle, who had recently come to court from Brittany, where her parents had a modest manor house near Brest. When Madame sent Louise de Kéroualle to fetch her jewel-case from her cabin to present Charles with a farewell present, the King went straight to the point. 'Forget about the jewels', he said. 'But I beg you let Mademoiselle de Kéroualle stay behind.' Henriette Anne was jealous of the impression the most insignificant member of her entourage had made on her brother. She said sharply it was impossible, that the girl was very young, and that she was responsible for her and had promised her parents to bring her safely back to France.

Before she left, Madame asked Charles to make Arlington an earl and Clifford a viscount. Neither at the time of the signing of the treaty were professed Catholics. Arlington made a death-bed conversion and Clifford announced his conversion on giving up his office of Lord High Treasurer when the Test Act was passed three years later. Charles agreed to these requests, and gave his sister 2,000 gold crowns for his mother's monument at Chaillot and for masses to be said for her there. Charles could not bear to tear himself away from his sister, although he had no reason to suppose they would not meet in the future.

Monsieur's behaviour was as bad as ever on her return to St Cloud; he insisted that as a reward for his letting her go to England she should ask the King to recall his friend the Chevalier de Lorraine from exile. When Louis sent for her to report on her mission, Monsieur went too and made a public scene. Henriette, exhausted by the excitement of her trip and the anticlimax of her return to domestic strife, left Versailles in tears.

During the next fortnight the heat was intense, and Madame was sad and listless. She often complained of a pain in her side and had no appetite, unable to face even her favourite strawberries. On 28 June she was so hot she bathed in the Seine and afterwards felt chilled. The next day, after dining at midday, she said she was tired and lay down with her head in Madame de La Fayette's lap. She woke up about five with agonizing pains in her side and was put to bed, and the royal physicians summoned. They bled her and administered emetics as she screamed in pain, and her room grew more and more crowded with her friends, the Prince de Condé, the Maréchal de Gramont, la Grande Mademoiselle, the Marquis de Bellefonds and his brother, and Charles's old mistress Bablon, now Duchesse de Mecklenburg. The Duc de Créqui rode over to tell the King at Versailles, and he arrived with members of the court about nine o'clock. He took his leave of her distraught with grief, while Monsieur sobbed hysterically at the bedside. She was still conscious enough when her old admirer Ralph Montagu, the English Ambassador, whispered to her in English the word 'poison'. She shook her head but told him urgently in English to destroy all the letters Charles had written to her, as they contained so many secret things. When he had found the box containing the letters and ciphers, she pulled off her ring and gave it to him to take back to England with her love to her brothers. Bossuet, who had been her spiritual adviser for years and who, through her influence, had converted both Turenne and her brother James to Catholicism, arrived in time to give her the last sacraments, and she died between three and four in the morning of 30 June. It was just two weeks after her twenty-sixth birthday.

Monsieur's other favourite, the Marquis d'Effiat, had brought her a silver goblet of iced chicory water to drink soon after she had collapsed, and there were strong rumours of poison, suspicion falling upon her estranged husband. Louis XIV ordered an autopsy, at which more than 100 people were present, including Ralph Montagu and his brother the Abbé Montagu. The surgeons said she had died of a perforated ulcer.

Charles accepted the findings of the autopsy, discounting the suspicion of poison, though the Stuart Princess's sudden death so soon after the signing of the Treaty of Dover caused feeling to run high in London. Three of the King's closest associates believed Madame was poisoned;

they were the Duke of Buckingham, Prince Rupert and Sir John Trevor, one of Charles's trusted messengers to Madame and a former Ambassador to France.

Louis XIV sent the Maréchal de Bellefonds to express his condolences to King Charles. He had been present at St Cloud during the Duchesse's agony and had seen her die. He had also been present at the autopsy. Monsieur's special envoy to his brother-in-law reached London first, but Charles kept him waiting until he had talked at length with Bellefonds, and then showed a marked coldness towards him and dismissed him abruptly. He could never forgive Monsieur for his public as well as his private ill-treatment of his 'deare, deare sister', who, on meeting Queen Catherine for the first time four weeks before, had said characteristically: 'She is not beautiful but she is a good woman and so amiable and kind, one cannot help loving her.'

Madame was buried with royal pomp at St Denis on 21 August 1670. Bossuet's oration, on the text 'Vanity, vanity, all is vanity', remains one of the masterpieces of this great preacher. In it he elaborated upon her qualities and her faults, making significant reference to her skilled diplomacy, which had joined the interests of the Kings of England and of France.

The Treaty of Dover, whose consequences were to cause the downfall of the Stuarts in 1688, was ratified in Paris in December 1670 by the Duke of Buckingham. In the ratification the terms that were published were confined to a pact of mutual assistance against the Dutch and made no mention of religion.

9

RESTORATION AND REVOLUTION

CHARLES WAS SO GRIEF-STRICKEN when he received Montagu's despatch announcing Henriette Anne's death that he had to take to his bed for several days. During the ten years of their exchange of letters, each week, or sometimes more often, dating from one of his earliest in 1661 ending, 'I do not write in French because my head is dosed with businesse and tis troublesome to write anything but English, I do intende to write to you very often in English that you may not quite forgett it', until the secret correspondence suddenly breaks off in June 1669. She was always his favourite sister, who helped to ease the essential loneliness of his restless nature. Mam was dead, and now Minette, with her death the very deep brother-sister relationship was gone forever. Even Frances Stuart whom he loved and who had known Henriette Anne since childhood could not replace her. Their last parting at Dover brought to mind the piquant face of his sister's Breton maid-of-honour. He still had need for a bilingual secret agent to send and receive messages from his cousin and ally the King of France. So, when Buckingham went to Paris for the ratification of the Treaty of Dover, Charles ordered him to bring Louise de Kéroualle back with him to Whitehall. The part she played in the King's subsequent negotiations with Louis XIV until the end of Charles's life was vital. She became an expensive item on the payroll of both kings, but she was worth it. She was created Duchess of Portsmouth in the peerage of England. She lived handsomely by her wits long after both Charles and Louis were dead.

Charles's first impression had not been false. She was even more voluptuous than he remembered. For the first few months at Whitehall she behaved with demure dignity. When the King approached her, she always turned the conversation to Henriette Anne and resisted any advances he made. Once she was sure of her power over him, it was she who offered to replace Madame as Charles's correspondent with Louis XIV before agreeing to become his mistress. This was in the autumn of

Louise de Kéroualle the Duchess of Portsmouth and, much later d'Aubigny, at the peak of her career at the court of Charles II.

1671, when she had been taken by the King to a house party at Euston in Suffolk, and to celebrate his conquest of Louise de Kéroualle, Charles rode his horse Woodcock to victory at Newmarket next day. Nine months later she bore her only child, whom she named Charles. The King created this bastard son Duke of Richmond, since Frances Stuart's drunken husband, the English Ambassador in Denmark, had died at Elsinore a few months before.

By the terms of the original donation of 1422 the estates of Aubigny and La Verrerie should have reverted to the French crown. Charles II, however, lost no time in claiming them as nearest Stuart heir male collateral through his great-grandfather Henry, Lord Darnley, and at the same time made an arrangement with his cousin Louis XIV that, for services rendered in his interest,[1] the Aubigny lands and titles should be given to the Duchess of Portsmouth and, after her death, to her son, the Duke of Richmond.[2] To this half-French bastard son Charles also gave the titles of Duke of Lennox, Earl of Darnley and Lord of Tarbolton. In August 1673 the inhabitants of Aubigny paid homage to the English Ambassador, 'having learned that the King [Louis XIV] had restored these lands to the King of England as a direct descendant of the first John Stuart, the Scottish Constable, the communal assembly names two representatives to offer the homage of the town to the English Ambassador to France'[3]

Although, for the most part, the Duchess of Portsmouth was an absentee landowner, she did visit her properties in Berry from time to time. She added her own coat-of-arms (greyhounds couchants) to the château of Aubigny, embellished the main salons with monumental fireplaces and supervised the laying out of the English gardens surrounding the château. The inhabitants of Aubigny flattered her with presents in the vain hope of having their feudal taxes reduced; but the baby-faced Louise de Kéroualle, for all her appealing ways, was nothing if not a hard-headed business woman and spent the greater part of her long life in litigation and writing begging letters for increases in the pensions and taxes due to her. She was twenty-two when she gave birth to her son, and saw to it that she had no more children. She finally ousted Castlemaine as the English King's principal mistress and confidante, and, while acting as his agent, never ceased to further the interests of France. Barbara Castlemaine, on the way out, was placated by the title of Duchess of Cleveland. Charles amused himself by naming his yachts after his various mistresses, so the *Portsmouth* joined the *Cleveland* but outsailed her.

For Portsmouth's services Louis XIV rewarded her in 1675 with the French title of Duchesse d'Aubigny and, in 1684, scandalized his leading nobles by upgrading the title of this suspect and notorious *femme galante* into one of the highest in the kingdom, making Aubigny a *duché-pairie* in favour of the upstart Louise and her royal bastard. The boy was then fourteen, a sulky self-centred youth resembling his mother in looks and character. The letters patent describe him as Prince Charles Lennox, Duke of Richmond, Master of the Horse to the King of England and Knight of the Garter. Signed by Louis XIV and witnessed by Colbert and Le Tellier, it was never in fact officially registered until 1777 because of the Duchess's equivocal position.

Even when Louise grew plump and middle-aged in her mid-thirties

Charles Lennox, Duke of Richmond, the son of Charles II and Louise de Kéroualle despite his parentage was never a Jacobite. In fact he became a member of the household of George I.

she kept her place in the King's affections, and her apartments at Whitehall were open at all times for the French envoys and aristocrats visiting London. When his passion had cooled, the King relied implicitly on her shrewd judgement and 'Fubbs', the affectionate nickname he invented for her, played her role brilliantly, managing to ensure England's neutrality when France went to war against the Dutch. It was she, acting under pressure from Louis XIV, who pushed Charles toward his death-bed conversion to Catholicism. It is incredible that a man as sceptical as Charles could have had a *crise de conscience* in the same way as his more serious brother James had experienced when he secretly embraced the Catholic faith in 1668. James had the example of his hero Turenne to follow and always had leanings toward Catholicism, but for the cynical man of science Charles to believe in hell and damnation and a one, true, exclusive faith, is hard to imagine. He had agreed to Louis's terms to declare himself a Catholic and to reimpose the old religion in his country in exchange for ready cash. But the only thing he had done was to issue a Declaration of Indulgence in 1673—the year in which the Duke of York openly professed himself a Catholic—which conveniently granted toleration to all Nonconformists, including Catholics, but followed it by the Test Act, which made them, including the Duke of York, resign offices of state and official appointments. During the Popish Plot and the Rye House Plot, Charles lay low and said nothing, but sent his unpopular Catholic brother into unofficial exile while he continued to keep his French Catholic mistress as his closest confidante.

The Duke of York, despite his stiffness and genuine piety, led a love life almost as hectic as his brother's. James was the coldest of lechers, clumsy and naive in his advances, and his mistresses were usually married women and invariably plain. The tall bony Arabella Churchill, who had come to court from Somerset with her ambitious younger brother John, was no exception in the matter of looks. She managed to have herself appointed one of the Duchess of York's maids-of-honour and was determined to gain the Duke's attentions. The Comte de Gramont records maliciously how James had ogled the plain Miss Churchill for a time but soon turned his roving eye on the handsome Jennings sisters, Frances and Sarah.[1] His waning interest, however, revived when he came upon Arabella sprawled upon the ground after a fall from her horse. He could not resist the tempting expanse of thigh and she quickly gained her ends. When she became noticeably pregnant, the embarassed Duke sent her off to France on the pretext of taking the waters at Bourbon.[2]

Miss Churchill obediently stayed there as she was told until, on 21 August 1670, she gave birth to a son in Moulins.[1] The long lean boy was baptized there as a Catholic and given the names of Jacques Fitzjames Stuart. His father wrote ordering his mistress to keep up the pretence of being on a health cure and to stay away as long as possible before returning to England. When the Duchess of York died in 1671, James sent for her and for his son, to whom he took an instant liking. Young Fitzjames was a remarkable child from the first and, as he grew older, showed a strength of purpose and more common sense and energy than all the legitimate Stuarts put together. He was so serious as a boy that the Comte de Gramont could not help remarking that this particular fruitof the Duke of York's amours was pure ice. Arabella Churchill had in all five children by her royal lover—another son called Henry and three daughters—before retiring to marry a worthy soldier called Colonel Godfrey.

Although Anne Hyde had died a Catholic convert, her two daughters, Mary and Anne, were brought up as Protestants. James's natural son Fitzjames, whom he later made Duke of Berwick, showed a great aptitude for the practical sciences, like his uncle Charles II and his father's cousin Prince Rupert of the Rhine. Later he specialized in military engeering and became as distinguished a soldier as his maternal uncle Marlborough, fighting against him as a naturalized Frenchman and Maréchal de France during the War of the Spanish Succession.

As King Charles had so far sired no legitimate heirs, and was showing no sign of changing his religion, Louis XIV decided by the summer of 1672 that the widowed heir-apparent, the Duke of York, must make a suitable Catholic marriage.[3] The French King consulted lists of available Princesses and soon narrowed down his choice to the fourteen-year-old daughter of his childhood friend Laura Martinozzi, a niece of Cardinal Mazarin and widow of Alfonso d'Este, Duke of Modena. He instructed the French Ambassador in London to present a description of the proposed bride to Charles and his brother. The Duke of York was approaching his fortieth birthday and found the idea of a nubile Italian bride twenty-five years younger distinctly appealing.

He agreed at once to his brother sending Lord Peterborough as his envoy to make the proposal of marriage to the Princess, who was described as being a beauty of docile disposition, well read and intelligent and, above all, very devout. The Marquis de Dangeau, whose sober day-by-day journals give a fascinating account of life at the French court, went with Peterborough on behalf of the matchmaker King Louis.

When Peterborough and Dangeau arrived in the little duchy of Modena, south of Parma, they found the Princess even prettier than her portraits. She was a tall graceful brunette with a creamy skin and the dark languorous eyes of her Mancini aunts, but with none of their wantonness. She received the French and English envoys with a composure astonishing for her age and disconcerted them completely by flatly refusing the Duke of York's offer of marriage. She said she had no wish for matrimony and had already decided upon an entirely different sort of life. Mary Beatrice d'Este was far from being the docile creature they had been led to expect. She told them with a certain amount of hauteur that she had set her heart on becoming a nun at the nearby Convent of the Visitation. Her cool refusal flabbergasted these two worldly men, who did not know what to make of the exaggerated virtue of this young woman, who was not only a great-niece of the opportunist Cardinal

Mazarin but on her father's side was descended from such notoriously unscrupulous figures as Lucrezia Borgia, her son the Cardinal Ippolito d'Este, Beatrice d'Este of Milan and her sister Isabella (Marchioness Gonzaga), and Duc Henri de Guise, whose mother Anne d'Este was a granddaughter of King Louis XII. For the impoverished daughter of the widowed Regent of a tiny Italian duchy to turn down the prospect of becoming Queen of England seemed eccentric, to say the least.

Dangeau had known the Duchess Laura well in her girlhood, and got her to help him convince her daughter that 'England had need of her to give princes to the world who would adorn it with virtue and merit'. Peterborough's eloquence ran away with him, and he promised that if she agreed to change her mind, she would be one of the happiest princesses in the world.

The difficult young girl finally yielded to family pressure and gave her reluctant consent. To make quite certain she would not change her mind, Peterborough arranged for her to be married by proxy at Modena on 30 September 1673. It had been agreed she would receive the sum of £15,000 a year as her marriage jointure, but, as it was Louis XIV who had to advance the first instalment, he had the English King more in his debt than ever.

A week after the ceremony the new Duchess of York celebrated her fifteenth birthday and, almost immediately afterwards, left for England before the weather got too bad to cross the Alps without danger. The Regent Laura escorted her daughter, who took with her two friends of her own age, the Countess Vittoria Montecuccoli-Davia and the Countess Molza, both of whom remained in her service for the rest of her life. Peterborough and Dangeau accompanied the bridal party to hand over the Princess to her husband. They sailed in English ships to Dover, where James, in his Lord High Admiral's uniform, was waiting to greet her. The pale leering face of the forty-year-old widower repelled her so much that she burst into tears, finding her middle-aged bridegroom cold and frightening. When his brother the King stepped forward to embrace his new sister-in-law, she cheered up considerably. Charles's dark Italian complexion, eyes with their heavy pouches, and amused smile, in spite of the deep sardonic lines on either side of his mouth, reassured her. From the moment of their first encounter he was spontaneously and consistently kind to her, treating her with the easy familiar relationship he had enjoyed with his dead sister Henriette Anne.

Many years later, as an inconsolable widow, Mary of Modena told the nuns at Chaillot about Charles: 'He was always kind to me and was so amiable and good-natured that I loved him very much, even before I became attached to my Lord, the Duke of York.'[4] The friendship she enjoyed with the King helped to make her life of almost continual pregnancies and miscarriages during the next twelve years bearable, while her haughty distant husband sought his pleasures in the company of his Protestant mistresses Arabella Churchill and Catherine Sedley. Mary Beatrice was a model wife, enduring two years in Scotland with the Duke and later exile in Brussels, when the unpopularity of their religion forced Charles to send them away from London. When they returned, they were given apartments at Whitehall that Mary Beatrice described many years later to the sister at Chaillot as being 'the draughtiest and most uncomfortable lodgings in the world'.[5]

By the beginning of 1685 King Charles was visibly ailing. He was only fifty-four and had always kept himself fit with fresh air and daily exercise, walking his dogs for two hours every day in St James's Park and saying wryly he preferred their company to that of human beings. He now suffered badly from gout, which kept him indoors and made him bad-tempered and introspective; he spent more and more of his time in his laboratory, trying to find a way to fix mercury.

On Sunday evening, 1 February, after spending a restless day on his own, he went to the apartments of the Duchess of Portsmouth and told her he would stay to supper, but he had no appetite and all he could take was a little soup. He drank little, left early and went to bed alone. Next morning he got up but collapsed while shaving. His personal physician, a Catholic named Short, went to fetch a surgeon. When he returned with the surgeon and Lord Peterborough, they found the King on the floor, writhing about in what seemed to be an apoplectic fit. The surgeon bled him while Peterborough went to fetch the Anglican bishops Sancroft and Kenn, and then sent for the Duchess of Portsmouth. She came at once and sat for the rest of the day at the King's bedside trying to soothe him. Next day he had another attack. The Duke of York had been summoned to his brother, who was by then unconscious. James and the Duchess of Portsmouth conferred together. It looked as though Charles could not last much longer. James sent for Father Huddleston, the Jesuit who had saved the King's life at Worcester and who had kept in touch with him ever since. The priest was waiting in a room below the royal bedchamber. The 'convenient moment' of the secret Treaty of Dover had come at last.

While the messenger was fetching the priest, the Duke of York ordered everyone to leave the room except the Lords Bath and Feversham (the latter was a Frenchman by birth named Duras). Then the door was locked and double-locked. It was only opened to allow Feversham to fetch a glass of water for the King when the Host stuck in his throat. The King had rallied when he saw Huddleston; he made his confession to him and received absolution. Afterwards he seemed more tranquil. He thanked the priest, saying he had saved him twice in his life, the first time his body, this time his soul; then he asked the priest if he thought the moment had come to declare himself a Catholic. Huddleston did not answer him directly but asked the King if he were telling him to make this public. Charles smiled but did not reply. Huddleston left again by the secret staircase, James had the doors unlocked and the others came in again. Everyone thought that the King had been making his will.

Bishop Kenn came forward and prepared to administer the Anglican communion, which he urged the King several times to receive, but Charles obstinately refused, saying he was too weak. The Bishop urged him at least to declare he believed and was dying in the Anglican faith. To this Charles made no response. Kenn proceeded to give him absolution for his sins, but the King remained silent, uttering no word of repentance for his past life nor any sign of contrition or intention to change.

The Duchess of Portsmouth, whom Shaftesbury, the head of the anti-James faction, had publicly called a common prostitute five years before, sent for her son the Duke of Richmond and got the Bishop to present the boy to his father to receive his blessing. There were some looks of shocked surprise among those in the room, then everyone murmured tactfully that the King was father to them all and knelt down to receive his blessing. By this time Charles was groaning in agony, saying his stomach was on fire. He managed to bid farewell to his brother, saying he left all in his hands and recommending to his protection the Duchess of Portsmouth and the young Duke of Richmond. There was never a word about the Queen, his subjects, his servants, his French pension, nor his debts, which amounted to something like 100,000 guineas. He died at 11 o'clock in the morning of Friday 6 February, with the curtains pulled back so that he could look upon the daylight for the last time. He had paid his debt to Louis XIV in changing his religion on his death-bed. In this the cynic, for whom the shrug and the curled lip characterized his life as the Merry Monarch, kept to his part of the Faust bargain. As far as Charles was concerned, it was 'après moi le déluge'.

The family of Charles I and Henrietta Maria were remarkable for their devotion to one another, in spite of their differences in character and temperament. Of those who survived adolescence, the Princess Mary of Orange and James, Duke of York, were lacking in humour, distant and stiff, taking after their father, while Charles, Henriette Anne and Harry were sociable, quick-witted and easy-going, sharing family jokes at James's expense; he was, for instance, absurdly credulous and invariably lost heavily when he gambled at Newmarket. He was a slow painstaking thinker, and once he got an idea into his head, he stuck to it obstinately. Charles was always loyal to his less popular brother, never forgetting the hardships and uncertainties they had shared in exile and was quite content that he should be his heir. His own leanings towards Catholicism, influenced by the Duchesse d'Orléans and later the Duchess of Portsmouth, and his commitment to that clause in the secret Treaty of Dover, was one reason for not divorcing his barren Portuguese Queen; he found it suited his indolent nature better to be succeeded in the natural course of events by an avowed Catholic.

It was no slight to his brother's memory that made James order Charles to be buried 'privately at twelve at night' in Westminster Abbey. The absence of public pomp and unsuitable witnesses got over the awkwardness of the exact form of religious rites performed at this ceremony, which took place within ten days of his death. Before the month was out the dissolute rakes and frivolous mistresses of the Restoration court had vanished now that their patron was gone from Whitehall, as though they had never been.

On the very day that Charles died the new King, with unexpected *sang-froid*, summoned the Privy Council and reassured them that his private religious beliefs would in no way alter the existing constitution. This first address to his Privy Council seemed perfectly reasonable. He took command of his stutter and said:

> My Lords, before proceeding to business, I believed it fitting to explain my feelings to you. Since it has pleased God to call me to this office and to succeed so gracious a King and so good a brother, I consider it my duty to declare to you that I am resolved to take him as my model above all in his wonted kindness and affection for his people. I have been represented as a man dedicated to absolute powers; and this is not the only calumny held against me. I shall do all I can to uphold the Government, in the Church as well as in the State, as it is established by law. I know that the principles of the Anglican Church are favourable to the Monarchy and that members of that Church have always shown themselves good and faithful subjects. I shall always be at pains to uphold and defend it. I shall never intrude upon the privileges of my subjects. I have, before now, many times, risked my life in defence of the Nation and am ready to risk it again to preserve her just rights and liberties.

Such were his intentions and, at the beginning of his reign, James set out to try the almost impossible compromise of being a devout Catholic ruling over a Protestant country. He knew he was unpopular but he was brave and honest, incapable of the late King's duplicity. He thought he could convince his people that his personal faith in no way threatened their liberties, and two days after his accession he made no secret of going to hear Mass in his chapel at St James's Palace. On 23 April he was crowned according to the rites of the Church of England, with the exception of the Communion Service. A month later he called his first

Parliament and repeated in more or less the same words the promises he had made to the Privy Council on 6 February. His brother-in-law Laurence Hyde, Earl of Rochester, a leading Anglican, was promoted to be Lord Treasurer, and most of his brother's ministers kept their old jobs. As the heir to the throne, his elder daughter Mary, married to the Protestant William of Orange, and her sister Anne, married to the Lutheran Danish Prince George, were both Anglicans, the Stuart Protestant succession seemed assured as, so far, all Queen Mary of Modena's children had died before they had reached the age of four.[6] Since then miscarriage had followed miscarriage, so that, although she was only twenty-seven, it seemed unlikely she would produce a Catholic heir.

Deluded by the idea that his actions would please all religious persuasions, while keeping him on good terms with the King of France, James underestimated the genuine fear of Papacy in the country. Within months of his accession two Protestant revolts broke out. A minor one in Scotland, under Argyll, was quickly crushed, but the other, a much more serious threat, began with the landing in Dorset of Charles II's favourite son, the Protestant Duke of Monmouth and 150 followers. At the end of June Monmouth found that his supporters had increased to 3,000, and at Taunton in Somerset he had himself proclaimed King. James still firmly believed in the support of William and Mary, and sent an urgent demand to Holland for the three Scottish and English regiments serving with the Dutch forces to be drafted back to help him deal with the rebels. Before they arrived, however, his own army defeated Monmouth at Sedgemoor, and the rebel Duke was found hiding in a ditch and brought before his uncle. In spite of Monmouth's desperate pleas for mercy, James hardened his heart and Monmouth, upon whom both his father and his aunt Henriette Anne had doted, was executed on Tower Hill. The harshness of Monmouth's fate and the Bloody Assizes that followed in the West Country, where Judge Jeffreys meted out savage punishment to the Protestants, were disastrous for James's image. It became worse when, to show his solidarity with his cousin Louis XIV's Revocation of the Edict of Nantes, by which their mutual grandfather Henri IV had granted civil and religious liberties to French Protestants, James idiotically made public Charles II's death-bed conversion to Catholicism.[1] He also defied the Test Act and inducted Roman Catholic regiments into the army. During the year following the Monmouth rebellion James began to lose all sense of proportion, limiting the powers of Parliament while asking for more subsidies to maintain his standing army and further ignoring the Test Act by admitting Roman Catholic peers to the Privy Council. Richard Talbot, Earl of Tyrconnell, a Catholic and a wild companion of

Wissing's painting of Mary of Modena, James II's second wife with her per dog also contains a Stuart identification: the white rose.

James's licentious days as Duke of York, was made Lord Deputy of Ireland, and in April 1687 James published a Declaration of Indulgence suspending all the penal laws and excluding office-holders from the Test Act. A further act of folly was to try to influence the Fellows of Magdalen College, Oxford, to appoint a worthless Catholic as their President. As the King continued to alienate the Church of England, which he had promised on his accession to uphold 'as by law established', his heirs-apparent in Holland took an alarmed look at the deteriorating situation. They feared a second overthrow of the Stuart monarchy and an end of their own hopes of succeeding, for, so far, James's second marriage had produced no son.

They became more alarmed, as did Princess Anne, when it was announced in the autumn of 1687 that Queen Mary of Modena was pregnant. Another girl would not matter, but what the two Protestant

This official portrait of James VII and II as King of Great Britain refers to his successful naval career.

Princesses feared was that their stepmother might at last produce a Catholic heir. As the tide of popular and family feeling rose against her husband, the Queen struggled through another difficult pregnancy, while James proceeded to commit the final outrage of arresting seven Anglican bishops who on 18 May 1688 had refused to read the Declaration of Indulgence and imprisoning them in the Tower of London.

Mary of Modena had never liked Whitehall and was determined that her child should be born at St James's Palace. The night before her confinement, when she felt her pains begin, she asked to be carried in a sedan chair across the park to the old Tudor palace. There, in the early hours of 10 June 1688, Prince James Francis Edward Stuart was born and immediately baptized by the Papal Nuncio, whose presence James had insisted on though several important witnesses were absent. These included the Archbishop of Canterbury, who was shut up in the Tower with the seven bishops, and Princess Anne, who was taking the waters at Bath. There were plenty of other witnesses, including the Queen Dowager, though of course she was a Catholic, to verify that the child was in fact the Stuart heir and no substitute smuggled in. By this time, however, the feeling in the country was so totally hostile to James because of his unconstitutional and irrational behaviour that the birth of a son caused dismay rather than rejoicings.

On 30 June the seven bishops were acquitted and that evening leading Anglican peers sent an invitation to William of Orange, with whom their agents had already been in touch, to come to England with an army to protect 'the religion, liberties and properties of the nineteen parts of twenty of the people who are desirous of a change'. This letter was signed by Shrewsbury, Devonshire, Danby, Lumley, the Bishop of London, Edward Russell and Henry Sidney, with the backing of the Duke of Beaufort, the Earls of Bath and Clarendon and Lord John Churchill. During that uneasy summer of 1688 James, through his own agents in Holland, was aware that an invasion was being planned. On 28 September he proclaimed: 'We have received undoubted advice that a great and sudden invasion from Holland, with armed force of foreigners and strangers will speedily be made upon this our kingdom.' As a former professional soldier and Lord High Admiral, he was, however, stubbornly confident in the loyalty of his army and navy, and unlike his cleverer brother Charles was diffident about asking his cousin Louis for more money and troops, as he knew the French King was deeply committed in his own war in Flanders. He bumbled on in this proclamation: 'Although we had notice for some time that a foreign force was preparing against us we have rather chosen (next to God) to rely upon the true and ancient courage, faith and allegiance of our own people, with whom we have often ventured our life and in whose defence we are firmly resolved to live and die'. By the time he had realized that French money and men would be necessary, it was too late. Louis was engaged in devastating the Palatinate and the way was clear for William to answer the call of the Protestant nobility and gentry in England who had had enough of James and his dangerous blunderings.

Evading the English fleet, which did remain loyal to James, William landed at Torbay on 5 November 1688, and immediately justified his action by proclaiming he had come at the request of leading Englishmen in order to call a free Parliament, to safeguard the rights of the Protestant church and to investigate the legitimacy of his half-brother-in-law, the Catholic Prince of Wales. The news of another nephew's attempt to usurp the crown, which he considered his by divine right, stunned James, and he began to lose his nerve. Worse was to come when he realized that many of those whom he, as a soldier, had counted upon most were deserting him, among them the soldier he had ennobled, Arabella Churchill's brother John Churchill. Churchill had the effrontery to try to win over James's half-Churchill natural son Fitzjames, whom his father had created Duke of Berwick. At eighteen Berwick was already a seasoned soldier, having fought in the Monmouth rebellion at the age of fifteen. In 1687 he had asked his father to send him to the Emperor to fight against the Turks. When the Emperor read the letter from the tall tight-mouthed young man, he found it hard to believe he was only sixteen and a half. He turned to his entourage saying, 'Here we have a new volunteer who is a natural son of the King of England but who is less remarkable for his birth than for his good sense and ideals and who, I am sure, will distinguish himself in the future by his exploits'. Berwick served under the Elector of Bavaria, the Commander-in-Chief of the Imperial Forces, and received his first wounds from a Turkish Pasha.

As soon as he heard of the Prince of Orange's invasion of England, he asked leave to go home to help his father. When Churchill's letter was brought to him suggesting that he too should join William, Berwick, disgusted that his uncle, who owed his advancement to the King, should desert him now, took the note straight to James. Berwick assured his father that he could count on his unfailing loyalty and he never went back on his word. He was as ambitious as any of the Churchills, but, just as there was not an ounce of spare flesh on his bones, so his character was devoid of any sentimentality and he was incapable of sacrificing any member of his family to further his own ends. He remained throughout his life cool and detached, and proved himself as brilliant and ruthless a tactician in the service of France as his uncle Marlborough on the opposing side. During those desperate days, when the memory of the fate of Charles I became a waking nightmare for James, Berwick sustained his father as more and more leading Englishmen abandoned him. They decided together that the Queen and the infant Prince of Wales must be sent for safety to France. For this enterprise they enlisted the help of the French Comte de Lauzun, who had fought with James at the Battle of the Dunes thirty years before and had shared the congratulation of Turenne.

Lauzun's life had been since then a series of scandals and hair-raising escapades. The impossible Grande Mademoiselle had fallen madly in love with him and he had finally consented to a secret marriage. But his insolence towards her and towards the reigning mistress at the French court, Madame de Montespan, had earned him his *lettres de cachet* for *lèse-majesté* and a sojourn for ten long years in the mountain fortress of

Pignerol, in the same prison as the disgraced finance minister Fouquet and the mysterious Man in the Iron Mask.

During his captivity Lauzun wrote incessantly to Louvois, the French Minister for War, begging for his release.[8] Finally in 1681 he was set at liberty, but had to continue living in disgrace away from the court. When, seven years later the news of the revolution in England reached Lauzun now no longer in disgrace, he asked and was given leave to go to England to help his old comrade-in-arms James II. Susceptible as ever, the ugly little Gascon, now in his middle fifties, fell passionately, but this time platonically, in love with Mary of Modena, and was an eager volunteer when James and Berwick called upon him to arrange the escape of the Queen and the Prince. It was just the kind of assignment to appeal to Lauzun's romantic nature. He also saw in the adventure, if it were successful, the means of maintaining himself in favour with Louis XIV.

So, on the night of 18 December 1688, Lauzun appeared in the Palace of Whitehall and entered the Queen's apartments by a secret staircase. The Queen was prepared for the flight, disguised as a washerwoman, with her Italian ladies-in-waiting, Molza and Montecuccoli-Davia, similarly dressed. A nurse and a valet-de-chambre brought the baby prince, warmly wrapped up against the cold. The tearful Queen had begged her husband to let her stay behind and share his fate while Lauzun took their son to safety, but James had insisted on her leaving at once, saying that he and Berwick would follow as soon as they could. Lauzun had a boat waiting on the river, which took them across to Lambeth, where a coach was waiting to take them to Gravesend. At Gravesend, where they were joined by the Catholic Lord Powis and his wife and three Irish officers, Lauzun had bribed the master of a small vessel to take the party across the Channel. He and the Irish officers stood guard over the captain throughout the voyage in case of treachery.

Since her first voyage to England as a bride of fifteen, the thirty-year-old queen had undertaken several hair-raising sea voyages to Scotland and to the Low Countries, but this crossing was the worst she had ever endured. She was frightened and seasick throughout, and had the added anxiety of knowing that the wet-nurse was too ill to feed the baby. At last they reached Calais, where the Governor of the town was waiting to welcome Mary with an escort sent by Louis XIV to take her to the Château of St Germain-en-Laye.

The Exiled Stuarts, 1688–1788

10

THE STUART COURT AT ST GERMAIN

In December 1688 as the news from England grew daily more alarming, Louis XIV ordered preparations to be made to house his cousin James and his family should they be forced to flee.[1] His first idea had been to put the Château de Vincennes at their disposal, but this grim fortress-like building on the far side of Paris from Versailles was also very cold and depressing in winter. He decided instead to refurnish his own apartments at St Germain for the royal couple, and thoughtfully had a magnificent nursery suite redecorated for the little Prince of Wales.

In spite of her protestations that she preferred to wait at Calais until she heard that James was safely out of England, the distressed Queen was persuaded first to move on to Boulogne and then, when there was still no news, to proceed directly to St Germain.

When, through the wintry landscape, the coach finally toiled up the steep approach to the old château the exiled Queen found the Sun King and his immediate family gathered there. They had driven from Versailles during the late afternoon to receive her. For Mary Beatrice, tired and frightened, it was her meeting with her brother-in-law Charles II all over again. Louis dropped all formality and embraced her, greeting her as his sister and taking the baby Prince tenderly in his arms. This was the beginning a friendship between the two that never wavered until his death. Louis regarded the deposed Stuart Queen with the same admiring affection he had felt for their mutual sister-in-law Henriette Anne, Duchesse d'Orléans. Dangeau, who never missed an occasion of this sort, recorded that at this first meeting, the French King remarked that the Queen of England had 'beaucoup d'esprit et grandeur d'âme' ('great character and nobility of spirit'); and added 'Tout pénétrée qu'elle est de sa douleur, elle se sent bien ce qu'elle est, et est tout-à-fait maîtresse d'elle-même' ('Although overcome with grief, she is very conscious of who she is, and is completely mistress of herself').

When the presentations had been made and compliments exchanged,

Mary of Modena begged leave to retire to her room, exhausted after the journey. She found a most welcome surprise waiting for her. Louis had placed on her dressing-table a casket containing 6,000 gold pistoles 'for her own immediate use'.

Meanwhile in London, James and Berwick had made an abortive attempt to flee the country the day after Mary and her party had left, throwing the Great Seal of England into the Thames before they quit the capital, but they had been recognized and arrested at Faversham. The last thing the self-styled liberator William of Orange wanted was another Stuart martyr on his hands. He therefore issued instructions to his troops guarding the house at Rochester to which his father-in-law had retired, to be lenient in their treatment of the King and to make no attempt at pursuit if he tried to escape. On 23 December James's French valet Labadie got hold of a fishing boat to take the King to France. The guards obeyed their orders while James, Berwick and a few others made their escape, and, after a night voyage on stormy seas, landed at Ambleteuse on Christmas Day 1688.

On the evening of 26 December Louis XIV drove from Versailles to receive his unfortunate cousin.[2] He brought with him his son, Monseigneur the Dauphin, and his nephew, the Duc de Chartres, the son of Monsieur and his second wife, Elisabeth Charlotte the outspoken but good-hearted German granddaughter of Elizabeth of Bohemia.

The party arrived at St Germain about nine o'clock to find that Mary of Modena, who did not know that her husband was expected so soon, had already gone to bed. Louis went straight to her bedroom and spent half an hour chatting with her, telling her that James was safe and would be arriving shortly. He was still in the Queen's bedroom when a messenger brought word that the coach with the English King was approaching the courtyard of the château. Louis went to the door of the Salle des Gardes to meet him. James was weary and in a state of shock after his long ordeal, but, a stickler for etiquette, he bowed low to the French King, who was considerably shorter than he, and made the gesture of embracing his knees. Louis at once raised him up and took him in his arms, kissing him on both cheeks and saying, 'Monsieur, how glad I am to see you here! I could not be happier than to see you safe and sound'.[3] He then went on to tell James that he must consider the château of St Germain as his home as long as he wished to stay. Then, leading the exhausted King by the hand, Louis brought James into his wife's bedroom, saying: 'I bring you a man I assure you you will be very glad to see.' The reunion of the husband and wife was so moving that many of those who witnessed it had difficulty in restraining their tears. According to the ubiquitous Dangeau, 'the King of England remained long in his wife's arms'.

Afterwards Louis presented his son the Dauphin, the red-faced sportsman who was to become James's constant hunting companion; his favourite child by Madame de Montespan, the Duc du Maine; and his clever nephew, the Duc de Chartres (the future Regent d'Orléans). Then he led his cousin to the nursery to see the sleeping Prince of Wales. 'You will find him in good health', he reassured the anxious father. 'I have taken great care of him for you'.

As they returned to join the Queen, Louis made James promise that he would let him know of anything else he could do to make life more comfortable for him. He then left the King and Queen together, saying they must both be very tired and that he would see himself out, and there was no need for James to escort him. 'Tomorrow, if you feel like it', he said as he left,'you will come to visit me at Versailles. I shall receive you there as you, from now on, will receive me as your guest at St Germain the next time I call on you. Et nous vivrons en suite sans façon (from now on we shall live like a family, without ceremony).'

The reunited pair were overwhelmed by the kindness of their host and hurried back to the nursery to visit their little son once more. Both wept with relief that the nightmares of the past weeks were over and that all three of them were safe, whatever the future might have in store for them.[1]

Reminiscing at Chaillot when her son was in exile and her daughter dead, Mary Beatrice as a widow recalled that when she first arrived in France the thought of even a short exile was appalling to her. 'How merciful is God to keep the future hidden from us', she told the nuns, 'If I had thought I would be here for the next twenty-three years I could not have endured it'. But she did endure all the trials, misfortunes and losses that beset her in France with courage and resilience, devoting herself to her elderly husband who, now that he had lost his kingdom, grew more and more dependent upon her.

James, like his grandfather James I, aged very quickly. He was only fifty-five when he was driven from his throne, but already he seemed an old man. Although he spoke good French, if not with the ease that his wife did, his stammer made communication with others difficult. The gallantries of his youth and middle age were now a thing of the past, and he strove by a genuine appreciation of his wife to make up for the unhappiness he had caused her by his earlier flagrant infidelities. His stiff awkward manner hindered his social life at the French court, though his passion for hunting made him popular with the Dauphin and his set.

Louis did all he could to make the Stuarts feel at home. In spite of their anxiety about the news from England, there was little time for boredom during the early months of their exile. For the first six weeks of 1689 they

James II and his Queen with their children, James Francis Edward (the Old Pretender) and Louise Marie, in exile at St. Germain-en-Laye.

enjoyed a round of visits, supper parties, card parties and hunting parties at Versailles, Fontainebleau and Marly. The French King was an unfailingly generous host to his Stuart cousins now that they were almost completely dependent upon him for financial support. James, like his brother Charles, had been more or less a pensioner of France ever since his father's execution. Now Louis allowed him 50,000 livres a month (about £3,000) and the use of the château of St Germain rent-free. This sum was no more than adequate, as ever-increasing numbers of impecunious Jacobites flocked to St Germain, expecting to be maintained. Privately James possessed about £23,000 invested in France. His wife had a small income from a salt-rent in the Ile-de-Ré that she had inherited from her mother, but the jointure of £15,000 a year that she had been voted on her marriage had never been paid.

One of the first visitors to St Germain was the pushing Louise de Kéroualle. The Duchess of Portsmouth and of Aubigny had come to France with her son soon after the death of King Charles. The sixteen-year-old Duke of Richmond complained to Louis XIV about 'the ill that had been done to himself and his mother by spreading false reports that she had held ill-natured talk about the circumstances of the birth of the Prince of Wales'. This spoilt bastard son of Charles II also protested about the reports that, if he were in England, he would choose to join the Prince of Orange; but, unlike the Duke of Berwick, the Duke of Richmond made no move at this or any other time to give active support to the Jacobite cause.

At forty, Louise de Kéroualle, was decidedly plump and matronly. She never married and managed her sex life with worldly discretion, producing no more children but devoting all her energy to increasing her pensions from Louis and James at every possible opportunity. The rest of her life was spent mainly in property deals and litigation over her estates in Berry and the family property she had inherited near Brest in Brittany. Mary of Modena found her impertinent and domineering and, although Portsmouth was the cleverer of the two, the Queen made it plain that she was not welcome at St Germain, dealing with the importunate Duchess firmly during the first month of 1689. The ex-royal mistress flounced off and bought herself a house in the rue de Petits Augustins (now the rue Bonaparte) in the parish of St Sulpice in Paris. For the next forty years she continued to plague the French court with demands for tax exemptions, and for more and more money for the services she had rendered in the past and was prepared to render in the future.

James and his friend the Dauphin were out hunting on 16 February when the news reached St Germain that William and Mary had accepted the crown of England three days before. The English Parliament, before accepting the couple as joint rulers, issued a Declaration of Rights by which they had to guarantee the Protestant succession, to agree not to maintain a standing army in peacetime, nor to suspend any laws, as James had done. Members of the Anglican clergy who protested against this Declaration of Rights were fined or imprisoned. Henceforth they were known as non-jurors, and soon the only future for them was to join the Jacobite exiles abroad.

Although he must have been expecting something of the sort, the brutal finality of his replacement by his own daughter and son-in-law stunned James. When he had recovered from the first shock, he drove to Versailles to consult Louis. The two kings spent the rest of that winter afternoon pacing up and down in the Orangery discussing the best course of action to take. The French King did not relish a Dutch Protestant in power across the Channel and promised James men, equipment and money, to undertake an expedition to Ireland, where it seemed reasonable to suppose that the Catholic population would rally to support him against the new régime in England.

Within a few days James sent for the Comte de Lauzun, who had agreed to act as commander-in-chief of the French troops to be sent to Ireland. James agreed to all the conditions and proposals made by the adventurous little Gascon and, in addition, invested him with the Order of the Garter in Notre Dame.

Liaison had been successfully established with the sympathetic Irish so that James, his son Berwick and Lauzun landed in Ireland with the greatest optimism early in March. Their hopes were further exalted by the enthusiastic welcome given to James and his troops when they entered Dublin on 24 March. One of the youngest Jacobites to follow James to Ireland as his page was his fourteen-year-old bastard grandson Thomas Sheridan. Sheridan's grandmother had been an Irish mistress of James's named Anne Jones, by whom he had a daughter who married James's former Secretary of State for Ireland, the eccentric and learned Thomas Sheridan. Sheridan senior was a Fellow of the Royal Society, a pioneer in education and the author of *Discourse on the Rise and Power of Parliament.* He was highly unpopular in England, where he had been implicated in the Popish Plot. He followed James to St Germain but died shortly after his arrival, leaving his young son in the King's protection. Young Sheridan's devoted service to the Stuarts began at the Battle of the Boyne, and only ended in 1746 after Culloden, at which he was present at the age of seventy.

To escape the loneliness of St Germain after her husband had left for Ireland, the Queen began to visit the Convent of Chaillot frequently. The Convent of the Visitation was only a short drive from St Germain and was a sister foundation to the one she had wanted to join as a girl in Modena instead of marrying James. She took her ladies Molza and Montecuccoli with her, and all three occupied the late Queen Henrietta Maria's apartments on the first floor overlooking the river. To make the Queen feel more at home, Louis XIV added books and pictures to the original furnishings, and, as he did for her at St Germain, ordered fresh flowers to be delivered to her daily from the royal gardens. Mary Beatrice and the Mother Superior, Soeur Angélique Priolo,[5] were soon firm friends, and the Queen became so popular with the nuns that they invited her to become their honorary head. The Queen refused, saying that she preferred to be treated like everyone else and to be free to share their simple meals in the refectory instead of being waited upon with ceremony in her own rooms. Starved of sympathetic company at St Germain, Mary Beatrice relaxed in the pleasant surroundings of Chaillot, where she was able to enjoy intelligent cultivated conversation instead of listening to the malicious back-biting gossip of the French court and the endless demands for places and preferment at St Germain.

When she was forced to return to her duties at St Germain, she kept up a regular correspondence with the sisters and the Superior of Chaillot. These letters, for the most part written in excellent French with only a few Italian misspellings,[6] give an almost day-by-day account of her life with all its happenings, serious and trivial. She had a natural unaffected style, and bundles of these letters in her sprawling generous handwriting reveal what it was like to be a poor relation at the French court, struggling to make ends meet, not only for her immediate family but also for those of her husband's subjects who had voluntarily followed him into exile. She managed her role superbly, with dignity and human warmth, only confiding her worst doubts and fears to the friends she could trust, the nuns at Chaillot.

It was during one of her visits there that she received her first letter from Ireland. James's optimism at this stage cheered her drooping spirits. But as the summer and autumn dragged on, the uncertain spasmodic news made her feel tired and depressed. She spent as much time as she could with the sympathetic nuns, walking in the gardens with Soeur Angélique and enjoying the conversation of the others after supper. After the badly cooked meals at St Germain, where the French chefs had been replaced by English cooks, the food at Chaillot seemed delicious. The farm attached to the convent produced fresh milk, butter and eggs; they had freshly-baked bread from the kitchens, fresh vegetables and salads from the *potager* and, in summer, cherries, strawberries, peaches and figs from the walled garden. In autumn there were grapes from the vineyard on the hill behind the convent and wine from their own wine-presses.

Donna Vittoria Montecuccoli, who dealt with the Queen's Italian correspondence, wrote to Duke Rinaldo of Modena: 'The departure of the King is the only thing that has power to pain his wife who shows indescribable courage and a total indifference to all her material losses.' In her own letters the Queen confirms this by saying more than once that she rather likes having fewer personal possessions, and that she only grieves for those she is unable to help in the way she formerly did. She repeatedly thanks the nuns for providing a much-needed refuge from the squabbling and intrigue at St Germain, where enforced idleness and petty rivalry made life unbearable.

The campaign in Ireland was a series of disasters. The last terrible confrontation for James was the Battle of the Boyne, on a glaring July day in 1690. William of Orange and his stiff Protestants rode away from the field in triumph and although the war was to continue for another year until the final slaughter at Aughrim, Ireland was lost to the Jacobites for ever.

James had to face this death blow to his hopes and return to St Germain with Berwick. After the Treaty of Limerick in 1691 they were followed by a flood of exiles to swell his already overflowing court. The atmosphere at St Germain was dismal, to say the least. Money was short and with the new batch of refugees from Ireland, accommodation became uncomfortably cramped. Not counting the royal apartments on the third floor, five crowded staircases had to house a motley collection of titles and temperaments, while the lesser members of the household and the domestic staff lodged in the ground floor rooms. Some of the distinguished members of the court occupying the first staircase included the Duke of Berwick; the Duke of Powis, the Lord Chamberlain; the Earl of Melfort, Catholic Joint-Secretary of State; the two Lords of the Bedchamber, Dumbarton and Abercorn; Frances Jennings, Duchess of Tyrconnell; the Countess Montecuccoli; Countess Molza, Lady Sophia Bulkeley; and John Caryll, the Queen's Scottish Private Secretary.

All credit must be given to Louis XIV for the kindness he continued to show towards the Stuarts. He was magnanimous enough to accept the defeat in Ireland, with the loss of his money and troops, as a gamble that had failed to come off. He tried hard to keep up the spirits of James and his wife by frequent invitations, entertaining them in great style when the hunting season opened at Fontainebleau and the forest was at its most romantic and beautiful. He organized stag-hunts and boar-hunts for the exiled King and picnics for the Queen in the rocky landscape bright with purple heather and tawny bracken. Each evening there was a different form of entertainment after supper—balls, music, and card-parties, of which Mary Beatrice was particularly fond.

The ardent champion of James II, the Comte, later Duc de Lauzun wearing the insignia of the Order of the Garter granted him by James II.

They were still at Fontainebleau when they heard that Lauzun had at last reached France safely from Ireland. Madame de Sévigné had written earlier about Lauzun: 'I marvel at Monsieur de Lauzun's lucky star which continues to shine on his good name which we had long thought buried in obscurity.' No blame was attached to him for the rout of the French troops in Ireland. Indeed two years later, when he was created a Duc at the age of sixty, when the jealous Grande Mademoiselle was dead, the pugnacious little Duc married a girl of sixteen, the sister-in-law of the Duc de St Simon. In spite of his insufferable conceit, Lauzun never lacked the courage of his convictions and remained loyal to the Stuarts in their adversity until the end of his days. He bought a curious double country house[7] in the village of Passy very near the Convent of Chaillot. His Duchesse was given her own part of the house while the Duc kept the other with several alternative entrances and exits to harbour his transitory amours. Later, when the need arose for a safe hiding place for the Stuart Pretender on his secret visits to Paris, he was always sure of a safe lodging in the Lauzun house in the Grande rue of Passy.

Lauzun was never a rich man—he had extravagant tastes and spent every penny he had—but he was unfailingly generous to James II and his family. His warm and respectful devotion to Mary of Modena sustained her until the end of her life.

Lauzun brought the latest news from England, and even he could not give much ground for optimism. At the end of the week's hunting at Fontainebleau, to cheer James up, Louis with his down-to-earth sister-in-law Liselotte, Duchesse d'Orléans, and Lauzun accompanied the English King and Queen as far as Chailly, where they all stopped for an elaborate picnic lunch.

At St Germain a new blow awaited James when the 150 Scottish officers who formed his military household, and who knew he could no longer afford to pay them, asked his permission to volunteer as ordinary recruits in the French army. These were all officers who had fought for him against William at Killiecrankie in 1689, and were the first to be called Jacobites. The King agreed reluctantly to their request and, on the appointed day, came down into the courtyard of the château to review his bodyguard for the last time. As he passed along their ranks, he thanked each man personally and wrote down his name in his pocket-book. Then, walking slowly back along the line, he took off his hat and bowed to them with tears in his eyes. The whole company then knelt down, bowed low and gave their sovereign the royal salute for the last time, before marching off to enlist as private soldiers fighting for the French, many of them to end their days in Catalonia in the War of the Spanish Succession.

After six months of idleness at St Germain, the twenty-year-old Duke of Berwick asked his father if he too could join the French army. Berwick's remarkable gifts as a military tactician had been noted by the French King, who was only too delighted to have such a useful volunteer. Louis commissioned him to serve in his personal entourage when the spring campaigning season began in Flanders. Berwick's birth and six years' military experience was taken into account, and the young man, luckier than the Jacobite officers, was given a suitably high rank.

On his return from Flanders early in the spring of 1692, Louis, reviewing the situation facing him there, decided to make one more attempt to use the Stuarts to oust his Dutch enemy from the throne of England. This time he intended to use the French fleet in a naval expedition to transport the fifteen Irish battalions now in France under Patrick Sarsfield, Lord Lucan, to invade England. Louis sent for James, who, as former High Admiral of the English fleet, was able to give him valuable first-hand information about their adversaries, although he could not help having painfully mixed feelings about attacking the navy he had once commanded so proudly. But then the English navy had been fighting the Dutch. Now the position was reversed, and his only hope of regaining the throne was to join forces with his French ally. Louis offered James an impressive force of 300 ships to transport the Irish troops. These were to be escorted by twelve French men-of-war commanded by the Comte d'Estrées. The French Grand Fleet was to stand by in the Channel under the Comte de Tourville.

On paper the enterprise seemed more than feasible, and James, the veteran of the Dutch Wars, was once more roused to optimism. He hoped against hope that it would succeed and he could leave St Germain and its eternal exhausting quarrels between his two groups of supporters, known as the Compounders and the Non-Compounders. These quarrels had reached their height with the prospect of this new attempt to regain England. The Compounders were in favour of a general amnesty and the safeguarding of civil and religious liberties if James were restored. Their leader was James's former Secretary-of-State in England, the conscientious Lord Middleton. The ultra-Catholic Non-Compounders, headed by James's Catholic Secretary-of-State Lord Melfort, were opposed to any sort of compromise. James sensibly agreed with the Compounders, and with them drafted a proclamation of a general amnesty even for those who had betrayed him, with very few exceptions, following the example of his brother Charles at his Restoration.

However good his intentions were, James need not have bothered. In spite of the favourable time of the year, the end of May, and the brilliant organization, everything went wrong. James and Berwick went to Brittany to review the Irish troops, leaving the Queen in the last stages of pregnancy at St Germain. She was now thirty-three, and both she and the King hoped for a brother for the heir Prince James Francis Edward.

The French fleet put to sea, but contrary winds prevented d'Estrées joining the King with his squadron and held up the Comte de Tourville. All this gave William time to summon Dutch ships to support his own fleet under Admiral Russell. The result was that Russell was able to smash and scatter the entire French fleet off Cap de la Hogue near Cherbourg in the first days of June. To finish the job, Russell sailed into the harbour of La Hogue and burned every French ship he could find there. For James this was the final humiliation. The King, who had fought so courageously against the Spaniards as a young man and had led the English fleet more than once to victory against the Dutch, was a broken man. Luckily Louis XIV was besieging Namur and his campaign ended with a spectacular victory for the French, which helped a little to offset the disaster of La Hogue.

James was too upset to return at once to St Germain and was absent for the fourth birthday of Prince James. The Queen was daily awaiting her confinement and, on 14 June, was brought the news of the destruction of the French fleet. In despair she wrote to Chaillot:

> What is there to say after all that has befallen and in the state in which I find myself except to marvel that the ways of God and man are so far apart. We see only too well in our late misfortunes and by these unforeseen and almost supernatural accidents how God has overthrown all our plans and so clearly seems to have set his face against us as to destroy us completely. [8]

James had still not returned and Louis XIV was in Flanders when Mary of Modena gave birth to a girl on 28 June at St Germain. When the news was brought to James, he hurried back to see his infant daughter, the last legitimate Stuart Princess. He was visibly moved as he took the child in his arms, saying 'God has given her to us to be our Consolation'. James now seemed to put all thoughts of earthly kingdoms from his mind, and devoted himself henceforth to atoning for his past sins and to becoming a kind and loving husband and father to his wife and to his two children.

The baby was christened Louise Marie Stuart a month later, when the victorious Louis returned from Namur. He held his god-daughter at the font in the Chapel Royal at St Germain assisted by the godmother, Monsieur's second wife, Liselotte, Duchesse d'Orléans, one of the kindest and also most eccentric members of the French royal family.[9]

Louis's composure and magnanimity over this second disastrous attempt to help the Stuarts regain their throne continued to astonish all. On 6 July, according to Dangeau, the King sent for Tourville, the French admiral and said to him: 'I am very pleased with you and with my Navy; we have been beaten; but you have won glory for yourself and for the whole nation; it has cost us a few ships, certainly, but that will be remedied in the coming year: and then surely we shall defeat our enemies'.

This last disappointment aged James considerably. He appeared to accept his fate with resignation and relied from now on for support from his wife. He became aloof from court life—apart from his insatiable appetite for hunting of all kinds, despite his failing physical powers. He loved to get out in the forest, following the hounds with the Dauphin or teaching his son the art of hawking and falconry when they were invited by Louis to Marly.[10]

All this fresh air and exercise was very necessary, as he otherwise spent most of his time at his devotions, repenting his past errors either in his chapel at St Germain or in increasingly frequent retreats to the Monastery of La Trappe, where he subjected himself to the most rigorous discipline. The impediment in his speech increased with age and nervousness. He began writing his memoirs to relieve his feelings of guilt. During his years of soldiering with Turenne as a young man he had kept a military journal, and so was used to committing his thoughts to paper. Now he took to religious self-examination of the sternest order. He tried to convince himself that it was infinitely less unhappy to be an exile and fugitive in the arms of friendship than to reign—and here an understandably acid note creeps in—over perfidious and ungrateful subjects.

The oddly assorted husband and wife shared a deep love of their children and a genuine piety. As the ageing King came to depend more and more upon his wife, the memory of his past coldness and hurtful infidelities faded from her mind and she too grew to have a tender affection for him. They were unusually good parents for those days. James, remembering his own exceptionally happy childhood at Whitehall up to the age of nine, was indulgent towards his young son and daughter. The widowed mother of Mary of Modena had been, on the contrary, the strictest of parents compared to Charles I and Henrietta Maria. Having been denied so many little pleasures as a child, Mary Beatrice was determined that her children should enjoy their youth as long as they could. She treated them like sensible human beings from an unusually early age and personally supervised their education and recreation. She used to tell the Chaillot nuns how wrong she thought it to forbid children sweets and little luxuries. 'If you deny them, it only teaches them to lie and deceive their parents, and lying is the one thing I abhor.'

When they were old enough, she let them choose their own doctors and confessors, because she knew how miserable it was for children to have unsympathetic people forced upon them. The Prince of Wales had the Duchess of Powis as his governess, and when Louise Marie was four, the Countess of Middleton, a handsome jolly woman, was appointed to be hers. James Drummond, Earl of Perth, governor to the Prince of Wales, was a good man, but unfortunately he was a Non-Compounder of the most uncompromising sort. The Compounders were mercifully always in the majority. From 1688 until the last Stuart Pretender died, two Protestant chaplains known as the Non-Jurors were always kept wherever the Jacobite court happened to be, even when eventually it went to Rome.

The Duke of Berwick (always pronounced Barwick in France) rose steadily as his ability warranted in the French army . He was a striking young man, six feet tall and as thin as a rake (the average height in eighteenth-century France was five foot six). He had a hard face but with a glint of humour in his penetrating eyes, which missed nothing. He was as fair as his father had been, and had the same reserved manner, but nerves of steel. There was nothing of his uncle Charles's indolence about him. He was constantly active, with all his energy directed towards furthering his career in the French army, because he liked military life and because he had no income except his officer's pay. The French description that fitted him best was *rusé*, cunning as a fox, but not *méchant*. He never missed paying a courtesy call at Versailles to keep in the good graces of the King and his Ministers, and in April 1694 was promoted Maréchal de Camp, the same rank as the King's favourite son, the Duc du Maine.[11]

The younger generation of the Jacobite families produced some exquisite beauties who were known for their flirtations as the nymphs of St Germain, but, despite their attentions, Berwick remained heart-free until he was nearly twenty-five. He had a name but no fortune, and seemed to have no particular inclination towards any of the women who found him attractive. Early in 1695 his father decided for him, choosing the young, well endowed widow of the heroic Patrick Sarsfield as a bride for his son. Honora de Burgh, Countess of Lucan, was a member of the rich and powerful Irish family of Clanricarde. She already had a son, christened Patrick after his dead father. The two were married at St Germain, where, a year later, the Duchess of Berwick gave birth to a son and heir christened Jacques François Fitzjames, to whom his royal grandfather gave the courtesy title of Earl of Tynemouth.

Two years after Berwick's marriage to Sarsfield's widow Louis XIV was forced to ask for peace terms in Flanders. The Treaty of Ryswick was drawn up and published in Paris in 1697. By its terms the French King had to recognize William of Orange as the lawful King of England. He only did so on the condition of refusing to expel the Stuarts from France. Louis also demanded that William III should see that the £15,000 yearly settlement voted by Parliament when Mary of Modena was crowned in 1685 should be paid to her. William agreed in principle but managed throughout his reign, just as his successors Queen Anne and George I did, to avoid doing so. Louis also cleverly managed to get William to agree to a secret clause naming the Prince of Wales as his successor after William's

Jacques Fitzjames Stuart, the son of James II and Arabella Churchill first Duke of Berwick in a Spanish portrait showing him wearing the Order of the Golden Fleece.

death. William agreed to do this on condition that James was educated in England as a Protestant. Berwick, who was kept closely informed on all Stuart political moves, was in favour of this, but the King and Queen opposed it. Lord Middleton wrote on James's behalf to the Pope, who said that such acceptance would entail the surrender of his claim by hereditary right. The refusal of James II and his wife to accept these terms cancelled out the secret clause, which the hard-headed Berwick thought was a major error on their part. Writing later in his memoirs, the practically minded Duke said he thought it 'a great imprudence to have refused such an offer'.

Ironically enough, Berwick was the only innocent victim of the Treaty of Ryswick. William of Orange insisted that he, as a Stuart, must leave the French army. Louis reluctantly sent for him and told him he had no choice but to dismiss him from his service. The thought of spending the rest of his life idling at the decaying court of St Germain was intolerable to him. He left Versailles, saying to his friend the Prince de Conti: 'Since I have nothing left to hope for here, I can only retire to live as a private individual in the provinces'.

Berwick had no country house of his own, and Conti generously offered him his own at Pézenas in Languedoc, rent-free. The Duke and Duchess of Berwick set off on the long journey south with their young family, Patrick, Earl of Lucan, and the one-year-old Earl of Tynemouth. On the edge of the flat coastal plain of Hérault, between Montpellier and the seaport of Sète, 500 miles south of Paris, they settled down to make the best of their virtual banishment from court. The Conti house in the picturesque old town of Pézenas was agreeable enough and they were well looked after, but the climate did not suit the Duchess, who sickened and died of fever a year later. The Duke stayed on with his son and stepson, fretting with grief and boredom, frustrated by his enforced inactivity. An English traveller visiting Pézenas was so shocked to see the state Berwick was reduced to, that, on his return to Paris, he went specially to St Germain to urge James to recall his son before he had a complete nervous collapse.

James had always been very close to Berwick and was eager to have him back. Before asking Louis to send for Berwick on compassionate grounds, he started looking round for another wife to console his son. He chose one of the nymphs of St Germain, Anne Bulkeley, known as Nanette, whose high spirits he thought would match Berwick's dynamic energy. She was the blonde beautiful daughter of the Jacobite Viscount Bulkeley and his wife Sophia, an elder sister of 'La Belle Stuart'.

Cool and detached as ever, the young widower accepted his father's choice for the second time, and the wedding took place at St Germain early in 1700. For once the gloomy old château took on a festive air. The Prince of Wales had his portrait painted at this time by François de Troy, which shows him as an unusually beautiful child with long curling brown hair, almond-shaped velvety dark eyes and clear complexion.

The year 1700, which opened with Berwick's remarriage, closed with internal political intrigue, for in November Charles II of Spain died,[12] bequeathing the Spanish Empire to the grandson of Louis XIV, the Duc d'Anjou, although the Habsburg Emperor claimed it for his own son, the Archduke Charles. On 16 November at Versailles, Philip of Anjou was proclaimed King of Spain by his grandfather, and James II and Mary of Modena went from St Germain to kiss their young kinsman's hand. In England, four months before, the death of Princess Anne's heir, the eleven-year-old Duke of Gloucester, had made the old Electress Sophia of Hanover the next Protestant successor to the throne, as she was the last surviving granddaughter of James I.

On 28 November Mary of Modena, who had been spending a few days at Chaillot, left hurriedly as her husband, who had been unwell, took a sudden turn for the worse. She wrote a note of apology[13] as soon as she could after her return to St Germain:

> Ma Chère Mère, Forgive me but I had no alternative. The King is in too bad a state for me to be far from his side. He was surprised and upset to see me return so unexpectedly. He has had some very bad nights and has suffered much during the last two or three days, but thank God, since yesterday, seems a little better. He has had a little fever but yesterday it was almost gone. Felix [one of the royal surgeons says that his malady is of the same sort suffered by the King his master two years ago in the form of a boil.
>
> It has been oozing pus for the last three days which smells horribly but the core remains. I spend my nights on a little bed in His Majesty's bedchamber. Up till now I passed such bad nights myself being apart from him. You can imagine how much it has pained me to see the King suffer so. But I hope the treatment will do him good. I attribute his recovery in great measure to your prayers at Chaillot. For these I thank you with all my heart and beg you to continue them. My own health is good. I recommend my son also to your prayers that he will be able to make his first communion at Christmas.

James II, who was sixty-seven, recovered in time to attend the Prince's first communion, but it was plain to all who saw him that he was failing. The following March, during Mass in the Chapel of St Germain, he fainted, suffering a first stroke, which left him feeble in his right hand and leg. A week later, on 13 March, his wife wrote to Soeur Angélique: 'I am snatching a moment while the King is sleeping to scribble you a note from his bedside. I read your letter to him and he told me to thank you and the sisters for your prayers and the concern you have all shown for his illness which is not painful but which he feels may be something serious. His head is still clear, thank God, but he is afraid that the paralysis which threatens his right hand and leg might affect his brain. I suffer more than he does, in a way, because, when I feel his limbs so cold, my heart is constricted with fear that the worst may happen.'[14]

Louis XIV, kind as always, sent his own physician, Fagon, to see what he could do for James. After the King had responded a little to the treatment, Fagon recommended the usual cure for paralytics in the eighteenth century—taking the waters at Bourbon.

Their journey was carefully arranged, and on 5 April 1701 the King and Queen set out with a small suite of their most intimate friends, including the Countess Montecuccoli, the Comte d'Autun and Françoise de Motteville, who had been a friend of James's mother and sister. Some of them kept diaries of the journey there and back. It took two weeks to reach Bourbon, with stops at Paris, Essonne, Fontainebleau, Montargis, Briare, Cosne-sur-Loire, La Charité, Nevers, St Pierre Moustier, and Moulins, where the Queen had a special reason for spending a night at the Convent of the Visitation. The foundress of the order, St Jeanne de Chantal, whom she so admired, had died there in 1644 and was buried in the magnificent chapel, which also contained the tomb of Duc Henri de Montmorency, beheaded at Toulouse for rebelling against Richelieu in 1632.

They finally reached Bourbon on 20 April and spent three weeks there, enjoying the spring weather while the King obediently drank the waters. They started back by the same route on 12 May, staying at convents and monasteries on the way. They spent longer on the homeward journey, stopping for a few days at Fontainebleau, and arrived back at St Germain at the end of June. James looked much better after his cure, but in July he had a second stroke during Mass. He recovered and on the warm evenings in August he was a familiar figure pacing the terrace of the château, leaning on his wife's arm. She never left him that last summer, watching him anxiously while her son and daughter romped about in the forest with their friends, the young Stricklands, the Middletons, the Plowdens and the Duke of Berwick's son and stepson. It was nearly twenty-eight years since Mary of Modena had married the Duke of York. She had been a pious young girl and he a middle-aged roué, but now, as her failing husband clung to her for support, she loved him dearly and could not bear to see him leave her.

James had come a long way from those days at the Restoration Court when his foolish lechery was a byword. He had written an autobiography in the last year, in which he made a full confession of his shortcomings as a man and as a sovereign. He had ended this by saying: 'It has pleased you my God to take from me my three kingdoms, in this way to rescue me from the sins of my life. It has been your will to banish me to a strange land where I have truly learned the realities of this life and my duties as a Christian.'

His end was indeed very near. On 2 September he had a third stroke while hearing Mass. His doctors were sent for and this time they pronounced his condition very grave. Dangeau was present to note in his journal that 'the poor King of England is dying like a saint. The Queen is in great desolation. Madame de Maintenon hurried over to St Germain and spent part of the day with her'.

James lay feeble and emaciated on his bed. He refused to be shaved and had a beard like a Capuchin friar. He said to the Prince of Wales: 'Be a good Catholic, fear God, obey your mother next after God and be entirely dependent upon the King of France. Never put the crown of England before your eternal salvation.'

He lingered on, and on 13 September Louis XIV came to see him. James asked him to recognize his son as King of England when he was dead. 'Sir', Louis assured his cousin, 'you can die in peace because I have decided that I will recognize the Prince of Wales as the next King of England.'

As James murmured his thanks, the Jacobites in the room knelt at Louis's feet, crying 'Vive le Roi'. Louis then turned to the thirteen-year-old Prince, put a hand on his shoulder and told him he would recognize him when the time came. James then asked Louis to continue to show affection to his wife and daughter and to his son the Duke of Berwick. Louis solemnly promised all these things and then, embracing the Queen and her children, took his leave of James for the last time. The King of France was forbidden by custom to look upon the face of a dead man, and James had already received the last sacraments. James remained conscious for three days more. He was lucid enough to ask to be buried without fuss, wishing only to have the tomb of a simple gentleman in the church of the English Benedictines, inscribed: 'Here lies Jacques second, roi de la Grande Bretagne.' He told his son that if God should find him worthy one day to regain his kingdom, he should not take revenge on his rebellious subjects. He prayed God to pardon his sins and those of his two daughters and his son-in-law for all they had done against him. He was quite resigned to his end, which came at three o'clock on the afternoon of Friday, 16 September.[15] Having made the customary homage to her son, the Queen said: 'Sir, I acknowledge you for my King but I hope you will not forget that you are my son.' She then left for Chaillot.

As he had wished, James's body was taken by the Duke of Berwick, Lord Middleton and other leading Jacobites from St Germain to the English Benedictines in the rue St Jacques, next to the great baroque church of Val-de-Grâce. His brain was deposited in an urn in the chapel of the Scots College in the rue Cardinal Lemoine, his heart in the chapel of Chaillot, and his entrails were buried in the parish church of St Germain, opposite the main entrance to the château that had been his home for thirteen years.

Four days later his widow returned to St Germain to receive the French King, who had come to declare publicly that he recognized the Prince of Wales as James III of England, Scotland and Ireland. He promised to continue his father's pension of 50,000 livres a month, and the use of the château of St Germain. At the same time Louis protected himself by writing to William III to explain that he had no intention of upsetting the status quo; his recognition of the Stuart Prince of Wales was simply his hereditary right as the legitimate son and heir of his late father.

There were diplomatic protests on both sides of the Channel. The English Ambassador immediately left Versailles without taking formal leave of the French King and, in London, William of Orange ordered the expulsion of Poussin, the French Ambassador to the Court of St James.

II

THE EARLY JACOBITE ATTEMPTS

On the day Louis's letter was despatched to England[1] the Stuart King rode to Versailles to pay his first ceremonial call. He had inherited his mother's equable temperament and his father's regard for etiquette and application to duty. At thirteen James was a serious youth with natural dignity and authority. Tall and slender in his violet cloak of mourning, he impressed Louis with his grave composure. The King of France greeted him as 'Mon frère', and motioned him to sit in the place of honour on his right hand. For some time the two kings, the young and the old, conversed earnestly.

Louis then formally presented the members of his immediate family whom James had known as long as he could remember: first the Dauphin, his father's hunting companion, as always at a loss for words; then Louis's grandson, the Duc de Bourgogne, and his chattering sixteen-year-old wife Marie-Adelaïde of Savoy. She was a grandchild of James's aunt, Henriette d'Orléans, and only three years older than he. She was high-spirited, outspoken and wilful, and ever since her marriage four years before had captivated Louis XIV, who spoiled her dreadfully and indulged her in all her whims. She was very fond of her Stuart relations, and saw that they were not left out of the court festivities.

The French King's gesture in proclaiming the exiled Prince of Wales James III, in recognition of his hereditary right, proved a costly one for France. Louis's example was followed by Spain, Savoy, the Duchy of Modena and by the Pope. As a result, England formed a Triple Alliance with Holland and Austria, which, less than a year later, led to the long War of the Spanish Succession.

When William III heard that James had issued a manifesto setting out his claims to the English throne, he put through a Bill of Attainder in Parliament stating that if the self-styled James III were to set foot in England, he would be executed without trial. He also made it a treasonable offence for any British subject to correspond with the

One of the staunchest friends of the Stuart family in exile was Duc Claude Louis Hector de Villars, Maréchal de France.

Pretender or to send money to him.[2] William of Orange could threaten as much as he pleased, but he realised that the King of France had insulted him openly from a position of strength following the six years of peace since the signing of the Treaty of Ryswick. During that time, through Louis's skilful manoeuvring, France had regained all the disputed territory in the Spanish Netherlands, and, by having his grandson the Duc d'Anjou proclaimed Philip V of Spain, Louis now had the whole Spanish

Empire on his side, plus all the continental Channel ports near England.

As one of his last acts before his death in March 1702, William appointed Marlborough, now well into his fifties, as commander of the Protestant forces in Europe. Louis countered this by promoting Marlborough's thirty-year-old nephew, the Duke of Berwick, as one of his six new lieutenant-generals under the Catholic commander-in-chief, the Maréchal de Villars. Claude Louis Hector de Villars was twenty years Berwick's senior. He was jolly in feature and plump with good living, but had a fiery Gascon temper like Lauzun, and, like him, was a fervent supporter of the exiled Stuarts.

In the month of William's death the War of the Spanish Succession began. It was to continue in Flanders, Spain, Portugal and the south of France for the next twelve years. From this date onwards Jacobite plots multiplied in France with the aim of restoring James as soon as possible or at least when his now childless half-sister, Queen Anne, died.

In March 1702 a proclamation was issued in the name of James III by his Protestant Secretary of State, Lord Middleton. It was addressed to James's British subjects and contained the following important passage:

> . . . that when it shall please God to put us in possession of our Kingdom of England we shall secure and protect all our subjects of the Church of England in the full enjoyment of their legal rights. And we shall leave it to our first Parliament to agree upon and settle a just and equitable moderation of the law now in force against the Roman Catholics. Given at our Court of St Germain, 3rd March, 1702, in the first year of our reign.[3]

This proclamation had the approval of Louis XIV. He knew it was meaningless in a sense, as James was still a minor, but it served as a useful warning to Anne, who was still the English heir-apparent, that the power of France did not necessarily accept the idea of the Hanoverian succession when she died.

With religion the main cause of the revolution of 1688 and the stumbling block to the restoration of any Catholic Stuart, it was most unfortunate that within weeks of this proclamation James's highly respected Protestant Secretary of State Middleton announced his conversion to the Catholic faith. He was renowned for his common sense, his stability of character and his long experience in his job, which went back to 1686. He was now an old man, and the death of James II whom he had served so long had affected him deeply. The Protestant Jacobites at St Germain were horrified when they heard of the step Middleton was proposing to take. He was suffering from high blood pressure and after a nervous breakdown retired from St Germain to a house he owned in Paris in the rue St Jacques, near the Convent of the English Benedictines, where the late King lay in the chapel awaiting ultimate burial in Westminster Abbey or at Windsor.

Middleton remained in his house in the rue St Jacques, brooding over his spiritual problems to the extent of believing he had a vision of his late master standing at the foot of his bed urging him to be converted. He went back to St Germain to confide in Queen Mary of Modena. She felt it was an answer to prayer and urged Middleton to follow the promptings of his conscience. She wrote to the Superior of Chaillot:

> I do not waste a second, ma chère mère, to send you the good news of Lord Middleton's conversion which I have known about for the last few days but was not at liberty to divulge until yesterday . . . I shall tell you the details when I see you, but, in the meantime, it is enough to know that Lord Middleton left St Germain at seven o'clock yesterday morning to enter the Seminary of the English Benedictines for several weeks to receive instruction from the superior who is a man remarkable for his intelligence. I have just written to Madame de Maintenon to tell her the news as I am expecting to see her tomorrow or the day after at St Germain.[4]

After his conversion Middleton felt it would be an embarrassment to his Protestant colleagues if he remained on the Council of Regency and offered to resign. He wrote:

> The first odour of conversion is so abominable to the English that one must be loaded with all reproach which wit, malice, indignation and zeal can devise. It would be a mighty prejudice to the Queen and her son to have one about them so universally obnoxious. I have heard her say that the King her son would do everything he could in conscience to please his Protestant subjects, and by them only could hope to be restored and supported, so here is now an opportunity of giving cheap proof of this by dismissing a useless servant.

Both James and his mother refused to accept his resignation and he was forced to remain at his post and endure the sneers and criticisms of his enemies.

While Middleton's dramatic conversion was the talk of St Germain, Louis XIV was faced with violent Protestant risings in the mountainous region of the Cévennes in the south-west of France. This was the last pocket of resistance against the King's revocation of the Edict of Nantes sixteen years before, and it was believed that the Huguenots in this area were receiving supplies of money and arms from England and Holland. When Louis had withdrawn all privileges and freedom of worship from the French Protestants in 1685, he had also decreed that the taxes levied against them were to be collected by priests, who were ordered to make forced conversions at the same time. With the Catholic French forces occupied in fighting the War of the Spanish Succession, the Protestant revolt in Languedoc became even more violent, and travelling in the Cévennes became impossible. Guerrilla bands of Protestants, called Camisards because of the loose white shirts they wore over their clothes, terrorized the countryside at night, burning Catholic houses and churches and hanging priests and tax collectors. During the next three years detachments of French troops were constantly being drafted from Spain to deal with the situation, but it made very little difference.

In 1703 the Duke of Berwick was commanding the French troops on the Portuguese border of Spain. He was summoned to Madrid by Philip V of Spain, whose wife, Marie-Louise, was a granddaughter of Henriette Anne d'Orléans and thus Berwick's second cousin. Berwick loathed the atmosphere of intrigue at the stiff Spanish court, where he discovered soon after his arrival that the French Ambassador, the Duc de Gramont, and the Queen's chief lady-in-waiting, the Princesse des Ursins, were determined to discredit him in every way possible. He longed to be back on active service, resenting bitterly the shabby treatment he was receiving at their hands. He wrote in his memoirs that Gramont had told the King of Spain that 'I was a singular, obstinate man, determined not to obey His Majesty's orders but as far as I pleased, so that it was absolutely necessary to get rid of me'. Word filtered through to Louis XIV that Berwick was impatient for his *congé* from the Spanish court, but by the time a letter from the French King could recall him to Versailles as soon as his replacement the Marquis de Tessé arrived in Madrid, he had been ordered by Philip V to return to the Portuguese front, as 20,000 troops had arrived from England under the French Protestant Ruvigny, now ennobled by William III as the Earl of Galway.

Berwick was, however, released from his obligations to the King of Spain and returned to Versailles, where he was received with every mark of affection and honour and invited, with his wife, to a special fête the French King had organized for the King of England and his sister, the Princess Louise Marie. Once this was over Berwick found himself hanging about at St Germain without a posting for the rest of the winter. Towards the end of 1704, after discussing the matter with Mary of Modena, Berwick applied for French nationality in order to further his military career and to stabilize the position of his family in France. Since James was still a minor, this permission was granted by the Queen Mother and the Council of Regency on the condition that Berwick would always be 'at James's service if required'. At this stage the half-brothers had always been on the best of terms, but there came a time when this clause led to a conflict of loyalties and a prolonged estrangement between the two.

The Duke and Duchess of Berwick took part in the New Year festivities at Versailles, ending with the traditional Twelfth Night Ball in the *galerie des glaces*. The Princess Louise Marie was escorted by her brother and wore a gown of amber velvet which enhanced the tawny lights in her chestnut hair and in her dark eyes. Old King Louis watched the young King and his sister with pleasure and fondness. The adolescent princess had something of the vivacious looks of her great-aunt Marie Mancini, who had been sent away to Rome to make an unhappy marriage with the Prince Colonna. The young Stuarts made a handsome couple, and danced until four o'clock in the morning.

In spite of their limited budget, life was less drab for them now that they were growing up. In the royal circle they could count on real friends in the Duc de Bourgogne, whose advanced and liberal ideas had been learned from his tutor Fénélon, and his warm-hearted wife Marie-Adelaïde. Philippe, Duc d'Orléans, shared James's passion for music and the theatre, and often took him and his sister to the opera or the Italian comedy in Paris. In addition, at the back of their minds the Stuarts kept cherishing the possibility of the Protestant Act of Settlement being reversed and of James becoming King of England when their half-sister Queen Anne died.

The New Year fêtes were barely over when Louis was alerted that Marlborough, whose troops had been in winter quarters on the Moselle, was planning to attack Metz, the key town of Lorraine, at the first sign of spring. This was obviously a move towards attacking France herself.

In Languedoc the Maréchal de Villars was still trying to stamp out the Camisard revolt in the Cévennes, now in its third year. His harsh punitive measures, known as the Dragonnades in this region stretching up from the flat coast at Sète, by Montpellier and Nîmes, into the wild ranges of the Massif Central, had begun to show results, and by the beginning of 1705 there was talk of a general amnesty. Villars had demanded that the Camisards laid down their arms and gave themselves up, and had finally succeeded in getting their leader Cavalier to come to Nîmes to talk with him. At this meeting Cavalier persuaded Villars to agree to issue passports to leading Camisards, so that they could leave the country, which seemed a workable solution, but, just at this point in the negotiations, Louis received news of Marlborough's intended attack on the eastern frontier and recalled Villars to take command of the French army on the Moselle.

He looked round for a replacement for Villars who would be tough enough for the job, and found the very man he needed at St Germain. Berwick with his driving energy and initiative and twenty years of soldiering behind him, although he was still only thirty-five, was waiting for a new posting. At the end of January, Berwick went south to

Montpellier to take over from Villars. He proved to be an even more ruthless persecutor of the Protestants than his predecessor.

Berwick's first action was to patrol the coast as far down as Narbonne to reconnoitre any likely landing place for Dutch or English troops and supplies. Picked squadrons of dragoons were sent into the High Cévennes and into the dry plains (the *garrigues*) around Uzès and Nîmes to hunt out rebels, and keep a sharp look-out for deserters from French regiments or foreign sympathizers who might be with them. Those rounded up were brought to the prison in Montpellier. Among these was the notorious Cavalier, who was overheard to say that the Duke of Berwick was to be seized and the town governor killed, and that already there were thirty men pledged to do this in Montpellier as soon as reinforcements led by the Camisards Ravanel and Catinat arrived. This information was brought to Berwick as he was getting ready for bed on the night of 19 April. He immediately issued orders for the guard on all the town gates to be doubled and any suspicious-looking characters arrested. At the same time he ordered a search of all the houses with known Camisard connections.

The town provost, entering one of these houses with six Irish soldiers, was fired upon. One shot pierced the provost's hat while another burned his wig. The provost fired back, killing the Camisard on the spot. A paper was found on his body giving a list of his accomplices. The other two in the house were arrested and brought to Berwick. One was a surgeon, a deserter from the Regiment of Firmaçon, and the other a deserter from a Swiss regiment, both natives of the Cévennes. The latter begged for his life, saying he could give Berwick important information. He gave the Duke the address of the house of a silk merchant in Nîmes where four other Camisard leaders were hiding. Berwick sent to Nîmes a detachment of troops who arrived at the silk merchant's house at nightfall and surrounded it. The Provost of Montpellier, who was with them, heard a voice inside saying, 'Serve God! I tell you that in three weeks the King will no longer be master of Languedoc nor of Dauphiné'. This was Ravanel speaking, and with him were another Villars (whose real name was Vila) and Jonquet, all three key figures among the Camisards. The troops rushed the door and all the Camisards were seized including the silk merchant, who was called Alison. Catinat was not caught, but when the Duke reached Nîmes after midnight he said he was sure that he was somewhere in the city.

Next morning, after searching all night, and having ordered that the town gates remained shut, Berwick offered a reward of 100 louis d'or to anyone handing over Catinat or supplying news of his whereabouts. He added the warning that if the owner of the house where he was found did not denounce him, he would be hanged at his own door, his family imprisoned, his goods confiscated and his house razed to the ground. Such was Berwick's reputation for ruthlessness that no one dared shelter Catinat, who was chased from his hiding place disguised as a watchman, and was just about to slip out of the town when he was recognized and arrested by an officer of the guard. He was brought before Berwick, who asked him why he had returned to Languedoc after being issued with a passport on his promise never to return or to take up arms against the French King. Catinat replied insolently that he had returned in the capacity of envoy-extraordinary of the Queen of England to the Protestants of France. He said that if Berwick would allow him to write to London, Her Majesty Queen Anne would undoubtedly agree to exchange him against the Marquis de Tallard.

Berwick's reply was one of horrifying savagery. He condemned him to be 'put to the question' along with Vila, Ravanel and Jonquet, during which torture Catinat broke down completely and confessed much more than the others. Their execution was postponed until the following day on account of the number of accomplices named by Catinat, who, with Ravanel, was burned alive, while Villars and Jonquet, after being broken on the wheel, were thrown, still alive, into the fire where the others were burning.

As a result of Catinat's information about 350 people were arrested, among them several bankers who had received money via Genoa, England and Holland. A considerable cache of rifles, bayonets, powder and other arms was discovered. The executions continued. The silk merchants Alison and Allègre were broken on the wheel, and their houses burned down, and many others were hanged. Some time afterwards mules driven by three deserters disguised as skin merchants from the Cévennes were seized, and were found to be carrying 30,000 louis d'or. These men were also put to death, but not before confessing in their dying testimonies that they were to have started an uprising on 25 May. In this the Governors of Montpellier and Nîmes, and all the officers they could lay their hands on, were to have their throats cut, and both towns then set on fire. The conspirators were to recognize each other by the green ribbons in their hats. This was confirmed by the discovery of a large quantity of green ribbon among the packages carried by the mules. The muleteers said that Alison and Allègre had dyed more than 300 pieces of green ribbon. They also confirmed that the English and Dutch had promised to land well equipped reinforcements at Sète. The Camisards from Montpellier were to join up with these troops on the plain of Frontignan; they had a list of those who were ready to be armed at Nîmes, Uzès, Alès and other towns and villages of Languedoc.

During the month of May Berwick had been patrolling the sea-coast from the mouth of the Rhône round as far as Perpignan. He sent detachments to hunt down Camisards who were believed to have fled into Ardèche, and during that summer brutal murders and hangings took place all over the region. To this day a solitary cypress tree in a field or by the roadside in the remote uplands marks the graves of these murdered Protestants. Those who could escape over the mountains left France. By the autumn of 1705 Berwick had ruthlessly dealt with the last pockets of resistance in the Cévennes. This earned him further favour with Louis XIV.

At the beginning of October Berwick was ordered to leave Languedoc, where his brutal repression had achieved an uneasy peace, and told to take over the siege of the citadel of Nice. The French were masters of the lower town but the citadel was still held by the Duke of Savoy, who had spent vast sums on fortifying it to make it one of the strongest fortresses in Europe. Usson, the French commander conducting the siege, had just died, and the Savoyard governor, the Marquis de Carail, had broken the truce he had made with him.

Berwick arrived with fifteen battalions augmented by thirty-two companies of grenadiers sent south from the army of the Rhine. His artillery was at Toulon, under orders to embark for Nice, but contrary winds drove the transports on to the Iles d'Hyères, and it was the first week of November before they were able to unload at Villefranche.

Berwick set up his batteries and began the siege. On 9 December he started a heavy bombardment of the château that crowned the citadel. His chief engineer and brigadier were killed by cannon-fire, the head and brains of the engineer being blown into the face of the Duke, who, as usual, was in the front line, checking every detail for himself. He kept the siege going for nearly three weeks until the besieged garrison mutinied and Carail was forced to capitulate. On 4 January 1706 Berwick was again forward with his batteries when he heard the enemy beating the retreat (*la chamade*). He ordered a ceasefire, took hostages, and set to work in a businesslike way to order the articles of surrender. He despatched his brother-in-law Lord Bulkeley, a Scottish Jacobite serving in the French army, to take the news of the victory to Versailles and to present the capitulation terms to the King.

On 6 January Carail left the citadel with 550 men and 80 officers, the survivors of his garrison, and the 1,400 civilians who had taken refuge there. They left behind 200 wounded, who were treated at the French King's expense.

In contrast to his harsh treatment of the Protestant rebels in the Cévennes, Berwick was generous in the surrender terms he offered his enemies in Nice. When the garrison left, he proclaimed an amnesty for all deserters who returned to their regiments. The conquest of the rest of the province of Nice was comparatively simple. It was completed by the end of January when Berwick returned to Versailles to receive Louis's congratulations. In his eyes, Berwick could do no wrong. He had accomplished his missions in Languedoc and Nice whereas in Flanders things were going badly for France. Marlborough had inflicted a heavy defeat on the Maréchal de Villeroi at Ramillies. In Piedmont Turin had been lost to the Savoyards, and in Catalonia the siege of Barcelona had been abandoned.

Louis decided that Berwick must go to Flanders, and sent his troops in advance of him. At this point, however, the Spanish Ambassador in France, the Duke of Alba, on behalf of Philip of Spain asked Louis for the Duke of Berwick to be given supreme command of the French army in Portugal. Louis was flattered by this request, and told Alba he could not think of anyone more suitable. Alba went straight back to Berwick and told him what had happened, and that his master expected him in Madrid in the least possible delay.

The next day Louis sent for Berwick and confirmed what Alba had said. He ordered the Duke to get ready to leave for Spain at once, but told him that before he took up his new appointment he wanted to recognize his outstanding services by making him a Maréchal de France. He said that his grandson the King of Spain would hand him the brevet of his new rank on his arrival in Madrid.

The new Maréchal's troops had to be recalled hastily from Flanders to be with Berwick when he arrived in Spain. Berwick went to take formal leave of Louis and the elder brother of the King of Spain, the Duc de Bourgogne. The latter, who was a close friend, asked Berwick to keep in touch with him, a request which the Duke, who was a great letter-writer, obeyed with scrupulous regularity. Berwick wrote with equal facility in French, English or Spanish according to the nationality of his correspondents. Tough and unsentimental though he was as a soldier, he reveals himself as endearingly human in his letters. He cared deeply for all his children and throughout his long life on active service kept in touch with their problems in warm practical letters, usually terse, to the point and entirely free of sermonizing or pomposity.

He arrived in Madrid on 11 March 1706 and the King of Spain at once presented him with his brevet and baton as Maréchal de France, backdated to 6 February. After a week in Madrid he went to Estremadura to join the combined French and Spanish forces and marched at their head to the Portuguese frontier. He spent the next eighteen months campaigning in Spain and Portugal. Philip V was so impressed by Berwick's personality and ability that in 1707 he made him a Grandee of Spain, first-class, and gave him the lands and titles of Duke of Liria and Xerica in Valencia, as well as bestowing upon him the Order of the Golden Fleece.

While Berwick was absent in Spain, his half-brother James III came of age, celebrating his eighteenth birthday on 10 June 1706. The Council of Regency was dissolved and James addressed himself to taking his new responsibilities very seriously indeed. Lord Middleton, who, after all, had not resigned as his chief Secretary-of-State, wrote to the French Foreign Minister, the Marquis de Torcy, saying, 'The King my master applies himself to business with all the address of a skilful workman'.

James was conscientious and had the same dedication to duty as his parents. Unlike his father he was a good letter-writer, a talent he inherited from his mother, expressing himself clearly in English or in faultless French or Italian. Letter-writing was to prove his main activity in the long years ahead governing his paper kingdom. But unlike Berwick's brisk brief notes, James's, equally filled with commonsense, tended to be earnest and long-winded, which exasperated many of the recipients, notably his elder son.

The exiled King's coming of age was followed, less than a year later, by the Union of the Parliaments of Scotland and England. By the Act of Union in May 1707 Scotland was only allowed to send sixteen representative peers and forty-five members to the combined British Parliament, compared with 500 English members. Scotland also had to agree to support the Hanoverian monarchy but was allowed to keep its own legal system. Among the commissioners who negotiated this highly unpopular union were the second Duke of Argyll, who was an anti-Jacobite and had fought for the English under Marlborough in the Low Countries, and the notorious Sir John Dalrymple. Queen Anne created him Earl of Stair, and later, when he was appointed the English Ambassador in Paris, he became the chief Hanoverian spy on the Stuart family in France.

The union caused riots on both sides of the border, a situation from which Louis XIV thought he might well profit. He had been watching reactions to the dissolution of the Scottish Parliament in March 1707, and, in that same month, he gave one of his agents, a naturalized Frenchman named Colonel Nathaniel Hook, plenipotentiary powers to treat with the Scottish Jacobite sympathizers.[5]

At the beginning of May 1707 eight Scottish nobles arrived secretly at St Germain. They assured James that if he came to Scotland now he would, in the present state of discontent with the union, find he had a considerable following. They begged him, in the name of the entire Scottish people, to come and be their leader. They were so persuasive that both James and Louis were won over. The eight Jacobite lords offered to remain in France as hostages for the truth of what they said and the success of the enterprise.[6]

Louis began to plan an expedition for January 1708. While the ships were being fitted out at Dunkirk, another agent, the Chevalier de Nangis, was despatched secretly to Edinburgh to sound out the feelings of the people in the capital. He was well received and reassured that all that had been said in France about the eagerness among the majority of the Scots for their exiled sovereign was true. The Chevalier, who was a ship's captain, handed over the arms and ammunition he had brought on his frigate to leading Jacobites to hold in readiness for the arrival of the King. The Jacobites he met told him England was in no state to oppose their scheme; and that, as soon as King James landed, he could count on 30,000 Scots ready to take up arms in his service.

The preparations for the expedition were carried out in such secrecy that the English seemed unaware of what was going on until the fleet was nearly ready to sail. This consisted of five men-of-war, two transports, twenty frigates and about 4,000 French troops, all to be assembled at Dunkirk under the command of the French Admiral Forbin, whose family had originally come from Scotland and had settled at Marseille in 1325. With these troops went arms, ammunition, saddles and bridles, plus uniforms for a company of guards for the King and a quantity of flags and standards.

James, within three months of his twentieth birthday, was overjoyed at the thought of action at last. Needless to say, the weather during the first two months of the year was too bad for the expedition to risk crossing the North Sea, but, towards the end of February, the King's governor, the Earl of Perth and his under-governor, Colonel Sheldon, with several other members of the Jacobite court, left in advance for Dunkirk.

On 5 March Louis XIV gave letters of credence to the Comte de Gassé to accompany James as Ambassador of France to Scotland. At the same time the French Foreign Minister had given Gassé his instructions for dealing with the Scottish and Irish Jacobite lords. Torcy also gave Gassé a letter of introduction to Colonel Hook and plans for the voyage of James, now officially called King of England in the French Foreign Office documents.[7]

On the following evening Louis XIV went to St Germain to take his leave of James. As he embraced him, he promised that he would never forsake him, and repeated the words he had used to his father on the eve of his expedition to Ireland: 'The best I can wish for you is that I may never see your face again'. He then presented James with clothes 'fit for a reigning monarch', a service of gold and silver plate and a casket containing 100,000 louis d'or. A large amount of bed linen and personal

James Edward as a young man of nineteen at Dunkirk pointing towards England across the Channel.

linen had already been sent to the ships at Dunkirk. James was overwhelmed by this unexpected generosity. He assured Louis he would never forget his kindness nor his obligations to him and to France.

His mother had given him 40,000 louis d'or and most of her jewels. The

Duke of Berwick returned from Spain and left in a private capacity for Dunkirk to help his half-brother, as he had promised when he was granted his French naturalization. The Princess Louise Marie was recovering from an attack of measles, but early next morning James insisted on seeing her to say goodbye before he set out from St Germain. The other Jacobites had all gone ahead of the King, so that, when he finally rode out from the château and headed north-west for the coast, only Lord Middleton, two gentlemen of his household and two valets accompanied him.

Queen Anne had by this time heard about the invasion preparations at Dunkirk. She had immediately issued orders that no one was to be allowed to land at a British port without a passport signed by her and her Secretary-of-State. She held back the troops and ships that had been ready to sail for Spain, and managed to assemble a fleet of forty-two English ships plus eight Dutch ships and an army of 25,000 men. Then she sent an army under the Earl of Leven north to Edinburgh, though, as events turned out, she need not have bothered.

By the time James reached Dunkirk on 9 March, ships of the English fleet were in sight of the port. The King had begun to feel unwell on the journey and was now running a high fever. His doctors diagnosed the symptoms as measles, which he had probably caught from his sister. They advised delaying the departure, which had been planned for 10 March, for another three days. Then, though his temperature was still very high, James insisted that they embark without delay and had himself carried aboard Admiral Forbin's flagship the *Mars*.

Then came an astonishing *volte-face* on the part of the French King. On 11 March, the day following the planned departure, Louis sent a letter to James countermanding the whole expedition. This letter orders the Prétendant to cancel his enterprise and return to St Germain, saying that it was Louis's intention to recall his fleet to Dunkirk and to order his troops back to their quarters.[8] If James ever received this letter, he deliberately ignored it, because on 17 March he wrote to his mother: 'At last I am on board. The body is very feeble but courage is good and will sustain the weakness of the body'. He went on: 'I hope not to write to you again until I do so from Edinburgh Castle where I expect to arrive on Saturday'.

James told his followers that during the voyage he wished to be addressed simply as the Chevalier de St Georges. He did not want the title of King to be used until he had landed in Scotland.

In spite of Louis's orders, the fleet sailed on the evening of 18 March. It now stood at seven men-of-war and twenty-one transports carrying 6,000 troops. The whole expedition was commanded by Admiral Forbin, with the land forces under the Maréchal de Matignon. Berwick sailed in a purely private capacity to be on hand as an observer.

The watching English fleet put to sea under Sir George Byng. In their pursuit they intercepted and captured the *Salisbury*, a former English man-of-war then belonging to the French, and among the prisoners taken were Lord Middleton's two sons. Several French transports were lost, with 800 men.

By 23 March Forbin's flagship and his fleet had anchored off the Firth of Forth, just north of Edinburgh. James demanded again and again to be put ashore, where he was convinced his supporters would rally to him, but Forbin obstinately refused, repeating enigmatically, 'Ce n'est pas possible'. He had obviously received secret instructions from Louis that James was on no account to be landed in Scotland. The object of the exercise, cruel as it was for the young King's hopes, was to threaten the Whig government in England and to frighten them into diverting troops from Spain. As such, it served its purpose, and it becomes clear that the choice of such an unimaginative defeatist as Forbin had been deliberate on the French King's part.

In the state of discontent Scotland was in at that moment, there is little doubt that, had he been permitted to land, James would have had a considerable popular following. Helpless and frustrated, he had to accept the humiliation of sailing back to France without a shot being fired.

In April 1708, Queen Anne proclaimed that all those who had followed the Pretender in the late expedition were guilty of treason. On 11 April, Louis XIV had the hypocrisy to send a letter to James expressing his sorrow at the failure of the expedition.[9]

James did not meet the French King until ten days later, when, making his first public appearance since his humiliating return, he went with his mother to Marly to visit the Duchesse de Bourgogne, who was sick. Louis happened to be there, and later he called James aside for a private talk. The two walked down the main avenue engaged in serious conversation, James looking very cast down.

Although it was mainly subsidized by the French King, the ill-fated expedition had eaten into the Stuarts' very limited funds. Princess Louise Marie, normally a cheerful girl, was heard for once to complain bitterly. 'We are reduced to such pitiable straits and live in such a humble way, that if it should ever please God to restore us to our natural rank, we should not know how to play our parts with becoming dignity.'

Restless and despondent after the abortive invasion attempt, James, like his father more than half a century before, asked permission from Louis to join the French army and to fight in Flanders. Louis, with apparently no qualms of conscience about his previous behaviour, said he was delighted to accept him as a volunteer.

Before leaving to join the French army, James sent for a trusted Jacobite, Charles Farquarson, and gave him a message for his disappointed supporters in Scotland. 'Tell them', he said, 'that far from being discouraged by what has happened, we are resolved to move heaven and earth to free ourselves and them and, to that end, we propose ourselves one day to come to the Highlands with money, arms and ammunition and to put ourselves at the head of our good subjects, if they are in arms for us.'

In the middle of May James, again using the title of the Chevalier de St Georges, set out from St Germain to fight as a mercenary soldier for the French against the allied troops under Marlborough. After a journey of two days he reached Valenciennes, where he joined his old friend the Duc de Bourgogne. James served with distinction throughout the Flanders campaign. He fought bravely at Oudenarde on 11 July 1708, and again in the terrible slaughter at Malplaquet on 11 September 1709, where he was slightly wounded. His commander-in-chief was the larger than life Maréchal de Villars, who had always been a partisan of the Stuarts and was honoured to have the young Stuart King as one of his staff officers.

James at the age of twenty-one was a dashing cavalier, and, wearing the pale blue ribbon of the Garter across his chest, led his own company of horse against the English under Marlborough. Malplaquet was the greatest catastrophe of a disastrous year for Louis. He lost 11,000 men, and this crushing defeat came after a terrible winter of cold and famine, leaving the French treasury almost completely drained. The King and the Princes sent their gold plate to be melted down, and the lesser nobility their silver plate. The summer was little better and ended, just before Malplaquet, with a very bad harvest, so that the prospects for the coming winter were grim. The only consolation for the defeat of Malplaquet was that the allies suffered even heavier casualties, losing 17,000 men.

After Malplaquet the Maréchal de Villars withdrew his remaining troops behind defensive lines in Flanders. Mons was still in French hands, but was besieged by the allies. Louis ordered the aged Maréchal Boufflers to break the siege and, at the end of September, the Duke of Berwick was to help Boufflers by reconnoitring Marlborough's positions. The allied forces were too strong for the French and, on 20 October, Mons surrendered. With this capitulation the campaign closed and both sides withdrew into winter quarters. The French were in such a bad way that they were forced to ask for an armistice. They were not, however, prepared to hand over the key towns they held in Spain. Marlborough thought that once he had dealt with France in the Low Countries he could carry on with his campaign to drive Philip of Anjou from the throne of Spain.

In November Marlborough made it a condition that Louis XIV should withdraw his troops from Spain within a time limit of two months, but the French King refused. In the spring of 1710 the war was resumed. France was so weak after her military losses and the terrible famine of the previous year that it seemed unlikely she could last longer than another campaign.

12

IF THE QUEEN OF ENGLAND SHOULD DIE

GRIM THOUGH ITS PROSPECTS were in the spring of 1710, the French army under the ebullient Villars faced the enemy in Flanders with stubborn resolution. The optimism of Villars transmitted itself to his men and gave them heart in this losing campaign against the superior strategy of Marlborough and the man he was to betray, Prince Eugène of Savoy.

For James the next six months were the freest and happiest of his life. As the Chevalier de St Georges he now had his own company directly under the Maréchal de Villars, and there was mutual admiration and affection between the two. Much as he loved his mother and sister, it was a relief to get away from his female family circle. He wrote to them regularly as a dutiful son, but to Lord Middleton as man to man. In one letter to him James confesses: 'I find it enough to be out of St Germain, to have one's health, for I cannot remember to have had it better than it is now. Our General (Villars) has organized a tavern for us where I go everywhere.'

As his personal entourage, James had taken with him his physician Mr St Paul, his confessor Father Eyre, and two servants, Richard Hamilton and his groom-in-waiting Charles Booth. Booth also acted as his secretary and made it his business to keep Middleton up to date with his master's activities. On 27 May Booth wrote from Arras: 'Our master rose at 4 a.m. and was on horseback by 4.30. He was eleven hours on horseback. He crossed the river near Arras with the Marshals and went to inspect the ground near Douay. French dragoons took 30 or 40 prisoners.' At Harcourt on 20 June James, attended by Booth, insisted on riding as far as the outposts. Seeing some of the enemy soldiers across the river, James was curious to know if any of his countrymen were among them. Booth found both Scottish and English troops, and when he told them he was in attendance upon the Chevalier de St Georges, the Stuart Pretender, he reported back that no animosity was expressed against him.

Marlborough's nephew, the Duke of Berwick, often visited his half-brother James in camp, and gave him sound fatherly advice on how to conduct himself in war. The relationship between the two was very good at this stage. Berwick was nearly twenty years older than James, and his long experience in the field had left him with few illusions. He was a shrewd judge of character and a wise counsellor when the young King found himself bewildered by the intrigues that inevitably surrounded him. Most of all Berwick warned him to beware of English government spies pretending to be Jacobites, who turned up from time to time and sometimes went on to try and glean information from the Queen Mother at St Germain. Mary of Modena kept her wits about her, suspecting all these unknown characters to be impostors until they proved their credentials.

James suffered from recurring bouts of fever during that damp summer in the plains of Flanders, but recovered when dosed with quinine. There was a lull in the fighting and rumours that peace proposals were being considered. About this time James met a man who was to have a lasting influence on his life; he was Fénélon, the Archbishop of Cambrai, who had been the Duc de Bourgogne's tutor and was responsible for the Duke's advanced ideas. Fénélon was now in his seventies, and was out of favour at the French court because of his doctrine of Quietism. He was attracted to the serious-minded James, and the ideas he passed on to him were to be a source of strength to the Stuart King during his long life of disappointment and exile. The thing that most impressed Fénélon about James was that he seemed to be entirely master of himself. He described him as

> . . . . acting like a man who always consults reason and obeys it in everything without yielding to the force of imagination or to the unequal fits of humour and fancy. He has dignity without haughtiness and suits his civilities to the merit and quality of everybody. He has a modest, peaceful gaiety like a man come to maturity; and he seems to yield himself up to his friends without enslaving himself to any one of them. He has a quick apprehension of truth, a perfect love for it, and a perfect relish of that divine virtue which is founded upon a submission to providence and this seems to be the governing principle of his life.

In spite of this eulogy, Fénélon was a realistic man of the world. He gave James sound advice on his conduct if he were ever to succeed Queen Anne as King of England. 'No human power can ever curtail the freedom of the mind', he insisted. As a Catholic King ruling over Protestant subjects, James should never try to force any to change their religion. 'You must allow tolerance to all.' James followed Fénélon's advice in all his subsequent proclamations, though he never had the chance to put these enlightened views into practice as a reigning monarch.

Fénélon also praised James's physical courage. 'I saw him leave Cambrai upon the rumour of a battle expected at a time when his strength was quite sunk and exhausted by several fits of long, continued fever. None about him durst oppose his resolution. If he had shown the least hesitation everyone was ready to make his court by pressing him to consider his health in the first place.'

The summer of 1710 had its lighter side. In one of his letters to Middleton, James wrote: 'I was last night at Monsieur de Rohan's who gave a great feste. There was play, music, and a very great and good supper. I left them at 12 o'clock with the resolution of staying up till daylight. Adieu. My compliments to Lady Middleton. Our Hector (Villars) doth talk of fighting in his chariot, but I do not believe him, especially now that the conferences of peace are certainly renewed'.

In August he wrote to Middleton thanking the old man for acting as his sister's escort: 'My sister is charmed with your complaisance in being her conductor in all her sorties. By what I can gather from her, she is as well pleased to be at Chaillot as I am to be out of St Germain.' He also told Middleton that, much as he longed to have his company in camp, he was indispensable at St Germain to keep an eye on things political and financial. James kept a sharp eye on his accounts. Writing to his Treasurer William Dicconson, he said: 'My expense in this campaign has not been extravagant. Before I went, none of you thought I would make it without retrenching or selling, but thank God, we have rubbed it out without either the Queen's help or your care.'

In the autumn of 1710, on his return to St Germain, James found his mother and sister in low spirits. Louise Marie was now eighteen. She was attractive and intelligent with an unusually sweet and considerate disposition, but, because of the uncertainty of the Stuarts' position and their lack of means, she had no suitors. She could not help hoping against hope that, on the death of their half-sister Anne, her brother might succeed to the English throne, and her own prospects for a happy future might brighten. However, she said philosophically to her friends at Chaillot: 'For my part, I am best pleased to remain in ignorance of the future. For it seems to me that persons like myself who have been born in adversity are less to be pitied than those who have suffered a reverse.'

A few weeks after this the election of a Tory government to replace the Whigs in England gave rise to fresh hopes among the exiles at St Germain. The Tory party was headed by Robert Harley, Lord Oxford, whose cousin Mrs Masham had replaced the Duchess of Marlborough in the Queen's confidence and affections. The new English Foreign Minister was Henry St John, Lord Bolingbroke, who had met the Duke of

Berwick when the Duke had been to England once or twice in disguise and already had had secret dealings with him.

The Tory government's first action was to reopen peace negotiations with France, and during the winter of 1710 the Duke of Berwick was visited by an agent of Lord Oxford with a plan to restore James to the English throne under the three following conditions: that, in its early stages, the plan should be kept secret from the Queen Mother because of the necessity of certain religious concessions; that Queen Anne should be allowed to retain the crown during her lifetime provided she agreed to its transference to James after her death; and, thirdly, provided that proper guarantees were given by James for the preservation of the Church of England and the civil liberties of his subjects.

On James's behalf Berwick agreed to these conditions, but during the next year he became more and more disenchanted with Oxford's procrastination. In the end he lost all faith in him, describing him as 'a man so dark and unpenetrable that he was tempted to believe him a knave'. His worst fears were confirmed when other agents told him that Oxford was also in touch with the Elector of Hanover on the same subject. On this occasion Middleton had been more shrewd than Berwick, having distrusted Oxford from the first.

Queen Anne's own feelings towards her half-brother were ambivalent. Past middle age, childless and grossly fat, she had a sentimental family feeling for her nearest surviving blood-relation as well as remorse for her unfilial conduct towards her father. She was, however, only too well aware that her subjects would never accept her Catholic half-brother as their King unless he agreed to renounce his religion. She had not seen James since he was an infant, but she had a pathological dislike of the eighty-two-year-old Electress Sophia of Hanover, whose only claim to succeed her lay in the fact that she was the nearest surviving Protestant descendant of James I, being the youngest child of James's daughter Elizabeth of Bohemia.

The year 1711 opened dismally, with the French King, for the first time in his long reign, giving no New Year presents because of the cost of the war. Then, on 16 April, the Dauphin died suddenly of smallpox at Meudon. He had been a dull uninspiring man, but had always been loyal and kind to James and his father. His son, the Duc de Bourgogne, succeeded him as heir to the French throne, and James's cousin, the flighty Marie-Adelaïde became the new Dauphine, a role that pleased her vanity immensely. She now felt almost on an equal footing with her sister Queen Marie-Louise of Spain, for whose position she had always felt a sisterly jealousy.

One month after the Duc de Bourgogne had become Dauphin of

France, the Emperor Joseph died in Vienna and the succession as Holy Roman Emperor of his son the Archduke Charles, rival to Philip V for the throne of Spain, marked the turning point of the war. England and Holland realized that for them to continue to back the new Austrian Emperor as candidate for the Spanish throne would fatally upset the balance of power in Europe.

Just about this time, James had taken the initiative of writing personally to Queen Anne from St Germain, begging her for reasons of the closest family ties to acknowledge his claims as her successor. A Jacobite agent took this letter and had it delivered to the Queen by Mrs Masham. In it James says:

> You may be assured, Madam, that though I can never abandon but with my life my own just right which you know is unalterably settled by the most fundamental laws of the land, yet I am most desirous rather to owe it to you than to anyone living, the recovery of it. It is for yourself that a work so just and glorious is reserved. The voice of God and Nature calls you to it, the promises you made to the King our father enjoin it, the preservation of our family and the preventing of unnatural wars require it.[1]

As no answer was forthcoming to this eloquent appeal, in June 1711 James set out on another military campaign, this time to serve under the Duke of Berwick in Dauphiné. During the summer he visited Languedoc and the Rhône Valley and, on his way north, at the end of the season, he took time off in Lyon to see the town. He visited the silk factories and chose a length of beautiful silk material to replenish his sister's very limited wardrobe.

During James's absence the new Dauphine Marie-Adelaïde went out of her way to entertain his mother and the Princess Louise Marie. She arranged visits to the theatre and opera and invited them to fêtes at Versailles and Marly. The Queen and the Princess spent as much time as they could at Chaillot, where one rainy Saturday morning in October two of the Dauphine's pages rode into the courtyard to warn them that the Dauphine was coming to visit them that afternoon.[2] At four o'clock Marie-Adelaïde arrived with the Duchesse de Berry and the Duchesse de Lauzun. The Dauphine told the Princess to show the other two round the convent while she stayed to chat to her mother. When they had gone, she told the Queen that she was planning a hunting party for the following Tuesday in the Bois de Boulogne and hoped very much she would allow the Princess of England to join them. The Queen thanked her but said her daughter had neither a horse nor suitable clothes. The Dauphine told her not to worry, for she would take care of everything.

Early in the morning on the day of the hunt the Dauphine sent a groom with a fine horse for the Princess and one of her own riding habits, which she said, in a note to the Queen, she was sure would fit Louise Marie perfectly. She apologized for not sending a new one, but there had not been time to have one made. The Princess was delighted, mounting the horse at once and trotting several times round the courtyard. At half past twelve the Duchesse de Lauzun and her sister-in-law, the Duchesse de Duras, arrived to fetch her to join the royal party. They both wore black and grey riding habits, as the court was still officially in mourning for the late Dauphin. The habit the Dauphine had sent for her cousin was, however, of fine scarlet cloth, trimmed with gold lace, which showed off her graceful figure and made a splendid contrast to the other members of the hunt in their sober grey and black. Louise Marie enjoyed an excellent day's sport, saw the stag swim and was in at the death. To round off the day the Dauphine had arranged that they would all have supper at the Lauzun house in Passy. The Princess was stiff and tired after her strenuous day in the open, and left for Chaillot shortly after nine, but Marie-Adelaïde and her husband were in such good form that they did not leave Passy for Versailles until well after midnight.

The following day, which was James II's birthday, Mary of Modena and her daughter had arranged to visit the church of the English Benedictines in Paris, where the late King was buried. To avoid attracting attention they went by hired coach, attended only by the Duchess of Perth and Lady Middleton. When the crowd pressing round the coach as it stopped in the narrow street asked the coachman the names of his passengers, all they could get out of him was that 'he had brought two old gentlewomen, a middle-aged woman and a young lady'.

The body of James II had been embalmed and placed in a lead coffin covered with a velvet pall. It remained in front of the altar of the chapel of the English Benedictines waiting for the day when it could be taken for burial to England. The Queen had been a widow for ten years and had never ceased to mourn her husband. In a letter[3] to Soeur Angélique at Chaillot, written on her birthday a week or so after his death, she had said: 'I feel more and more the loss and separation from him who was dearer to me than my own life and who alone rendered that life supportable. I miss him more and more each day. To begin with I felt a sort of calm in my grief but now I feel it even more profoundly.' Since then she had behaved with admirable courage. She relied on her two children for support and all her prayers were directed towards their personal happiness.

The Queen and her daughter drove down the steep rue St Jacques and across the Seine by the Pont Neuf back to Chaillot. There they waited for James to return from his military service to spend the winter with them at

St Germain, hoping and fearing for the future.

Next day, after Mass, a message arrived for them, but not from James. It was from the Duc de Lauzun warning them that the preliminaries of peace were on the point of being signed between England and France. Lauzun himself came over later in the day to break the distressing news to the Queen that, by the terms of the proposed treaty, Louis XIV would almost certainly be forced to repudiate James and order him to leave French territory. Mary of Modena stoically heard out what her old friend had to say, but Louise Marie broke down completely. The future for them seemed too bleak and pointless to contemplate.

James was already on his way home from Lyon after his six months in Dauphiné with Berwick. On 4 November 1711 he appeared unexpectedly at Chaillot, having spent the previous night at Chartres and stopped to hear early Mass at the English Benedictines on hisway through Paris. He dined with his mother and sister and afterwards invited the nuns to join them in his mother's sitting-room, when he described the campaign in Dauphiné and his impressions of the French provinces. He told them he was very glad to be back in Paris, as he had seen nothing in Provence or Gascony to compare with the Ile-de-France. The countryside of Languedoc was too harsh and dry, and the towns of Montpellier and Lyon disappointing. He then excused himself to reurn to St Germain and from there went to announce his return to the King and the Dauphin at Versailles.

The court was still in mourning but Marie-Adelaïde kept the crotchety old King from fretting in spite of the gloomy progress of the war. She was overjoyed to see her cousin James again, and told him not to be too depressed or to cross bridges before he came to them. With her optimistic nature she was sure that some solution would be found to his problems. The three Stuarts were invited to the Christmas and New Year parties at Versailles and Marly, which Marie-Adelaïde contrived to make even gayer than usual.

James was twenty-two and Marie-Adelaïde just twenty-five. In a portrait of the Dauphine in hunting costume she looks very much like her cousin, with the same long face, mobile mouth and dark Italianate eyes. The lightness and optimism of Marie-Adelaïde had the same tonic effect upon the reflective James as it had on the pompous Louis, and both Kings adored her. As the mother of two little boys, the Dauphine had done her duty by France, but at the beginning of 1712 she was once more pregnant. She found Marly too draughty and uncomfortable in winter, so, to please her, the court returned to Versailles early in February.

On 9 February she was struck down by a severe attack of measles, always dangerous in a pregnant woman. The doctors diagnosed it as purple fever and tried all the known drastic remedies. She was plunged into baths of hot water to try and sweat out the infection: she was bled in the foot and given special powders. Nothing did any good, and within twenty-four hours the light and life of the French court was dead. The old King was grief-stricken, but worse was to come. Four days later, while his wife still lay in state in the chapel at Versailles awaiting burial, her husband fell a victim to the same fever, the same purple rash spreading over his face. By 18 February he too was dead.

The court was stunned by this double blow. As the Duc de Bourgogne, the Dauphin had been as intelligent and farseeing politically as his wife had been popular. Three weeks later their elder son, the four-year-old Dauphin, died of the same disease, and by the end of March 1712, after a reign of seventy years, the Grand Roi Louis XIV was left with only a sickly great-grandson of two as his heir. If he too were to succumb, the next in succession to the French throne would be Louis's other grandson, the former Duc d'Anjou, who was Philip V of Spain. Louis was so sunk in apathy and despair that it seemed likely he would agree to the harshest possible terms in the proposed peace treaty.

At this critical stage James, in desperation, wrote once more to Queen Anne, endorsing in his own hand the letter that is filed in the French Foreign Office archives as 'Protestation—Spain—letter to my sister':

> In the present situation of affairs, it is impossible for me dr. sister [Madame is crossed out], to be any longer silent and not to put you in mind of the honour and preservation of your family and to assure you at the same time of my eternal acknowledgement and gratitude if you use your most efficacious endeavours towards both. I shall always be ready to agree to whatever you shall think most convenient to my interest which, after all, is inseparable from yours, being fully resolved to make use of our mutual happiness and to the general welfare of our country.

He signs this 'Your most entirely affectionate brother', instead of with his usual signature 'James R.'

Queen Anne apparently consulted Buckingham, who was in secret correspondence with Middleton. She said that if only her half-brother would consent to change his religion, she would do what she could. But James, writing to friends in England had insisted:

> Plain dealing is best in all things, especially in matters of religion, so I shall never tempt others to change. I am well satisfied with the truth of my own religion yet I shall never look worse upon any person because in this they chance to differ from me. But they must not take it ill if I use the same liberty I allow others to adhere to the religion which I, in my conscience think the best,

and I may reasonably expect that liberty of conscience for myself which I deny to none.

They were fatal words, spoken with a fatal stubbornness inherited from his parents and from his grandfather Charles I. James was too honest to play the political games necessary to regain his birthright. Poor Anne was in an impossible situation. There was nothing she could do without breaking the law, which she respected more than any other member of her family, to prevent herself being succeeded by the Electress Sophia, whom she loathed, or the equally unappealing Hanoverian heir George.

During the last week of March Mary of Modena and Louise Marie went to stay at Chaillot to be with Soeur Angélique Priolo, who was ill. James was restless and moody, lost without his friends Marie-Adelaïde and her husband. By 29 March he could stand it no longer and rode to Chaillot to beg his mother and sister to return with him to St Germain. He seemed so agitated that they agreed to go back with him that same evening. Two days later James was really ill, with a rash on his face that was diagnosed as the dreaded smallpox. It turned out to be a relatively mild attack, and with careful nursing he recovered, with his face only slightly marked. But ten days later his sister noticed a rash on her own face. She did not worry too much, as her brother had survived the illness without too much disfigurement. She was bled in the foot but that only seemed to aggravate the symptoms. The Queen never left her daughter's bedside, but the Princess did not respond to any of the prescribed treatments. She asked her mother to send for her confessor Father Gaillans. She was quite clear in her mind and, after she had confessed, she said to her mother: 'If I am to die now, I resign myself into the hands of God'.

'My daughter', said the Queen, weeping, 'I only entreat God to prolong your life that you may be able to serve Him better than you have done.'

'If I desire to live', said the Princess, 'it is for that alone and to be of some comfort to you.' This was on the night of Sunday, 17 April. The doctors gave both the Queen and the Princess sleeping powders, but the Princess awoke in the early hours of 18 April, and by nine o'clock in the morning she was dead before her mother was awake. The Queen and her son were so prostrate with grief that neither was in a fit state to attend the funeral. The Duke of Berwick, the Earl of Tynemouth, Lord and Lady Middleton, all the officers of the household from St Germain and some from Versailles followed the last Stuart Princess up the rue St Jacques to see her coffin placed beside that of her father in the English Benedictines. Louise Marie was only nineteen, and the steep narrow street was packed with the coaches of those who had known and loved La Consolatrice ever since her birth at St Germain just after the disaster of La Hogue. Her heart was buried in the chapel at Chaillot, and the length of embroidered silk her brother had chosen for her in Lyon was presented by her mother to the convent to be used as an altar cloth.

St Germain without Louise Marie became unbearable for the Queen. She spent as much time as she could afford as a paying guest at Chaillot. 'You cannot possibly imagine what my life is like at St Germain', she confided one day to Soeur Angélique. 'After supper there is absolutely nothing to do except go to my room to read or write letters. The rest of the time I am constantly being asked to take sides in disputes and quarrels so that I long for the peace and good company I only find here with you.'[4]

During the summer of 1712 Louis XIV decided to make a final bid to retrieve his losses before agreeing to peace terms. he put his most experienced commander, Villars, in charge of his forces against the allies under Prince Eugène. At the end of July Villars defeated Prince Eugène at Denain and followed up his victory on 8 September by taking Douai. These successes in no way altered the expulsion order for James and, on 16 September, as the Chevalier de St Georges, he had to take leave of his mother, who was in a state of the deepest depression. Dressed in a coat of scarlet cloth, he came to say goodbye to her in the chapel at Chaillot. His destination was Châlons-sur-Marne in Champagne, where Louis had arranged for him to stay pending the signing of the peace treaty. From Châlons James wrote two letters of thanks, one to the King of France and another, on the same day, to Madame de Maintenon.[5] In both he recommends his mother to their protection, describing her as 'the only person who is left of those who were most dear to me and who deserves so much of me as the best of mothers'. Madame de Maintenon showed the letters to his mother, saying that they 'combined the polish of an academician, the tenderness of a son and the dignity of a King'.[1]

By the end of October Villars had forced Prince Eugène, who had lost fifty-three battalions, to retreat to Brussels. In this last opetation of the war Villars succeeded in liberating all French soil. By the time the conference of Utrecht opened in January 1713 Louis was in a position to negotiate an honourable peace and to retain for France the main issue of the war, which was that his grandson Philip of Anjou should remain as Philip V of Spain. Having gained this point, he conceded the allies' demand that, as the former Duc d'Anjou, Philip of Spain should renounce any claim to the French throne; and that France should formally recognize Queen Anne as the rightful sovereign of England and give no further assistance to the Pretender James, the Chevalier de St Georges, nor harbour him within the kingdom.

James was the greatest sufferer by this treaty, as each of the allied powers—Holland, Portugal, Savoy and Prussia—guaranteed the Protestant succession in England. He arrived at Bar-le-Duc in Lorraine from Châlons on 22 February 1713. Duke Leopold, the ruler of Lorraine, whose duchy had been restored to him by the Treaty of Ryswick in 1697, was well disposed towards the Stuarts. His wife was a daughter of Liselotte, Duchesse d'Orléans, princess of the Palatinate. James spent the next two years very agreeably in Lorraine, either as a guest of the Duke and Duchess or at the château of Commercy, the home of his friend the Prince de Vaudemont.

The treaty of Utrecht was signed on 11 April 1713 and the terms published in Paris on 22 May. France, in spite of everything, had managed to gain the main point of the war, namely that Louis's grandson Philip of Anjou, of whom he had said provocatively in November 1700, 'I present to you the King of Spain', was at last accepted as such by the allied powers. But for the Stuarts, by the terms of Article Four, it seemed to be the end of the close association they had enjoyed with France for nearly 300 years.

This was not the case, however, as the secret memoirs and documents in the archives of the French Foreign Ministry reveal. Whenever it suited the French government, the Stuarts were still to be supported and used in all wars against England up to the end of the eighteenth century.

Bar-le-Duc was now the second Jacobite court in exile. Duke Leopold of Lorraine was a Catholic, like James, but he was a tolerant and realistic man. He put a room in his château at the disposal of the Protestant Jacobites where the two Non-jurors could hold Anglican services. These Protestant chaplains were permanently attached to the court and travelled to Avignon and finally to Rome with the exiled King. This tactful gesture by Duke Leopold worried Mary of Modena. She was afraid her son might be yielding to pressure to change his religion. If only he had done so, the English succession on Queen Anne's death might well have passed to him without too much opposition, as there was no great enthusiasm for the Hanoverians. However, James was not the devout Mary of Modena's son for nothing. In one of his many letters to England at this time he says: 'I neither want counsel, nor advice to remain unalterable in my fixt resolution of never dissembling any religion, but rather to abandon all than act against my conscience and honour, cost what it will'.

Dr Leslie, one of the Scottish Episcopalian chaplains, describes James in Lorraine as being 'tall, strait, clean-limbed and slender, his bones very large. He has a graceful mien, walks fast, is cheerful but seldom merry, thoughtful but not dejected and bears his misfortunes with magnanimity of spirit. There is no sort of bigotry about him. He has a great application to business, spends much of his time in his closet, writes much, which no man does better or more succinctly. I have often admired his criticalness in his choice of words.'

Many of the Protestant Jacobites in Lorraine wanted to get rid of Middleton as Secretary-of-State because he was a Catholic convert. They were jealous of him because he enjoyed the confidence, not only of the King, but of the Queen Mother and the Duke of Berwick as well. James was finally, much against his will, forced by this Protestant pressure to ask for Middleton's resignation. He told the Duke of Lorraine apologetically that in any case Middleton, who was now over seventy, wanted to retire. But it was with a sad heart and misgivings that he saw him off to St Germain. In his place he was persuaded to appoint a Protestant of mediocre ability named Higgins.

Mary of Modena was very pleased to have her old friend back at St Germain. She was now in her middle fifties and suffering from cancer of the breast, which was slowly killing her. They talked over old times as they walked together on the terrace and in the gardens of the château, sharing the news that came in reply to the Queen's many letters to her relations scattered throughout Europe. In October 1713 she was one of the first to be informed of the birth of a son and heir to Philip of Spain and her Stuart great-niece, Marie-Louise of Savoy. She wrote back at once to the Spanish queen's chief lady-in-waiting, who was still the trouble-making Princesse des Ursins, telling her to embrace the baby Prince Ferdinand of the Asturias for her. 'His great-aunt who promises to love him as tenderly as her own son', was how she signed this warm family letter.[6]

From the beginning of 1714 onwards James was involved in secret correspondence with Tory Jacobite sympathizers in England. There are no fewer than five letters written by James on the same day, 3 March 1714, on this subject.[7] One was addressed to Queen Anne, one to Bolingbroke, one to the Earl of Oxford, one to Lord Paulet and one to the Abbé Gaulthier, a dubious character who had been acting as agent and go-between for months past. Ever faithful to his family, the Duke of Berwick was also corresponding secretly with Bolingbroke on the chances of a Jacobite restoration, and made another incognito visit to England about this time.

When the Electress Sophia finally died in June 1714 at the age of eighty-four, Berwick's reaction was to increase his correspondence with members of Queen Anne's Tory Ministry. He also wrote to James Butler, second Duke of Ormonde, who had taken over command of the British army in place of the disgraced Marlborough, and to other leading noblemen telling them to 'awake from their lethargy and to take precautions against the misfortune which would surely befall them if the Queen of England should die'.

Ormonde was the son of the first Duke, who had shared the exile of Charles II and had become Master of the Household at the Restoration Court. After his own secret visit to England, Berwick tried to persuade James that he too should risk a trip to London during the summer to try and obtain a reversal of his attainder while there was still time. Berwick felt if only, under some pretext, James could meet his impressionable half-sister she would be convinced that the succession of this serious intelligent young man, her nearest blood-relative, would be preferable to that of a distant kinsman, the boorish George of Hanover, known to be entirely ignorant of the English language and whose treatment of his wife, Dorothea of Zell, was a public scandal. Unfortunately it was not possible for James to travel to England, and although, as Queen Anne lay dying at Kensington Palace at the end of July, she was heard to murmur repeatedly 'My brother, my poor brother', her words went unheeded. On the day of her death, 1 August 1714 a Council of State was held at Kensington Palace at which The Duke of Buckingham is said to have whispered to Ormonde, 'My Lord, you have twenty-four hours to do our business and to make yourself master of the kingdom'. But although he had strong family sympathies for the House of Stuart, Ormonde was no General Monk. He was popular with the army but lacked the power of quick decision. At this vital moment he hesitated, and, when Queen Anne died a few hours later, the Elector of Hanover was promptly proclaimed George I of England, Scotland, Ireland and Wales.

13

EXILE IN LORRAINE AND AVIGNON

As soon as James heard of his half-sister's death, he wrote to the French Foreign Minister Torcy, telling him he was leaving Lorraine immediately for Paris. He ends the letter, 'ever since my birth, the King (Louis XIV) has been my support and protector and now, more than ever, I have need of everything he can do on my behalf . . . On arriving in Paris I shall go straight to the Duke of Lauzun's house in Passy and remain hidden there. I shall send you news of my arrival and wait there for the advice of the King'.[1]

He travelled incognito from Bar-le-Duc in the middle of August, but his plan of crossing to England before the Elector George had time to set out from Hanover was flatly turned down. Torcy warned James that Louis XIV was in no position to give him any backing this time, morally or materially. After conferring with his mother and with Lauzun he had no alternative but to return disconsolately to Lorraine. On 29 August he issued a manifesto in English, French and Latin, protesting against the proclamation of the Elector of Hanover as George I, and describing him as 'the Elector of Brunswick, one of our remotest relations, ignorant of our laws, manners, customs and language'. Of himself he says, 'I am the only born Englishman now left of the royal family'.[2]

Bolingbroke disappeared from the English political scene shortly before George, leaving his wife under house arrest in Hanover, landed at Greenwich, with his two mistresses, on 29 September. Although there had been encouraging outbreaks of pro-Jacobite rioting in several cities, Bolingbroke was afraid that his secret negotiations with James and Berwick in the months before Queen Anne's death might come to light and that he would be impeached. He remained in hiding until he was able to slip away to France.

The first act of the new English King was to get his Parliament to offer a reward of £100,000 to 'any person who shall seize and secure the Pretender in case he shall land or attempt to land in any one of His

Majesty's Dominions'. This insulting order was never forgiven by James and his sons, and, on landing in Scotland in 1745, Prince Charles Edward issued a similarly worded reward for the capture of the Elector of Hanover.

With George I *de facto* King of England, James had to resign himself once more to accepting the hospitality of the Duke of Lorraine and to be content with receiving regular intelligence of the situation across the Channel through his correspondents and Jacobite agents.

Six months later Bolingbroke appeared in Paris and went straight to call on the Duke of Berwick. Berwick was very pleased to see him, as he had always wanted Bolingbroke to succeed Middleton as James's Secretary-of-State. Both were highly sophisticated men but Berwick, though more intelligent, was at a disadvantage, as Bolingbroke was self-seeking, unreliable and dangerously indiscreet.

At the end of July 1715 the Duke of Ormonde finally decided to throw in his lot with the Jacobites and abandoned his Richmond headquarters to escape to France. A letter in the French archives from a Jacobite agent describes the panic in London when the desertion of the head of the British armed forces became known: 'When the Duke of Ormonde left Richmond at the latter end of July, the Hanoverian Court then at St James's, determined to have His Grace seized in the night following the morning of the day on which he had left. For that end they had drawn their troops gradually nearer to Richmond. When they heard he was gone, they were in great consternation and held a Cabinet Council to consider what was to be done'.[3]

While England was in this state of unrest, Mary of Modena was invited to spend the summer in Lorraine with her son. This was her first holiday since the visit she and her husband had made to Bourbon fourteen years before. At the end of June she travelled to Bar-le-Duc to stay with the Duke and Duchess of Lorraine in their château high above the River Ornain. From there James and his mother went on to the luxurious château of Commercy, which the Prince de Vaudemont had placed at their disposal. On 29 June James wrote to thank their host, who was on duty at Versailles:

> I could no longer defer writing to you since, for a week now, my mother and I have been united, enjoying thank God perfect health and rejoicing to find ourselves in such a beautiful spot. God be praised for the good health of the King. We are on the eve of great events in England but the curtain is not yet drawn aside and you can well judge that my thoughts and my hands are fully occupied. Nothing is yet positively decided, but it cannot be much longer delayed and the result may arrive sooner than you think. You will be well informed.[4]

From Vaudemont they returned to Bar-le-Duc, where Bolingbroke and Ormonde went to see them. James, schooled by Villars and Fénélon, distrusted Bolingbroke instinctively, but the Queen, relaxed after her holiday, for once made an error of judgement and responded to Bolingbroke's easy charm. She listened to his accounts of the anti-Hanoverian riots during the last few months and was impressed by his schemes for restoring her son. He told her that one of the signatories of the unpopular Act of Union, the Earl of Mar, had been snubbed by George I and was now sounding out leading personalities in Scotland on the Stuarts' behalf. Bolingbroke was so convincing that the Queen managed to persuade James to appoint him Secretary-of-State in place of the dreary Sir Thomas Higgins. In this she had the backing of Berwick and Ormonde. The King and his mother went on to Nancy and then to Lunéville, where, on the first of September 1715, they learned of the death of Louis XIV. The clever pleasure-loving rake the Duc d'Orléans took over as Regent for the four-year-old Louis XV. Bolingbroke, in his new office of Secretary-of-State, wrote to inform James that the Regent was the absolute master of France.

On 10 September, the day the Sun King was buried at St Denis, the Earl of Mar precipitated events in Scotland by taking matters into his own hands, summoning all the Jacobites he could muster in Aberdeenshire, and, on the pretext of a hunting party, raising the Stuart standard at Braemar. He proclaimed his sovereign James the Eighth King of Scotland and Third of England, and started to march south to challenge the unpopular George I of England. There is no evidence that Mar received any direct encouragement from James in Lorraine. However, when he heard that rebellion had broken out in the Highlands, instead of dissociating himself with Mar, he appointed him commander-in-chief of the Jacobite army. On the very day that James authorized this appointment, the lowland Scottish Lord Stair, the Hanoverian Ambassador in Paris, complained to the French Foreign Office about the facilities the Duke of Ormonde and Lord Bolingbroke had obtained in France for encouraging the Pretender's enterprise in Scotland.

The season was kind to Mar's Highlanders and, at first, their surprise tactics succeeded in frightening the stolid citizens of Perth into surrendering the town. From Perth Mar issued a high-sounding proclamation in the name of King James III. All his army needed now to boost its morale was the Jacobite King to come over the water and lead them into England. James was eager to go but worried about the lack of preparation and funds. He wrote to Bolingbroke at St Germain: 'All seems ripe in that country, the dangers of delay are great, the proposals of foreign help are uncertain and tedious.' Both Bolingbroke and Berwick sensing the mood of the Regent with regard to the terms of the Peace of Utrecht, advised caution. But James was now determined to follow up this opportunity, however ill-timed. Letters flew backwards and forwards between Lorraine and St Germain. Up to the middle of October James had hoped to persuade Berwick to accompany him and act as his commander-in-chief instead of the inexperienced Mar. Berwick was no fool and frankly had no intention of chancing his own brilliant military career on such a risky enterprise. He wrote firmly to James on 7 October: 'The instant it is in my power either to accompany Your Majesty or to follow, I will do it, but Your Majesty knows where the difficulty lies and I am not my own master.' His meaning was clear enough for James to write to Bolingbroke on 10 October: 'Ralph [Berwick] is so incommunicate and incomprehensible that I have directed D.O. [Ormonde] to say nothing to him of the present resolution. Ralph is now a cypher and can do no more harm, and if he withdraws his duty from me, I may well my confidence from him. Suspicions breed like bats.'

That he was, for the first time in his life, deeply hurt by Berwick's attitude, is shown in a letter shortly after this to Bolingbroke: 'I must confess that I cannot but suspect that he [Berwick] hath been sooner or later the cause of the strange diffidence they have of me at the French court where he never did me any good'. This was one of the few occasions when James showed a lack of generosity and fairness to his half-brother. But he was bewildered and resentful at what he considered was Berwick's betrayal of him when he needed him. Berwick's position was impossible. He was a naturalized French subject and a Maréchal de France. To leave France without the Regent's permission would have meant the end of his career. He had no other resources to fall back on, and he had a large, deeply loved family to support. With his thirty years' military experience he knew that an attempt to over-throw the English government at that moment was futile.

James, in his bitterness, persisted in quoting the clause Berwick had sworn to when he had applied to take out French nationality. He sent the following peremptory order to his half-brother: 'Our will and pleasure is, that immediately upon receipt of this order you will repair in the most private and speedy manner you can to our ancient Kingdom of Scotland and there take upon you the command given you by virtue of our commission of this date'.

Berwick's reply was that he had consulted lawyers and men of sense 'with a full resolution to go as far for Your Majesty's service as I can in honour and conscience, but I find the reason against my leaving France without the Regent's consent so strong that it is with the deepest concern I am forced to ask Your Majesty's pardon for not complying with Your

Majesty's commands'. This refusal caused an estrangement between the two that lasted twelve years. But Berwick's eldest son, the Earl of Tynemouth, who was nineteen, did go with James to Scotland.

The Regent d'Orléans behaved very well to James in other respects, paying him his pension regularly and seeing that he was allowed to stay on in Lorraine. His policy was to support the Hanoverian régime in England, though he was constantly being irked by criticisms from Lord Stair, who was not only Hanoverian Ambassador to France but the head of a highly organized spy system on his master's behalf. In November Stair quoted Article Four of the Treaty of Utrecht to the Regent, reminding him that it forbade him to let the Pretender pass through French territory.

While James was making his own arrangements to sail to Scotland, the Rising of 1715 was pursuing its doomed course. After taking Perth, Mar procrastinated long enough to give George time to rally the lowland clans, led by the Campbells, and to bring over reinforcements from Holland. Ten miles south of Perth, on a bleak stretch of moorland called Sheriffmuir, a battle was fought on 13 November. In spite of the tactics of an ancient one-eyed veteran of Killiecrankie, Macintosh of Borlum, and the bravery of his highlanders, the battle was a defeat for the Jacobites. The rising in the north of England was equally disastrous, ending with another defeat at Preston.

But by this time James was already on his way to Scotland. On 29 October he slipped away from a masked ball at Commercy and, disguised as an abbé, reached the Lauzun house in Paris the following day. The Duke, who was now eighty-two, had Mary of Modena brought secretly to his house to say goodbye to her son. Then, once more in disguise, James left by one of the secret entrances to the house and rode off through Normandy to join the Duke of Ormonde at St Malo.[6] At the little town of Nonancourt, near Evreux, he narrowly escaped assassination by one of Stair's agents, a former colonel in an Irish regiment named Douglas. The sympathy and quick wits of the wife of the owner of the staging post saved his life. She hid him in one of the outbuildings for three days and sent his would-be killer on a false trail.[7]

There was no ship available at St Malo, so James left Ormonde there and rode with Tynemouth north to Dunkirk, where they were told that a gift of 200,000 gold crowns sent by Philip of Spain had been shipped ahead of them to Scotland. James and Tynemouth at last made the North Sea crossing in rough weather and landed at Peterhead, a small fishing port north of Aberdeen on 22 December. Their first news on stepping ashore, weak from seasickness, was that the ship with the Spanish gold had been wrecked on the way. This was a bad enough omen, but a crippling attack of the ague, brought on by the harsh north-east winds, laid the King low for three days and did not improve matters. The news Mar brought was disquieting. He had to admit that his army of 12,000 men had dwindled to 3,000. James accepted this stoically and set off south, getting as far as Glamis Castle in Angus, where the young Lord Strathmore, whose father had been killed six weeks before at Sheriffmuir, received him. The Jacobites who rallied to him were all pleased with their King, but openly disappointed that he had brought neither money nor foreign troops to help them. By the beginning of February a price of £100,000 had been put by King George on the Pretender's head, and the Duke of Argyll was heading for Perth with a large force of English and Dutch regular troops. The highlanders were vanishing daily into the hills. James realized that for him to remain in Scotland as things were going was pure folly. From Glamis it was only a few miles to the coast, so, after publishing a message telling each man to shift for himself, James and Mar boarded a French ship at Montrose and sailed away from Scotland for ever.

Before he left, James appointed Gordon of Auchintoul as commander-in-chief to replace Mar, with full powers to negotiate the articles of capitulation with the Hanoverian government. The Earl of Tynemouth and his cousin Francis Bulkeley made their way to Edinburgh, where they chartered a ship to take them to Holland.

After six days on the North Sea James and Mar landed at Gravelines, north of Calais, and from there went straight to St Germain. For several days James tried to get an audience with the Regent, but was always refused. Since the Fifteen had proved a fiasco, the Duc d'Orléans, always a realist, had decided to support the existing régime in England, and was now hand in glove with Lord Stair. He told James bluntly that he must leave French territory immediately. Duke Leopold of Lorraine was in the embarrassing position of being almost wholly dependent on France, and was no longer in a position to offer hospitality to the Stuarts. He was a kind man, genuinely upset by James's predicament, and suggested he might try for asylum at Deux-Ponts (Zweibrucken) part of the Palatinate belonging to the violently anti-Hanoverian Swedish King Charles XII.

James did try, and found Charles of Sweden sympathetic, but he was unable to obtain a safe-conduct to go there. There remained the Papal city of Avignon. James wrote to Pope Clement XI, and his mother to her old friend Cardinal Gualterio. Ormonde and Mar were both in favour of Avignon, considering it a convenient rallying point for Jacobite exiles as well as having a pleasant climate and an agreeable atmosphere. While James was waiting for the Pope's reply, George I, determined to make life as difficult as possible for his rival, ordered the Swiss States to forbid the Pretender to stay in their territories or even to pass through them. The

Pope sent a favourable reply, and before going south to set up his little court at Avignon, James arranged for five ships to be sent to Scotland to transport as many of his followers as possible to safety.

At the end of March 1716 the King, accompanied by Mar, whom he had created a Duke, and officers of his Household, were on the road to Lyon. At Vienne on the Rhône they were met by the Papal Vice-Legate's Captain of Cavalry, who escorted them down the right bank of the Rhône until they crossed it at Pont Saint-Esprit. This was done at James's request, to avoid passing through the town of Orange, which had painful associations with the Dutch Prince who had deposed his father. Then they travelled down the left bank of the Rhône until they reached Villeneuve-les-Avignon, the Pope's summer residence, with its fine view of the Papal city.

James had decided that his entry into Avignon should be as unostentatious as possible, as befitted an exiled fugitive. At Villeneuve he changed into a post-chaise, with Mar riding on one side of him and the Captain of the Papal Cavalry on the other. They entered the walled city by the gate nearest to the old Pont Saint Benezet, called then the Porte du Mail (now the Porte d'Oulle). James's suite followed in two carriages, one berline, one chaise and on thirty-six horses.

As soon as the Pope's invitation had been received, James's Master of the Household had gone ahead to find suitable accommodation. He chose a fine seventeenth-century mansion belonging to a Monsieur de Serre, in the parish of St Didier. The Hôtel de Serre[8] in the rue St Marc was rented to James for the sum of 800 écus a year. Once he was installed, James made an arrangement with the owner of the adjoining Hôtel d'Entraigues to rent part of his house as well. For this he agreed to pay Monsieur d'Entraigues 700 écus a year.

The Papal Vice-Legate was waiting to greet James with all due ceremony on his arrival at the Hôtel de Serre. James politely invited him to dine but the Vice-Legate excused himself because of Lenten abstinence. In this miniature Vatican James, with his strict Catholic upbringing, felt completely at home, but the behaviour of many of his Protestant followers was soon to cause him trouble with his hosts.

Two days later the Duke of Ormonde reached Avignon, followed by the Lords Nithsdale, Panmure, Tullibardine and Drummond, and by the Jacobite Treasurer, Sir William Ellis, bringing with him the very welcome sum of 80,000 écus in gold. Jacobites rich and poor, the majority of them the latter, arrived daily in Avignon. Soon James found himself surrounded by a court of over 500 exiles.

After adventurous wanderings in the Low Countries, the young Earl of Tynemouth and Francis Bulkeley finally arrived in April. Tynemouth

The Duke of Liria, eldest son and heir to the Spanish titles of the Duke of Berwick.

was another victim of George I's vengeance. For his part in the Fifteen Rising, on the English King's representations to the Regent, he was dismissed from the French army, in which he held the rank of Brigadier, and expelled from France. The Duke of Berwick was hard-headed enough to see there was no future for his eldest son except in Spain. He discussed the matter with the Regent, with whom he was still on good terms, and they agreed that the best solution was for Tynemouth to ask for Spanish nationality and to assume his father's titles and lands in Spain.[9] This, in fact, eased family problems for Berwick, as his second wife, Anne

Bulkeley, and her stepson did not get on well. In July 1716 Tynemouth took up the title of Duke of Liria and, by his twentieth birthday on 19 October, was planning to marry a rich young Portuguese widow, Catalina Ventura Colon, Duchess of Veragua. James, as his sovereign and head of the Stuart family, granted permission for the marriage.

Berwick's letters to his son in the months preceding the wedding are all to do with the financial side of the transaction. Referring to the chronic state of penury in which Berwick and the Fitzjames family lived, the Maréchal advised his son to go, if necessary, to Jewish moneylenders, so that this advantageous marriage should not be held up by shortage of the necessary 'dineros' on Liria's side.[10] Berwick also told his son to find out exactly what the bride-to-be had been left by her late husband. Berwick had been given the château of Warty, near Compiègne (whose name he changed to Fitzjames in 1710) by Louis XIV, but its upkeep made it more of a liability than an asset.

By the time Liria had departed for Spain, the Duke of Mar's brother-in-law, Colonel John Hay, and his wife Marjory had arrived in Avignon. They became lifelong friends of James and his family.

The inhabitants of Avignon were fascinated by the constantly changing spectacle of Scots, English and Irish exiles, whose means were as varied as their dress and accents. Although most of them were nearly penniless, having lost everything in the Rising, they managed to enjoy life with enviable panache. Even the King shook off his worries and depression and lost some of his reserve. The leading families in the town invited him to dinners and balls, to which James responded by giving, for the first time in his life, receptions at the Hôtel de Serre. His most intimate friends, who brought out the hidden gaiety in his character, were the Donis, a rich cultivated family of Roman origin. They owned a magnificent house near the Hôtel de Serre to which the best society of Avignon flocked for music and card-parties. James honoured the Donis with invitations to ride in his carriage, and in return the Donis organized excursions and picnics to local beauty spots such as the Fontaine de Vaucluse, and to the classical sites of the Pont du Gard, Nîmes, Arles and St Rémy.

One familiar face was missing from James's entourage, for Bolingbroke had been dismissed from office in March 1716. James had learned before he sailed to Scotland that Bolingbroke, when he saw that the Fifteen had failed, had been in touch with Ambassador Stair offering his allegiance to King George. The Swedish and Spanish ambassadors in Paris had confirmed this when James had returned to Paris, and told him that Bolingbroke had already betrayed him earlier by passing on details of his plans to the English government. This damning factor James was generous enough to put down to Bolingbroke's notorious indiscretion. He was known to share a mistress with the untrustworthy Abbé Dubois, who was a well known double agent. It is possible too that Claudine Alexandrine de Tencin was on the same intimate terms with the Regent and with Stair. James gave as his reason for dismissing Bolingbroke culpable negligence in failing to send vital supplies of arms and money to Scotland. Horace Walpole summed up the affair in his waspish way: 'And so poor Harry is turned out from being Secretary of State and the seals are given to Mar, and they use poor Harry most unmercifully and call him a knave and a traitor and God knows what. He had a mistress at Paris and got drunk now and then, and he spent the money upon his mistress that he should have bought powder with, and neglected buying and sending the powder and arms and never went near the Queen' [Mary of Modena at St Germain].

Bolingbroke had many friends to commiserate with him. Even Berwick reproached James for having dismissed his friend in what he considered the most disgraceful manner. Berwick maintained that Ormonde was behind the dismissal, through jealousy of Bolingbroke as a man of superior genius. Bolingbroke stayed on in Paris, where he was on extremely friendly terms with the Regent, sharing his debauches. Like the Regent, he was superficially cultivated, and for a time took to writing philosophical treatises, the best of which was *Reflections upon Exile*. Although he had no official position at either the Stuart or the Hanoverian courts, he managed to lead a more amusing existence than he would have done in Avignon.

Ambassador Stair, acting on instructions from London, and following King George's note to the French government expressing his displeasure that the Pretender should be in Avignon, sent agent after agent to assassinate James. Soon the whole affair became comic opera. George, through the Regent, let James know that he was willing to pay his mother's long-overdue dowry if only he would agree to move to Italy. James did not bother to reply.

The agents sent by Stair proved unbelievably inept. James went about his business unperturbed. Once, when walking alone outside the city walls, one of these hired killers, named La Grange, caught sight of him, a perfect target, only to realise as he clapped his hand to his holster that he had left his pistols at home that day and so had missed 'la plus belle occasion du monde'. Many of James's friends, including the Papal Vice-Legate Salviati, were worried about his disregard for his safety and urged him to keep a detachment of Swiss permanently on guard outside the Hôtel de Serre. Outwardly calm and self-possessed, James continued to hear Mass daily at the fourteenth-century church of St Didier, dined out, held musical evenings at his house, and attended the Opera. The Président de Brosses described him at this period, when he was the focal point of social life in Avignon. 'The Pretender is easily recognized as a Stuart. He has the typical features. He is tall and slender and with his graceful figure and grave melancholy he resembles the figures painted by Watteau in his scenes of court gallantry.' But in spite of his appearance, James remained distant and aloof from the gallantries that surrounded him; he enjoyed the friendship and admiration of the women in his circle but never lost his heart nor his head, in contrast to his father and uncle in similar circumstances.

In July 1716 the influx of refugees reached it peak. Most of them, to the great alarm of the Papal authorities, were Protestants. These newcomers were mostly Scottish Episcopalians, and had as their chaplains the two Non-jurors, Leslie and Hamilton, who had followed the King from Lorraine, and had accepted willingly the restrictions placed upon their religion. Even so, the higher ecclesiastics were worried that the native Catholics might be tempted to lapse into Protestant bad habits such as non-observance of fasting and feast-days.

After one of the most agreeable summers he had known, James became seriously ill in September 1716, with a very painful anal fistula. At first he was treated by two local doctors, Gastaldy and Parreli, as his own physician, Dr Wood, had been captured in the Fifteen and was still a prisoner in London. His mother was beside herself with worry and persuaded Guerin, one of the court surgeons at Versailles, to go to Avignon to operate on her son. The operation took place on 20 October, and Guerin had hopes that if all went well his patient would be up and about in a fortnight. He said the wound should have healed sufficiently for James to be able to ride again in six weeks' time. But James's recovery was much slower than expected and he was still in bed on 20 November. One month after his operation he was able to receive his first visitors. He awaited them eagerly but the news they brought was not good. During the weeks James had been ill the Regent, to secure his right as heir-apparent to the young Louis XV against the claims of his cousin Philip of Spain, had decided it was necessary to have the English and Dutch Governments on his side. As Peter the Great of Russia had chosen to move his troops into Mecklenburg and so threatened Hanover, George I was also anxious to have the Dutch on his side. At the Hague the English Whig Secretary-of-State, Lord Stanhope, and the Regent's envoy, the Abbé Dubois, met to negotiate an alliance with the Dutch.

James had his first outing on 10 December, and on the fifteenth accepted an invitation to dinner with the Donis. The news in the *Gazette de Hollande* that it was only a matter of days before the Anglo-French alliance would be concluded was the main topic of conversation. By Christmas all the Jacobites who had the means to do so had left Avignon for Italy and, by the end of the year, of the 500 who had made up the court in the summer, only 150 remained. The King kept up a show of optimism and gave dinner parties to celebrate Christmas and the New Year. He was hoping that Pope Clement's power would prevail against the pressures put on the Regent by George I. When the Dutch finally joined the Triple Alliance on 4 January 1717, all hope vanished. By Articles 2 and 3, the Regent agreed to expel the Pretender from Avignon and to give him no help of any kind henceforth.

The Regent, who was genuinely fond of Mary of Modena, was deeply embarrassed by his position in relation to her. Pressed by Lord Stair, he finally let the English Ambassador convey the terms of the treaty to the Papal Nuncio and left him to break the news to the Queen at St Germain. The Papal Nuncio refused to do this, saying firmly that the Pope recognized no other King of England but James III. In desperation the Regent asked the Maréchal de Villars, the most popular man in France, to convey his orders to the court of St Germain. Villars was sure enough of himself to refuse bluntly, saying the Regent knew very well where his sentiments lay and that he personally would never abandon the Stuarts. Finally it was another Maréchal, Villeroi, who informed the Queen. She was, as everyone knew she would be, overcome with grief. She had endured nearly twenty years of misfortune with incredible patience and courage, but this was the final blow. All their hopes had rested on France and now France was rejecting them completely. She was growing old, she was sick, and none of her immediate family were left with her—only dependants. Even her unfailing friend the Superior of Chaillot was dead. The poor woman was dazed with misery. When she had recovered, she accepted the inevitable with her usual dignity and resignation, and wrote to the Vice-Legate Salviati in Avignon to convey the Regent's wishes to her son.

The Pope, with the best will in the world, could not afford to clash with the Regent as he had at all costs to preserve his right to the Papal city on French territory. Avignon society received the news with dismay. The bustle of the Stuart court had been a welcome relief from the cramping censorious influence of the Church.

'The King and the Duke of Ormonde are shattered' was the comment of a French friend of the King and the Duke in Avignon. Three short weeks had been allowed for James and his suite to pack up and plan their long journey to Italy. It was out of the question for the ailing Queen Mother to make the midwinter journey south to say goodbye to her son, whom she knew she would never see again. Thoughtful as ever, she sent presents for him to give as farewell tokens to the friends who had been so kind to him in Avignon. She sent English clocks and watches for the Doni family, to the Abbé Curnier, Canon of St Didier and to Father Vignangué, his Avignonese confessor.

The time of the year could not have been worse for a journey over the Alps. Snow was falling even in Avignon when the last fête took place at the Palace of the Vice-Legate on 4 February 1717. The King and the remaining members of his court, about 100 in all, were the guests of honour.

On Saturday, 6 February, at nine o'clock in the morning James went to hear Mass for the last time at his parish church of St Didier. Afterwards a crowd of well-wishers gathered to watch him get into his carriage with Ormonde and Mar on either side of him, followed by the Vice-Legate Salviati. Then, followed by about seventy officers and carriages carrying the Donis and other leading local families, they drove north from Avignon to Gentilly, where they stopped for lunch. After lunch the Vice-Legate took leave of James, embracing his knees as though he were indeed an anointed sovereign. James raised him up and embraced him affectionately, thanking him for all his kindness and hospitality during the past ten months. The faithful Donis drove as far as Orange with James, where they dined and slept the night. After hearing Mass in the Cathedral next day they had a farewell lunch and then went their separate ways. Before the final parting James presented miniatures of himself to Monsieur Doni and Monsieur d'Entraigues.

James had been so pleased with the servants he had engaged during his stay at Avignon that he invited them to remain in his service. He took nearly all of them, including the kitchen boys and the laundress, to Rome, sending the household staff with the linen, silver and plate by the Rhône to Marseille and then on by sea to Leghorn.

The journey over the mountains was one long agony for James after his recent illness. The party of seventy struggled over the passes in coaches, escorted by the Marquis de Cavaillac, who had been sent to guide them by the Duke of Savoy. At last, on 27 February, they reached the palace of the Duke and Duchess of Savoy in Turin, where they rested thankfully for several days. Mar, true to his selfish and unstable character, had abandoned the party during the early stages of the journey and gone back to Paris.

Leaving his Savoy relations in Turin, James moved south to Modena, his mother's birthplace, where he stayed with his uncle, the Duke Rinaldo. There he found letters from his mother in which she asked eagerly for his impressions of Modena and for news of her family. She begged him to visit Sassuolo, the Este summer villa in the hills where she had spent her childhood summers, but the weather was unsuitable and James preferred to remain in the comfort of the ducal palace. He had another reason for staying. Duke Rinaldo was an elderly widower with three attractive daughters. James was by this time twenty-eight and, in spite of the temptations of the beauties of Avignon, had so far never shown himself susceptible to feminine charms. The eldest Este girl, the Princess Benedetta, reminded him of his mother, and for the first time in his life James fancied himself in love. He wrote enthusiastically to his mother:

> I arrived at Modena on Friday March 12th and went straight to the Palace where the Duke received me with all imaginable friendliness. He has the best and frankest heart I ever met and in half-an-hour we became so well acquainted as if we had lived a year together. I then went to the Duchess of Brunswick [Rinaldo's mother-in-law] where I found the three princesses. I may say, without flattery, that they are very agreeable. The two elder may surely pass for beauties. The eldest of the three is very like you. They are tall and well made and have had a perfect education.

In a postscript he confided that he had proposed to Benedetta, the eldest of the three. This news brought great joy to the poor Queen, and for once she let her heart run away with her head. Her brother Rinaldo was less pleased. He was not a rich man, and he knew he must find a son-in-law with more to offer than a romantic name that would expose Modena to the combined hostility of King George of England and the Emperor of Austria. He felt, quite rightly, that James was unbelievably naive for his age, and received the 'love at first sight' proposal with reserve. He suggested tactfully that while he was considering James's offer, the best thing would be for the Jacobite party to move on to Pesaro, where Cardinal Davia, a cousin of the Countess Montecuccoli-Davia, was ready to place his palace at their disposal. Unwillingly James accepted Rinaldo's advice and went to Pesaro, which he described gloomily in letters to his mother as 'a sad, dirty little town where the wine was detestable'. The climate did not suit his health and, after a boring month waiting for news from Modena which never came, he wrote desperately to his mother to see if her friend Cardinal Gualterio could invite him to stay with him in Rome.

Mary of Modena's friends seldom let her down. The Cardinal sent the invitation she asked for, and came to meet James with two coaches and six when he reached Rome on 25 May. It was the height of the season and the Cardinal had ordered the Palazzo Gualterio to be specially decorated and illuminated for the occasion. Three days later, when he was sufficiently rested, the Cardinal took James for an audience with the Pope to thank him for his hospitality and kindness to him in Avignon. James described Clement XI as being 'mighty easy and kind'. He confided to him his desire to marry his cousin the Princess Benedetta d'Este, and the Pope promised to do all he could to being about the match.

Cardinal Gualterio was an untiring guide to the treasures of Rome. He spent hours in the Vatican library showing James the paintings and sculptures. Together they visited St Peter's and all the famous Roman churches. Another day they drove out to the Villa d'Este at Tivoli, with its gardens and fountains, the creation of one of James's ancestors, the Cardinal Ippolito d'Este.

From there Cardinal Gualterio took him to spend three days at Castel Gandolfo, the Pope's summer residence. During a private conversation with the Pope, James plucked up the courage to ask for a Cardinal's hat for Alberoni, the Spanish Prime Minister, who, with the new Queen of Spain, Elisabeth Farnese, was a strong supporter of the Stuarts. It was a bold request to make, as the Pope had always resented the rise to power of the humble curate from Parma, but a well timed letter from Mary of Modena thanking the Pope for his kindness to her son softened his attitude, and he told James he would consider the matter carefully.

Mary of Modena's impeccable conduct throughout her widowhood had made her a legend in her own lifetime. She had the rare quality among the great personages by whom she was surrounded of never speaking ill of anyone. Without being disapproving, like Madame de Maintenon, she refused to be drawn into malicious intrigues. 'If it's something nasty, please don't tell me', she used to say to brush off the spiteful gossips at the court. 'I don't like stories that damage reputations.' However depressed or irritated she was herself, she always tried to respond with understanding and warm humanity to the many who importuned her.

While her son was sightseeing in Rome, she received an unexpected and amusing visitor at St Germain in the larger than life person of Peter the Great of Russia. The Czar arrived in Paris from Amsterdam in May 1717. He lodged with his suite at the Hotel Lesdiguières in the Marais and proceeded to shock courtiers and citizens alike by his eccentric and uncouth behaviour. After getting so drunk after a royal dinner at Fontainebleau that it took four strong men to carry him back to his coach, vomiting all the way, no one knew what he might do next. He was a violent man who hated pretentiousness and hypocrisy. Since the age of seventeen, when he had drastically suppressed his unruly boyars, his chief military adviser and friend had been a Scottish mercenary, General Patrick Gordon, who acted as his chief of staff. His personal physician, who travelled everywhere with him, was another Scotsman, Robert

Erskine, a member of a traditionally Jacobite family. Peter's antipathy to the German Elector who ruled as King of England was pathological. The Czar had frightened him a few years before by sending Russian troops to occupy Stettin not very far from Hanover. To spite King George further, Peter drove over one day to St Germain to pay a state call on the exiled Stuart Queen.

The visit planned out of defiance and contempt turned out to be one of the rare occasions during his stay in France when the boisterous giant behaved himself in a seemly manner.[11] When Peter, with his nervous tic and compelling eyes and his reputation for wildness and cruelty, was presented to the pale unassuming Mary Beatrice, he was drawn to her unaffected dignity and goodness. She was fifty-eight, a dying woman, and he was a robust forty-five. After all the flutterings, contemptuous asides and artificiality of the court coquettes at Versailles, the outlandish Czar felt at home. They made a strange pair, conversing in a mélange of languages, the Queen a sympathetic and fascinated listener to his tales of adventure as a common workman in the shipyards of Amsterdam and London. He had heard about her sad life from Scottish friends in St Petersburg, and marvelled at her acceptance of her lot and the sweetness of her nature. As they walked together in the gardens of St Germain, Mary Beatrice was transformed, seeming to shrug off her ill health and loneliness. Before he left, Peter impulsively offered one of his daughters as a bride for her son; but James was still waiting to hear if his proposal to the Princess Benedetta had been accepted, and so the Czar's daughter, Anna Petrovna, married a dim Holstein prince instead.

There was still no answer from Modena, and James began to feel he was outstaying his welcome in Rome. His instinct was right. At the beginning of July the Pope told him that the ducal palace of Urbino in the hills above the Adriatic would be placed at his disposal as a permanent residence for his court. James, attended by Colonel John Hay and Charles Booth, left for Urbino with a parting gift from the Pope of 10,000 Roman scudi. They crossed the wild countryside of central Italy, and a week later reached the little medieval town of Urbino. The palace had been built in 1468 by the broken-nosed condottiere Federigo da Montefeltro, immortalized by Piero della Francesca. The Duke's study, decorated with *trompe l'oeil* paintings, looks across the craggy mountains towards the sea. The palace, small and intimate, is one of the marvels of Renaissance architecture, with its beautiful shallow staircase leading up to a magnificent library.

At first James was enchanted with his new home, set in such romantic surroundings, but there was still no news of his princess and, after a few months, the isolation of Urbino got on his nerves. He was in this state of mind when a messenger arrived one autumn morning to tell him that Duke Rinaldo had definitely turned down his offer. At the end of November the arrival of Mar from Paris broke the monotony of life in the palace. He brought with him the latest news from France, for which the bored Jacobites were all avid. Mar was also quite a good musician, a talent he shared with the King. They formed a chamber orchestra to enliven the long winter evenings. Describing his musicians, Mar said in a letter to his brother: 'We have an excellent violin, one that plays well on the harpsichord and one voice tolerably good.' Before the snow came to keep them almost prisoners, James and Mar would sometimes slip away to hear an opera at the nearest town, Fano, on the coast. Mar, however, had not earned the nickname of 'Bobbing John' for nothing. He was a born intriguer, and for the first time in their lives managed tragically to stir up trouble between the King and his mother, who only had a few months to live.

Mar disliked the head of the Scots College in Paris, the Abbé Lewis Innes, who was also the Queen's trusted almoner, and complained to James that Innes had deliberately put a false interpretation on one of James's letters to his Protestant supporters in England. He influenced James sufficiently for him to order Innes's dismissal. The Queen knew that this attack on one of her oldest friends was unjust, but the King refused to listen to her pleadings and Mar's jealousy triumphed. The Queen had been dying of cancer for the last five years, making light of the pain she suffered and the discomfort of the treatment, saying that she could not see that the preservation of one life was so important. Life at St Germain after her two children had gone was sad and wearisome for her, though she still had the friendship of Middleton and Lauzun, of Madame de Maintenon when it suited that lady, and of the Palatine Princess Liselotte, Duchesse d'Orléans. They all took the news of Innes's dismissal badly but were in no position to countermand the King's orders from Italy. The Abbé Innes left Paris and went to live at St Germain, and was with the Queen when she died on 7 May 1718, within four months of her sixtieth birthday. Her last instructions were given to the Countess Molza, who had been with her ever since she had left Modena as a bride of fifteen. She said to her: 'Molza, I pray you, when I am dead, send this crucifix to the King, my son.' Colonel Dominic Sheldon, Master of the Household at St Germain, took the crucifix, the ruby ring James II had worn at his coronation and the diamond earrings Louis XIV had given Mary as a wedding present with the news of his mother's death to James at Urbino.

The Regent's brusque German mother Liselotte a granddaughter of Elizabeth of Bohemia, summed up the feelings of Mary of Modena's many friends at the French court when she wrote the following day: 'I was very fond of this Queen and her death grieves me.'[2] She was missed by different generations of the French royal family, legitimate and illegitimate alike; even Liselotte's most hated enemy, the tough old spider Madame de Maintenon, who remembered how the Stuart Queen had come over to comfort her on the death of Louis XIV, mourned her as one of her true friends, who had never changed towards her in her retirement.

At Chaillot the Queen was given the simple funeral she wished. When the convent was destroyed at the Revolution, her heart and that of her husband and daughter were transferred to the chapel of the Scots College in Paris, where most of the leading members of the Jacobite court finally found burial.

When Colonel Sheldon arrived at Urbino with the sad news, James realized what it was to be really alone in the world, without a close relative to care about him.[13] The letter Sheldon brought with him from his mother's confessor increased his misery, for, in it, the priest did not spare his words in telling the King how much his unjust dismissal of the Abbé Innes had hurt the Queen in the last weeks of her life.

'You must not ignore the pain she felt at the last order she received from Your Majesty, but, persuaded of your affection, she ordered me to tell you that whatever came from you, although it might be contrary to her ideas and wishes, made no contrary impression upon her love for you and that she was in no way displeased with you.' When Cardinal Gualterio arrived at Urbino from Rome to console the King in his loss, he also confirmed the injustice of James's action. James now realized how he had been manipulated by Mar, and almost immediately reinstated Innes as Principal of the Scots College, a post which he held until his death in 1734.

Cardinal Gualterio also stressed the straits in which the court of St Germain found itself, now that its benefactress was dead. Mary of Modena had supported entire Jacobite families out of her dwindling resources. She kept nothing for herself and was mother to them all. In the last stages of her illness her greatest worry was what would become of them after she was gone. James, on Gualterio's prompting, wrote to William Dicconson, the Treasurer at St Germain, telling him that he would continue to do all he could for those left behind. He also said he would in no way be opposed to any of them who felt like it applying to the French court for subsistence. 'Would to God they could get bread anywhere', he said to Dicconson, and went on to instruct him to provide money for clothes for particularly needy retainers. 'As long as you have anything', he said, 'you must not let my people starve.'[14]

James was now nearing his thirtieth birthday. He reproached himself for not having married sooner and produced a Stuart heir before his mother died. He turned again to the lists of suitable princesses, which had been drawn up by John Hay, Ormonde and Mar. The sixteen-year-old Maria Clementina, granddaughter of the Polish King John Sobieski, who had saved Vienna from the Turks, sounded promising. Her miniature showed her to be a piquant blonde beauty with dark eyes. At the end of June the King sent James Murray to Ohlau to ask Prince James Sobieski for his daughter's hand. The Princess Clementina was both romantic and imperious, and the thought of perhaps one day being Queen of England pleased her vanity. The proposal was accepted, and in September 1718 Colonel John Hay was despatched to bring the bride down through Austria to Italy where James had the equally grand and romantic idea of marrying her in the imposing Este Palace in Ferrara.

For some time after the party had set out from Ohlau there was no news until the dramatic announcement that the Emperor, acting on instructions of his ally, King George of England, had seized and imprisoned the Princess and her mother in the castle of Innsbruck. George I was determined at all costs to prevent the tiresome Stuart Pretender marrying and producing troublesome heirs. The Sobieskis, mother and daughter, closely guarded in the Schloss Innsbruck, were unable to communicate with Urbino, where James, the frustrated bridegroom, paced the terraces, sunk in melancholy. Since his mother's death, the isolation of Urbino, picturesque though it was, had been growing steadily on his nerves. When he could stand it no longer, he wrote to the Pope, begging leave to be allowed to return to Rome.

James set out as soon as he could, travelling by way of Bologna, where he had an invitation to stay. He had been so emotionally unbalanced by the prospect of marriage that, in his overwrought state, he found himself swept off his feet by a Bolognese heiress, Donna Maria di Caprara. Never having made love to a woman, at the advanced age of thirty he lost his head completely, and soon after his arrival in Bologna became obsessed with the idea of breaking off his engagement to the imprisoned Polish princess, whom he had never seen, in order to marry this captivating Italian girl who had no royal blood. He wrote to the Pope and to Cardinal Gualterio, who were naturally shocked by his capricious behaviour. They expressed their disapproval in no uncertain terms, advising James to leave Bologna without delay to avoid ruining his reputation for integrity. They urged him to come to Rome at once to await the release of Maria Clementina, whom he was in honour bound to marry.

They also told him they had leased the Palazzo Muti, where he and his bride could settle down in a style befitting his royal status. This palazzo still stands in the narrow Piazza dei Santi Apostoli, and although originally leased for the Stuarts for three years, in fact housed them for the rest of their lives.

James obeyed reluctantly and left for Rome. Once installed, he found himself occupied with intrigues designed to break up the alliance of the Emperor, Holland, France and England against Spain. James's protegé, Alberoni, was now a Cardinal and the most powerful figure in Spain, with the backing of an unlikely pair of allies in Peter the Great of Russia and Charles XII of Sweden.

In November 1718 Alberoni invited the Duke of Ormonde to Madrid to plan a Spanish invasion of England to dethrone their common enemy George I. Ormonde asked for arms to be sent to the highland chiefs, who had sworn to create a diverson in Scotland, to be backed up by Swedish troops, while Alberoni would send a new Armada to land in the West of England. Alberoni also persuaded James to come to Madrid. In spite of the activities of the Hanoverian spies in Rome, James got away, and after a hazardous sea voyage reached Spain. The first news that met him on his arrival at Madrid was that during his weeks at sea his supporter Charles XII of Sweden had been killed at Fredrikshall in Norway. This meant that no help could now be expected from that quarter. James held a council of war with Cardinal Alberoni, Ormonde and the Duke of Liria, and decided to go ahead with the invasion without the Swedish troops they had counted on for Scotland. Liria was to accompany James, and in April 1719 they set out for the west coast of Spain. A Spanish fleet set sail but without Liria and James, and was wrecked off the French coast at Finisterre. A few Spanish troops did succeed in reaching the Hebrides, to join the waiting highlanders on the mainland opposite the southern tip of Skye, but they were routed by English redcoats at Loch Duich on James's thirty-first birthday, 10 June 1719. News of this fiasco reached James, who was now back in Madrid, at the same time as an announcement by the Pope that his fiancée had been rescued at last and, on the Pope's instructions, had been married by proxy to James on her arrival in Italy and now awaited her husband there.

James's reaction was scarcely that of an ardent bridegroom. He insisted on staying on in Madrid throughout that long hot summer, hoping against hope that Alberoni would devise some other plan. It was the beginning of September before he returned to Italy, met Maria Clementina for the first time, and married her himself at Montefiascone.

He was delighted with her looks and spirit, and wrote an official letter to the French Regent announcing his marriage. As much as it flattered her to become the wife of the rightful King of England, Maria Clementina was disappointed to find that James, although handsome, was sober and reserved, and after the months of waiting the highly strung bride of seventeen gave alarming signs of a difficult Polish temper beneath her fragile appearance.

Both, however, made the best of the match, and for the first few months seemed happy enough in their new state. But by Christmas Clementina had begun to complain that James was neglecting her by spending so much of his time in his study writing letters. She felt she was missing all the gaiety of Rome during the carnival, which started in December and lasted until February. James abstractedly urged her to go out and enjoy herself, chaperoned by members of the court, but this was not what the romantic Clementina wanted. She demanded imperiously that James should be seen with her more often, and when he said he was too busy, she felt herself slighted. She soon realized what it was to be a Queen in name only, without a country and surrounded by exiles of varying degrees of poverty with whom she could not even converse in a common language. Her Polish pride was humiliated and she felt lonely, thwarted and thoroughly miserable.

The King's private secretary was James Edgar, a native of Angus who had escaped after the Fifteen to Avignon and followed James to Rome, and became James's devoted servant for the rest of his life. He had a vivid eye for detail and in his correspondence gave an almost day-to-day account of the hard realities of life at the exiled court. In one of his many letters to his brother he said: 'Nobody is in a fixed way for suppers here. Mr Erskine and I come whiles home and take only a glass of wine and a bit of bread or sometimes go to a place like an English ordinary where the lords and ladies are for the most part at night. There we endeavour to keep our hearts up as well as we can.' More philosophically than James's disappointed young bride, he added: 'But Rome is a place nobody can weary in; go where we please, we meet something wonderful, and I believe I'll wear out a pair of shoes here in a fortnight.'

Things were much better than this at the King's table, which was always set for a dozen at least and well supplied with French and Italian wines. James liked his glass of champagne, and kept up the custom he had instituted at Urbino of having musicians play for him during and after dinner.[15] His most intimate friends soon became John Hay and his wife Marjory, who shared the King's love of music. The Duke of Mar was back in Paris, and disturbing rumours were circulating about his behaviour there. He was said to be in touch with agents of the Hanoverian government. James sent John Hay to Paris to investigate 'Bobbing John's' activities and, as a result, Mar was asked to resign his office as Jacobite Secretary-of-State. When Hay returned to Rome, James created him Earl of Inverness, and made him Secretary-of-State in Mar's place. During Hay's stay in Paris Lord Middleton, who had served James and his father as Secretary-of-State for nearly forty years, died at St Germain at the age of eighty-one.

In 1720 the plague hit the south-west of France. Starting in the slums of Marseille, it spread up through Arles to Avignon and west to Languedoc. The Regent called upon the Duke of Berwick, who knew this part of the country well from the dragonnades he had organized there at the beginning of the century, to try to control the outbreak. This Berwick did with his usual efficiency, establishing *cordons sanitaires* and burning down the most badly infected villages.

In Rome on New Year's Eve, which was always celebrated by the Scottish exiles, there were even greater rejoicings when Queen Clementina gave birth to a son and heir at the Palazzo Muti. On the following day, the first of January 1721, the proud father wrote two letters to the French court, one to the eleven-year-old Louis XV and one to the Regent d'Orléans, informing them of the birth of Prince Charles Edward Louis John Casimir Sylvester Maria Sobieski Stuart.[16]

The news of the arrival of a 'strong, healthy boy' certainly gladdened the heart and revived old memories for the Duc de Lauzun. The birth of the Young Pretender, as the Hanoverians called him, had the opposite effect on Lord Stair, who at once redoubled the efforts of his spies and agents against any new attempt the Stuarts might make against his master George I. Only a few months before George I had instructed Stair to see that the Regent expelled any British subjects resident in France known to be in favour of restoring the Pretender, an order that the Regent, although a crony of Stair's, had chosen to ignore.

To celebrate the first birthday of Prince Charles Edward, James issued, on 31 December 1721, a nine-page proclamation setting out his son's claim to be heir to the kingdoms of England, Scotland and Ireland. Three months later the Stuarts' protector Pope Clement XI died and was succeeded by Benedict XII, the former Cardinal Orsini. James continued to receive his papal pension, but this was far from adequate to maintain his dependents.

In February 1723 he wrote to the Cardinal de Rohan at Versailles to claim the 6,000 louis d'or of his mother's dowry that had been promised by the court of France. Within days of this letter being received, the Regent d'Orléans died of a stroke, and a few months later in the same year the apparently immortal Lauzun died peacefully at the age of ninety.

For managing his affairs James now relied almost entirely on Lord Inverness, who, unlike Mar, the man of straw, was realistic, honest and capable. His ability was taken so seriously that the ablest of the Hanoverian spies in Rome, the Baron von Stosch, reported that it was essential to get rid of him. Inverness had another enemy in the young Queen, who was neurotically jealous of the pleasure her husband enjoyed in the company of Lady Inverness. But neither the plots of his enemies nor the irrational behaviour of the Queen had any effect on the King's relations with Inverness and his wife. He left Maria Clementina to her tantrums and, perhaps rather insensitively, went off to the opera with Lord and Lady Inverness.

After the birth of a second son, Henry Benedict Stuart, in March 1725, the Queen became even more impossible. Her rage against the considerably older and less attractive Lady Inverness, with whom James was quite obviously only on platonic terms, led her to retire dramatically to a convent in the Trastevere, where she pouted and sulked with a few chosen sympathizers. This separation caused such a scandal among the Stuart supporters that, early in 1727, Lord Inverness offered his resignation and begged leave to retire with his wife to Avignon. The King accepted his departure, and with much sorrow saw his two closest friends leave Rome. In Avignon they rented the Hôtel d'Ancezune at No 4 rue Dorée, now called the rue Chauffard. Like Lauzun, Lord Inverness and his wife remained ultra-loyal Jacobites for the rest of their lives, putting everything they possessed at the disposal of the King and his sons, and harbouring them in their house in Avignon whenever the need arose.

After they had gone, Maria Clementina calmed down and rejoined her husband at the Palazzo Muti. She tried to become an exemplary wife and mother, accepting the fact that her husband would never be a passionate man, and for the remainder of her short life she devoted herself to rigorous piety and severe mortification of the body and spirit. James was a sensible father who loved his children without giving in to their whims, but Maria Clementina was unable to cope with them and her situation. In time she became a remote figure given to inexplicable outbursts of temper.

In 1727 Berwick's eldest son, the Duke of Liria, who bore a strong family resemblance to James, called on his uncle and Clementina on his way to St Petersburg as Ambassador for the King of Spain. James had always been fond of Liria, and had never forgotten what he had risked in following him to Scotland in 1715. He took this opportunity of conferring the Order of the Garter on him, which prompted Liria to heal the breach that had existed between his father and the King for the last twelve years. He wrote to Berwick from Rome: 'His Majesty has been pleased to treat me with the utmost kindness since I am here. I assure Your Grace that his esteem for you has not little contributed to the undeserved favours I have received from him.' Liria at thirty obviously had all the polish and tact essential for his career as a diplomat.

In July 1727 James received the news of the death in Hanover of his enemy George I. He reacted in exactly the same way as he had done on hearing that Queen Anne was dead. He left Rome immediately for

Lorraine to consult his old friend Duke Leopold at Nancy. After three weeks, the new British Ambassador in Paris succeeded in forcing the Duke to get rid of the Pretender. Versailles was out of the question, so, for the last time in his life, James headed south for Avignon. He arrived there on 19 August and spent three months as the guest of Lord and Lady Inverness. But although he kept very quiet and they were the most discreet of hosts, protests were sent by George II to the French Foreign Minister, Cardinal Fleury, and to the Pope, demanding the Pretender's instant removal from France. Sadly the Pope had to agree, and once again it was the high road over the Alps to Italy for James. He could not remember England, his birthplace; he had seen Scotland for only three bleak winter months during the Fifteen; and now France, which had been his home for the first twenty-five years of his life, was barred to him forever.

Like his father, James never ceased to think of himself as completely English by virtue of his birth in London, in spite of his Scottish, Italian, French and Danish blood. He felt the same about his sons, who had in addition Polish blood and, in Charles's case, a highly strung temperament. James wrote to Ormonde, who had made the fruitless journey with him to Avignon and decided to stay on there permanently: 'My brave, lusty boy shall be dressed and looked after, as much as the climate will allow, in the English way; for though I can't help his being born in Italy, yet, as much as in me lives, he shall be English for the rest all over.'

Prince Charles Edward was now seven years old, courageous and excelling in all outdoor sports, but headstrong and wilful like his mother. He grew up speaking English and French with a strong Scots-Irish accent, which he never lost, and his spelling, in spite of the efforts of his tutors, was deplorable in all three languages. Like his father James II, indeed like all the Stuarts, in contrast to the Hanoverians, who hated their offspring, James III adored his two sons and let them run wild in the grounds of the Savelli Palace, a country house in the Alban Hills that had been lent to them by the Pope. In the autumn of 1729 James wrote to Lord Inverness: 'My children give me a great deal of comfort. I am really in love with the little Duke. He is the finest child that can be seen.'

In the same year Clementina's cousin Marie Leczinska, the Polish wife of Louis XV, gave birth to an heir. James describes the fêtes in Rome to celebrate this occasion[17] as taking place 'the year Harry was breeched'.

14

THE YOUTH OF PRINCE CHARLES EDWARD

AT SEVEN O'CLOCK IN THE MORNING of 12 June 1734 the Maréchal Duke of Berwick was killed at the siege of Philipsbourg. While inspecting the trenches to settle a dispute between two of his engineers, he had his head blown off by a cannonball. He was nearly sixty-four, had been Governor of Strasbourg since 1730 and had occupied Lorraine for France in 1731.

His eldest son, the Duke of Liria, writing to tell his uncle King James of his father's death, suggested that Prince Charles, now nearly fourteen, might like a taste of military life, and offered to take him under his wing. In Italy the Spaniards were sweeping down from Tuscany, driving their Austrian enemies before them. James gave his consent and, at the end of July, Charles left Rome to join his cousin Liria at Naples. His Protestant Governor Lord Dunbar, Lady Inverness's brother, and his Catholic Under-governor Sir Thomas Sheridan went with him.

During the campaign he took the title his father had used before him, the Chevalier de St Georges. For six weeks Charles took part in the siege of Gaeta, where he gave his guardians many anxious moments but impressed the troops by his utter disregard for danger and his infectious high spirits. On 12 September he returned to Rome with a guard of fifty men and two fine Spanish horses, a gift from the King of Spain. Naturally he was full of his exploits, and his father was disturbed to see how easily the boy's head could be turned. His brother Henry, at nine, was and was to remain always much cooler by temperament.

This short episode in Italy was the only military experience the Prince was to have before, just over ten years later, sailing optimistically to Scotland with an oddly assorted bunch of seven followers to lead his highlanders in a country very different from the hot plains round Naples.

Later that same year, 1734, the eighty-two year old Maréchal de Villars, James's old commander and champion of the Stuarts to his last breath, died commanding the French troops in northern Italy. 'He always had the luck that one!' had been his envious comment on hearing the news of Berwick's spectacular end. Hector Villars himself died in bed. Their joint adversary from the days of the War of the Spanish Succession, Prince Eugène of Savoy, who had brought up Imperial troops to relieve Philippsbourg immediately after Berwick's death, died the following year at the age of seventy-two.

The last and oldest of these survivors of the Restoration Court in England and that of Louis XIV at Versailles, Louise de Kéroualle, Duchess of Portsmouth and of Aubigny, had died a few months before at her house in Paris after a turbulent life of intrigue and non-stop litigation. She had outlived her royal bastard son,[1] was still attractive and as full of verve as ever—so much so that soon after George II's coronation in 1729, when she was eighty, she wrote asking for a pension, Hanoverian though he was.

Marlborough, Berwick, Villars and Prince Eugène were all gone but the situation in Europe was much as it had been in their day. France and Britain were still antagonists, but both had astute, peace-loving Prime Ministers in the aged Cardinal Fleury and the laissez-faire Sir Robert Walpole. Walpole found himself on the verge of having to side with Spain against the Emperor in 1730, but cleverly managed to avoid it by accepting the Pragmatic Sanction he had refused six years earlier. This was the Emperor Charles VI's decree that, failing male heirs, his only daughter Maria Teresa could succeed him as ruler of his dominions, though as a woman she was not eligible to become the next Holy Roman Emperor. Walpole finally agreed, but only on condition that George II should be given the disputed bishoprics of Bremen and Verden. This arrangement suited George, whose Hanoverian territories bordered on these two bishoprics. The Tory squires and indeed the majority of the electorate in Britain could not have cared less about the problems of Hanover. The rich Whig merchants were incensed that by Walpole's 'peace' the French could get away with attacking their trading vessels on their way home from the colonies in the East.

So far France had refused to recognize the Pragmatic Sanction, but when the question of who was to succeed to the crown of Poland on the death of Augustus II of Saxony in February 1733, Louis XV decided to support the claims of his father-in-law Stanislas Leczinski. He got Fleury to make an alliance with Spain and Sardinia with the aim of expelling the Austrians from Italy and curbing British overseas trade and colonization. The Emperor Charles clearly had to oppose this alliance, as France, if successful, would threaten his empire on two sides. The only Polish part of this war was the siege of Danzig, which ended in the summer of 1734 with the humiliating defeat of Stanislas and his escape to Lorraine.

In 1735 Queen Maria Clementina died in Rome at the early age of thirty-five. In spite of their temperamental differences and frequent estrangements because of her unsatisfactory sex life with the King, James missed his difficult Polish wife, whose hysterical outbursts he had treated with firm dignity instead of the passion she craved. Through his marriage James was related to Stanislas, the unsuccessful claimant to the Polish throne.

Soon after Clementina's death the Archduchess Maria Teresa of Austria was betrothed to Duke Francis of Lorraine. It was agreed that if Stanislas renounced his claims to the Polish crown, he would be granted the Duchy of Lorraine with the title of King for his lifetime and that, after his death, Lorraine was to revert to France as the belated dowry of his daughter Marie Leczinska. In return for this reasonable and peaceful annexation, France had to accept the Pragmatic Sanction and promise to vote for Duke Francis of Lorraine as the next Holy Roman Emperor when Charles VI died.

During this time secret correspondence was building up in France to convince Louis XV and Cardinal Fleury that discontent was growing in England against their enemy George II. At the beginning of 1738 the French King and his Prime Minister received the copy of a nine-page memoir sent by the Catholic Lord Sempill to James in Rome reporting the state of feeling in England. In this he reported that 'towards the end of 1737 the zeal of James's Scottish subjects was so strong that it seemed to him the Highlanders could withstand any Government forces, and that, even without foreign help, they could succeed.' Sempill continued: 'As I happened to be in London on business, several noted Royalists, speaking of the King's letter, were much more enthusiastic than I would have believed. I saw clearly that the Royalist party was much stronger than I thought; that nearly all the country squires were attached to the old principles of monarchy and that the majority of those who were opposed to the Hanoverian court in Parliament would not oppose the restoration of the legitimate sovereign.'[2]

All this was optimistic stuff, but the truth of Lord Sempill's observations was borne out in a letter brought by MacGregor of Balhady from seven well known Scottish chiefs to Cardinal Fleury in March 1741.[3] The signatories had formed a conspiracy as early as 1738 with the object of restoring the Stuarts, but were waiting for an opportune moment to declare themselves to France. Two events decided their timing: the death of the Emperor Charles in October 1740 and the invasion of Silesia in December 1740 by Frederick the Great, violating the Pragmatic Sanction and sparking off the War of the Austrian Succession. The original of this letter, in perfect French, is filed in the archives of the quai d'Orsay, and bears the autograph signatures of 'le Duc de Perth, le Lord Jean Drummond de Perth, My Lord Lovat, Milord Linton, Cameron, Baron de Lochiel, the Chevalier Campbell d'Auchinbreak and MacGriegor, Baron de Balhadies'. In translation the letter begins:

> Having learned from Monsieur le Baron de Balhadies the pleasure of our legitimate sovereign, we hasten to send back this Baron with the pledge of our gratitude and with our most solemn assurance both on our own part and on the part of our supporters to take up arms against the usurper and that we are ready to fulfill all that has been conveyed in the memoir of Lords Sempill and Balhadies. The chiefs of our Highland clans whose names were submitted to them along with the number of men each one could put in the field, remain pledged to their promises and we can assure Your Eminence that 20,000 men are available for the service of our only true King James the Eighth of Scotland, if it would please His Most Christian Majesty to send us arms and munitions with the troops necessary to protect these arms until such time as we are able to assemble.

In the parliamentary election of November 1741 Walpole at last suffered defeat. Carteret, who was an enthusiastic supporter of Maria Teresa, was put in charge of foreign affairs. The archives of the quai d'Orsay for this date contain accurate and penetrating character sketches of Walpole and Carteret, with speculation as to their worth and real aims. Antagonism to France was a continuous thread running through Carteret's policy, but his mistake was to limit his horizon to Europe. He tried to get Maria Teresa to make peace with the brilliant, but unscrupulous, Frederick of Prussia in order to concentrate against England's enemy France. He sent British troops to Holland to join the Dutch and Hanoverians. The taxes levied to pay for this 'Pragmatic' army made, in the words of more than one French memo on the subject, 'the House of Hanover more odious to the English than ever'. Pitt emerged as leader of the opposition, strongly attacking this added burden on British taxpayers, who were disgusted to learn that George II had chosen to wear Hanoverian instead of British uniform when his combined forces won the Battle of Dettingen in June 1743.

Less than a month later Cardinal Fleury died in Paris at the age of ninety. His place was taken by Tencin who, like the notorious Alberoni in Spain, owed his Cardinal's hat to the good offices of King James III in Rome.

On 23 December James hopefully issued another of his proclamations, in which he promised to maintain the existing form of government and named his elder son Charles as Prince Regent. He underlined the promise that the foreign troops that might be employed to aid his restoration would be subject to the strictest discipline in England, and would be sent home as soon as 'public tranquillity was judged by Parliament to allow it'.[4] He also said that as it was impossible, for a variety of reasons, for him to lead his troops personally, he hoped that the youth and vigour of the Prince of Wales would take his place.

James was a man with a good and honest heart—too honest ever to be a successful politician. He went on to add magnanimously about the House of Hanover, should he ever be restored: 'I thank God I have no resentment against them, nor against anyone living. I shall never repine at their living happily in their own country after I am in possession of my Kingdom and, should they fall into my power upon any attempt for my restoration, I shall certainly not touch a hair of their heads.'

France was still officially at peace with England, although it was obviously French troops to which James was referring in his proclamation. Cardinal Tencin kept prodding the indolent Louis XV about using the Stuarts to further the interests of France. Finally, at the end of 1743, Louis agreed to invite Prince Charles Edward to Paris. Charles was elated at the prospect, but his father was cautious and sceptical. 'As long as France has not committed herself to declare war on England, it means she intends to make use of us instead of assisting us.' The French insisted that the Prince's journey should take place in the strictest secrecy, and that, when he reached France, he was to remain incognito to await further orders.

On 2 January 1744 James wrote to Lord Sempill, who was to be his son's host in Paris:

> I received on Tuesday yours of December 16th and have since had the pleasure of hearing from Balhady who I hope may be with you before the end of the week. I have fixed on the road by Genoa and Antibes as the least exposed to danger and accident. The Prince will probably be at Antibes about the 20th of the month, for he is to part from hence Tuesday the 9th, before day. I did not forget that the day named for the beginning of the journey was the 12th, but I thought I might take it upon me to anticipate three days to make a party of chase serve more naturally to cover the journey. Besides being once determined and settled, the sooner it is executed the better. The King of France has called for the Prince and he shall part. I take the case to be now or never in relation to France, and therefore we must all act accordingly. I don't remember that I have any more to say but the assurance of my constant kindness to you and to Balhady.

On 9 January 1744, before dawn, the Prince and his brother left Rome, supposedly on a shooting trip. 'Be careful my dearest Carluccio', James said as he took what was to be his last farewell of his son. Poised eagerly for his great adventure, Charles answered theatrically: 'I go Sir, in search of three crowns which I doubt not but to have the happiness of laying at Your Majesty's feet.'

Henry had been deliberately kept in the dark about his brother's real plans, and when he woke up next morning, he found him gone. The servants said that Charles and Lord Dunbar had left early to go shooting. It was not until the Prince and his tutor, disguised in the uniforms of Spanish officers, were thought to be well past Genoa that Henry was told the truth. Crossing the French frontier at Antibes, Charles made first for Avignon to stay with Lord Dunbar's sister, the widowed Lady Inverness. Lord Inverness had died of a heart attack in a tobacconist's shop in Avignon in 1740. After a few days with Lady Inverness the pair headed north by Lyon to Paris, and found Lord Sempill at the house he had rented in Montmartre, then a picturesque village on a hill to the north of the city.

Hanoverian agents warned the British government of the Young Pretender's arrival in Paris, and George II arranged for Dutch troops to be drafted to England. There was no move on the part of Louis XV to receive Charles. A month passed and in February King James wrote to Lord Sempill that the promises of France were not to be reconciled with her negligence and indifferent behaviour towards the Prince.

However, during the month of February Louis XV was building up a substantial expedition of twenty battalions of infantry plus some cavalry regiments on the Channel coast between Dunkirk and Gravelines. He planned that the hero of the Flanders campaign, the Maréchal de Saxe, would lead the invasion force against England. The landing place selected was Maldon on the coast of Essex. The Maréchal de Saxe, like Berwick, was a royal bastard, son of Augustus II of Saxony, the late King of Poland. Like Berwick he had become a naturalized French subject and had risen to the highest rank in the French army. But just as ill-luck had dogged James in his youth at Dunkirk at the same season, violent storms struck and wrecked most of the French transports, so that Saxe estimated it would take at least six months to repair the damage. Knowing that this delay would give the English time to recall their fleet from the Mediterranean, the Maréchal abandoned the project and returned to Flanders. With his retiring from the scene, the plan for Charles to accompany the expedition as Prince Regent for his father fell through.

James kept writing anxiously from Rome: 'This week has been the longest of any I have passed in my life.' When he heard the bad news, remembering his own disappointment in 1708, he urged his son to join the French army and to follow the Maréchal de Saxe to Flanders. Louis XV refused Charles permission to do this, and on 5 March 1744 declared that France was at war with England.

During March and April, Louis was in constant correspondence with Philip of Spain. He assured him that he had not abandoned the Stuarts but for the moment it was essential that Charles remained hidden. So, much against his will, the Prince had to stay in the background, chafing against inaction and deeply unhappy in his relations with Sempill and Balhady, both of whom got on his nerves. The secret was so well kept that it was 9 May 1744 before the French Foreign Minister, d'Argenson, received an official letter from Lord Sempill informing him of the arrival incognito of the Prince of Wales in Paris. He ends this letter: 'The Prince awaits His Most Christian Majesty's instructions and begs to be sent on active service in the French army or to embark upon an expedition to Scotland.'[5]

The Prince's sojourn in Paris was already costing the French King considerable expense, and Charles constantly overran his allowance. On 24 May D'Argenson was writing to Louis XV: 'On the stay of the Prince of Wales in Paris. Financial aid needed by him.'[6] The next day D'Argenson wrote to Maurepas, Master of the Household, saying that the King approved the arrangements made for the Prince of Wales to take up his residence in a well hidden and isolated house.[7] The petulance and moodiness the Prince had inherited from his mother made it extremely difficult for him to be patient at this stage. His father, knowing how impressionable Charles could be, was unhappy about the influence some of his less desirable companions might have on the frustrated young man. But, inevitably, the more his father fussed over him, the more did the Prince, with his mixture of Stuart and Sobieski blood, pursue his own wilful way, and his father's anxious letters went unanswered.

He could not bear to be lectured and resented it when James wrote: 'For God's sake, dear child, be on your guard as to wine and play. These are two points of great consequence.' Then James was censorious about one of the Prince's English Jacobite cronies, Francis Strickland: 'I have no scruple to say that he is an ill man, and conjure you to forget, if possible, whatever he may have said to you on any subject.' Even Charles's confessor, Father Kelly, revealed himself to be another disreputable character. He certainly was a drunkard and a lecher, and the Prince's sexual coolness, if not coldness, must have exasperated him as they hung about aimlessly in Paris.

In May the King sent the fussy old bachelor, Sir Thomas Sheridan, who doted on the Prince, to keep an eye on the behaviour of Charles and his companions. Sheridan made up for the Prince's deficiencies as a correspondent. He kept the King informed of every detail of their daily life in his neat spiky hand, so unlike Charles' big forward-sloping ill-spelt scrawls.

His brother Henry, whose lot was always to be left behind, was, on the contrary, a great letter-writer. When he had to return alone disconsolately to Rome, he sent the following touching letter by the courier to Lord Sempill for the Prince:

> Dear Brother, I really had not the heart to write to you before I heard of your safe arrival at Antibes, but, as soon as I got the comfortable news, I seized on the first occasion for to return you many thanks for the great goodness you have showed me on this occasion. I can assure you, Dear Brother, that I am here without you, like a fish out of water. I also thank you particularly for not having told me the secret of your journey beforehand, for certainly, the great love I have for you could not but have showed itself maybe imprudently on that occasion. The secret has been kept here much longer I believe than you expected, for it was the eleventh day before the courier went off. I have already been on thorns until I heard you had safely landed and particularly when I heard you were locked up at Savona, for certainly you were there in a very ugly situation. I can assure you, Dear Brother, were the King but to permit me, the love I have for you would make me fly through fire and water to be with you. I have nothing else to say to you, Dear Brother, at present, but wait patiently for that happy day in which we shall meet again wherever it may be. I am with all respect your most loving brother
>
> Henry.[8]

On 8 June 1744 Sheridan sent off one of his weekly bulletins:[9]

> The Prince is lodged in a pretty little house near Montmartre where the prospect and air are good. He has all his conveniency and room enough for so small a company as his. I found him in very good health and he seemed to me taller and broader than when I saw him last. He is certainly increased in bulk and his height, when I seemed surprised at it, he let me into the secret. He showed me ye heels of his shoes which he weares now of the usual size, whereas before he wore them remarkably lower than other people. In fine, he has altogether a more manly air than he had when he began his travels. His sentiments towards Yr Majesty are such as could be wished.

Sheridan glossed over the continual rows that shook the house in Montmartre. Somehow the discordant little band got through the summer of 1744. The Prince got into debt and borrowed from the English and Scottish bankers in Paris. Sheridan acted as housekeeper and did all he could to make ends meet. All were waiting for something exciting to happen, but nothing did. The bored Prince sulked and complained endlessly of the neglect of the French court.

To remove him from the irritation caused by Sempill and Balhady, and to try and counteract the deplorable influence of Strickland, Townley and Father Kelly, Sheridan succeeded in persuading the Prince to lodge for a time at the house of Aeneas Macdonald, a Paris banker who was a younger brother of a leading Jacobite chief, Macdonald of Kinlochmoidart.

Meanwhile the French Foreign Office was deluged with memoranda on the state of affairs in England. In January 1745 d'Argenson was noting:

> It is apposite to examine the ministry of Sir Robert Walpole, to pass to that of Milord Carteret and then to give a fair idea of the present Government to gain from that what is most favourable to France in the circumstances of the present war. Walpole managed to avoid with great skill anything that would have caused a war with France. Two major reasons determined him on this course: 1) To confirm by this means the House of Hanover on the throne of Britain which could not be endangered by the Tories, the enemies of this House, unless they were backed up by foreign troops which could only happen in the event of an open war with France. 2) To disconcert by such means any attempt by the Tories to encourage discontent and to form cabals against the Government... Walpole's wise policy had the desired effect on the Tories but, since the genius of the English leads them to persevere stubbornly to achieve their goal, they will not let themselves be rebuffed by obstacles which seem to spoil their plans, and their only idea was to get rid of Walpole and continue in their efforts to bring back the legitimate claimant to the throne, having first prepared the Nation in his favour. This was the reason why Walpole was accused in Parliament of taking bribes and mishandling public subsidies. This affair could have proved so serious for the King and his ministers that George II believed it would be too dangerous to investigate the accusations too deeply. An arrangement was made whereby Walpole was removed from office, to give the King the necessary time to pardon the Minister before the affair reached a public hearing. The balance of power in Europe and the support of the Queen of Hungary (Maria Teresa) are the excuses given by the English government for the heavy expenditure demanded by this war, the weight of which falls on the ordinary people and which makes the House of Hanover even more odious to them.[10]

15

FRENCH POLICY BEFORE 1745

IN 1744 on the Feast of St Sylvester, as New Year's Eve is called in France, the Prince celebrated his twenty-fourth birthday, feeling that after ten months in Paris he was no nearer achieving the restoration of the Stuarts. Although Louis XV had invited him to come to France, he had never once been received by the French King or by any of his ministers. All negotiations with the French court had been conducted by Lord Sempill, whom he had grown to distrust and dislike intensely, or by a much more interesting and able character, the Irish Colonel Daniel O'Bryen. O'Bryen had been in the secret service of James III for many years; he spoke fluent French and could almost pass for a Frenchman.

On 22 February 1745 James wrote O'Bryen's official letter[1] of introduction to the French Foreign Minister, d'Argenson.

> His Most Christian Majesty having approved that I employ Monsieur O'Bryen on my behalf as in the past, I hereby introduce him to you as someone who enjoys my full confidence and whom I beg you to listen on all matters concerning my side of affairs. For intelligence on how matters stand in England, however, I recommend Milord Sempill to you who is in constant touch with my friends in that country. It is he who has been dealing with relations on that side of the Channel for some years past—since 1737 in fact—and was in communication with the French court before the Prince, my son, left for France. I thank you for the welcome you have given Monsieur O'Bryen which he merits, having served me faithfully for a number of years. I have long experience of his worth; he is wise and, above all, has sound common-sense, and I flatter myself you will be pleased with his services. The confidence which I have in your friendship equals the esteem in which I hold you. France is at war with the Elector of Hanover who is the main support of the House of Austria. From this combination of circumstances I have much to hope from a wise and generous King and his enlightened Minister. Assuring you of my sincere friendship,
>
> Jacques III.

Charles Edward, the Young Pretender, 'Bonnie Prince Charlie' in 1739.
(Reproduced by gracious permission of Her Majesty The Queen.)

By the same courier he sent a brief letter introducing Sempill officially to d'Argenson.[2] D'Argenson, of course, already knew Sempill well. Ever since the Prince's arrival in Paris he had been plagued by him with requests for maintenance money.

While these letters were on their way from Rome to Versailles, Charles at last seemed to be enjoying some kind of social life, however limited. He even hired a coach and went to the Ball of the Clipped Yew Trees at Versailles, given to celebrate the Dauphin's marriage to the Princesse

Marie-Josephé. This was a masked ball with abundant food and wine and, conveniently for the Prince, who was still incognito, there was such a crush that no one knew who was who. There were balls all over Paris the following Sunday, also with free food and wine, which cheered the Prince's spirits so much that he actually sat down and on 28 February, for the first time in weeks, wrote to his father:

> Sir, I have received yrs. of ye 1st and 7th current. As I have been so much hurrid between Balls and business, I shall refer to my next. It would be a great comfort to me to have real business on my hands, but I see little of that at the present as I shall explen in another. It is something surprising to me not to have heard from Lumley [Lord Sempill] this two weeks and even he owe me an answer to one of mine of that standing but I easily conceive the reason on't which is, that after making such a noise of his being able to do a great deal, he does nothing—or does not care to let me into the confidence of his managements which I believe happened before now to more than he, for I see here everybody thinks himself to be the wisest man in the world.
>
> I lay myself at your Majesty's feet and most humbly ask blessing.
>
> Your dutiful son,
>
> Charles P.

The strained relations between Lord Sempill and the Prince were obviously at breaking point, and even Aeneas Macdonald was beginning to have more than enough of Charles. A letter from Sheridan to O'Bryen, dated 4 March, paints a dismal picture of the hardships they were suffering now that they had moved to the Hôtel de Bretagne in the rue de Croix de Petits Champs, shows that money was once again the trouble. The local tradesmen were rude and reluctant to supply them on credit, and the harassed old man—he was now nearly seventy—had to go out marketing before eight in the morning and haggle like any housewife before struggling back with live chickens and wine for the Prince's table. When he was lodging in the Petits Champs, Charles used the titles of Baron de Renfrew or Baron de Ziveebach. These were the first of the many aliases he was to employ during his subsequent wanderings around Europe. The Baron de Renfrew was quite genuine, being one of the most ancient titles borne by each Prince of Wales, along with that of High Steward of Scotland. Sheridan ended this particular letter of complaint with a hint of his master's new social life, saying: 'The Baron [the Prince] returned last night from Versailles in good spirits and is not yet awake.'[3]

This note from Sheridan had been despatched to O'Bryen at eight o'clock in the morning. Preserved in the French Foreign Office archives, it is marked 'répondu le même jour', so O'Bryen, efficient as ever, seems to have responded to the old man's S.O.S. and saved the situation while the Prince was sleeping off the effects of yet another incognito sortie.

In March 1745 the French diplomatic archives note with satisfaction the death of Sir Robert Walpole, and comment that 'this event, instead of prejudicing our affairs, could be favourable'.[4] In March, too, Sempill submitted a long memorandum to the French court that contains a typical instance of the jealousy and intrigue unfortunately rampant among the Jacobites in France. He describes the bad treatment received by the Chevalier Maclean, son of a Maclean chief whose estates had been forfeited after the Fifteen. Hector Maclean had been asked to take over as Lieutenant-Colonel of the Royal Ecossais, a regiment in which exiled Scots could serve with the French army. Lord John Drummond, one of the seven signatories of the letter sent to Cardinal Fleury in 1741, had somehow managed to get Louis XV to countermand the appointment, but only after Maclean had got in touch with new recruits from Scotland and had been presented to the existing regimental officers and to the French Minister of War as their Lieutenant-Colonel. The reason Lord John gave was that up to this time Maclean himself had not served in the French army.[5]

When he heard this, James wrote at once from Rome protesting against this slight to a distinguished Highland chieftain:

> Quite apart from the personal merits of the Chevalier, you know as well as I do, how much I owe to his family's devoted service. You can judge better than I can the amount of ill-feeling this change will cause among the Scots in France and, as the Chevalier Maclean is the chief of an important Highland clan, it is certain to make a very unfavourable impression in Scotland and, in consequence, detrimental to my interests. So I should be glad if, without loss of time, you would explain the situation to the Comte d'Argenson [the Minister of War] and get him to do all in his power to remedy this insult. For I would rather a Scottish regiment had not been raised at all than that the displacement of Maclean were to result in such bad feeling.[6]

Sempill backed up the King's letter with his own version of the affair, and Louis XV confirmed Maclean as Lieutenant-Colonel of the Regiment, which a year later sailed to Scotland and fought at Culloden.

In the early spring of 1745 Sir Hector Maclean and Lord Sempill were at Versailles and introduced to d'Argenson a Jacobite agent recently arrived from Scotland, John Blaw of Castlehill. Blaw asked the French War Minister straight out for 10,000 men for England. The Comte d'Argenson then asked how many were wanted for Scotland. Blaw answered that if the above number were sent against England, Scotland could very well manage her own affairs, though, if there were two or three thousand to spare, she would take them. D'Argenson told Lord Sempill in Blaw's presence that had they asked for these men two months sooner, they could have got them, but that at present there was not one regiment in France but had their operations assigned to them for the campaign in Flanders. Blaw replied that if the French answered their present demand, they would have England immediately on their side, which would enable France to do with the Empress Queen (Maria Teresa) what she pleased. According to Blaw's narrative,[7] 'D'Argenson retired into the nixt room where King Louis XV was and returned saying that I might assure my Master's friends in Scotland that His Most Christian Majesty should give the men demanded against the month of October nixt, if the campaign was in any way successful to France'.

At the end of March Blaw returned to Scotland, where he was joined a month later by Sir Hector Maclean who came to deliver the French King's answer to the Duke of Perth on 1 May. On 5 May Sir Hector and Blaw were arrested in Edinburgh and transferred to, the Tower of London.

From this date onwards the archives of the quai d'Orsay are crammed with documents, memoranda and secret correspondence covering the French side of the Forty-five rebellion. Until the end of July the Prince, for some unfathomable reason, was kept in complete ignorance of this behind-the-scenes diplomacy. When he sailed for Scotland with his handful of followers, his two ships were frigates he had hired at his own expense from gentlemen privateers of Irish origin. The arms and ammunition taken had been bought by the Prince with borrowed money. After the landing in Scotland and his first successes, the French archives change tone and contain instructions for the Prince's support in men, arms, ammunition and money, as well as detailed information on all the leading personalities taking part in the Jacobite Rebellion in Scotland. Finally, almost to the very day mentioned to John Blaw, Louis XV signed the Treaty of Fontainebleau, the last Franco-Scottish military alliance, at the end of October 1745.

The squabbling among the Jacobites in Paris during the spring of 1745 made Charles decide to leave the rue des Petits Champs and go to stay with his cousin the Duc de Fitzjames at his château of Fitzjames north of Paris near Compiègne. The Duke, eight years older than the Prince, was a son of Berwick, and therefore a grandson of James II and Arabella Churchill. He was also a friend of both the Marquis and the Comte d'Argenson, the French Foreign Minister and the Minister for War respectively. Letters from his father disapproving of the Prince's disreputable companions, whom he had now left in Paris, were forwarded to him at Fitzjames. For once, on 12 April, Charles replied: 'Sir, I have received yours of 23 March. I am very sorry to see by it that Strickland has given you occasion again of mentioning his name . . . I am very young and it is very hard for me to foresee many things, in which all I aim at is at leste not to do harm, not being able to do good.'

On the same date he was writing a much more important letter to an ambitious shipowner of Irish origin, Antoine Walsh,[8] on the subject of getting together money, arms and ships for a secret expedition to Scotland: 'From Fitzjames le 12 avril 1745. The offers which you have already made of your services give me reason to hope that I shall shortly be able to make use of them. M. Rutlidge [another Irish shipowner] will explain more fully to you what is necessary. You can rely on his word but I myself assure you that I shall always remember the zeal you have shown towards me on this occasion. I swear you, as I have him, to the utmost secrecy. A Dieu. Charles P.'

A week later, still from Fitzjames, he wrote again to his father, stressing his lack of experience: 'My want of experience is what I too much know and would fain get as soon as possible, for, to be able to serve you and our country more effectually and to the purpose, is all I am put into this world for. It would be endless for me to write and for you to read, if I were to enter into all the little Malicious doings of Lumley [Lord Sempill] and Mallock [Balhady], their heads are filled with nothing but malice and spite.' The Prince's distrust of these two men, upon whose judgement, with the exception of O'Bryen in Paris, his father relied upon implicitly, grew almost pathological. But in the meantime, unknown to Charles, the French watch on developments in the English political situation was growing even more vigilant.

On 4 May O'Bryen wrote to d'Argenson asking for a passport for yet another Jacobite agent, John Douglas, who had landed at Boulogne with messages from Scotland. Dated 5 May at Versailles, d'Argenson wrote out, 'permission for John Douglas, a Scottish gentleman, arriving in France from England by Boulogne to regain his own country by way of Holland'.[9]

On receipt of the messages brought by this agent, Charles decided that, whatever the French did or did not do to help him, he was sick of inactivity and would go to Scotland alone if necessary. He moved from Fitzjames to Normandy, where another cousin, the Duc de Bouillon, had a property near Rouen with the propitious name of Navarre. From Navarre he got in touch with Antoine Walsh, who had been introduced to him by the Irish Lord Clare, and was then based at Nantes, whence his fleet traded in sugar and spices from the West Indies. The fortune accumulated in a relatively short space of time by this ex-naval officer was said to have come from his shadier sideline as a slave-trader (*négrier*). The mother of the Duc de Bouillon was a Sobieski princess, the sister of Maria Clementina, while yet another Polish princess was married to a neighbouring seigneur, the Prince de Talmont, who was related by marriage to Antoine Walsh.

By borrowing money from the Waters father and son, an accommodating pair of English bankers in Paris, Charles ordered small arms and ammunition to be delivered to Antoine Walsh's headquarters at Nantes. A victory by the French under the Maréchal de Saxe, who defeated the Duke of Cumberland at Fontenoy in May 1745, spurred the Prince on to making his final plans. During the first weeks of June he wrote more letters than he did at any other time in his life.

The most important batch was written on 12 June 1745 from Navarre, with instructions that they were not to be forwarded until after he had sailed for Scotland. To his father he wrote four pages, of which the gist is the following:

> Sir, I believe your Majesty little expected a courier at this time and much less from me, to tell you a thing which will be a great surprise to you. I have, above six months ago, been invited by our friends to go to Scotland, and to carry what money and arms I could conveniently get, this being, they are fully persuaded, the only way of restoring you to the crown, and them to their liberties. After so much scandalous usage as I have received from the French Court, had I not given my word to do so, or got so many encouragements from time to time as I have had, I should have been obliged in honour, and for my own reputation to have flung myself into the arms of my friends and die with them, rather than live longer in a miserable way here, or be obliged to return to Rome, which would be giving up all hopes. I cannot but mention a parable here which is, if that a horse which is to be sold, if spurred, does not skip, nobody would care to have him, even for nothing. Just so, my friends would care very little to have me, if after such usage as all the world is sensible of, I should not show life in me. Your Majesty cannot disapprove a son's following the example of his father. You yourself did the like in the year '15; but the circumstances now are indeed very different by being much more encouraging.
>
> I have tried all possible means and stratagems to get access to the King of France or his Minister. Now I have been obliged to steal off without letting the King of France so much as suspect it, for which I make proper excuse in my letter to him, by saying it was a great mortification to me never to be able to speak and to open my heart to him. That this thing was of such a nature that it could not be communicated to any one of his Ministers by writing, but to himself alone—in whom, after Almighty God, my resting lies—and that the least help would make the affair infallible. If I had let the French Court know beforehand, it might have had the following bad effects: 1st. It is possible they might have stopped me, having a mind to keep measures with the Elector, and then to cover it over, they would have made a merit of it to you by saying they had hindered me from doing a wild and desperate thing. 2ndly:— My being invited by my friends would not be believed, or at least would have made little or no impression on the French Court.

I have sent Henry Stafford to Spain and Sir Thomas Geraldine to demand succours in my name. Let what will happen, the stroke is struck, and I have taken a firm resolution to conquer or die, and stand by my ground as long as I shall have a man remaining with me.

I think it is of the greatest importance that Your Majesty should come as soon as possible to Avignon, but take the liberty to advise you not to ask leave of the French Court; for if I be not immediately succoured, they will certainly refuse you.

Your Majesty may now see my reason for pressing so much to pawn my jewels, which I should have been glad to have done immediately, for I never intend to come back, and money, next to troops, will be the greatest help to me. I owe old Waters about 60,000 livres and the young one about 120,000 livres [in all about £3,500].

I and Sir Thomas Sheridan will write more fully to James Edgar about these matters, both as to the sum I carry with me and the arms, as also how I go. I write this from Navarre but it won't be sent until I am on ship-board. I have wrote a note to the Lord Marischal, telling him to come immediately, giving him credentials to treat with d'Argenson for succours. To the Duke of Ormonde I have writ a civil letter, showing a desire of his coming here immediately, but at the same time, leaving it to his discretion to do so. I should think it proper if Your Majesty pleases to be put at His Holiness's feet, asking his blessing on this occasion. But what I chiefly ask is your own which I hope will produce me that of Almighty God upon my endeavours to serve you, my family and my country, which will ever be the only view of Your Majesty's most dutiful son. Charles P.

Charles then wrote to his father's secretary, James Edgar, giving details of the arms and equipment he had bought:

Navarre. 12 June 1745.
Having writ a long letter to the King, I add that I owe Waters the banker about 60,000 livres part of which went to the payment of my debts last winter which the F.C. [French court] did not think fit to complete. Young Waters advanced me a hundred and twenty thousand livres and promised to pay several other things which I had referred to him. It is absolutely necessary to remit the two sums immediately. Young Waters desires that his money be sent by Beloni [the King's banker in Rome] directly to himself, without letting the old man know he made any such advance, and whatever other money may be remitted for my use the best way will be to send it to the young one, for the other I believe, will be glad to be eased of the trouble. All this money I have employed in my present undertaking, having bought 1,500 fuses, eteen [eighteen] hundred broad-swords, mounted a good quantity of powder, balls, flints, Durks, Brandy etc.[10] and some hundred more of the fuses and broadswords of which I cannot at present tell the exact number. I have also got twenty small field pieces, two of which a mule can carry, and my cassette which will be near 4,000 louis d'or.[11] All these things will go to the frigate which carries myself. She has twenty odd guns and is an excellent sailor and will be escorted by one

and perhaps two men of war of about 70 guns each. It will appear strange to you how I should get these things without the knowledge of the F.C. I employed one Rutlidge and one Walsh who are subjects. The first got a grant of a man-of-war from the F.C. to cruise on the coast of Scotland and is luckily obliged to go as far north as I do, so that she will escort me without appearing to do it. Walsh understands his business perfectly and is an excellent seaman; he has offered to go with me himself, the vessel being his own that I go aboard of. He also has a man-of-war that will likewise go with me if she can be got ready in time and a frigate of 44 guns which he took lately from the English and is manning to send out with all expedition. He lives at Nantes and I expect a courier every moment from him with an account that all is ready and that I must lose no time to get there and go directly on board. If there be no danger of being stopt or discovered I shall write from there. Adieu friend. I hope it will not be long before you hear comfortable news; in the meantime be assured of my constant friendship. Charles P. P.S. I send you here enclosed an authentick copy of what is to be printed and dispersed at my landing. I also forgot to mention that I intend to land at or about the Isle of Mull.

I enclose here also five letters and one open to yourself, all from Sir Thomas. I here enclose the King's and the Duke's letters,one for Lord Dunbar and another for B. Tencin. If the bearer be one Pierre I know him to be very honest and a good servant, Macdonald [Aeneas] is his master, whom I carry with me, so the servant deserves to be taken care of.

In a letter to O'Bryen Sheridan explains the Prince's arrangements whereby his letters to his father were to take so long on the way that there could be no possibility of a reply reaching him before he left. The messenger Pierre was to go to Rome via Avignon to invite the aged Duke of Ormonde to join the expedition, also the Earl Marischal. The purpose of Henry Stafford's mission to Spain was to obtain money rather than troops. But like the French subsidies, it arrived too late.

Having got these domestic epistles off his chest, Charles took the plunge and wrote to Louis XV:

A Navarre ce 12 juin 1745.

Monsieur mon oncle,

After vainly trying all means of reaching Your Majesty in the hope of obtaining from your generosity the necessary help to enable me to play a part worthy of my birth, I have made up my mind to make myself known by my actions, and undertake alone a project which some small aid would make certain of success. I venture to hope that Your Majesty will not refuse me such aid. I should never have come to France if the expedition planned more than a year ago had not bade me to recognize Your Majesty's good intentions on my behalf, and I trust that the unforeseen accidents which rendered that expedition impracticable for the time being have in no way changed these intentions of yours.

May I not trust, at the same time, that the signal victory[12] which Your

Majesty has just won over your enemies and mine (for they are one and the same) has resulted in some change of affairs; and that I may derive some advantage from this new blaze of glory which surrounds you? I beg Your Majesty most urgently to consider that, by upholding the justice of my rights, you will be putting yourself in a position to achieve a stable and enduring peace, the sole object of the war in which you are now engaged.[13] In any case, I intend to try my fate, which after God's hands, is in Your Majesty's. If you help me to success you will find a faithful ally in a kinsman who has the honour to remain, with the most respectful attachment, Monsieur my uncle,

Your Majesty's most affectionate nephew,
Charles P.

Unlike these official farewell letters of 12 June, those addressed to O'Bryen went direct to him at St Germain. On 16 June the Prince replied to one of these: 'I have received yours of ye 13th and in it the news of the Battle of Fontenoy. It is not easy to foresee if it will prove good or bad for our affairs. I find the situation and the country here so agreeable as also the people here procuring me all diversions possible that has made me prolong this jaunt of mine here. I expect a distincter account of this battle which, if you get, you will send to me under cover to Mr Kelly as I mentioned to you in my last. My compliments to yr Lady. Charles P.'

In his next letter to O'Bryen, still from Navarre, the Prince acknowledges one from O'Bryen on 18 June. In this he says: 'I design to go today to a party of pleasure which is to see a little of the country herabouts at La Trappe nearby Rowan [Rouen].' He goes on to say that he means to go to Paris for a few days. This was a deliberate blind, as instead he went straight to Nantes, where his chosen companions had been told to join him, one by one, during the last week of June. Antoine Walsh, who had been in charge of the arrangements for the expedition, was waiting for him there. Walsh had his armed frigate the *Du Teillay* equipped for the voyage and was himself ready to sail with the Prince to Scotland. The lending of Walsh's frigate and the hiring of the armed escort vessel the *Elizabeth* from Walter Ruttledge of Dunkirk, had finally been approved by the French Minister of the Marine, the Comte de Maurepas.

As a cover, Walsh gave out that his ship had been chartered to pick up a cargo of spices from the Antilles. The *Elizabeth*, originally an English warship that had been captured by the French years before during the War of the Spanish Succession, was given permission by Maurepas to cruise off the west coast of Scotland, as Charles had explained in his letter to James Edgar.

Captain Durbé, the French commandant of the frigate *Du Teillay* began his log on Friday 2 July 1745 in the traditional fashion 'in the name of God and the Holy Trinity', describing himself as the commandant of the armed sloop *Du Teillay* of Nantes, carrying eighteen guns and a crew of sixty-seven for the voyage to Scotland.[14]

From five o'clock on the morning of that day Durbé awaited his passengers, who arrived one by one in small boats. The embarkation went so well that by seven o'clock in the evening he was ready to take on board his last three passengers, whom he listed quite simply as His Royal Highness the Prince of Wales, the Chevalier Sheridan and Monsieur Walsh. The Prince was dressed as a student of the Scots College in Paris and the seventy-year-old Sir Thomas Sheridan posed as his father. Those who sailed with him and have since been immortalized as the Seven men of Moidart were none of them particularly young or warlike. They were the Duke of Athol (the former Marquis of Tullibardine)and Aeneas Macdonald the banker, both Scots; Sir John Macdonnell, an Irish officer serving in the French army; John William O'Sullivan and Father Kelly, also Irish; the drunkard Francis Strickland, so detested by James III, the only Englishman in the party; and the Abbé James Butler, said to be an illegitimate son sent by his father, the old, sick Duke of Ormonde, to report on the voyage. As his personal servants the Prince took Ned O'Kelly, to whom he gave the high-sounding title of Master of the Household and, as his valet, the tried and trusted Michele Vezzosi, the Italian who had served James III in the same capacity in the Fifteen. There was, in addition, a Gaelic-speaking boatman, Donald Cameron, who had been sent to France by Lochiel, to act as the Prince's pilot when the two frigates got into West Highland waters.

Before embarking, the Prince dashed off another letter[15] to his father, dated 'St Nazaire at ye mouth of ye Loire ye 2nd July 1745':

> Sir,
>
> The contrary winds that have been blowing hitherto have differed my embarking which will be this afternoon at Seven. I keep this open and do not send it until I am ferely set off from Belle Isle, the Randeevous, so that I may add a note to it if being sea-sick does not hinder; if it does, Sir Thomas will supply in mentioning what more may occur . . .

Later he added, to go by the same courier (12 July) to Edgar.

> This being the last note I shall write on this side of ye seas, I do not fail to give you adieu in it, making my compliments to Lord Dunbar and to as many of my friends as you shall think convenient and proper.
>
> I enclose here letters for the King and the Duke which will go off together in the great packet of the 12th last, as soon as I am freely sailed off from Belle Isle. I hope in God we shall soon meet which I am resolved will not be but at home. In the meantime I remain all yours.
>
> Charles P.

For a week there was no sign of the other ship, the *Elizabeth*, and Charles was writing again to James Edgar.

Belle Isle, à la Rade ye 12 July 1745.

After having waited a week here, not without a little anxiety, we have at last got ye escort [the *Elizabeth*] I expected, which has just now arrived. Id est a ship of 68 guns and 700 men on board. I am, thank God, in very good health, but have been a little seasick and expect to be more so, but it does not keep me much abed. I find the more I struggle against it the better. Pray make my excuses along with my most humble duty to the King for not writing, not having anything more particular to add but what is here. My excuses also to the dear Duke with many compliments. My compliments again to all my friends and I give you adieu with nothing more to add and being in a great hurry. C.P.

This was, in fact, his last letter before leaving France. The *Du Teillay* and the *Elizabeth* finally weighed anchor and sailed from Brittany for Scotland on 15 July. On 20 July they crossed the path of a patrolling British man-of-war called the *Lion* off the Lizard. She gave chase and engaged the *Elizabeth*, whose Commandant d'O and 156 men were killed or wounded. Her flag-lieutenant, the Chevalier Bart, descendant of the Dunkirk pirate Jean Bart, advised Antoine Walsh to continue the voyage alone, while her escort, the badly damaged *Elizabeth*, limped back to Brest.

It was only when the *Elizabeth* arrived back in this Breton harbour that the news of the Prince's departure leaked out. On 22 July an Irish Jacobite agent informed O'Bryen that he had seen the Prince of Wales sail from Belle Isle. O'Bryen lost no time in informing the French Foreign Minister. This letter, in French, dated Paris 22 July 1745, in O'Bryen's own hand to d'Argenson, gives vivid send-off to the Forty-five: 'Monsieur, I have just this moment received a visit from an Irish gentleman who swears that he saw the Prince of Wales set sail from the Brittany coast.'[16]

O'Bryen then goes on to tell the Foreign Minister that Charles had himself ordered the Irish agent to take the news to O'Bryen, assuring him that he had written to him at length on the subject of his departure. O'Bryen says that he has so far received no letters and gives d'Argenson his word of honour that he had absolutely no idea of the Prince's plans; nor he emphasizes had King James. 'But the Minister can judge for himself from the Prince's bold action just how far he is prepared to go to regain the crown of England for his family. He can only add that his courage and enterprise is worthy of a great-great-grandson of Henri IV of France.' O'Bryen hopes that, far from displeasing the King of France, His

Majesty will be generous enough to support him in every way possible.

Colonel O'Bryen ends by saying that, according to the information he has received, the Prince embarked with no more than five or six gentlemen on a small frigate carrying eighteen guns. 'I imagine that his plan is to go to Scotland. And this Sir, is all I am able to tell you for the moment.'

16

THE 1745 – A WILD AND DESPERATE THING

As he had promised, the Abbé James Butler wrote an account of the voyage of the *Du Teillay* for the old Duke of Ormonde, anxiously waiting for news in Avignon. Butler's journal corroborates Captain Durbé's description of the fight between the *Lion* and the *Elizabeth*. He says:

> The English man-of-war attacked us about 5.30 in the evening and the battle continued until 10 at night. I was on board the small frigate with the Prince. Mr Walse who was owner and chief on board did not think it proper for us to fire our guns and engage in battle for fear the Prince might come to any mischance. With much ado we gained upon the Prince to retire. When the battle was over we spoke to the Elizabeth who told us they had about 300 men killed or wounded and were obliged to go back to Brest. We took our leave of them, choosing rather to dye than to return that way and committed ourselves to Providence and after several alarms from different ships we met with, conducted ourselves to the Isle of Barra in Scotland. Being a very wet and dirty night, and the wind not favourable for coming in, it was not possible to land. Besides, a strange man-of-war which had been following us closely, kept off and on about two leagues from ye harbour.

The weather was so bad and the seas so high that they were forced to land on the flat little island of Eriskay, where they spent the night in a 'black house'—a croft of rough stones, heather-thatched, whose only ventilation was a hole in the roof. After making a fire, which filled the one room with suffocating smoke, they 'roasted some flounders which Aeneas Macdonald had catched' and washed down with a dram of malt whisky. Charles insisted that old Sir Thomas Sheridan, with his frail health and rheumatism, sleep in the only bed available. He and the others sat up and played cards all night.

'Next morning, Macdonald of Boisdale came to visit the Prince and assured us that the matter had been discovered.' Boisdale insisted they turned back, saying positively he had received such orders from the Prince's friends and well-wishers. The Prince refused, replying with dignity, 'I am come home sir'.

> We all came on board and held a council of war on what was to be done. The Prince declared he would rather die than depart upon so slight a motive and said he was resolved not to return until he had seen his friends. This concluded, our difficulty was how to escape the ship that lay cruizing off and on for us. After deliberation, we resolved at all hazard to go for Scotland and got under sail when it grew dark, though the other ship was in sight of us at sunset. As fortune pleased, we got into a bay on the mainland called Loughanou [Loch-nan-Uamh][1] meaning in English, the loch of the caves right opposite to the Island of Eigg. There we announced the arrival of the Prince to the first who appeared, Macdonald of Keppoch, Macdonald of Kinlochmoidart [brother of Aeneas Macdonald] and Young Clanranald. We told them what the Prince had risked on their account and expected they would adhere to their promises.

The Prince received them wearing the Highland dress he had been sent in 1740 by the Duke of Perth—the kilt with a short tartan coat, without the plaid, and on his breast the cross of the Order of St Andrew. He was tall, fresh-complexioned, fair-haired and brown-eyed, with his father's air of distinction and authority. Butler continues:

> Macdonald of Borrodale and other local notables appeared soon afterwards, rowed out to the Du Teillay in small boats. They answered him that their lives and their fortune were at his disposal but entreated him to remain quiet until they advised all their friends. This the Prince assented to. Immediately, Macdonald of Kinlochmoidart parted for Edinburgh and the low country to communicate the Prince's arrival. We then asked for a place to disembark our arms. We emptied all our barrels of salt water and filled them with fresh.[2]

The next day Captain Durbé took the *Du Teillay* round to the narrow sea loch of Loch Ailort to the south, in Cameron country.

From nightfall until 3 a.m. on 6 August they landed all the arms and ammunition. The *Du Teillay* remained in Loch Ailort for a week, while the Prince's party set up camp further south at Kinlochiel. To this camp, his first headquarters in Scotland, came the neighbouring clans—the Camerons, the Stewarts of Appin and other septs of the Macdonalds. There were so many that the Abbé Butler could not recollect all their outlandish names. His narrative continues:

> Mr Clanranald parted for the Isle of Skye to engage Sir Alexander Macdonald and Mr Macleod who, in a few days, despatched a messenger to know if the Prince had a power signed by his father. He said he had [though he did not]. Mr Murray of Broughton was hourly expected with an account of how matters stood in the low country.

> What people complain of mostly is that the Prince did not bring arms or money enough. I assure Your Grace [Ormonde] both articles would be very requisite. We left them 18 small field pieces. The affairs have a very promising look and numbers are crowding daily to offer themselves. They complain that they have no man of note to lead them but the Prince, which greatly dispirits them. Provisions are also very scant, the moisture of the year having occasioned a very late harvest, but God seems to favour them in all things, for the very day we parted [Butler and Walsh sailed back on the *Du Teillay* on 16 August] we met three English ships loaded with oatmeal.
>
> We took 'em as Prizes and despatched 'em to the Prince which will be sufficient supply for some time. The Prince shows a vast deal of resolution and undauntedness which prodigiously pleases the people and we supposed the disaffection of Sir Alex Macdonald and Macleod was but a feint to know if the Prince was steadfast and determined and, as they find him to their wish, there is no doubt they will soon joyn him [but these two chiefs did not]. The Prince told the people that he hoped by their bravery and fidelity to surmount all difficulties and, for his part, he would give them daily proof of his love and tenderness.
>
> Sir Hector Maclean had been taken prisoner at Edinburgh and conducted to London, letters from France having been found at his lodgings. This accident imperilled the Prince's party before his arrival, but, as the Government could make no sense of what they contained, Maclean, immediately after his first trial which took place a little before we parted for Scotland, was remitted to the Tower of London. About two days before we left [Butler and Walsh] an attempt was made to seize the Duke of Perth but luckily he escaped. All this was merely upon suspicion as not one of the opposite party knew of the Prince's being in the country. It is evident and moralely probable that the least assistance from France or Spain at the present happy conjuncture would entirely terminate our misfortunes and crown our glorious attempt with success, and we are persuaded by the situation of affairs in Europe and the divisions and dissatisfactions in Great Britain that a very small supply would be sufficient. We arrived in Scotland the 3rd August, and parted, the Prince and his company in perfect health, the 19th, and after a difficult journey, arrived safely at Amsterdam, the 3rd of 7 bre N.S.

At Amsterdam, Antoine Walsh sold the *Du Teillay*, and with the money hired a coach in which he and the Abbé Butler returned to Versailles, bringing the news of the landing in Scotland and a personal letter dated 6 August 1745 from Loch Ailort from the Prince to Louis XV.[1] In this letter he stresses the importance of help from 'Monsieur mon oncle', now that he is in Scotland and ready to act: 'The success of my enterprise depends uniquely upon Your Majesty and help which would cost Louis very little would enable the Prince to invade England and crown the glorious enterprise with victory.'[3]

When James III finally received the Prince's letter of 12 June, he wrote at once to Louis XV protesting his ignorance of the whole escapade and his embarrassment in relation to the King of France. He ended, however, on a note of paternal pride in Charles's daring and initiative. With key phrases heavily underlined, he says, writing on 11 August 1745: 'It is only a few days ago that I learned to my great astonishment that *my son* had actually left the French coast to sail to Scotland. He has planned and carried out this enterprise *without consulting me*, knowing full well that I would never have approved that he should embark on such an expedition *above all without Your Majesty's knowledge*. I was entirely ignorant of it: but now that it is done, I must confess in all sincerity, that I cannot help but admire him . . .'[4]

On 19 August 1745, the day the *Du Teillay* sailed away from Scotland, Prince Charles Edward raised the Stuart standard at Glenfinnan at the head of Loch Shiel in Lochaber, in the heart of the Cameron country. Donald Cameron of Lochiel, one of the original signatories of the letter to Cardinal Fleury in 1741, brought 500 of his clansmen. Three days later, on 22 August, Charles, styling himself Prince of Wales and Regent of the Kingdoms of Scotland, England, France and Ireland and the Dominions thereunto belonging, issued a printed declaration offering 'a reward of £30,000 sterling for the capture of the Elector of Hanover, whether landing or attempting to land in any part of His Majesty's Dominions.[5] Should any fatal accident happen from thence, let the Blame ly entirely at the door of those who first set the infamous example'. The Prince was not without humour of a macabre sort.

The clans were now forming into a considerable army as more of the chiefs rallied to the Prince's standard. By 28 August the enthusiastic if undisciplined Jacobite forces had marched south over the Corrieyairack Pass to Blair Atholl, reaching Perth on the evening of 4 September. After a week in Perth, when he was joined by Lord Ogilvy and Lord George Murray and their followers, Charles moved on to Edinburgh, still unchallenged.

On Monday, 16 September, Charles issued surrender terms to the Provost and Magistrates of the city, and on the following day entered the Scottish capital, having his father proclaimed James VIII of Scotland and himself as Prince Regent at the Mercat Cross. As he rode on a white horse into the courtyard of the palace of Holyrood House, white cockades, the Jacobite emblem, were distributed to the cheering crowds who thronged around him. Later the Prince gave a ball in the old palace, which had last been occupied by his grandparents James II and Mary of Modena when they were Duke and Duchess of York. Although the castle on its rock dominating the city was still garrisoned by government troops, they remained inactive, making no move to suppress the general enthusiasm for the Young Chevalier.

When the news reached London that another Charles Stuart had appeared in the Highlands, the English High Command sent a tetchy little General, Sir John Cope, to deal with the situation. Cope embarked with his Hanoverian troops for Aberdeen, but the Prince had moved too quickly for him, and Cope, hearing of the triumphal entry into Edinburgh, re-embarked and landed south of the capital at Dunbar.

Exhilarated by his success, the Prince sallied forth very early in the morning of 19 September at the head of his Highlanders and surprised and routed Cope and his regular soldiers at Prestonpans near Musselburgh. 'They ran like rabets,' Charles wrote that same night to his father, a vivid enough description of one of the shortest battles in history. The Prince had stayed on the battlefield late into the evening, personally supervising the care of the wounded and the burial of the dead. 'For I could not suffer an Englishman to rot above ground', he told his father in the same letter. It grieved him that necessity had made him cause the death of his own subjects, 'who being regular soldiers were only doing their duty. I could have wished the Hanoverians had sent Dutch or foreign troops against me so that I did not have to take my own blood'.[6] As a victor, Charles revealed himself to be as humane and magnanimous as his adversary and contemporary, the Duke of Cumberland, was brutal.

The news of the Jacobite victory at Prestonpans reached the French King through yet another Irish shipowner named O'Heguerty. On 21 September he wrote to Versailles saying 'two smugglers had arrived at Boulogne with the agreable news of General Cope's defeat by His Royal Highness. All the town of Boulogne gives credit to it'.[7] O'Heguerty continued:

> We see Mr Walsh daily. He proposed to M. de Maurepas [the French Navy Minister] the manadgement of the troops passage if there were fair wind to get over he engages to land them in 12 or 14 hours at the furthest. If a man rich with millions dread not the storm in a fishing boat, a soldjer ought not to dread it and yet, Sir, I greatly fear disobedience among the French soldjers when they be commanded to embark in stormy weather.

Antoine Walsh, who had received, as previously agreed between him and the Prince, the title of Comte de Serrant[8] before returning from Scotland, wrote to thank King James. He said: 'The Abbé Butler who had the honour of accompanying His Royal Highness to Scotland and who returned with me is on his way to Rome to give Your Majesty an exact account of the voyage and the state in which he found the chiefs and clansmen in the Highlands'. Yet another Irish Jacobite living in Leghorn wrote to James Edgar to tell him that 'the town was agog with the rumour that a young man, in the dress of an Abbé, but undoubtedly Prince Henry Stuart, had passed through Leghorn riding north in the direction of France, and that the gentlemen-merchants here are full of the news of the Prince's landing in Scotland'.

By the end of September 1745 Louis XV was so encouraged by the way things were going in Scotland that he at last ordered French troops to prepare to embark at Dunkirk. His special envoy on the progress of the Jacobite rising was Alexandre de Boyer, the Marquis D'Eguilles, a lawyer from Aix-en-Provence. His mission for Louis was a secret one and his official rank was Capitaine au Regiment de la Marine. D'Eguilles sent detailed reports of every phase of the campaign, with assessments of the leading Jacobites and the general feeling in the country. All this secret information, in D'Eguilles's handwriting, is filed in the quai d'Orsay archives.

The preliminary invasion force sailed for Scotland on 1 October 1745. On that day D'Eguilles wrote two letters to the French King. The first, addressed to the Marquis d'Argenson and written early that day says:[9]

> This morning a ship of almost the same size as the one in which we are to embark, entered this port, but it is an infinitely better sailor. She has just escaped two English privateers which have the reputation of being faster.
>
> As this one is completely armed and as the ammunition has not yet been put on board, we consider it more sensible to use this new ship. She should be ready by this evening so that our departure will not be held up and our navigation less dangerous. The ship in which we should have sailed will leave 5 or 6 days after us. It is necessary to check on the weight of the cargo though we can only take half the number of cases and packages we meant to. The sum of 4,000 guineas has arrived. This is not an enormous sum. It is to be hoped the next consigments will be more substantial.
>
> I am with profound respect,
>
> Your very humble and obedient servant,
>
> D'Eguilles.
>
> A Dunkerque ce 1^{er}8bre, 1745
>
> To the Marquis d'Argenson,
> Secretary of State for Foreign Affairs
> Versailles.

Later that same day he wrote:[10]

> Monseigneur, We shall leave today if the wind permits. It is blowing from the northeast and it is very cold, it is to be feared it won't change quickly. We have embarked on the Espérance, on which I shall sail, almost all the powder and 11,000 rifles, bayonets etc. The Hareng Couronné which will leave five days

later and which is already loaded with 1300 rifles and other munitions in the proportion that the two vessels can only take half the quantity we hoped to embark. This, despite the fact that the ships are much bigger than we anticipated. They are between 100 and 110 tons. The others cannot be more than 40 tons. We shall therefore need eight ships to carry out what we had hoped to do in three. The Brown brothers and Sheridan [Michael Sheridan, a nephew of Sir Thomas] who will embark on the Espérance, are the only Irishmen Mr Rutlidge recommended here to Walsh. He accepted them without hesitation since, without them, we should be forced to land on the coast of Scotland with neither guide or interpreters. It seems from the letter from the Comte de Maurepas to the Chevalier Bart that he should have kept Messrs Brown and Sheridan behind for the second embarkation, but not having been forewarned, Bart could not do anything but let them go.

Each day small craft and even quite big ships approach the harbour entrance to spy on us and to search the Dutch ships for incriminating letters. We try to hold up any Dutch vessels in port on the pretext of investigating the customs dues they should pay, but all these precautions cannot prevent the English from knowing that there are two French ships here loaded with arms and ready to sail and will do everything they can to prevent our crossing if we are not lucky with a favourable wind to speed our departure.

Monsieur Dromont [Lord John Drummond] commandant of the Royal Ecossois who will also embark on the Espérance has been put in charge of the troops by the Minister for War. I have been unable to avoid being seen by these three Irishmen [the Browns and young Sheridan] as they are always around, but M. Charron has given them to understand that I am a Frenchman to be trusted, devoted to their cause and determined to serve their Prince and hero to the best of my ability. They find this resolution admirable and none of them has the slightest suspicion that I have any ulterior motive [namely that of acting as a secret agent for the King of France]. When it is necessary for me to question them on any matter, M. Charron acts as my go-between. By the letters we have received here via Holland, it seems almost certain that the Prince is very near Edinburgh, if he has not already entered that city; this must be a very great event over there.

I am with profound respect etc.
Monseigneur, D'Eguilles.

By the same post a letter written on 27 September arrived for Louis XV from Henry, Duke of York,[11] who had reached Avignon and was staying with Lady Inverness. After the usual polite preliminaries the twenty-year-old Prince makes his excuses for the delay in writing to the French King:

The difficulties of the journey and the great distance I had to cover in an extremely short time has held me up till now. Taking all this into account, I hope you will approve my journey. The King my father impressed upon me the necessity for secrecy and to avoid recognition before reaching Your

Majesty and learning from you what you consider the best course of action which will not embarrass you. I await your instructions and beg you to assist me to act in such a way as to convince you of my esteem and friendship.

Your good friend,
Henry.

The *Espérance* and the *Hareng Couronné* sailed as planned, making port safely at Montrose on the east coast of Scotland. By the end of the first week of October D'Eguilles had arrived at Holyrood.

The French court had now moved to Fontainebleau for the hunting season. On 8 October the Jacobite successes occasioned another secret memorandum from d'Argenson, in which the French Foreign Secretary debates the pros and cons of aiding the rebellion across the Channel. In translation this reads:

France, according to all the laws of war has just as much right openly to excite a revolution in England and to support the rebels with all necessary forces just as England would, if she could, make a descent at La Rochelle, Bordeaux, or any other port in the kingdom to aid the French Protestants.

It matters very little to France whether it is King James or any other competitor who furnished the pretext, the main thing is to use whoever seems most likely to succeed. There can be no doubt that a prince who has on his own, without the aid of another power, found the means to raise the greater part of Scotland to maintain his position and even to make progress, presents a favourable opportunity for France, but it is also certain that this opportunity will pass her by if King George has time to assemble his Parliament and to send a considerable body of troops to Scotland when that country will be forced to sue for peace and those English, most opposed to the present Government, seeing themselves without any hope of support, will be the first to offer their lives and property to uphold a King they detest whose throne will be more secure than ever. Before going on to propose the question of an invasion (since everything is ready and it is only a question of deciding the best way of going about it) it will not be out of place to enumerate here the advantages likely to rebound on France from such an invasion of England whether it does or does not succeed.

If it succeeds:—New masters, new ministers, new Parliament, occupation of the interior of the kingdom, suspension of naval activity; no more subsidies to the Queen of Hungary [Maria Teresa] and to the King of Sardinia; peace with Spain; Holland crushed; the Queen of Hungary and the King of Sardinia reduced by impotence to continue the war which the King [of France] is pleased to impose upon them.

If it does not succeed:—France will have sent 10,000 men to England in order to occupy 50,000 inhabitants. From the day these 10,000 men will have disembarked, there is not the slightest doubt that, fearing the worst, the Bank of London will have closed immediately. Once the Bank of England is closed, there will be no means by which the Hanoverian government can collect the

> necessary funds as their money is nearly all in notes, and the letters of credit from Vienna and Turin will be held up while these two courts await developments. These 10,000 men sent at the request of a party in England it is presumable that they will shortly be joined by considerable forces of sympathizers. The country is open, the natural resources abundant, so that everywhere they can take up advantageous positions and await reinforcements from the sympathetic provinces. Besides, they can also get in touch with France either for money or for military supplies.
>
> If the outcome is the opposite (which I don't for a moment believe) they can always resort to surrender and France will have had the advantage of having prevented England for a considerable time from sending troops to help the common enemy.[12]
>
> But an invasion *IS* necessary, and I shall try to show that this is easily possible without risk and at very little cost.

On 15 October 1745 the *Gazette d'Amsterdam*,[1] the source of most of the news from England and avidly read by all Jacobite exiles in France, published this item: 'The passports which the Young Pretender is issuing are signed Charles, Regent of Scotland, England, France and Ireland and dependent states: they are counter-signed by a Secretary-of-State [John Murray of Broughton] and sealed with the royal seal.'

By 24 October 1745 the Treaty of Fontainebleau[13] between Louis XV, King of France, and Charles, Prince Regent of Scotland, acting on behalf of his father King James III, had been drawn up, signed and ratified. This military alliance was the last treaty of the old alliance between the two kingdoms, which went back to 1165. It contained six articles and begins in very much the same terms as the Treaty of Corbeil in 1326 between Robert the Bruce of Scotland and Charles le Bel of France.

> Prince Charles Edward of the Royal House of Stuart, having been proclaimed Regent of Scotland at Edinburgh, seeing that His Most Christian Majesty is at war with King George, the Elector of Hanover, has asked for reinforcements to be sent to him to be used against their common enemy, and for a treaty of alliance in their common interest. His Most Christian Majesty having agreed to this proposal, the undersigned Ministers are duly authorized to agree to the following articles.

Then followed the six articles. France pledged to send immediate military aid, comprising a body of French troops as well as the Scottish and Irish Regiments in the French service, to the Prince. Article 5 said that, to cement the union and intelligence between the two countries following the restoration of his father to his rightful throne, a treaty dealing with commerce would be established and that the French King would see that the Scottish nation would once again enjoy the special privileges that had existed between France and Scotland when Scotland was ruled by her own Kings. It was agreed that the terms of the treaty should come into force within two months from the date of ratification or earlier if that was possible. The Treaty was signed at Fontainebleau by the Marquis d'Argenson on behalf of Louis XV, and by Colonel Daniel O'Bryen on behalf of Prince Charles Edward, Regent of the Kingdom of Scotland. The text of the treaty was found among the Prince's private papers captured after Culloden.

On the day the treaty was signed at Fontainebleau Charles dictated the following letter in French to Sheridan for his agent, James Stuart of Goodtrees to take to the king of France, and sealed it with his ring.[14]

> Monsieur mon oncle,
> The affection which Your Majesty has already shown towards me and the further pledge he has given me through the Marquis D'Eguilles, prompts me to send the Chevalier Stuart to thank Your Majesty and at the same time to give him a first-hand account of the progress of my affairs. I beg Your Majesty to listen to all he has to say on my behalf and especially to receive the assurances I send with him of the Respect and attachment I have for Your Majesty. Monsieur mon oncle
>
> de Votre Majesté
>
> le très Affectioné Neveu Charles P.R.
>
> Edimbourg le 24 octobre 1745.

On the following day Sheridan added a covering note to introduce Stuart as the Prince's accredited agent at the French Court; he was to be the counterpart of D'Eguilles in Scotland. The Chevalier Stuart sailed for France on 31 October and remained there until his death in 1748.

D'Eguilles was the most conscientious of agents. Attached to his routine letter to Louis XV on 3 November 1745 were two carefully annotated lists, the first of leading Jacobites,[15] noblemen and Highland chieftains, with shrewd observations as to their character and worth, and the other an estimation of the number of troops[16] in the Prince's army on the eve of the march into England (see Appendices, 1 and 2).

The Duke of Perth was described by D'Eguilles as 'a man of some worth' and the Earl of Kelly as 'a good and zealous man for the cause' but Mylord Georges Murray (Lieutenant-General), though a man of real ability and guiding spirit of the Jacobite army, was in the Frenchman's opinion of suspect loyalty. D'Eguilles ends his report with the name of the Chevalier Stuart 'who brings this letter; followed by Sullivan who has the role of Quarter-Master General; Strickland (an Englishman) who is Master of the Horse; Mr John Murray of Broughton, a relative of the Duke of Athol, a man of ability who acts as the Prince's Secretary-of-

State and Sir Thomas Sheridan, undergovernor to the Prince who acts as assistant secretary to Murray. Here Monseigneur, is what I know at the time of writing of the leading personalities during the eight days I have been in Scotland. It is certain there will not be so many of worth in the forces who march against us'.

Charles set out on his march to London at the head of his army, which was grossly overestimated by D'Eguilles to be about 8,000 foot and 600 horse, at the beginning of November when many of the promised reinforcements had not shown up. Carlisle surrendered on 14 November and the Jacobites moved south to Lancaster and Preston and on to Manchester, where they were greeted by cheering crowds, many of them wearing the white cockade. Few, however, volunteered to join the Prince. French intelligence seemed to think he would make for Wales, but instead the Jacobite army continued south to Derby. When the Prince reached Derby, he received the news that Lord John Drummond had just disembarked at Montrose with his infantry regiment, the Royal Eccossais, whose officers and men enjoyed the privileges of dual Scottish and French nationality. Detachments from the Irish Brigade had landed at Stonehaven and Peterhead, but these French reinforcements only amounted in all to 750 men.

News of the occupation of Derby on 4 December caused panic in London. Rumours flew about that George II and his family had chartered a yacht to take them back to Hanover. As d'Argenson had prophesied, the Bank of England was refusing payment. Special prayers were ordered to be said in all the churches, and a detachment of volunteers (sketched for posterity by Hogarth) started to construct defences on the outskirts of the capital at Finchley. Charles, buoyed up by this news from Scotland and London, was all for continuing the advance. At this moment, if his commanders had been less cautious, and allowed him to enter London with the pipes skirling, at the head of his picturesque army of Scots, he might well have captured the imagination of the panic-stricken or romantically inclined public. The young and handsome Prince made such a contrast to the uninspiring Hanoverian royal family, with their bad manners and constant family rows, that if Charles at this stage had been able to follow Montrose's maxim of daring to win or lose it all, he might have won—at least for a time.

But his commanders, headed by Lord George Murray, refused to go any further without considerable more French support in troops and arms. Murray advised retreating to the Highlands for the winter and launching a new campaign in the spring when the promised French aid had arrived. At the council of war held on 5 December the Prince was overruled by the majority, and the heartbreaking decision to retreat was taken. Charles never forgave Lord George Murray for this, and grew to dislike and distrust him more and more. Murray and his supporters had argued that the Duke of Cumberland's army, about 10,000 strong, was in front of them and that General Wade's experienced troops were approaching from the rear. They also rightly pointed out that in England very few people had rallied to the Stuart standard, and that it would be suicide to attack London with 5,000 primitively armed, undisciplined foot-soldiers and a few hundred cavalry.

So, on 6 December, the Prince, sick at heart, headed north once more. His instinct had been right, and his generals had been fatally over-cautious. They grossly overestimated the military resources of the government at that time and underestimated how many people detested the House of Hanover. The Highland army returned as it had come, by Carlisle. They crossed the border on 19 December and made for Dumfries and then Glasgow.

On the very day of the fatal decision to retreat from Derby, O'Bryen had written to d'Argenson describing the Prince's bold march into England with the seeming project of making for the 'pays de Galles': 'All these provinces [those in the north-west of England and Wales] having a long tradition of loyalty to the House of Stuart. There can be no doubt that revolution in England is imminent but it is essential to seize the moment'. He stressed once again the urgent need for arms, money and, above all, troops from France.[17]

On 6 December Prince Henry Stuart, using his second title of Count of Albany, arrived at Versailles to present his brother's Scottish envoy, the Chevalier James Stuart. On 18 December O'Bryen was writing to Maurepas, forwarding a letter from Henry, who was now calling himself Duke of York, asking for the sum of 60,000 louis d'or, which had been promised him by the French King. On 20 December O'Bryen was writing direct to Louis on the subject of the Duc de Richelieu,[8] great-nephew of the Cardinal, being appointed commander-in-chief of the French invasion force to help the Jacobites. On the same day, the Duke of York had at last been received by the King and the homely Queen Marie Leczinska, who was his mother's cousin.

In Scotland Charles had reached Glasgow, a bastion of Whig respectability. Despite the hostility of the citizens of Scotland's second city, the Prince reviewed his troops on Glasgow Green with such panache that his courage and debonair appearance won over a large section of the population. One of the rich tobacco lords of the city entertained him at his mansion in the Trongate. There the Prince gave public dinners during Christmas and the New Year, and even took a day off to go shooting in the grounds of Hamilton Palace, a few miles from the city.

Sixty miles north, at Perth, Lord John Drummond was waiting with the French troops that had landed on the east coast of Scotland. The Prince sent orders for Drummond to join him at Glasgow, but Lord John, handicapped by the cautious instructions he had received from the French court, failed to obey. Charles was put out by his refusal, and decided to meet the French troops half-way, commanding them to join him at Stirling. Unfortunately the castle there was in Hanoverian hands. The French military engineers were ordered to proceed immediately to Stirling to start besieging the fortress. On 3 January, three days after celebrating his twenty-fifth birthday in Glasgow, the Prince and his army marched northwards out of the city, drums beating, pipes playing and the Jacobite flag flying bravely.

He took up his headquarters at Bannockburn House, feeling that the name alone was a good omen. His host was a widower, Sir Hugh Paterson, whose niece Clementina Walkinshaw, was his hostess; she was the rather gawky youngest daughter of the late Colonel John Walkinshaw, who had been the Jacobite secret agent in Vienna in 1718. Clementina was about the same age as the Prince, big-boned with long features and a freckled complexion. Because of her father's connection with the drama of the Sobieski princess's imprisonment and escape from Innsbruck, the youngest of his nine daughters had been baptized as a Catholic and named Clementina after the Prince's mother. During the two weeks he spent at Bannockburn Charles fell ill with influenza and was nursed by Miss Walkinshaw. The Prince, who had turned all heads with his charm and good looks, was remarkably unsusceptible to feminine beauty. Some kind of romantic relationship sprang up between the two at this time, but it was six years before they met again during his exile on the continent, when the sandy-haired Clementina became his mistress and mother of his only child.

On New Year's Day the faithful Lady Inverness had written her usual greetings from Avignon to the King's secretary, James Edgar, in Rome: 'Many thanks good sir for your kind compliments of the season. Receive mine, pray, upon the same occasion. We have reason to flatter ourselves that this year will put an end to the misfortunes of the Royal family. I hope in God it will and that I shall soon hear that the King has left Rome for England. I wish you with all my heart a good journey, and am, Sir, your most humble servant. M. Inverness.'

The Prince was still at Bannockburn on 14 January when the news came that English troops under the martinet General Hawley were advancing from Edinburgh, which had been reoccupied by government forces under Lieutenant General Handasyde. By 17 January the Prince was well enough to lead his Highlanders and French to face the enemy at Falkirk.

The Jacobite army fought in a very primitive way in three ranks. The first rank comprised the clans, each occupying their traditional positions to the left or right of the centre. The Macdonalds were on the right, while the Camerons, Macintoshes, Stuarts and Gordons fought on the left of the front line. The second rank was composed of the Lowland regiments under Lord Lewis Gordon, with Lord John Drummond's French troops, the Royal Ecossais, behind them. They charged as fiercely as they had done at Prestonpans, but this was no surprise victory. They were up against highly trained professional soldiers and just managed to hold their own. The siege of Stirling Castle was still going on, but the government garrison was holding out stubbornly. After Falkirk, many of the Highlanders started to drift off northwards. Lord George Murray and the clan chiefs held an urgent council with the Prince and told him that a retreat to the north was vital. General Hawley, rumoured to be the natural son of George II, had only been nominally defeated at Falkirk, and it was known that the Duke of Cumberland was after them with forces far outnumbering their own. Once more the Prince had to submit to the will of Lord George Murray. He wrote before setting out for Inverness on 1 February: 'I know that I have an army I cannot command further than the chief officers please, and there, if they are resolved upon it, I must yield—but I take my God to witness that it is with the greatest reluctance, and that I wash my hands of the fatal consequences which I foresee but cannot help'.

At the head of his army the Prince marched north through the same terrible weather as Montrose had known a century before. They stopped at Blair Castle, seat of the Duke of Athol, before going on in a blizzard through the Cairngorms to Dalwhinnie, and eventually reached Moy Hall on Loch Ness, the home of the Macintosh, Chief of Clan Chattan. Here Charles found a curious situation. The Macintosh was actually serving with the government forces under the Lowland Lord Loudon at Inverness, but his wife Anne had raised her husband's clan for the Prince. Lady Anne billeted Charles and his suite at Moy when he arrived on 16 February. When her husband received word of this, he decided to capture the Prince by night. However, the Chief's mother, old Lady Macintosh, sent a young kinsman, Lachlan Macintosh, to warn her daughter-in-law. The fifteen-year-old boy took a short cut and roused the blacksmith of Moy and local stalwarts, who fell upon their Chief and his men when they arrived, killing several of them. During the Rout of Moy the Prince escaped to Inverness, and there, reinforced by 200 French officers, took over the castle. Among these officers was D'Eguilles, who continued to send his despatches to King Louis via the French sloops that were coming to out of the way places on the north-east and north-west coasts.

Sir Thomas Sheridan wrote to d'Argenson from Inverness Castle on 2 March 1745. The translation of his letter reads:

> We understand that funds have been sent from France but it is a bit too late. The Enemy are in possession of all the coasts or will be. We are very much afraid the money will fall into the hands of the English. As for men, all that has arrived are 26 men of the Regiment of Fitzjames and a small box of gold which was landed and buried in the ground. God knows if it will ever be found again. We live in fear of being forced to fight another battle very shortly. If we win we shall once more be masters of the coast. In the meantime it is essential that the French ships bringing the arms and money land it at the mouth of the River Spey. Money is what we need most, although the arms and men are vital too. If, instead of small ships, you could send vessels of 30 or 40 guns, they could defend themselves, for the English, so far, have not sent larger than this. They say that an officer of those who landed from the last frigate speaks of an embarkation from Brest for the West of England—but, as always, one doesn't know what to believe. The Prince has at least done more than he promised in spite of all the difficulties he has had to surmount.[19]

During these five weeks before the final reckoning at Culloden on 16 April the Prince's natural extrovert spirits asserted themselves, and he made the most of this waiting period. Unlike his father, he never believed in giving way to despair. In Inverness he dined, wined and danced, impressing all who came in contact with him with his energy and unaffected charm.

On 6 April, only ten days before the fatal battle, D'Eguilles sent another list to France, giving the characters of the leading personages in Scotland attached to the House of Stuart. He ends with a comment on the impression made by the Prince on the Scottish women.[20] He himself had great success in this sphere, and it was from first-hand knowledge he wrote to Versailles that 'in general, all the young or pretty women are Jacobites, and have only become so since the arrival of the young Prince. It is not because he is gallant with them but rather the opposite which attracts the Scottish women who are by temperament serious and passionate, feeling he is a man of depth and constancy, not frivolous by nature. It was a woman who told me this'.

Unfortunately the Prince's female admirers could not fight for him against the Butcher Cumberland on the battlefield of Culloden where, after a night march without sufficient rations, his Highlanders charged as bravely and ferociously as ever, but this time against murderous cannon-fire and grapeshot. Those who were not blown to bits were ripped to pieces by bayonets. Cumberland, who had issued extra rations to his 'brave boys' to celebrate his twenty-fifth birthday the day before, gave the order 'No Quarter', and this was carried out to the letter. Men, women and children, the living, the wounded and the dead, were slaughtered in the most savage way imaginable. Culloden was not only the last battle on British soil, it was the bloodiest and most discreditable in the history of the British army.

When the Prince saw that all was lost, he was persuaded to leave the scene of carnage, mounted on a fresh horse. Along with the seventy-year-old Sir Thomas Sheridan, who had remained by his side throughout the action, Lord Elcho, the badly wounded Lochiel, O'Sullivan and some others, he crossed the Water of Nairn and rode south in the direction of Loch Ness, where they found shelter for the night at Aird, the house of a member of the Fraser clan. The Prince and Lochiel had their wounds dressed while they drank three glasses of claret and discussed the best course to take. In the end they decided to make for Achnacarry, Lochiel's family home in Lochaber. When they got there, Lochiel (who had been wounded in the leg), the Duke of Perth (who was a sick man) and old Sir Thomas Sheridan stayed in hiding while the Prince and the others made for the coast.

Back in Inverness the 222 French and 326 Scots forming the garrison were forced to capitulate to the English Major-General Bland. He received the surrender and the *parole d'honneur* from the officers that they would not attempt to escape. This was in an odd mixture of French and English: 'Les officiers et les soldats françois qui sont à Inverness surrender as prisoners of war to his Royal Highness the Duke of Cumberland and promise to submit themselves to the generosity of the English. Signed:–Le Marquis D'Eguilles, Cusack, Murphy, Dehan, O'Brien, Macdonald etc.'[21] On the following day a *billet d'honneur* was signed by the foreign officers taken prisoner at Inverness: 'We, the undersigned in the service of His Most Christian Majesty, recognize ourselves to be prisoners of war of His Britannic Majesty, and we promise on our honour not to leave the town of Inverness without the permission of His Royal Highness the Duke of Cumberland. In pledge whereof we have signed this billet d'honneur and sealed it with our regimental arms. Given at G.H.Q. Inverness the 28 April 1746 [continental dating, 17 April Old Style].[22] The officers who put their names to the surrender order came from the Royal Ecossais, and the regiments of Berwick, Bulkeley, Dillon, Fitzjames, Lally and Ross, and included French army engineers and surgeons, and officers in the service of the King of Spain. A fuller list of these prisoners is given in Appendix 3.

The Prince's five months of wandering and eventual escape to France is too old a story to be recounted here, but the fate of his original companions, the Seven Men of Moidart, is less well known.[23] Scarcely had Charles left the Scottish mainland for the Hebrides, to escape the redcoats combing the sea coast to capture him, than two frigates from Nantes arrived in Loch-nan-Uamh to look for him. These were the *Bellona* and the *Mars*, bringing more French gold, which was buried at Loch Arkaig. This sum was reputed to amount to 36,000 louis d'or, and it has since become a legend, for it has never been seen since. At Loch Arkaig the French found the Duke of Perth, Sheridan and Lochiel, all by now in pretty bad shape after taking refuge in the heather and sleeping rough in the open while Hanoverian soldiers, before Lochiel's eyes, burned Achnacarry and its library, the finest in the highlands. The French officers took the three survivors back with them to Arisaig, where they boarded the *Bellona*. After a sea fight with three ships of the British navy at the mouth of the loch, the *Mars* and the *Bellona* sailed back to France. Sheridan was beside himself with grief at having to leave before they had found the Prince, but there were hundreds of little Hebridean islands to search, and after their bloody encounter with the English sloops the French frigates could not afford to risk another battle with the ships of King George's navy, which were patrolling the Minch searching for the Stuart pretender.

The Duke of Perth was in such a bad state that he died on the voyage and Lochiel only had a few months to live after he had reached the safety of France. But Sheridan's fate was the hardest that could befall an old man after a lifetime of single-minded devotion to the Prince, to his father and to his grandfather, his own blood-relations. On his arrival at Navarre to report the failure of the rising to the Duc de Bouillon, he received a furious letter from James III, written from Rome on 25 July:

> This is to require you to come and joyn me here with all speed. Your silence since your return from Scotland has been a matter of much surprise to me when you could have given many satisfactory, though not agreeable informations.
>
> When you went from hence you know how much reason you had to be persuaded of my confidence and good opinion. I think it of absolute necessity for mine and for the Prince's service that I should have some free discourse with you, for I am unwilling to think that you are altered towards me and should be sorry to have reason to be it towards you, after all the pains you have taken in the service of a son so dear to me, and to whom I shall write about your coming here that he may not wonder to find you not in France. Mr Waters has my orders to give you 1,500 livres for your journey when you call for it.

Poor Sheridan replied to this cruel rebuke in a detailed letter explaining the facts of the case:

Navarre, August 14 1746.
Sir,
On Thursday the 12th I received the honour of Your Majesty's commands with which I shall not fail to complie. Tomorrow I intend to return to Paris and shall set out from there towards the end of the week. The pleasure of laying myself at Your Majesty's feet would make the journey more agreeable to, me were I not all the time under the cruel uncertainty in which I have been so long as to the Prince. This has been the only reason for my silence, for once having given an account of all I knew concerning his Royal Highness and how I came to part with him, which I did in my first letter to Lord Dunbar, I could not find anything else to say that I could think worthy of Your Majesty's notice. I must now, Sir, in the humblest manner, beg leave to tell Your Majesty that I could not without the greatest mortification, observe something in your letter which looked as if you had conceived some umbrage against myself. Upon the severest recollection I can find nothing that could give occasion for it, but my having concealed the Prince's design of going to Scotland. I now think that tho' the event proved so fatal, our first successes were sufficient to shew that they might have been compleat had they been tolerably seconded from abroad. As for my own Person, I never shrank from any danger which might have put an end to my days, but could not find an opportunity of perishing unless I had either shot myself with my own hands or wilfully thrown myself into those of the Enemy, of neither of which expedients I believe Your Majesty would have approved. . . . That I may still have the happiness to enjoy your good opinion is, next to the Prince's safety, the sincerest wish of Sir, Your Majestie's most humble, most obedient, most dutiful subject and servant,

Tho. Sheridan.[24]

The old man then set off alone to make the long journey across France to Rome to explain his conduct to King James. He was still without news of the Prince, and before he left Paris he wrote a letter to Scotland, which he hoped might reach his beloved Charles, giving an account of his return voyage to France. Dated 19 August, exactly one year from the raising of the Stuart standard at Glenfinnan, the letter reads:

Sir, Notwithstanding a letter I wrote some days ago which you will probably receive at the same time as this, I shall begin with my own departure from Scotland. Upon receipt of your last letter dated April 23rd which was delivered to me by Mr Hay, together with one for the Chiefs, I repaired to the side of Lough-nan-Uamh where I found Mr Murray and Logheil with his brother the Doctor [Archie Cameron], Major Kennedy and Sir Stuart Threpland. I shewed Murray and Logheil your letter to the Chiefs, and whilst they were deliberating how to draw the remains of our broken forces together, an express from Lord John [Drummond] found me out and brought me letters from the Abbé Butler and Nick Brown, giving me an account of their arrival on the coast with some arms, ammunition and with a considerable sum of money, none of which they said they would consign to anyone but me, conjuring me withal to make all haste possible, for otherwise they should be obliged to make off, for fear of being blocked up in ye Bay by English shipping. Upon perusal of this letter Logheil and Murray both desired me to make all haste I could to get the cargo put on Shoar, and then to go on board myself in order to follow you, in case I should arrive before you, to represent their condition to the Duke of York and the French Court.

Accordingly I went to the seaside, where the first thing I saw there were three English ships making for the Bay. That evening I got the money put on Shoar, the arms and ammunition having been landed already. By this time I found news of your departure was becomepublick, and everybody was persuaded you were already in the Orkneys. But it was judged entirely wrong to look for you there, as I had mind to, for it was alleged that would be the way to draw all English shipping after us and, by pointing out the place where you were supposed to be, render your escape impossible if you had not already gone off. Besides our frigates were foul and short of provisions. So we resolved to go immediately on board, as we did a little before break of day. Within half an hour the English vessels bore down on us, and an obstinate fight began which lasted until noon when the English thought fit to bear away. After that engagement, the reasons which had prevailed the night before for making the best of our way to France were become much stronger. Our ships had suffered considerably and were now in a much worse condition. So the rest of the day and the following night were spent in repairing them and early in the morning we set sail, and with much difficulty reached Nantes after a voyage of three and twenty days.

Within two or three days of my arrival at Paris, O'Bryen came to see me from Flanders where he had been sent to wait on the Duke of York at the siege of Antwerp. We went together to Versailles where I saw the Ministers and gave them the best account I could of how matters were when I left Scotland. All the answer I got from them was that till they knew what was become of your Royal Highness, for whose safety they expressed a great deal of concern, they could come to no resolution; but the truth is they were so bent on the hopes of a Peace that they seemed to think little of taking any rigorous measures towards renewing the war. They have since sent several ships from different places to bring you off, all of which you will have sufficient accounts from themselves, O'Bryen and others.

But I must not omit to inform you that Cardinal Tencin told me 'that we had made many mistakes'; one of the things which he instanced was that you had sent too many Agents and particularly he wondered what occasion there was for sending the Sieur James Stuart. I replied that there was nothing more natural than when we were in the hands of the Scots and had found so many friends among them, to send one of them, a gentleman of such distinction to take care of your affairs here. Besides the King of France had sent you a Minister [D'Eguilles] and had you sent none in return would that not have been cryed out upon as an unpardonable omission. I was likewise informed by several persons, amongst them O'Byren, that his Eminence had found a great fault that you did not write oftener to the King of France. To this I replied that should I write myself to the greatest Prince in Christendom and that several times and, not only, receive no answer from him, but not the least acknowledgement from a Secretary to ye receipt of any of my letters, should I not have reason to conclude that they importuned him, and that both in Prudence and good manners, I ought to cease writing. But, not satisfied with having represented this, I got the Duc de Bouillon to know of the King himself whether he took it ill of you that you had not writ oftener to him and his answer was 'Far from that, his letters flattered and embarrassed me because I was unable to reply to him as I should have wished'.

O'Bryen likewise asked the Cardinal in my presence whether, if your Highness had privately acquainted the Court of France with your intention of going to Scotland, they would not readily have furnished you with all necessaries for such an expedition? But to this the Cardinal answered with great earnestness:— 'No, certainly not, we should have prevented him from going'.

I took occasion to tell the Comte d'Argenson[25] that, as there would probably be a good many of yr. friends that would be obliged to retire out of Scotland and for whom you would be obliged to provide in some shape or other, I thought it could not be better done than by forming two new Scots Regiments, to which he answered that there would most certainly be some Provision made for such people, and that he would do all in his power to facilitate the matter.

I must now beg leave to tell your Royal Highness that I think you would do well, immediately upon your arrival here to send for Lally[26] and employ him in your negotiations with the Court of France. He is very well acquainted there, and nobody is more zealously affected for you. Bulkeley, by all that I can hear, has likewise behaved himself extremely well on this occasion and I think your Royal Highness ought to shew particular regard to him. Ld. Clincarty [Lord Clancarty, the one-eyed old rogue, who was actually *très mal vu* at the French court] is certainly full of zeal for yr. service and will wait upon you as soon as he hears of your arrival. He is by birth a man of the greatest distinction in Ireland where he lost an immense estate by the Revolution. He has passed all his life in England where he is very well known and has great relations. He has been so active during embarkation that I believe he cannot think of returning any more home—at least for some years.

Thos. Sheridan.

After his long and painful journey to Rome, the Prince's old tutor had to endure the humiliation of being reproached by James, who, with uncharacteristic sharpness, blamed Sheridan's bad advice to his son as being the main cause of the failure of the Forty-five. In his seventy-second year Sheridan left the King's presence a broken man. He sank into a deep melancholy and the only thing that consoled him in his disgrace was the news that the Prince had landed safely at Roscoff in Brittany on 10 October 1746. He roused himself from his sorrow to write a last letter to Charles:[27]

Sir,

I hope your Royal Highness will give me leave to congratulate you on your safe arrival in France, after all the Dangers and Hardships to which you have been so long exposed. I should not have been obliged to do so from this distance had I not received the King's positive orders to attend him here. I shall not trouble your Royal Highness with representing to you the cruel anxiety under which I have laboured ever since that unfortunate day that tore me from your presence. I flatter myself that you will more easily imagine than I can express what I have suffered, and I am sure if my services for so many years past does not convince your Royal Highness of it, all the expressions I could make use of on this occasion would prove superfluous. That your Royal Highness may long enjoy the Reputation you have so justly acquired, and one day reap the fruit of your labours, is the sincerest wish of Sir.

Your Royal Highness's most humble, most dutiful and most Obedient servant.

Albano. 3 November 1746. Thos. Sheridan.

Three weeks after writing this letter Sir Thomas collapsed and died of a stroke in Rome. The poor old man never knew that the Prince had written to James Edgar asking for Sheridan to be sent to join him in Paris. On 6 November 1746 Charles had written a covering note to Edgar from Clichy, the district near Montmartre:

I enclose here a letter for ye King. My kind compliments to Lord Dunbar and all my friends there. I say nothing to Sir Thomas because I am in hopes he is already set out for to join me. My wanting of him gives me a good deal of trouble for tho I have a very good opinion of Kelly and must do him justice of saying that I am very well pleased with him, yet neither he, nor anybody else much less, I would absolutely trust my secrets as I would in Sir Thomas which occasions me a great deal of toil and labour.

I remain at present assuring you of my constant friendship,

Charles P.

On 25 November King James wrote to his son telling him that his old friend had died of apoplexy on 23 November, adding, 'I had him buried with all decency in our own parish of S.S. Apostoli'. A few days later, on the King's instructions, James Edgar wrote to Sheridan's two aged sisters, who were still living at St Germain, in very straitened circumstances.

To Les Dames Sheridan. Rome 28 November 1746.

Mesdames,

I am sorry to give you the melancholy news of yr. Brother Sir Thomas Sheridan's death on the 23rd. I write now particulars of it to Mr Kelly, and send him an account of the money and effects found in his custody. He will no doubt inform you what I say on those heads. Not to encroche upon your grief, I shall further say that the King is graciously pleased to direct Mr Waters to continue to pay the pension he gives you as formerly ordered...

It was a sad end to a career of fifty-six years of unstinted devotion and loyalty to three generations of Stuarts. In many ways it was typical of so many who believed in the Jacobite cause whose dedication was only to be rewarded by insolence, indifference and demands for money and hospitality.

17

THE PRINCE IN PARIS

DURING THE FIVE MONTHS Charles was a fugitive in the highlands, his brother Henry had joined the French army and taken part in the siege of Antwerp. He stayed in Flanders until the end of August, when he was given leave to return to the Bouillon château of Navarre in Normandy to wait for news from Scotland. During the past months weekly letters had been arriving for the Stuart brothers from their father in Rome. Those addressed to Charles were kept by O'Bryen for the Prince's return. In one of these James mentioned 'remittances from Spain being put into O'Bryen's hands through the agency of the Chevalier Stuart'. The King talks about a sum of 450,000 livres to be kept apart: 'When I saw that affairs in Scotland were lost I ordered young Waters to return that money to me here as soon as it arrives. With it I shall redeem yours and your brother's jewels which were put in pawn, by which I shall save the expense of paying interest on the said money, and the jewels themselves will always be at yours and your brother's disposal.' Then, to the still missing Charles:

> When you are back in France I hope you will let yourself be advised by Cardinal Tencin and O'Bryen. The first is the only sincere friend we can trust amongst those ministers. You know my good opinion of the last and as he is agreeable to and has access to them, nobody is better able than he to serve us at the French Court. It is impossible for me, my dearest Carluccio, to say all I would like by writing, but what I have chiefly to recommend to you consists in three points. The first, to be always kind and loving to your Brother and never let anyone try and sow discord between you. The second is to behave with prudence and moderation in relation to the Court of France on whom we are forced to depend. And the third is to keep our people in due subordination, without allowing them to break your head with accusations and invectives against one another, but showing them that you are master and will act in your own way without being unkind, much less unjust, to any.

At last, on 15 October 1746, a short letter from Cardinal Tencin at

Fontainebleau told the King of his son's safe arrival in France: 'Sire, I draw breath. The Prince is saved; he arrived safe and sound at Roscoff which is the old harbour between Rennes and Morlaix'.[1] Tencin said he had received the news from the Irish shipowner Warren and that he, the Cardinal, would do everything in his power to be of service to the Prince. The Duke of York was staying at Clichy when he received word of his brother's return. On 14 October he wrote to his father:

> Your Majesty may judge how happy I am with the news I send you. I long so much to have this courier arrive that you may be rid of all the pains and anxieties you have been under for so long. I am very impatient to see my dearest Brother, and am in hopes it will be tomorrow. The Chevalier Stuart has just gone to meet him for the reasons that O'Bryen mentions. As I have slept but three hours last night, my head does not permit me to write long. By the next post I shall probably make it up. Your most dutiful son, Henry.

The Jacobite Secretary-of-State at St Germain, Sir John Graeme, wrote to Rome on the same date. 'This being the happiest day of my life, I beg leave to rejoice with Your Majesty on the Prince's safe arrival.'

Three days later, on his return from Brittany with the Prince, Graeme wrote another letter to Rome:

> Your Majesty will be glad to know that the Prince is arrived at Paris in perfect health and high spirits. Tho' the fatigue, the want of all necessaries and the dangers he has undergone are beyond imagination, yet he looks as well as when I had the honour to see him more than two years ago. Nothing was ever so tender as his first interview with the Duke. It is an unspeakable pleasure to me to see how much they love one another, and I hope in God it will always continue so. Col. O'Bryen is gone to Fontainebleau to concert his interview with the King of France. We wait his return with impatience to know the manner of it, tho' by some letters already writ from thence we have reason to fear that the Court will insist upon its being done privately, which will not be to the Prince's taste, and it is no wonder.
>
> Besides Messrs. Warren, Michael Sheridan, O'Brien and Lynch that went to look for H.R.H., there are come over with him Lochiel's brother Doctor Cameron, Lochgarry and Roy Steuart. He also brought over one Macdonald of Barastal [Barrisdale, a traitor to both sides] against whom there were proofs that his intentions were treacherous and he has been handed over to the Intendant of Brittany. H.R.H. has been very private in Paris since his arrival, and will be for some days longer. The Duke dined with him on Saturday and yesterday and after dinner they came out together to this place [St Germain] where the Prince stayed about an hour and returned again to town.

Louis XV received Charles at Fontainebleau 'with every mark of tender affection'. The returned hero, still thin and weatherbeaten after his five months on the run, dressed himself in a dandified way for the occasion. He wore a coat of rose-velvet, embroidered with silver, over a waistcoat in scalloped gold brocade. With his fashionably powdered wig and lace ruffles, none of his fellow fugitives would have recognized him as the ragged figure in the threadbare kilt and old black jacket of three months before.

He made a great impression on his mother's cousin, the kindly Queen Marie Leczinska, and her six daughters, who clustered round him avid for all the details of his adventures in Scotland. Later the Prince excused himself from this domestic scene, as he had been invited to a private supper by the King and his new mistress Jeanne Antoinette Poisson, now the Marquise de Pompadour. Madame de Pompadour and Charles did not take to one another. Charles, like many members of the French court, was snobbish about the Pompadour's bourgeois origins, and made it plain he thought she was rather common. On the other hand, as the Prince showed no signs of responding to the sexual magnetism to which she owed her position, the reigning mistress dismissed him, quite rightly, as a cold fish. For the penniless Prince it was *une occasion manquée*, and the animosity between the two was to prove disastrous for him during the next two years.

Meanwhile his father was writing from Albano:

> I cannot express to you, my dearest Carluccio, the joy and comfort I felt in receiving your letter from Morlaix of 10th October, after all I have suffered on your account for so many months past . . . I had promised Mr Warren that if he brought you back safe from Scotland I would make him a knight baronet, and accordingly you will find here enclosed a Warrant for that effect. I wish however that he would keep his warrant secret, because I am resolved to give no more such, or any Commissions, as long as our affairs remain in the situation they now are.

Having snubbed La Pompadour, the Prince for the only time in his life expressed a serious interest in marriage. He was attracted to the Princess Anne-Henriette, one of the six half-Polish royal princesses of France. But he wrote sadly to his father: 'My opinion is that I cannot as yet marry unless I get the King's daughter'. He was in no position, however, to ask for her hand.

The Marquis D'Eguilles, who had finally been released along with the other French troops in Scotland, presented Louis XV with a list of 240 Jacobite officers[2] to whom, at the Prince's request, the French King gave sums of money. Among these, as early as 25 October 1746 were the following:[3]

Milord Ogilvie. Brigadier and Colonel.	4,000 livres
Lochiel, Chef de Camerons, Brigadier.	4,000 livres
Colonel Archie Cameron (Lochiel's brother)	3,000 livres

This list was followed by D'Eguilles' statement concerning the numbers of English, Scots and Irish who had arrived in Paris as followers of Prince Edward.[4]

Baron Lochiel died at Bourges shortly after his arrival in France, and his eldest son, young Lochiel, was granted permission by Louis XV to raise a third Scottish Regiment for service with the King of France;[5] the other two were the Royal Ecossais and the Regiment of Ogilvie. D'Eguilles noted that young Lochiel was in Paris with two of his uncles: 'He is only seventeen or eighteen years of age and was a child when I knew him. I saw his father at the head of 1100 of his clansmen. Old Lochiel was an impressive man, head of the largest Jacobite clan with a great reputation for integrity which he well deserved, highly esteemed and loved by all who knew him. His death was a great loss to the House of Stuart.'

D'Eguilles' list of other leading Jacobites then permanently in exile in France included the following:

> Le Docteur Cameron, Lochiel's brother, and, since his death, guardian of Young Lochiel. The Doctor is in France to present his nephew, an estimable young man who has no other resources but the King of France. All his relations are proscribed and his home Achnacarry was burned before his eyes by Hanoverian troops . . . M. Jacques Hay, Major-Domo of the King's Household . . . He is a very gentle, unassuming man who does not know what will become of him. He had to leave his two children behind in Scotland to be brought up on charity. M. Macdonnell of Glenghari, the second son the Chieftain of the Macdonalds of Glengarry. He is only a boy of sixteen but nonetheless commanded his clan of 250 men from the day his elder brother was killed. M. Kelly, Irlandois, deacon of the Anglican church [D'Eguilles must be confusing the two Kellys, who were intimates of the Prince; both were disreputable, and one was a priest and the Prince's confessor].

The Regiments of Lochiel and Ogilvy were eventually raised and, with the Royal Ecossais, absorbed most of the able-bodied Jacobites. The original Scots Guards during the seventeenth and eighteenth century had gradually become almost entirely French. These new fighting regiments campaigned with the French army in Flanders against the Dutch, Hanoverians and Austrians for the remainder of the War of the Austrian Succession and later in the Seven Years War. Some of these first and second generation Scottish exiles made great names and fortunes for themselves in the French army under the *ancien régime* and later, after the revolution, in Napoleon's Grand Army. Macnabs and Macdonalds settled at Sancerre, near Aubigny in Berry, and the Uist schoolmaster who helped the Prince escape with Flora Macdonald to Skye, Niall MacEachain Macdonald, married a French wife at Sancerre and their son, the Maréchal Macdonald, became one of Napoleon's most famous Marshals, Prince de Tarente, and the victor of Wagram.

By the beginning of November 1746 Charles had finished his round of ceremonial calls at Versailles, and had returned to join his brother at Clichy—not, as it is now, the red-light district of Paris, but an attractive little village clustering on the slopes of Montmartre. After the first excitement of their reunion both brothers became quickly disillusioned. Their habits and temperaments were too dissimilar for them to endure living at close quarters for long. During his wanderings in the highlands Charles had grown addicted to the local whisky when his supplies of brandy had run out. Back in France, with little to occupy his time, he began drinking heavily again and was irritated by Henry's disapproval. As the Prince drank the spelling and punctuation of his letters grew worse. On 6 November he wrote to his father:

> I had been a little out of order, it being an indigestion but am entirely recovered, as I have had all the Kiks [Quacks?] of the Facalty, except bleeding, that has hindered me from wryting this week. I have as yet no positive answer from ye F.C. [French court] in regard to our manner of living here, except a regiro of M. d'Argenson sending his clark with a verbal message to Obrien, and making a most scandalous arrangement for us . . . I find it and am absolutely convinced of it that ye only way of dealing with this bloody Government is to give as short and sharp an answer as one can, at the same time paying them in their own coin by loding them with civilities and compliments, setting apart business, for that kind of Vermin, the more you give them, the more they'll take: as also the more room you give them the more they have to grapple at, which makes it necessary to be Laconick with them, which is the only way of passifying them and putting all shame on their backs which they would fairly try to shift with rigiros . . .

The King's private secretary, James Edgar, had the complicated task of dealing with rude, muddled and practically incomprehensible letters of this sort from the Prince, a task the gentle scholarly Edgar did with infinite patience. In the course of his routine correspondence with Sir John Graeme at St Germain Edgar learned that several gentlemen from his native county of Angus had arrived to join the regiment of Ogilvy. He asked Graeme to convey respects to Lord Ogilvy and to wish his regiment well in the Flanders campaign.

Charles's next letter to his father was both offhand and insolent:

> I have received yrs. of 12 November, which, as its being so long a-missing I gave it up for lost. I must owne my fault but I have not yet red all yr old letters that I received in one bundle upon my arrival in this country, my only excuse is I really did not imagine there was anything in them that needed to be answered immediately, had I thought otherwise I would have read them notwithstanding my being hurried in a manner every day mostly with trifles which notwithstanding cannot be neglected. Not being able to find Lord Sempill's cyphers which I have mislaid or lost, this hinders me from reading yrs of 19 April and 25 July you point out to me, but I shall certainly be able to answer them by the next post for I have immediately sent to Lord Sempill for his copy.

Relations were now very strained between the brothers. Henry complained to his father about the bad company Charles was keeping. This provoked a stream of censorious letters from James that infuriated the Prince, making him go from bad to worse. By the beginning of 1747 his behaviour was becoming a public scandal, and there was no longer any question of his being received in good society. He had made an implacable enemy in the now all-powerful Pompadour, who had never forgotten how he had slighted her at their first meeting.

On 3 February his harassed father wrote: 'When I consider your present situation, it is a subject of no small grief to me, because I see that you are misled and deluded to your great and universal prejudice by the craft of ill and designing men. I must tell you, my dear Charles, very plainly that, if you don't alter your ways, I see you lost in all respects.' On receipt of this Charles moved from Clichy to Poissy, further out in the country to the west of Paris, where he was joined by Sir John Graeme.

Graeme was beset with applications for money from the Jacobite exiles. On 27 February he wrote to James to tell him:

> Lord Ogilvy is at Versailles these eight days past waiting for a final decision concerning his Regiment. This will be an occasion for placing several of our unfortunate countrymen. Also there is a private letter from London which gives some hope that there may soon be an Act of Indemnity, in which case, I suppose many of those who are not attainted and have anything to return to, will go home.

This more optimistic news was counteracted by more accounts of the Prince's bad behaviour in Paris. He was said to have publicly insulted Madame de Pompadour, encouraged by the unscrupulous, designing schemer, the Polish-born Princesse de Talmont, who was at least twenty years older than Charles but was doing her best to seduce him. On receiving news of this latest scandal, James implored his son to mend his ways: 'Our misfortunes hinder us from being on an equal footing with the French court; they cannot but feel it and we cannot expect that they should have the same respect for us as if we were in England, and how are we ever to get their goodwill and assistance? Believe me there is nothing to be got by hectoring them.'

In spite of Charles's continual indiscretions, Louis XV was very generous to him, paying him a regular pension of 8,000 livres a month from 1 October 1746 onwards,[6] and allowing him 3,600 livres a month to maintain his immediate entourage. By January 1748 Charles had received 222,000 livres in all.

To the relief of everyone connected with him, the Prince left Paris in the spring of 1747 to look up old friends in Avignon, and to visit his cousin the King of Spain. In Avignon he stayed with Lady Inverness, who, as always, was ready to lend him any money she had. The new King of Spain, Ferdinand VI, through his mother Marie-Louise of Savoy, was a great-grandson of Henriette Anne, Duchesse d'Orléans and a great-nephew of Charles's own grandmother, Mary of Modena, who had greeted his birth with such joy in October 1713. The Queen Dowager, Elisabeth Farnese, who had worked for the restoration of the Stuarts with Cardinal Alberoni, welcomed Charles, but otherwise his reception in Madrid was distinctly cool. He called on his Berwick relations at the Palacio Liria, and returned to France with the promise of some sort of pension from the Spanish King.

During his brother's absence in Spain Henry, who was now twenty-two and sick and tired of the life he was being forced to lead in Paris, slipped away to Rome. He had been in correspondence with the Pope for some months about his desire to enter the Church. The younger Stuart brother, who had a much sounder head on his shoulders than Charles, had decided once and for all that their cause was hopeless, and preferred to renounce all claims to an earthly crown by becoming a Prince of the Roman Catholic Church.

Charles was kept completely ignorant of what was happening. The first he knew of Henry's desertion was a letter from his father of 13 June 1747:

> I know not whether you will be surprised, my dearest Carluccio, when I tell you that your brother will be made a Cardinal in the first days of next month. Naturally speaking you should have been consulted about a resolution of that kind before it had been executed, but as the Duke and I were unalterably determined on that matter, and foresaw you might probably not approve, we thought it should be done before your answer could come here, and to have it in your power to say it was done without your knowledge or approbation.

The news came as a shock to Charles who rightly saw it (as the exiled Charles II before him had regarded the possible apostasy of Harry, Duke of Gloucester) as a mortal blow to his chances of ever becoming King of Protestant England. Those two spiteful bachelors Horace Walpole and Horace Mann, in letters to each other on the subject, could not contain their glee that the younger Stuart brother, by his action, had irreparably damaged the Jacobite cause.

Henry's decision to become the Cardinal York was the beginning of a long estrangement between the brothers, who were not on speaking terms for the next eighteen years. The estrangement came from Charles's side, not Henry's. On 20 June 1747 the newly ordained prelate wrote from their father's villa outside Rome to assure the Prince of his most respectful love and tender affection. Charles did not answer Henry, but wrote angrily to his father instead: 'I have received yrs of the 13th and 20th June and had I got a dagger throw my heart I would not have been more sensible at ye contents. I hope your Majesty will forgive me not entering any further on so disagreeable a subject the shock of which I am scarce out of . . .'

The unanimous reaction of the Jacobites in Paris is summed up in a letter from one of their number to James. 'The general distraction is only equal to the confusion in your Majesty's subjects here in agreeing it a mortal, deadly stroke to the Cause. His R.H. (I am told, for I don't go near him) has shut himself up for several hours alone upon hearing the news, and the Duke's health is no more drunk nor his name mentioned at table.'

Charles reacted to his brother's betrayal by ostentatiously frequenting the fashionable free-thinking circles of the *philosophes* in Paris. He became an habitué of these anti-religious avant-garde salons, into which he was introduced by the Princess de Talmont. He ran even deeper into debt, borrowing from the ever-obliging young Waters, and left nearly all his father's letters unanswered.

The news from Scotland was heartbreaking. The Prince who had lived, as he would never live again, an outdoor life of action during his year in the Highlands, now heard nothing but accounts of the savage oppression of those left behind in that beautiful tragic country: the merciless hunting down of the clans, the proscribing of the chiefs and the Jacobite landowners, and the shipping off of clansmen in batches to the plantations in North Carolina and the West Indies as the clearances of the glens began. The wearing of the tartan was forbidden, and military roads linked the chain of forts from Fort William on the west coast of Inverness-shire up the Great Glen by Fort Augustus to Fort George (the names are indicative enough) on the Moray Firth near Inverness.

In spite of his worldly life in Paris society, Charles felt utterly bereft without the companions who had helped to plan and who had shared his great adventure. He missed the restraining influence of old Sir Thomas

Sheridan, his friend and mentor since childhood. Aeneas Macdonald had been forced to surrender to General Campbell, and was first imprisoned in Dumbarton Castle before being transferred to Edinburgh and then by sea to London. There, contrary to the terms of surrender, he was imprisoned in Newgate along with Flora Macdonald. He was tried and condemned to death but subsequently pardoned. In 1747 he was still a prisoner, along with many of the Prince's closest associates. Strickland, an emaciated wreck, had died at Carlisle.

The Prince drank even more heavily to ease his sense of failure, guilt and loss, and the uncertainty about the future. When he drank, it was always to excess, and he became offensive to friends and enemies alike. Many of his other Jacobite friends were fighting in the War of the Austrian Succession. By the spring of 1748 the French had suffered heavy losses, and the preliminaries of the Peace of Aix-la-Chapelle were being discussed.

One of the terms insisted upon by the English Government was the expulsion of the Young Pretender from France. When Charles was informed of this condition of the Treaty, he exploded with indignation. On 20 August 1748 he wrote in the strongest terms, in French with his usual mis-spellings, to Louis XV through his Secretary-of-State, the Marquis de Puysieulx.[7]

> I oppose and shall oppose absolutely all that will be said, done and stipulated at Aix-la-Chapelle or anywhere else. I hope that His Most Christian Majesty will think seriously about my position. I regard this agreement as being more dangerous for his interests than mine. I beg Your Majesty with all my respect and devotion. Nothing is nearer my heart than to be of use to him one day and to prove to him that his true interests are dearer to me than to his Ministers. Charles P.[8]

The Treaty of Aix-la-Chapelle was finally signed in the middle of September and ratified in the middle of October 1784. Since Charles showed not the slightest intention of moving from Paris with his entourage, the French King was compelled to send him a copy of the terms of the Treaty, ordering him to leave France without further delay. There was no ambiguity about the King's wishes in this matter:

> My Ministers Plenipotentiary having signed at Aix-la-Chapelle on the 18th of last month the definite Treaty of peace by which all the European powers have renewed the engagements they have contracted on different occasions on the subject of the succession to the throne of Great Britain, my intention is to carry out what has been agreed in this matter. I shall be obliged if the Prince Charles Edward will make this easy for me by definitely quitting all the

territories of my Dominions. I have too good an opinion of his wisdom and good sense to think he will act against my wishes. My cousin the Duc de Gesvres will explain to him in detail my instructions. I hope that Prince Charles Edward will respond in a way which will justify the esteem and affection in which I hold him. Given at Fontainebleau the 4th October 1748.

Signed. Louis.

Like a defiant child, the Prince remained stupidly obstinate, ignoring with gross discourtesy this order from his host and benefactor. He did not reply to the King's letter but continued to be seen at public gatherings, accepting invitations to dinners and balls (even if these were not of the highest class) and attending the opera, of which he was particularly fond. Louis XV had no other course open to him but to write a stiff letter to James III in Rome ordering him to command his son and heir to remove himself from France immediately.

James, deeply mortified, acted at once, sending a five-page letter to Charles on 23 November 1748. The translation of the copy made for the French Foreign Office archives leaves no doubt as to the King's feelings about the Prince's behaviour:

However carefully you have concealed, my dear son, what has passed between the French Court and you since the signing of the Peace, I am nevertheless informed of all, and I tell you that I read with surprise and sorrow your letter to the Duc de Gesvres on the 6th of this month. Neither you nor anyone else could imagine that you could remain in France against the will of the King.

Certainly no sane and reasonable person however much they may be hostile to France, if he really wanted your good, would counsel you, above all in the situation in which you find yourself, to break with a power which is respected throughout Europe. . . . You know very well your conduct towards me has not been what it should, and you also know with what patience and moderation I have borne with you and the entire liberty I have always given you but, in the present circumstances I can remain silent no longer, seeing you on the brink of a precipice and about to fall into the abyss. I should be an unnatural father if I did not do the least I can to save you from yourself, and that is why I find myself obliged to order you as your father and as your Sovereign to conform without delay to His Most Christian Majesty's will, in leaving his dominions with good grace . . .

Finally, my dear son, consider seriously what you are going to do if you disobey my orders and the orders of His Most Christian Majesty. I foresee that they will make you do by force if necessary what you will not do of your own free will. And, if it comes to violence, naturally they will bring you to this place [Rome] which I am sure would not be to your taste nor in your interest. What a scandal it will cause and what will you gain from it except a bad name and character which will lose for you in an instant all the reputation and admiration you have built up for yourself; for virtue and courage that does not show itself wise in adversity will never be regarded as true and enduring.

Judge for yourself the pain and anxiety which your behaviour causes me, in which state I shall remain until I know the effects of this letter upon you. It is written by a father who feels nothing but tenderness for you and whose only concern is your good and your true glory.

I pray God to enlighten you and embrace you with all my heart.

James R.[9]

Every word in his father's letter made sense, but its effect on the truculent Charles was that of an old preacher droning on and on, and it antagonized him even more. He took no notice of it and continued his round of pleasures and distractions in Paris. What he thought would be the outcome, if he thought at all, no one knows.

Retribution came swiftly and unexpectedly on the night of 10 December 1748, on his way to attend a performance of the Italian opera at the Palais Royal. As his coach trundled down the crowded rue St Honoré, a well-wisher pushed a scribbled paper through the window warning the Prince to expect trouble. He shrugged his shoulders and the coach drove on. As he was getting out in the narrow cul-de-sac at the entrance to the Opera, four sergeants of the guard of the Governor of Paris set upon him, bound his hands behind his back with cords, removed his sword as he continued to struggle, and placed him under arrest, along with the friends who were with him in the carriage. To add insult to injury, the officer in charge of the operation was one of the Prince's acquaintances, a Monsieur de Vaudreuil, who was acting under the orders of the Marquis de Chatelet, the Governor of Paris.

The Prince was not taken to the Bastille but to the château de Vincennes to the east of the city. There he was shut up in a bare little room without a fire, although the weather was freezing cold. The Captain of the Guard sent a report to the Foreign Secretary at Versailles: 'Monseigneur, I have the honour to inform Your Excellency that M. de Vaudreuil has arrested the Prince Edward in the cul-de-sac of the Opera. M. de Vaudreuil had him seized by four sergeants. The members of his suite were also arrested.'[10] Another note adds the details of his hands being tied and of his being left for two hours in the room without a fire at Vincennes, as no orders had been received there for dealing with the distinguished prisoner.

The scandal of the Prince's arrest ran round Paris like wildfire. For the first two days of his imprisonment he was not allowed to communicate with anyone outside. But as soon as his cousin the Duc de Fitzjames, who was a member of the King and Madame de Pompadour's intimate circle, heard the news, he wrote to the Secretary-of-State Maurepas asking him to try and get the King's permission for him to visit his cousin with other members of the Fitzjames family. This letter, in the Duke's small neat handwriting, states in French: 'You are aware, Monsieur, of my attachment, my duty and my respect for the Prince who was yesterday imprisoned at Vincennes. I beg you to authorize if at all possible, the visit of my mother and myself and the rest of our family to the Prince to pay him the duty and respect we owe him."[11]

This letter is marked that the King had not judged it suitable to grant the permission requested by Fitzjames. The next note in the dossier on the Prince's arrest in the French Foreign Office Archives is one addressed to Cardinal Tencin, reporting to him the steps that were being taken to force Prince Charles Edward to leave all territory under the jurisdiction of the French King.[12]

At last, on 12 December, the injured Prince managed to obtain some writing paper and a pen and sat down to pour out an impassioned scrawl to Louis XV. He protested against his ignominious arrest and avowed his 'unalterable attachment for the sacred person of His Most Christian Majesty. I cannot express to Your Majesty the state of extreme anxiety in which I have been all this time'. He continued contritely, 'I am ready to leave immediately from Your Majesty's territories if that is what He wishes', and finished, with a mixture of exaggerated politeness and familiarity, 'I have the honour to be, Monsieur my Brother and Cousin, Your Majesty's good Brother and Cousin, Charles. P.R.'[13]

This epistle was followed up the next day, 13 December 1748, by an incredibly badly spelt, ill-punctuated letter, in a huge childish scrawl to Maurepas: 'Du Donjon de Vensaine le 13 décembre [from the fortress of Vincennes]. Having seen, Sir, your letter of yesterday to the Marquis of Chatelet by which I am obliged to leave here accompanied by an individual who will escort me as far as the Alps, my health does not permit any further delay and so I beg you, Sir, to send this person immediately and I shall leave the same evening. Your good friend, Charles. Prince Regent.'[14] On receiving this appeal, Maurepas who had been Charles's friend at the time of the Forty-five, when he was French Minister of Marine, got in touch with the Foreign Secretary and gave the following pledges if the Prince could be released immediately. The conditions Maurepas drew up for Charles to sign were as follows:

1 To retire within the space of eight days from all territories under the domination of the King of France, leaving by the Pont de Beauvoisin.
2 That he will no account pass through Paris.
3 That he will not stay in Lyon or in any other town of consequence in France.

4 That he will be accompanied on his journey only by those persons specified on the list he has presented and which His Majesty has been pleased to approve.

The Marquis de Derussy will communicate these conditions to the Prince Edouard and will ask for his reply in the presence of the Marquis de Chatelet and the officers of the guard and have them signed by the Prince before they are put into force.

The Prince gave his word of honour and signed the articles. The next day, 15 December, he was released from Vincennes and allowed to leave for the Papal States in Italy.

He left wearing the uniform of an Irish officer in the Spanish army,[15] the same disguise he had used nearly five years before when he had set out from Italy for France to prepare the Forty-five rising. He was accompanied by the few members of his personal suite who had been arrested with him. The little party left the outskirts of Paris under escort and were put on the road south in the direction of the Alps. It was midwinter and bitterly cold. After two years of riotous living in the French capital, the Prince no longer had the resistance of the wiry young man who had tramped the Scottish glens and scrambled over mountain passes, sleeping in the open, wrapped in an old plaid. He had grown soft and pampered, and was sulky and ill-tempered after his humiliation at the hands of the French King; he fumed against any idea of returning to be fussed over and scolded by his father and patronized by his virtuous younger brother in Rome.

They got as far as St Marcellin on the route for Savoy and the Alpine passes, but there Charles suddenly decided he could not face the prospect of leaving France. He told his followers abruptly that they were returning to Avignon. He insisted stubbornly that Avignon was still Papal territory, so that he was not breaking his word of honour.

They abandoned their worn-out horses at St Marcellin, where they hired post-horses that were not much better and made an uncomfortable journey through blizzards on icy roads until they reached Orange in the Rhône valley. They left the post-horses at Orange and hired a post-chaise for the Prince and two of his friends, who set out ahead of the others for Avignon. There they went straight to the house of Lady Inverness, and received the warm welcome they had counted on. Charles was even more delighted to find that his former Governor, Lord Dunbar, was staying with his sister.

The Military Governor of Avignon wrote to Versailles on 28 December 1748, giving news of the Prince's arrival.[16] His letter to the Secretary-of-State says: 'Sir, I have the honour to inform you that the Prince Edward arrived this morning incognito in this town. After the 31st he will stay with the Papal Legate while a residence worthy of His Royal Highness is made ready to receive him. He has still seen neither the Legate nor the Archbishop . . .'

The Prince celebrated his twenty-eighth birthday on New Year's Eve at the house of Lady Inverness in the rue Dorée. All the Jacobite exiles in Avignon were invited to the house to toast the occasion with copious drams, for which Charles had developed too much of a liking. A few days later accommodation was found for him in the Palais des Papes, where he set up his minuscule court. He rode to take up residence to the sound of a royal salute of fifty-two guns. His official arrival in Avignon was celebrated in verse by several local poets who enthusiastically turned out doggerel of the most banal sort.[17]

The news was less joyfully received in Rome. On 31 December, the Prince's birthday, James Edgar was occupied in writing to Waters, the banker in Paris:

> Sir, A courier arrived here on Thursday night from Paris bringing an account of the Prince's being forced to leave France. This is so moving a subject and swells my heart to such a degree that I cannot express what I feel upon it. I earnestly pray to God to preserve and support H.R.H. in all the tryalls and hardships he is put to, and I beg, when you hear anything particular about him personally you would let me know it. You will find enclosed an order of the King's for paying 200 livres to the order of Mrs Stewart, the Colonel's widow [widow of the Chevalier James Stuart of Goodtrees].

By 21 January 1749 James Edgar was a little less anxious about the fate of Charles. Writing to O'Sullivan in Paris, he says: 'You may be sure I shared with you in your uneasiness occasioned by what happened lately to the Prince but understanding last week he was at Avignon and in good health, I am now much easier on that article, and I pray God he may be allowed to stay there undisturbed as long as he finds it convenient for him.'

However, this was not to be. The Prince's dubious associates from Paris followed him to Avignon, and the old round of drinking and quarrelling in public places began again and soon became the talk of the town. Charles had no known romances during his stay in the Papal city, but instead, to relieve his boredom, he introduced the English sport of boxing, which was viewed with grave disfavour by the church authorities. By this time he had moved out of the Palais des Papes and had acquired a house of his own, where he laid down an impressive wine cellar. Sir Thomas Sheridan's nephew Michael and another survivor of the Forty-five, Henry Stafford—the one who had gone to Spain to raise money—were in charge of the household arrangements. The Prince gave wild drinking parties in these bachelor quarters and generally made a nuisance of himself in the city.

The Hanoverian Government, which had been protesting to the French King about the Young Stuart Pretender remaining on French territory ever since his departure from Paris, now put pressure on the Pope to expel him. They threatened to send the British Navy to bombard Civitavecchia if Benedict XII did not order Charles to leave Avignon immediately. The Prince's excesses and continual disturbances of the peace provoked the Pope to submit to these demands.

So, early in February 1749, once more in the depths of winter, Prince Charles Edward, accompanied only by his bosom friend Henry Goring, rode out of Avignon and headed for the snowbound Alps, just as his father had done thirty years before but in rather more dignified circumstances. His house and retainers were kept on in Avignon, supervised from time to time, by Lady Inverness. The Scottish Countess had changed her first name of Marjory to Marie-Marcelle, and grew more and more French in her manners and way of living. She and her brother, Lord Dunbar, both ended their days in Avignon. Her devotion to the Prince, as to his father, was remarkable; she always treated him with the tenderness she would have given to a difficult son. When she died two years after James III in 1768, she left all she possessed, 100 louis d'or, to the Prince, whom she described in her will as her rightful sovereign King Charles III. Lord Dunbar, who survived his sister, wrote a wry little note on the occasion of her death, informing the Prince of the legacy, saying he was 'extremely concerned at the account you give me of your circumstances which make so small a sum left to you by my poor sister of such consequence to you'.

After crossing the Alps, Charles and Goring stopped to consider where they should go. The thought of paternal advice and disapproval made them avoid Rome, where the long-suffering James waited in vain for the son he longed so much to see.

The carnival in Venice was still in progress so the pair decided to head there. This was the start of the Prince's mysterious wanderings about Europe, during which he tapped any source he could for financial support, and used a series of pseudonyms to sign the endless notes he scribbled to agents and associates everywhere except in Rome. He seldom bothered to reply to any letters he received from his father and, in fact, never set eyes on him again.

The official connection of the royal Stuarts with France was now at an end, though the oldest and poorest of the Jacobite exiles lingered on at St Germain for the next twenty years.

18

THE WANDERING PRINCE

DURING THE TWENTY YEARS he spent travelling round Europe, Charles kept his eye on England, ever hopeful that at the appropriate moment his 'cher Oncle et Cousin' the King of France might, in spite of all that had gone before, use him once again to discomfit their old enemy. Louis XV lived on until 1774, growing less and less the 'bien aimé' of his disgruntled subjects. In the Seven Years War France's loss of her possessions in Canada and India did nothing to restore confidence in his power. In 1759, Pitt's year of victory at Quebec, serious plans were made by Louis and his Foreign Minister, the Duc de Choiseul, for another attempt in Scotland,[1] but these plans were abandoned after the defeat of the entire French fleet by Admiral Hawke off Quiberon Bay. This date finally ended all Stuart hopes of a restoration with French help.

During the ten years after his departure from Avignon on the last day of February 1749 the Prince seldom stayed longer than a few months in any one place. His first port of call, with his boon companion and equerry, Henry Goring, was Venice. The pair found the place greatly to their liking, and would have been delighted to prolong their stay in this amusing unshockable city, where every pleasure was catered for, at a price. As usual, shortage of cash was their problem rather than the disapproval of their public behaviour by the Church. In Venice the Church had been conveniently tamed by the secular government of the Doge. Dashing off one of his rare brief notes to his father from 'Venise, ye 17th May 1749', Charles says gaily: 'My health is perfect and I hope soon to give notice to Your Majesty of my being well received and protected here. In ye mean time I keep myself absolutely private for iff there was the least sent of it, many oppositions would be made to hinder me from remaining in a place that, next to France, is best for my Interest and the only one in Italy'. However, someone was put on his scent, and he was asked to leave Venice by the end of that month.

What he really needed were sympathizers who would be willing to harbour him secretly in France, but this was not so easy. Neither his Fitzjames relations nor the family of the Duc de Bouillon could risk incurring the King's displeasure on his account. Through the ever-ardent Princesse de Talmont, however, Charles was able to make a convenient arrangement with two wealthy 'dames pensionnaires' in a fashionable convent in the Faubourg St Germain in Paris. These were an attractive young widow, Madame de Vassé, and her blue-stocking friend Mademoiselle Ferrand, who had adjoining rooms in St Joseph's Convent, the worldly religious establishment in the rue St Dominique to which Madame de Montespan had retired after being implicated in the scandalous affair of the poisons. Charles had most probably met these two young women when he had frequented the *philosophe* salons before he was expelled from Paris.

In June 1749 the Prince got in touch with Mademoiselle Ferrand and asked if she would act as a *poste-restante* for him under the name of Monsieur John Douglas. As well as using these women as a postal service, he also commissioned them to obtain for him such luxuries from England as soap, razors and the latest novels. His other vital contact in Paris was young Waters the banker, and it was most likely at Waters' house in the rue de Verneuil that the Prince stayed when he visited the capital incognito. Aeneas Macdonald seems to have been dropped in a callous manner by Charles when he was eventually released from Newgate after the Forty-five, although he returned to end his days in Paris and died during the Revolution.

In spite of the admiration of the ladies in St Joseph's Convent, there were still no signs of any serious love interest in the Prince's life. The Princesse de Talmont, much as she would have liked the rôle, was no Diane de Poitiers. For all his Stuart-Sobieski good looks and seeming virility, there is no evidence of any homosexual attachments; Charles, like his father and great-grandfather Charles I was simply cold sexually. He attracted the deepest devotion from both sexes, but either through excessive spoiling as a child or an exaggerated egotism in relation to his rank and aspirations, he remained immune from the tender passion all his life. For his thirtieth birthday he received the inevitable boring letter from his father, urging him for God's sake to marry and settle down for the sake of continuing the Stuart dynasty.

> Tomorrow you end your thirtieth year. May you see many more than double that number and happier ones than those already past. The hardships you have gone through and do perhaps still undergo are not small and it is to be hoped they will contribute at last to what they are chiefly directed. But in the darkness you keep me as to all that relates to you, I can neither judge nor

> advise, except on one single article which is so obvious and so important and that is securing the succession of our family by marrying . . . I am so much convinced of the necessity of your marrying that I could almost say I would rather see you marryed to a private gentlewoman than that you should not be it at all. I recommend you earnestly to think seriously on this matter and, as you now cannot hope to make a marriage suteable to yourself, to endeavour to make one as little unequal as possible.[2]

The Prince ignored this letter, as he had all the others on the same subject. But by September 1752, in a fit of optimism, he had decided the best step for him to take if he was ever to become King of England was to follow the example of his French ancestor Henri of Navarre and change his inconvenient religion. He sailed from Antwerp and arrived in London on 16 September, turning up unannounced at the house of a well known hostess, Lady Primrose, in Essex Street, just off the Strand. Lady Primrose was the widow of the Jacobite Sir Archibald Primrose, executed at Carlisle in 1746. Since the general amnesty she had blossomed in fashionable society and was giving a card-party when the Prince walked in that afternoon. It is probable that he stayed at her house, for before the month was out he had been received into the Anglican communion at the Church of St Mary-le-Strand, less than five minutes' walk from Essex Street. There is no official record of Charles's conversion, but the church has always had Stuart connections. It contains a beautiful diptych on wood of Charles I and Henrietta Maria, and it is there that the annual commemoration service for King Charles the Martyr is held on the anniversary of his execution on 30 January.

Having agreed to abide by the Thirty-nine Articles of the Church of England, which his father and grandfather could never accept for themselves, and for which his great-grandfather had died, the Prince strolled off to have a look at the defences of the Tower of London. He ended the day by dining in Pall Mall with two highly placed Jacobite sympathizers, the Duke of Beaufort and the Earl of Westmorland. They ate well and lingered over the wine and brandy, but the unsatisfactory outcome of the evening was that these gentlemen did not consider the time ripe for action.

Disappointed, Charles left for the continent as mysteriously as he had come. A week or so after his departure Lady Primrose made a trip to Antwerp with a message for the Prince that Clementina Walkinshaw, with whom he had spent a romantic few days in Scotland in 1746, was arriving shortly to enter a chapter of Honorary Canonesses at Douai. Clementina's eldest sister Janet was well known at the Hanoverian Court, where she occupied the post of woman-of-the-bedchamber to the

Princess Augusta, widow of Frederick George, Prince of Wales, who had died in 1751, and who, true to family tradition, had hated and was hated by his father George II. It is more than probable that Clementina was on a visit to London and that Charles had renewed his acquaintance with her at the house in Essex Street. The daughter of a Jacobite spy, she could well have been useful to the Prince as a source of information about the internal politics of the Hanoverian royal family. She was no beauty and at thirty-two was still a spinster. Whatever the reason, she travelled to Antwerp about the same time as Lady Primrose and met Charles in October 1752. She apparently agreed to become his mistress, living with him in Paris and Flanders, and moving with him from Brussels to Ghent and then to Liége.

At first the liaison was as happy as could be expected with someone of the Prince's indifferent and difficult temperament, but their shared memories of a brief encounter during the Forty-five soon lost their charm for Charles. When Clementina became pregnant, the Prince grew bored and irritated and started to drink heavily again. The frequent quarrels of the obviously ill matched pair became a source of embarrassment to the Jacobites until the discovery of the Elibank Conspiracy in March 1753 diverted their attention from the unsavoury personal life of the Prince.

This was an absurd plot to kidnap the whole Hanoverian royal family. The ill prepared affair was betrayed by a Jacobite traitor, Young Glengarry, and the scapegoat, although he had nothing to do with this crazy scheme, was Doctor Archibald Cameron, brother of the dead Lochiel. Since 1746 he had been living in France, and had served as surgeon to the Regiment of Ogilvy stationed at Orléans. In 1751 he had returned to Scotland after the general amnesty on a secret mission with Macdonald of Glengarry to try to recover the French gold sent to the Prince in 1746 and buried at Loch Arkaig near the Cameron house of Achnacarry. Doctor Cameron was seized and thrown into the Tower of London, where he was condemned to be hanged, drawn and quartered at Tyburn, although he protested on his honour to the last moment that he had nothing to do with the Elibank Conspiracy, and had only returned to Scotland to recover the money left behind by Prince Charles Edward.

To his eldest son in France, the night before his execution, the last Jacobite martyr wrote on slips of paper with a blunt pencil that broke before he had finished the letter:

> My dear Child, I am far less concerned about myself than about my friends and my ruined country. I thank God I am hearty and in much better health than I have been for some years past, more especially since I saw that letter which gives me such hopes of your future conduct from the desire you express in it that I should rather sacrifice my life than save it on dishonourable terms. I

> thank God I was always easier ashamed than frightened. It is with the highest satisfaction that I have for some time observed in you a sense of honour and loyalty much beyond what could have been expected in a boy of your years, and tho' death will soon deprive me of the power of being of farther service to my king, my prince and my country, yet, what greatly adds to my satisfaction is the principle you shew in your letter to your mother on the news of my being in custody, and the confidence you have in my fidelity to the royal cause.
>
> I have no money to leave you as a legacy, but take what is of infinite more value viz: above all things, first serve God, next your king, prince and country: and then always be in your duty to your mother, brothers and sisters: act honestly by your neighbour: meddle in no party quarrels, but when you are personally wronged, demand justice with coolness, regularity and resolution without personal reflections. Beware of ever speaking to the disadvantage of the absent, even though they should deserve it. I recommend you in a particular manner in the care of your health. Observe great moderation in eating: at any rate abstain from heavy and late suppers: and above all avoid drinking and whoring. Be a good economist of your little money and clothes. Let the company you frequent be your betters rather than your inferiors. My time and writing implements allow me only to recommend my most hearty thanks to my Colonel [Lord Ogilvy]. Don't neglect your duty to him. My love and dying benediction to my children, affection to my brother's children, best wishes to all my friends and hearty compliments to all my good acquaintance . . .[3]

Here he was obliged to leave off for want of a knife to cut his bit of pencil, pen, ink and proper writing paper having been refused him.

On the next day, before being dragged through the streets of London on a sledge to be tortured and hanged, he sent a pair of shoe-buckles to his son with the message: 'Tell him from me that I send him these and not my silver ones and that if I had gold I would not send him gold but these steel ones which I wore when sculking. For as steel is hard and of small value, it is therefore an emblem of constancy and disinterestedness. So I would have him constant and disinterested in the service of his king, prince and his country, and neither be bribed nor frightened from his duty.'

The Scottish Episcopal clergyman chosen to attend him on the scaffold has left this account of Dr Cameron's behaviour there: 'When this gentleman came to the place of execution he looked on the officers and spectators with undaunted and composed countenance; and as soon as he was loosed from the sledge, he stept up into the cart with the help of one of his executioners, whence, looking round at the awful apparatus of death, he smiled, and seeing the clergyman who attended him coming up the steps, he came forward to meet him and endeavoured with his fettered hands to help him up, saying, "So you are come?" '

At the special pleading of the widowed Hanoverian Princess of Wales (mother of the future George III) the last horror of being cut down and having his heart and bowels torn out and burned before his eyes was spared him. Princess Augusta of Saxe-Gotha's request that Dr Cameron should be given a decent burial in the Queen's Chapel of the Savoy was respected. The closest adviser of George II's daughter-in-law was John Stuart, Earl of Bute; and Lord Waldegrave, grandson of an illegitimate daughter of James II and Arabella Churchill, acted as Governor to the Hanoverian heir. George III and his son the Prince Regent were always as sympathetic as they could be to the Stuarts.

The news of Dr Archie Cameron's death reached Charles at Ghent and sent him into a deep depression that did not make him any easier to live with. A few months later, in October 1753, his Scottish mistress gave birth to a daughter at Liége, the only child the Prince ever had. She was baptized as a Roman Catholic at the Church of Our Lady of the Fountains, where the parish register records the infant as being the daughter of the noble Seigneur William Johnston and the noble Dame Charlotte Pitt. The godfather was James Keith, the brother of Earl Marischal, who appears under the pseudonym of the noble Seigneur Andrew Giffard. The Prince took his daughter from the arms of Clementina Walkinshaw and held her himself at the font, giving her the uncomplicated name of Charlotte Stuart.

The arrival of a squalling infant, and a female one at that, did not crown the happiness of the couple—rather the reverse. Their quarrels in public taverns became the talk of Liége. Less than two weeks after Lady Charlotte Stuart's christening, her father was writing in a furious temper to his equerry Henry Goring:

> I have wrote to Avignon for to discard all my Papist servants. I shall maintain ye two gentlemen Henry Stafford and Michael Sheridan and all ye Protestant servants on the same footing as usual. My mistress has behaved so unworthily that she has put me out of all patience and, as she is a Papist too, I discard her also!!! P.S. She told me she has friends that would maintain her, so that, after such a declaration and other impertinences, makes me abandon her. I hereby desire you to find out who her friends are, that she may be delivered into their hands. Daniel [the Prince's valet] is charged to conduct her to Paris.
>
> I remain anew your sincere friend,
>
> John Douglas.

From Avignon Stafford and Sheridan, who were in charge of his house and possessions there, replied with justifiable indignation:

> Yesterday we received a letter without a name desiring us to send Daniel to Paris. We followed your instructions. We should have informed you sooner had we known your address that we changed lodgings, sold the coach and eight horses. The coach for 1,976 livres, seven horses at 600 livres each and an

eighth for 16 louis d'or. One dyed of the staggers. Another we still have on our hands. Shall we sell him to the first that bids money for him? The letter desires us to give the money to John Stuart. You know that you ordered us to put all your effects into the Vice-Legate's custody which we did accordingly; except the papers in Mr Sheridan's keeping. When you think it proper to give us your address, shall lett you know what passes here. Sir James has wrote for his books.

Your most obedient servants,
H. Stafford. M. Sheridan.

On 10 April 1754 the Prince again wrote to the pair at Avignon:

Mr Stafford and Mr Sheridan,

My last was of ye 18 Janry. This is to let you know that as I am extremely necessitous for want of money, it engages me out of Economy to send for Daniell Obrions clothes which you are to pack up in his own trunc and send it addressed to Mr Woulfe [the Prince] at Paris, but let there be in ye trunc none of Daniell's papers or anything else except his Close. I expect daily accounts from your parts. In the meantime I remain yr sincere friend,

John Douglas.

In the summer following the birth of his daughter the Prince made a desperate appeal to James Edgar in Rome: 'My situation is terrible, the more that, in reality I cannot see any method or appearance of its Bettering. Shall give an account to my Master of all my proceedings as soon as in my power, for the present it is not possible to put severall things in writing: you cannot imagine how many Crosses I meet with, but never shall any hinder me from doing what I think to be the best.'

James III heard with dismay that his son and heir was living openly with a commoner mistress, by whom he had had an illegitimate daughter. However, as this fact proved that at least the Prince, if he chose, was capable of continuing the Stuart line with legitimate heirs, it made the old King harp on the same old theme in those birthday letters Charles had come to dread:

December 31st 1754. King James to Mr John Douglas.[4]
Though it is always a comfort to me to receive my Deare Friend's letters, yet I own that yours of 24 November was at the same time of great concern and affliction to me. What you had writ some months ago made me hope you were beginning to open your eyes to your present situation, but from what you now say, you appear more fixed than ever in your former scheme. In that case you will pass your life in obscurity and will let our Family end for the want of providing for its succession. All this cannot be your own thoughts or work, but those of others. You look upon them to be your friends and I cannot say they are otherwise, because I know them not. But I can see, and so may all the

world, that if they were your greatest enemies they could not take more effective measures to ruin both your interest and your reputation and to put you under a sort of necessity of never getting out of their hands. They have drove you into a labyrinth out of which it will be hard to extricate yourself.

The harassed Prince, with his railing mistress and bastard child, moved from Flanders to Switzerland. In 1755 Lord Elcho, to whom the Prince had owed a considerable sum of money since September 1745, wrote spitefully in his journal: 'While I was at Neuchâtel, the Prince Stuart was living in Basle with a Miss Walkinshaw who passed herself off as his wife and he posed as an English doctor of the name of Thomson. They remained undiscovered for a long time until a print-seller displaying a portrait of Prince Charles Edouard in his window, attracted attention to the resemblance between the Prince and the supposed Dr Thomson.' Elcho went on: 'He changed his religion at Basle and made it publicly known that henceforth he was a Protestant. He treats Miss Walkinshaw very badly and at Basle is regarded as the worst of husbands.'

From Switzerland the unhappy ménage returned to Lorraine where they were invited by the Prince's first cousin, the childless Duc de Bouillon to stay at the Château de Bouillon near Sedan. The Prince was even more weighed down by his financial difficulties. Henry Stafford kept writing from Avignon for permission to sell more and more of his master's possessions in order to keep himself and Sheridan alive. It was months since they had been paid any wages. In answer to the Prince's grand instructions to sell the contents of his wine cellar, Stafford wrote back: 'The wine can't be sold, as the good can't be distinguished from the bad, nobody will buy altogether. I believe it best to keep them till you can drink them yourself.' Another curt note from Stafford said on 31 October:

Sir, I received the honour of yours of the 21st and shan't miss the first opportunity of selling the Chair (Sedan chair), it may lye on my hands for many months without I sell it at under price. I have a gold watch and some other moveables which I'll sell or pledge, as for credit, I have none. If you could employ the footman elsewhere, it would lessen the expense, he is quite useless to me. I only have enough wood to boil my pot, and shall endeavour to pass the winter without fire. I am with due respect. H. Stafford.
P.S. If I am hear on the 1st Feb. I must pay 6 months rent for my lodgings.

The Prince replied:

Mr Stafford. I received yours of 31 October and ye contents give me concern. You should apply to Lady Inverness to lend you one hundred Louidors. Shure Shee won't refuse you when I answer to get it remitted to her in six months—

the servant may still be kept in this manner and yr self too as usuall. Do not delay answering.

Yr sincere friend. J. Douglas. Bouillon. 11 november.

Stafford wrote on 23 November 1757:

Sir, I yesterday received the honour of yours. Lady Inverness is at present in the country. Shall take horse and ask her in your name for the money. Shall let you know her answer. In case she refuses shall either pledge or sell everything I have, even to the last shirt, for yr. Service. [Then from Avignon on 3 December 1757:] In consequence of this letter I received the hundred louis d'or from Lady Inverness. H.S.

By this time Michael Sheridan had already left. He had had enough of penury in Avignon and had rejoined the French army. Later he married a French heiress and ended his life comfortably enough in obscurity in a small château on the Loire.

The physician Gastaldy, who had treated James III as long ago as 1717 for fistula in Avignon, was now keeping the King supplied with scurvy-grass water for soreness of the gums, from which both the Cardinal York and Lord Lismore (the former Colonel O'Bryen) were also suffering. This was a common Jacobite complaint in Rome, probably caused by the diet.

The next year Alexander Murray of Elibank wrote to warn the Prince, who was expecting the visit of some English Jacobites at Bouillon, to behave himself:

That infamous creature Lady Primrose is spreading it about the whole kingdom that you are a drunkard. The only way to convince your friends of the falsity and malice of her lies is to drink very little while these gentlemen are with you, in case any of them should propose drinking, for God's sake evite it yourself because your character and success depends upon the report of these gentlemen at their return.

This damaging gossip, spread by his former champion, was no doubt quite simply due to female jealousy, because the Prince had preferred her plain protegée, the now notorious Miss Walkinshaw, to Lady Primrose's more mature charms.

The accounts reaching Rome of Charles's behaviour forced James to send his under-secretary, Andrew Lumisden, to Bouillon to try and bring the Prince to his senses, both with regard to his drinking habits and the irregular life he was leading with his Scottish mistress. With winter approaching Lumisden had a journey of more than 1,000 miles in front of him. He reached Lyon on 6 November and boarded the diligence, which took another week to reach Paris, where he had to contact Waters the banker. Waters' instructions were that he had to take the stage-coach for Lorraine, which meant another six days on the road. Lumisden wrote from Paris: 'I have a few zeckins [Florentine sequins] still remaining which I shall keep for my return to Italy and have therefore taken 600 livres from Mr Waters.'

When he got to Sedan, the town nearest Bouillon, he met with extreme discourtesy from the Prince, who refused to see him and sent word for him to put anything he wanted to say in writing. So, without appearing to have accomplished anything, he had to return to Rome at the worst time of year.

By 1759 Charles was outwardly behaving more soberly to impress the French while yet another plan for a 'descente en Ecosse' was being considered by the Duc de Choiseul. But late in November Admiral Hawke's annihilation of the French Fleet at Quiberon Bay brought these proposals to nothing.[5]

Charles had been in Brittany during this period, leaving Clementina at Bouillon. She had decided that she could stand her wretched existence no longer. When the dispirited Prince returned from Brittany, he found the news waiting for him that his father was so ill in Rome that he was not expected to recover, and he set off to visit him. The moment he was gone, Clementina took the seven-year-old Charlotte and fled with her to Paris. She left a letter for the Prince complaining of

> . . . the repeated bad treatment I have matte with these eight years past and the daily risque of losing my life. Your Royal Highness is too great and just when you reflect, not to think that you have pushed me to the greatest extremitie and there is not one woman in the world that would have suffered so long as I have done. However it shall never hinder me from having for your Royalle persone all the attachment and respect, and hope in time coming, by my conduct to merit your protection and friendship for me and my child . . .

Unfortunately the Prince changed his mind about going to Rome and returned to Bouillon within a few days to find his mistress and child gone. He exploded with rage, and refused to eat or see anyone until his daughter was restored to him. Clementina had taken the coach to Paris, with a vague idea of finding a haven at the Scots College in the Latin Quarter. The Principal, John Gordon, told her firmly that this was out of the question, and she then found a lodging at the Hôtel St Louis in the rue des Grand Augustins, down by the Seine near St Germain-des-Près. The Prince wrote to everyone he could think of, including the Abbé Gordon, ordering him to instruct the Paris police to search the city for the missing mother and child. His list of people he suspected of harbouring the runaways was quite wild: Waters the banker; Richard Warren, the Irishman who had brought him back from Scotland; O'Sullivan; Eleanor Oglethorpe, the daughter of a Jacobite general and now the Mother Superior of a Paris convent; and lastly 'Madame O'Bryen if she is still in Paris'. This last name shows how out of touch Charles was. He had always admired O'Bryen's wife since he had first met her in Paris in 1744, but Madame O'Bryen was now Lady Lismore and lived in Rome, where her husband had been James's Secretary-of-State up till the time of his death in October 1759.[6]

By the end of October 1760 there was still no news of the missing pair. Gordon, worn out with making fruitless enquiries, wrote wearily to the Prince: 'Time will make known where she is. I suspect Venise or Nice more than any other part—if the mother and child are in Paris they cannot escape to Flanders or elsewhere as all the police are warned to look out for them.' But Clementina was, in fact, very much in Paris. From there she had courageously written to King James to put her case before him. He replied promptly and generously. He offered to provide funds to maintain the child and herself if she agreed to remain quietly in a suitable Paris convent, where Charlotte could be given a decent education. He was only too thankful that the mistress who had been living openly with his heir, to the detriment of his reputation among the Jacobites, had taken matters into her own hands and left him.

For the next twenty-four years, therefore, Clementina Walkinshaw and her daughter Charlotte Stuart lived in Paris as 'dames pensionnaires'. During the lifetime of King James, who allowed them 12,000 livres annually (about £4,000), they could afford to stay in the fashionable rue St Jacques at the Convent of the Visitation,[7] near the English Benedictines where the embalmed bodies of Charlotte's great-grandfather James II and the Princess Louis Marie still lay in the chapel. In recognition of the services of Clementina's father as his envoy to the Habsburg Emperor in Vienna, James allowed Clementina to conceal her identity under the courtesy title of the Countess Albestroff.

In January 1766, when James III died, it was not Charlotte's father the Prince who continued their allowance but the Cardinal Duke of York. The Cardinal, however, reduced the pension of his brother's ex-mistress and her daughter by half, so that they were obliged to leave the comparatively expensive convent, a sister one to Chaillot, in the lively rue St Jacques for a much cheaper one in the country to the south of Paris. The two found the Couvent de la Miséricorde at Meaux-en-Brie dreadfully dull and uncomfortable, and it was also cut off from society.

Charles, for all his storming and raging, was in fact relieved to see them go. When he had calmed down, he made no real effort to pursue them or, more important, to maintain them.

James III died on New Year's Day 1766,[8] and was given a magnificent funeral in St Peter's, paid for by the Pope. Charles failed to arrive in time to be reconciled with his father, not reaching Rome until the end of the month. So once again it was Henry who had to deal with all the diplomatic and financial problems arising out of his father's death. This he did as efficiently as always, and by 8 January had sent off a note to the French Ambassador in Rome, informing him of the approaches he was making to the Holy See to have his brother recognized as King Charles III and the next legitimate sovereign of Great Britain.[9] On the same day he wrote to Louis XV, informing him of his father's death.[10] The Pope replied on 14 January that, for the present, he was unable to recognize the Prince Charles Edward as King Charles III, but that he considered it essential that His Royal Highness should come to Rome without delay. When Charles did appear on 29 January, he also officially informed the French King that he had succeeded his father.[11] For the remaining eight years of his reign Louis XV obeyed the Pope's ruling. He never insulted Charles with the name of Pretender but simply referred to him as the Prince Edouard Stuart.

According to the French Foreign Office archives, 'The House of Stuart only received from France an annual pension of 132,000 livres'. This ceased automatically with the death of James III. In addition to this personal pension, the sum of 40,000 livres had been distributed annually among the neediest Jacobites left in France.[12] After his father died, Charles was dependent on his brother's charity, which Henry, the rich prelate at that time, could well afford.

Jacobites everywhere were more anxious than ever that their last hope, now nearly fifty, should make a suitable and if possible an advantageous marriage. Lists of princesses were submitted and scrutinized, but with no visible effect upon the once dashing Young Chevalier, whom middle age had made even more choleric and awkward to deal with.

Minor German princesses, the best that an impecunious monarch without recognized title or kingdom could hope for, were submitted by the Irish Colonel Ryan to Charles. All were rudely dismissed because of face, figure or general dreariness. At last, in 1771, Ryan discovered that the widowed Princess Elisabeth de Stolberg, of impeccable lineage, had two remaining unmarried daughters. Her second daughter Caroline had recently married a Spanish Stuart, the Marquis of Jamaica, the eldest grandson of the Duke of Berwick.[13] Caroline was the pick of the Stolberg girls and only sixteen. Her mother was half-Scottish, the daughter of the Prince de Hornes, a

Louise Maxmilienne de Stolberg, Comtesse d'Albany, wife of Charles Edward, holding a Stuart white rose; an English engraving of 1773.

descendant of the Horne who was executed with Egmont in Brussels by Philip II, in the sixteenth century, and the Lady Charlotte Bruce, a collateral descendant of King Robert the Bruce. Colonel Ryan wrote from Brussels that Louise Maximilienne de Stolberg, although she was twenty, had a good figure, a pretty face and excellent teeth, in fact 'all the qualities Your Majesty can desire'—except, alas, money! The Duc de

Fitzjames, uncle of the Marquis of Jamaica, added that if Charles preferred a bride of fifteen, he was sure the Princess de Stolberg would let him have her third daughter instead. But Charles said Louise would do and, by February 1772, the Duc de Fitzjames was negotiating the marriage allowance to be offered by the French court.

The Princess Louise-Maximilienne de Stolberg was a determined young woman. The idea of being Queen at least in name in Rome appealed to her more than a convent in Mons and eventual marriage to some German princeling. She accepted the proposal, and, in a letter from Count François-Jacques Walsh de Serrant,[14] brother of Antoine Walsh, who had died in 1763, one learns the sequel:

> I spoke about the marriage of the Prince Edouard. It's perfectly true. They are saying that it took place the day before yesterday and that the Duc de Fitzjames stood proxy. That was not so. Here is the true account. The marriage took place at midday on the 27th March and the Duke of Berwick [Liria] acted as proxy and Mademoiselle de Stolberg, elder sister of the Marquise de Jamaique was there in person. At five o'clock on the same day she left accompanied by Monsieur Ryan of Berwick's Regiment. I am going to Versailles today and if I hear any further details I shall let you have them.

After this proxy ceremony Louise travelled under Ryan's protection to Venice, where they embarked for Ancona. The bridegroom and Lord Caryll went from Rome to Macerata and the marriage was celebrated there on Good Friday, 17 April 1772.[15]

Whether Louise regarded her stout elderly husband—he was fifty-one, she was twenty—with repugnance is hard to say. However, she not only betrayed him within the first years of their marriage, but did so under his very nose, at the Palazzo Clemente in Florence.

The news of the marriage came as a great shock to the Prince's daughter, who was the same age as Louise, and to her mother. They were very hard up financially, having no other income than the Cardinal York's allowance. Unwisely but understandably from the emotional point of view, and to get away from the boredom of their provincial convent, they decided to make the journey to Rome to confront the newly married couple. The trip was wearisome and costly, and, when they got there, the Prince, disillusioned as he already was with conjugal harmony, was curious to see his grown-up daughter but refused point-blank to receive his discarded mistress. Charlotte, with commendable pride but silly stubbornness, refused to meet her father unless she could bring Clementina too, so that the meeting never took place, and sadly the two women had to make the long journey back to Paris, returning by Genoa, Antibes, Aix-en-Provence and Avignon. To add insult to injury

Henry Stuart, Cardinal York painted in 1786 possibly by the Scots painter H. D. Hamilton.

they had been told they must go back to their cheap convent or forfeit their pension: 'The Cardinal York does not care where they go, provided they remain in a nunnery.' As the fruitless journey had eaten so much into the slender resources, they had no alternative.

Two years later, when it had become painfully clear that her father had no intention of doing anything for her in the way of providing money, dowry or a suitable husband, Charlotte addressed a long appeal to Louis XV, begging for his financial support.[16] She wrote an effusive 3,000-word description of her plight, saying she was the natural and only daughter of Prince Charles Edward Stuart and that her mother was of the noble Scottish family of Walkinshaw, many of whom had laid down their lives not only for the House of Stuart but also for France. She says that since 1760 she and her mother were supported by her paternal grandfather, the late King James III of England, and that, since his death, a pension of half that amount has been allowed them by her uncle, the Cardinal York. She states that she and her mother live as 'dames pensionnaires' at the Couvent de la Miséricorde at Meaux, outside Paris. She ends this long and touching appeal by saying, 'the daughter of Prince Charles must remain without relations, without friends, without a name, unacknowledged and without a home', and in this pitiable state dares to approach the Court of France for support. She does not know if it will be to the political advantage of France to interest itself in her case, but she appeals personally to His Most Christian Majesty as the sole and last heir of the House of Stuart. Finally, as none of the later Stuarts failed to do, she reminds King Louis of their shared descent from the great Henri IV of France, and asks for his help in maintaining her in a position worthy of her birth.

Louis XV was a dying man when this long-winded epistle was sent to him, and no known answer exists. He may never have seen it, as he died a week or so later.

When she wrote it, Charlotte was twenty-three. She was quite a striking-looking girl, tall like her father and big-boned like her mother, with dark blond hair, a pink complexion and blue eyes. As a 'dame pensionnaire' she merely paid for her board and lodging, and was free to come and go as she pleased. The Convent at Meaux bored her stiff. She was shallow and frivolous by nature and a snob, very conscious of her semi-royal status. When invitations came for her to visit the princely family of Rohan in Paris, she accepted them as being no more than her due. This proud Breton family had been connected with the Stuarts by marriage since the fifteenth century, when James I's daughter, the Princess Isabel of Scotland, became Duchess of Brittany. Since then the various branches of the family, the Rohan-Chabot, the Rohan-Guéménée, the Rohan-Montbazon, the Rohan-Soubise and the Rohan-Gié, had held the highest offices in the Church and State. For the most part they led scandalous colourful lives, and were notorious trouble-makers at court. The fact of being cardinals or archbishops did not interfere with their tastes for gallantry and debauchery, though this squandering of their substance was offset by the lasting monuments they left in the shape of the magnificent palaces they built throughout France. The Prince Louis de Rohan-Guéménée, when he became a cardinal, built himself a splendid palace at Strasbourg, and his younger brother Prince Ferdinand, as Archbishop of Bordeaux, built the house of palatial proportions that is now the Hôtel de Ville of that city.

Two years after the accession of Louis XVI Charlotte was still without the financial support she had requested from the French King. Although styling himself, against the Pope's wishes, as King Charles III, her father gave her no money at all, and would not even write a letter in her favour to Versailles, although the French Foreign Minister had been heard to say that if he had such a letter, he could probably obtain a pension for Charlotte and her mother. As she was now nearly twenty-five, with no dowry and no prospect of marrying, Charlotte decided to take the normal way out for girls of noble blood in her position, and to apply to be admitted as an Honorary Canoness of the Noble Chapter of Migette, a convent near Besançon. In this she was following in the footsteps of her own mother Clementina and her stepmother Louise de Stolberg.

Charlotte travelled to Besançon in Franche-Comté in the summer of 1776. At the dinner given after her reception Lord Elcho, who was still on the trail of the money her father owed him, was present and noted in his journal that one of the distinguished guests on this occasion was the Archbishop Prince Ferdinand of Rohan, who was presented to the new Canoness, the Lady Charlotte Stuart. Charlotte was introduced as the daughter of the Stuart Pretender and treated as a princess.

Since she returned to Paris shortly afterwards instead of staying on in the convent at Besançon, it is more than likely that the worldly Archbishop found her nubile charms to his taste, and that they had formed an attachment. Like his brother, the Cardinal of Strasbourg, who moved on to become the Keeper of the Privy Purse at Versailles and to be involved in the Diamond Necklace scandal, the Archbishop of Bordeaux was a great womanizer with no real depth of feeling. He treated Charlotte in a cynical offhand way, and took little or no trouble to conceal the fact that he had several other mistresses at the same time. Her own mother's equivocal situation made her an understanding accomplice in her daughter's subsequent love life; and whenever Charlotte became pregnant, it was Clementina who looked after her, and arranged to have the babies put out to wet-nurses in the country, the normal practice in those days. The Prince rented a small house in the rue St Jacques for his Stuart mistress, near the Convent of the Visitation, to which she and her mother had returned after this liaison began. Rohan also provided a modest house in the country at Antony, about seven miles south of Paris in the direction of Fontainebleau, where their offspring could be housed discreetly.

Charlotte had three children by the Prince Ferdinand de Rohan. The eldest Aglaë (named after one of the six daughters of Louis XV) was born in 1778 and a second daughter, Marie, in 1780. The Archbishop of Bordeaux then became Archbishop of Cambrai, and found that he had less and less time for the Stuart girl. Although she reveals herself in her letters as dull and self-centred, with an excessive idea of her own importance, Charlotte stoically bore the cavalier treatment inflicted upon her by her inconstant lover. In her many letters to the Archbishop she always refers to him coyly as her 'ami' and to their children as 'the flowers they had planted in their garden'. There is no record that their father ever bothered to visit the Rohan-Stuart children at Antony.

In 1781 Louise de Stolberg finally left her husband and ran off to Rome with her lover, the sentimental Italian poet Vittorio Alfieri. There she had the effrontery to ask for financial support from her brother-in-law, the Cardinal York, carefully concealing her true relationship with 'Alfi'. The marriage of Charles and Louise had been a disaster from the start, but his wife's desertion affected the morose old man as deeply as Clementina Walkinshaw's had done twenty years before. He shut himself up in his room, feeling betrayed and utterly abandoned. After more than a year of misery, however, Charles let himself be persuaded by his new friend, the dapper King Gustavus III, of Sweden to agree to a formal separation from the unrepentant Louise and to send for his daughter Charlotte to comfort his declining years.

It is clear that the Prince knew nothing about her liaison or her illegitimate children when, on 30 March 1783, he solemnly executed an act of legitimacy in favour of his only child. (At this time Charlotte was in the embarrassing position of being again pregnant by the Archbishop de Rohan.) In this act Charles exercised his prerogative as *de jure* sovereign of Great Britain, and had it recognized by the French government. He created Charlotte Duchess of Albany, which greatly annoyed his brother Henry, who, as the younger son of a King of Scotland, rightly considered this as his own hereditary second title.

On his own account Louis XVI promulgated a further act of legitimization dated Paris, 7 September 1784, calling her the Lady Charlotte Albany. He granted her the privileges of a royal duchess in France, which meant the 'droit du tabouret', the right of remaining seated in the Queen's presence, socially very important at Versailles.

All this was like a dream come true for Charlotte, though it in no way altered her embarrassing situation with regard to her ecclesiastical lover. Three months before her promotion at the French court, in June 1784, she had secretly given birth to a son named Charles Edward, who was immediately removed to a wet-nurse. When her father first sent for her, she had to make excuses for delaying her departure. Back in the Convent in the rue St Jacques, six weeks after the birth of her son, she wrote to her father in French to express her pleasure and gratitude at her new status. She could not resist trying to impress him with the connections she had made with important people and highly placed ministers in France, especially the members of the House of Rohan.

To bring his daughter to him in Italy, Charles sent his Master of the

Charlotte Stuart, the only child of Charles Edward, created Duchess of Albany by her father and recognized by Louis XVI.

Household, John Stewart of Ardvorlich. When the time came to go, she apparently had no qualms about leaving her three children in the care of her mother. She never set eyes on them again. In Florence, just after her thirty-first birthday, Charlotte was reunited with the father she had not seen since she was seven years old.

The *Gazette de Leyden*, a newsheet with a wide circulation among the Jacobite exiles, gave the details of Charlotte's change of fortune on 21 September, though with no hint of any scandalous gossip about her.

> We spoke in our last number of the Pretender's daughter, brought up and educated in Paris under the name of Lady Charlotte Stuart, being recognized by her father and named as his heiress. Lady Charlotte, today Duchess of

> Albany, the daughter of the Pretender and a Scottish lady of quality has up till now been neglected by her father. She lived at the Convent of the Visitation of Sainte Marie in the rue St Jacques on an annual pension paid to her by her uncle, the Cardinal York. She was not a little surprised to receive a month ago a letter from her father, summoning her to comfort him in his old age. With this letter were the acts of legitimacy and her title of Duchess plus a copy of her father's will naming her as his heir. Among other things, all his possessions in France [in fact very few—all sold at Avignon by Sheridan and Stafford]. The French Parliament has, in her case, exempted her from the *droit d'aubaine* by which the property of a foreigner who has not been naturalized reverts to the French crown on death

The *Gazette de Leyden* affirmed, quite mistakenly, that the Prince's possessions in France, including furniture and diamonds, amounted to about two million livres!

The contents of the will and her new title of Duchess cheered Charlotte considerably, just as the arrival of his long-lost daughter, the same age as his erring wife, put the Prince, to begin with, in an excellent humour. He had settled in Florence and now started to entertain lavishly again, and arranged receptions and dinners for her to meet Florentine society and distinguished visiting foreigners. On 30 November, St Andrew's Day, the Prince, calling himself King Charles III, gave a gala dinner at which he bestowed the Order of the Thistle upon his daughter.

Like his father and brother, Charles liked music, and in his younger days had played the 'cello. After his wife had eloped with her lover, he used to enliven his lonely evenings by having musicians come in to play to him after dinner while he drowsed over his brandy. Now, with Charlotte as his companion, he took to going out whenever possible, seldom missing a performance at the theatre or at the opera. He became so regular a patron that the Grand Duke of Tuscany had boxes specially redecorated for the Stuarts. The one at the opera was relined in crimson damask and that at the theatre in yellow brocade. The pair became one of the sights of Florence, the Prince, enormously bloated and heavy, nodding off throughout most of the performances, more often than not, but thoroughly enjoying his outings none the less. He suffered terribly from gout, and his legs were so swollen that he had to be carried everywhere in his chair. Nevertheless he insisted on watching the carnival while it lasted, in Florence, as in Venice, from before Christmas until Lent.

In spite of the constant scenes he created with his shouting and rage over trifles, Charles in his last years appears as a much more endearing character than his daughter. Her deprived childhood and youth had worn the bloom, if there ever had been any, off very early, and turned her into a hard mercenary woman at her worst, and a superficial and vapid one at

The Young Pretender towards the end of his life.

her best. Her main preoccupation was ordering the latest fashions from Paris to impress the English visitors, who, out of curiosity, made a point of asking to be presented to the Pretender's daughter. She shamelessly made use of her mother to shop for her, and brief messages and kisses to her three children were scribbled as postscripts to her detailed orders for dresses and hats.

On 25 March 1785 she alluded significantly to 'one who will no doubt soon be returning to Paris, it is quite time that he did so. I count on you, chère maman, to watch over his health and see that he wants for nothing'. This was almost exactly nine months after the birth of her son Charles Edward, who would then have been of an age to be weaned and brought back from his foster-mother to the care of his grandmother. In the same letter Charlotte, an insatiable gossip, passed on to Clementina the latest scandal about her stepmother being joined at Innsbruck by 'Alfi' and that it was rumoured the couple planned to go to Paris.

Clementina, now nearly seventy, took the two girls and the baby Charles to the country house at Antony in April. Writing to her mother there, Charlotte said she had at last heard from her 'ami' in Cambrai, adding naively, 'he seems fonder of me now that I am farther away from him'. Her letters to Paris were now almost entirely devoted to money matters. She and her father were waiting impatiently to hear whether Lord Caryll, grandson of the old man who had been Mary of Modena's private secretary more than fifty years ago at St Germain, had managed to get the money due to them from the English government. Caryll had been sent to London to try to collect the arrears on the dead Queen's dowry, which had been owing since 1685. The sum had been voted by an Act of Parliament on the accession of James II, and the act had never been repealed. In the Treaty of Utrecht Queen Anne had reaffirmed that this money should be paid to her stepmother. Now, nearly 100 years later, Mary of Modena's grandson lived in the optimistic false hopes of inheriting this comfortable amount of money. But for all Caryll's efforts, it never materialized. The exiled Stuarts had to subsist on charity for the rest of their lives, and the Cardinal York, losing his Church revenues when French troops invaded Rome during the Napoleonic Wars, was grateful for a grant made to him by the often-maligned but always generous George III of England.

In the meantime Charles fell deeper and deeper into debt in Florence, 'throwing away his money', as Charlotte described it with some annoyance to her mother, adding spitefully: 'My Lord Nairn and my father dispute and quarrel all day long. Il n'a plus de tête! [He's completely gaga].' In this same letter (September 1785) Charlotte asked eagerly for the latest news about the Diamond Necklace scandal in Paris, in which her Archbishop's elder brother, the Cardinal Louis de Rohan, was implicated. He had been arrested in the Galerie des Glaces at Versailles on 15 August and imprisoned in the Bastille. He was not acquitted until nearly a year later, after which he was exiled to Ettenheim in Germany.

In September 1785 Charlotte persuaded her father much against his will, as old grudges died hard with him, to let her meet her uncle and try and patch up the rift between the brothers. He finally agreed. Charlotte and the Cardinal met in Perugia and immediately took to one another, sharing hard-headedness and a lack of sentimentality. The estrangement that had lasted for nearly forty years was ended when Charlotte achieved her goal and got her father to move from Florence, which she considered provincial and boring, back to Rome. She persuaded Henry to arrange for them to reoccupy the Palazzo Muti, her father's birthplace, and to use his considerable influence with the Pope to have the old Prince treated with the dignity becoming to a legitimate monarch. They left Florence on 1 December 1785, travelling to Rome by way of Siena and Viterbo. The Pope kept his word to Henry, granting the Prince the right to use the royal tribune in St Peter's, as his father King James had always done. He and Charlotte made their first appearance there on Christmas Day 1785.

During the next two years his health grew steadily worse. He went red in the face and fell into hysterical fits of rage when tactless visitors reminded him of painful incidents in his past. Towards the end of 1786 the Duchesse de Polignac, on a visit to Rome, brought the young Comte de Vaudreuil to pay his respects to the Prince. Charles realized that he was the son of the man who had arrested him with such indignity outside the Paris Opera on that December night nearly forty years ago, when his hands had been tied and his sword taken from him by Vaudreuil's militia. He fell into such a demented frenzy that Charlotte thought he could not possibly survive it.

But recover he did, only to become even more difficult to control, flying into ungovernable rages on the slightest pretext. Knowing that his life, three-quarters of it wasted, was nearing its end, the Prince used to prowl about the rooms of his palace, restlessly asking the time and resorting more and more to the solace of the brandy bottle.

On 23 January 1788 he collapsed again, and this time did not rally. The attack was the first of three strokes, which robbed him of his speech. He lingered on, half-paralysed in his great curtained bed for another week. As the icy winds from the mountains howled round the shabby Palazzo Muti on the night of 30 January, the anniversary of his great-grandfather's execution, the last hope of the House of Stuart died.

EPILOGUE

THE LAST OF THE LINE

As soon as Charles had been buried in the same vault as his father, though with less ceremony, Charlotte wrote briskly to Clementina to tell her grandly that she was putting the Prince's household of twenty-six retainers into mourning as had been done 'pour le roi Jacques'. She advised her mother to follow her example, saying if she was too hard up, to ask the Prior of the English Benedictines for the money. This was absurd pretentiousness on Charlotte's part, since her mother had no retainers, as well as no money. The Duchess of Albany told her that, much as she longed to, it was out of the question for her to return to Paris, as there was so much legal business to be dealt with following her father's death. The Pope, she added with some satisfaction, was very kind and was allowing her to continue to use the royal tribune in St Peter's. Charlotte was very much concerned with the outward forms of mourning, though it was quite evident that the loss of her father was a relief rather than a cause for sorrow. Her letters to her mother, who genuinely grieved for the one love of her life, were still filled with trivial requests for mourning buttons, mourning earrings and mourning ribbons.

As the Pretender's sole heir, the Duchess of Albany emerged as a sharp businesswoman in dealing with the complicated question of succession duties. She applied without loss of time to the French government to continue the Stuart pension, and so successfully that she got it raised from 10,000 to 20,000 livres; and she persuaded the Grand Duke of Tuscany to let her off paying taxes on the property she had inherited in Florence.

The anniversary of Culloden on 16 April held no meaning for her. Instead, on this historic date, Bonnie Prince Charlie's daughter was writing busily to Paris about her plans for selling her father's old home, the Palazzo Clemente in Florence, and ended this letter with her usual self-pitying complaints about the heartlessness of her 'ami'. At the end of April 1788 problems about the sale of the house in the rue St Jacques arose.

Charlotte, although extravagant over trifles, was stingy by nature, and though she was quite well off, refused to buy it for her mother and children. The Archbishop had always paid the rent, and Charlotte had no intention of letting him out of his obligations. She did, however, sign a lease for another three years on this modest house, which had been rented from the Abbé de la Villette. When her mother told her that the Abbé had suggested taking a room in the house as a boarder, and sharing the expenses of a carriage with her, Charlotte put her foot down firmly, telling her mother sharply it was a proposition not *digne* for the Countess d'Albestroff. They had enough scandals in the family already.

Charlotte had no illusions about the Archbishop de Rohan's meanness. She kept warning her mother not to let him know how much was being allowed her through Busoni, her father's banker in Paris.

The Cardinal York was now sixty-four and suffering from a persistent cough and weakness of the chest. Charlotte visited her uncle regularly at Frascati, because, as she said, naively or callously, she did not want him to die before she had paid all her debts. During one of these visits she arranged for the Cardinal to make over to her all his rights to any money that might eventually come to him from England.

In June 1788 she succeeded in getting a good price for the Palazzo Clemente, selling it for 40,000 écus. As her father had only paid 18,000 écus for it in 1770, and as she had got tax exemption on the sale from the Grand Duke of Tuscany, she felt she had done very well. She was so pleased with herself that in July she commissioned her portrait to be drawn in pastel by a Scottish artist in Rome, Hugh Douglas Hamilton. She promised her mother a copy of the best of the three sittings, which shows her plump-faced, in profile, wearing a simple diadem of pearls. In a later one, drawn in September, Charlotte's obsession with the latest fashions is seen to her disadvantage. She is wearing a top-heavy Tipoo Sahib turban, the rage of pre-revolutionary Paris but vastly unbecoming to her.

The Duchess of Albany was now approaching her thirty-fifth birthday. She was still handsome, but definitely middle-aged in appearance and growing stouter each year. Her reaction to her mother's letter telling her that the Archbishop Prince Ferdinand de Rohan was infatuated with a new and glamorous mistress called Pitfara was to cast round desperately for a husband for herself before it was too late. For once Charlotte seemed really concerned about her children, especially her eldest daughter Agläe, who was now ten years old and might be subjected to the bad influence of this Parisian courtesan.

The wife of the Stuart's first cousin, the Duc de Bouillon, had recently died. The widower was sixty-two, childless and ugly, but Charlotte, who had known him when she was a small girl, seriously considered marrying him. She wrote him a letter of condolence and waited for a reply, but none was forthcoming. The Duke, Charles Godfrey de La Tour d'Auvergne, remained a widower and died, the last of his line, in 1791.

The arrival in Rome of another Stuart cousin on the Spanish side of the family, the young Duke of Berwick, great-grandson of the Maréchal, gave rise to new hopes. He was a Grandee of Spain, the immensely rich owner of the magnificent Palacio Liria in Madrid and had vast estates in the country. The young Berwick was twice related to the Duchess of Albany, through her father and through her stepmother, whose sister Caroline de Stolberg was the Duke's mother. Berwick was duly presented to Charlotte and to her uncle Henry. The Cardinal was delighted with his charming young relation, as he had always admired the family of Berwick and Fitzjames, descendants of the great soldier. The Duke was both intelligent and handsome. Unfortunately he was only nineteen, so that poor Charlotte's hopes were dashed once more, and, to add insult to injury, just about the time of Berwick's visit she received an uncalled for reprimand from her fickle lover. The Archbishop wrote pontificating about their children's future, exhorting her 'to remember her obligations'. Charlotte was rightly furious, and replied heatedly that, absentee mother though she was, 'she knew them full well and would willingly follow his example: it was for him to set it. It would be disgraceful if he, on his side, did nothing'.

Meanwhile in France, in November 1788, Andrew Stuart of Castlemilk, the Tory member of Parliament for Weymouth,[1] who traced his descent from Sir William Stuart of Castlemilk, the brother of the Constable John Stuart of Darnley, was visiting Aubigny. He had taken a year off from his Parliamentary duties to compile a genealogical history of the Stuart family, and planned to spend some months in Paris and Berry before going on to Rome. He stayed at the Château of Aubigny, then the property of the Duke of Richmond and Lennox, great-grandson of Charles II and Louise de Kéroualle. On this occasion he saw in the salon, a large oval gilt frame containing portrait heads of eight of the eleven seigneurs of Aubigny. Less than a year later this composite portrait, together with most of the contents of the châteaux of Aubigny and La Verrerie were seized at the Revolution and sold as 'biens publics'.

The Duke of Richmond was placed on the list of emigrés and the châteaux of Aubigny and La Verrerie sequestrated twice, once during the Revolution and once by Napoleon, the second time during the blockade in 1805, because it was the property of an English family. The châteaux were restored to the Richmond family in 1814, but the château of Aubigny remained, as it is today, the Hôtel de Ville of the town. La

Verrerie remained in the possession of the Stuart descendants, who only visited France occasionally to use it as a hunting lodge.

Andrew Stuart was still in France on the anniversary of the death of Prince Charles Edward in January 1789. Like another English traveller, Arthur Young, who recorded his impressions of rural and provincial France at the end of the *ancien régime,* he too was caught up in the turmoil of the Revolution the following summer. Andrew Stuart went on, as he had planned, to Rome, but never met Charlotte, who was dying of cancer of the liver. In spite of the pain she was suffering, she was still preoccupied with money matters and the latest Paris fashions. In March she had hopefully sent another portrait of herself to the Prince de Rohan. She still had the strength, conscious of her rank as a royal duchess, to scribble a letter of introduction for a good-looking young Englishman who had paid his respects to her in Rome, asking her mother, the Countess d'Albestroff, to present the young man to her friend the Princesse de Rohan in Paris.

The news from Paris of the Fall of the Bastille in July 1789 naturally alarmed her. She wrote agitated notes to her mother, begging her to take the children to some safer place. She suggested Switzerland, and even asked if it were not possible for them all to come to Rome at her expense. But that was as far as it went. Charlotte was now suffering visibly from her incurable disease. Her doctors recommended the inevitable change of air, and in September she travelled as far as Ancona, stopping on the way at the shrine of Loretto, where her great-great-grandmother, the Duchess Laure of Modena, had gone to pray that her daughter Mary Beatrice, the wife of James II, might bear the longed-for Stuart heir.

When Charlotte reached Bologna on her return journey at the beginning of October, she was too ill to move from the house of her friend the Marchesa Giulia Lambertini-Bovio, who nursed her devotedly during the last weeks of her life. Charlotte mercifully can have had no idea that her death was so near, as she wrote from Bologna to ask her poor old mother to search revolutionary Paris for bargains in dress materials. The second last letter she ever wrote was on this frivolous note, though she did remember to add her usual greeting to her children, 'embrasse pour moi mes chères amies'. Her very last letter to Clementina was dated 10 October 1789 and was little more than a *petit mot.*

Although he was kept informed of the progress of his niece's fatal illness, the Cardinal York made no move to visit her in Bologna. On 14 November Charlotte made her will, naming her uncle the universal heir of all her goods and jewels, including the Garter jewel worn by Charles I at his execution and the diamonds given as a wedding present by Louis XIV to her great-grandmother Mary of Modena. She made no mention in her will of her three children, nor of their father, the Prince Ferdinand de Rohan. But she did leave an annual pension of 15,000 livres for life to her mother, giving her the right to dispose at her death of 50,000 livres in favour of her needy dependants. She left personal bequests to all the members of her household, and asked to be buried in the neighbouring Church of San Biagio in Bologna and for the customary alms to be distributed to the poor of the parish.

Charlotte Stuart, Duchess of Albany, died unmarried but the mother of three children on 17 November 1789, aged thirty-six.

In France, during the summer of 1789, all the aristocrats who were able to escape the fury of the revolutionary mobs had begun to emigrate in the direction of the Rhine, where the Prince de Condé was trying to organize an émigré army at Coblenz. Members of the Rohan-Guéménée family, to which the Archbishop Prince Ferdinand belonged, went to Germany at this time. His brother, the disgraced Cardinal de Rohan, was still living at Ettenheim, the headquarters of another group of French émigrés, and he died there in 1803.

Nothing more was heard about the two Stuart girls beyond the fact that they both died unmarried at the Château de Beaumanoir near Tours. Aglaë died in 1823 and Marie in 1825, and they were buried at St Cyr-sur-Loire. Their grandmother, Clementina Walkinshaw, still using the title of Countess d'Albestroff, eventually succeeded in reaching Switzerland, where she died in poverty and obscurity at Fribourg in 1802.

During the Napoleonic Wars Bonaparte tried to make use of the Prince's brother Henry, the last surviving legitimate male Stuart, against England. But as a Prince of the Catholic Church, and through his own sharp sense of realism—a rare Stuart quality—the aged and impoverished Cardinal York, eking out his existence on a pension paid to him, ironically enough, by George III, remained stubbornly immune to any temptations Napoleon had to offer.

The Emperor also made another, rather half-hearted, attempt to win over the widow of Prince Charles Edward. Louise de Stolberg, Countess of Albany, had been estranged from her elderly husband from the earliest days of their incompatible childless marriage. She had led a happy enough life in Florence with her lovers, first with her dear 'Alfi', the poet-dramatist with whom she had cuckolded her husband under his own roof before eloping with him to Rome; and after Count Vittorio Alfieri's death with a French painter very much younger than herself, François-Xavier Fabre.[2] She too refused to be used as a pawn in the Anglo-French War, and so nothing came of that last attempt from France to use the Stuarts against England.

The Cardinal York died in 1807 at Frascati, and was buried with his father and brother in St Peter's. He left his papers and his possessions, including Charles I's Garter jewel, in the hands of his executor, Cardinal Gonsalvi, who in turn handed over some crown jewels to the Prince Regent. A further immense collection of papers relating to the Stuarts, including 10,000 autograph letters addressed by members of the exiled family to the different sovereigns in Europe and to Jacobites in Scotland and England, was discovered in Rome in the attics of the Palazzo Monserati in 1816. These were presented to the Prince Regent and are now at Windsor.

The son of Charlotte, Duchess of Albany, and the Archbishop Prince de Rohan disappeared from Paris during the emigration when he was about nine years old. From his own account of his early life, given many years later in a memorial he presented to the Prince Regent when he came to London, he said that he had spent the first twenty-five years of his life in Germany. He called himself the Chevalier de Roehanstart (surely a combination of Rohan and Stuart).

From the correspondence of Prince Ferdinand de Rohan it appears that he took a great interest in the education of some boy in the last decade of the eighteenth century, though this boy was never precisely named. The Archbishop himself had gone to Germany during the Terror but returned to Paris during Napoleon's Consulate, when he became a favourite of Josephine de Beauharnais. He was appointed her almoner when she became Empress in December 1804. In 1805 he conveniently renounced Holy Orders, which can hardly have caused him any *crise de conscience*, and, once officially back in secular life, accepted the title of Count of the Empire. He died in 1807, the same year as the Cardinal York.

Charles Edward de Roehanstart, the doubly illegitimate grandson of Bonnie Prince Charlie, lived from the age of seventeen to twenty-one in the household of Prince Alexander of Wurtemberg, Cavalry Commander in the Russian army. Roehanstart was a fluent linguist, speaking French, English, German and Russian, and fought in the Napoleonic Wars against France before coming to England in 1816. He went first to Edinburgh, where he took rooms in student lodgings and supported himself by giving French lessons to law students. One of these students passed on the details of Roehanstart's adventurous life to an advocate in Stirling, who in turn related them to Lord Hardwicke. The Chevalier de Roehanstart, then a man in his middle thirties, had said that he had fought against France in the recent European wars and that he was a grandson of Prince Charles Edward Stuart and a Miss Walkinshaw of Stirling. His mother, he claimed, was their only child, the Lady Charlotte Stuart, Duchess of Albany. Roehanstart told the students he taught in Edinburgh that he had come to Scotland 'to make acquaintance of the brave people who had fought so well for his grandfather. He said it was his intention to learn Gaelic, the language of his grandfather's most faithful followers'.

Later in 1816 the Chevalier de Roehanstart went to London to present a petition to the Prince Regent claiming his mother's estate, which had passed to the Cardinal York. Roehanstart gave the date of his birth more or less accurately as 11 June 1784, though the place was wrong. He said he was born in Rome but Charlotte at that time was still in Paris. She did not leave France to join her father until October of that year.

Thomas Coutts of the banking family, who had lived in Paris before the Revolution and was now a leading figure in the City of London, commented on Roehanstart's likeness to Clementina Walkinshaw, the old Countess d'Albestroff. Coutts had not only known her well but had been the executor of her will.[3] In this way the letters to Clementina from Charlotte had come into the possession of the Coutts family and, eventually, through one of Thomas Coutts' daughters, passed to the family of Lord North. Fanny Coutts, another daughter, married the Marquis of Bute and so became a Stuart by marriage. She described Roehanstart when she met him as 'a gentlemanlike man and very like Madame d'Albestroff'.

The Prince Regent, who liked nothing better than a romantic story, was a sympathetic listener. He was a great admirer of Sir Walter Scott, and had read his Jacobite novel *Waverley* when it first came out in 1814. But much as he would have liked to help the Chevalier, his own position was too delicate for him to take action.

Having failed to obtain any material satisfaction in London, the Chevalier then went to Paris, which was under allied occupation. There he had the usual trouble with his *papiers* and made a declaration to the French police on 3 July 1817, a copy of which is among the Stuart documents at Windsor, together with a copy of the letter sent by the French authorities to the French Ambassador in London. In their report the French police said that 'they found Roehanstart perfectly harmless, neither interested in politics nor proud of his noble birth, but a humble and submissive individual who seeks in study, a consolation for the hardness of his fate. The British Government need have no fear of him'.

He returned to London the following year and married Marie-Antoinette Barbuoni, the daughter of a French émigré, who died without children in 1821. She was buried in Marylebone Church, in the parish that housed most of the French émigrés in London. In 1826 Roehanstart married his second wife, an Englishwoman with the unromantic name of Louisa Smith. She always called herself Madame Stuart and she too had no children.

The Chevalier then disappeared from the English scene, presumably returning to Austria, where his father's branch of the Rohan family had settled. He had a double set of connections there, dating back to his great-grandfather Walkinshaw's time as Jacobite envoy to the Imperial Court in Vienna in 1718.

The next twenty-five years of his life were spent as a mercenary soldier in the Austrian army. In 1854 the Chevalier de Roehanstart, or, as he now called himself, the Count de Roehanstart, returned to Scotland as an old man. Whether he meant, as he had hoped in 1816, to buy an estate in the Highlands and to settle there, or whether it was merely a sentimental pilgrimage to the scenes of his grandfather's victory and defeat in the Forty-five is a mystery. All that is known about him is that he was killed in a stage-coach accident in Perthshire on 28 October 1854. He is buried in the churchyard of Dunkeld Cathedral, where a stone was erected to his memory by an unnamed Scottish nobleman. It describes him as General Charles Edward Stuart, Count Roehanstart, who died at Dunkeld on 28 October 1854, aged 73 years, and underneath the name and dates is the inscription 'Sic transit gloria mundi'. Following the appearance of the obituary notice in the *Scotsman* for 1 November 1854, a second notice appeared a week later, describing the dead man as a general in the Austrian army who claimed to be a lineal descendant of Prince Charles Edward Stuart.

The race of royal Stuarts was doomed to extinction, but it left behind a legend that persists in the two countries inextricably linked by this ill-starred family and by the unique alliance that lasted unbroken for six centuries. France used Scotland as a backdoor to attack England until the end of the eighteenth century: but France also received, housed and pensioned the penniless exiles who followed the misfortunes of these Stuarts, who, with the exception of Charles II, found compromise impossible, however much their blood was mixed, and so made such hopeless politicians. In the world's terms they were all failures. They possessed, however, a fascinating blend of qualities that gave each one of them an indefinable magnetism, only made more human by their faults. They often lacked wisdom but never courage, and they in their turn inspired courage and self-sacrifice among their followers, Scottish, Irish, English and French, to a remarkable degree.

The French Stuarts have vanished without trace, but to this day in France their name evokes an instant response and recognition. Three castles in France today remain very much as they were when they housed the Stuarts. St Germain-en-Laye, high on its hill, with its great terrace and superb view of distant Paris and the River Seine winding far below, where, in the last months of his life James II used to take his evening walk leaning on the arm of his admirable wife Mary of Modena, has not changed except for the fact of now being a mere fifteen minutes from the centre of the capital. The chestnuts and elms in the park are as old as the exiled court crowded with Scottish, English and Irish Jacobites who had lost everything following the fall of the Catholic house of Stuart.

The other two castles of Aubigny and La Verrerie in the green rolling countryside of Berry, which the Constable of the Scottish Army, the first John Stuart, knew during the Hundred Years War, are the only properties left of those the Stuart family owned in France. After the French Revolution the château of Aubigny remained public property, becoming the Hôtel de Ville of the town, while La Verrerie, sadly neglected, was visited rarely by the quarrelsome descendants of the Duke of Richmond. In 1841 it was bought from them by the present owners, the Vogüé family, and gradually restored to what it was in the time of the Maréchal Robert Stuart d'Aubigny, the friend of François I. It rises, faded rose-pink, out of its woods and informal gardens on the edge of a rippling lake, blending into the pastel greens of the forest like a castle in a tapestry. The château and the nearby town of Aubigny-sur-Nère give a sense of immediacy to the Stuart legend that persists in France to this day. At Roscoff, Morlaix, at Dol-de-Bretagne, in the sea-port of Nantes, in Berry, in Orléans, Bourges and Avignon, in the old convents and in the elegant black and white chapel of the Scots College in the Latin Quarter of Paris, and at St Germain-en-Laye, the Stuarts are friendly ghosts known familiarly and without rancour by their Christian names. Of what other dynasty in Europe can one say this?

APPENDIX I

D'Eguilles' List of Jacobite Leaders

THE MARQUIS D'EGUILLES' list of Jacobite leaders is preserved in his own handwriting in the Archives of the Quai d'Orsay, and reads as follows:

The Duke of Athol (Governor of East Scotland.)

The Duke of Perth (Lieutenant-General. A man of some worth.)

Mylord Georges Murray (Lieutenant-General, a man of real ability, the guiding spirit of the Jacobite army but of suspect loyalty.)

The Earl of Kilmarnock, whose eldest son is in the service of the Elector of Hanover and is, through his mother, Hereditary Constable of Scotland. This Earl is an able man and was a member of the Hanoverian Court. It was an agreeable surprise when he arrived in Edinburgh with his second son two days ago.

The Earl of Kelly. A good and zealous man for the Cause.

The Earl of Strathallan, Governor of Perth, a wise man and well thought of. His eldest son who is in the service of France, commands the Duke of Perth's Regiment.

The Viscount Kenmure, whose father was banished for his part in the '15 Rising.

Mylord Pitsligo who brought 130 mounted followers with him.

Mylord Nairne. Strathallan's brother-in-law.

Mylord Elcho.

Mylord Ogilvie eldest son of the Earl of that name. These last two are Episcopalians, also Strathallan, Gordon, Kelly and Kilmarnock.

Guillaume Murray brother of the Earl of Duras serving with the Elector in Flanders.

Charles Boid younger son of the Earl of Kilmarnock.

The eldest son of the Magdonells of Clanranald.

The second son of Magdonnell of Glenghari whose brother Aeneas is in France.[1]

The father and chief of the Magdonnells of Keppoch.

The Chief of the Camerons [Lochiel].

The paternal uncle of the Chief of the Stuarts of Ochil.

The Chief of the Robertsons: two Chiefs of the two branches of the Clan Robertson.

Mackinnon: the chief of the MacGregors: the eldest son of the Chief of the Macphersons: Gordon of Glenbucket who brought 200 men with him.

The Chief of the Fraesers.

The Chief of the Macintosh.

The Chevalier Magdonnell who commanded a Brigade of Caribiniers in France.[2]

The Chevalier Stuart who brings this letter.

Sullivan, formerly A.D.C. to M. Maillebois and who has the tole of Quarter-Master here.

Strickland, an Englishman who is master of the Horse. M. Murray, a relative of the Duke of Athol, a man of ability who acts as the Prince's Secretary-of-State.[3]

Sheridan, Under-governor to the Prince who acts as assistant secretary to Murray.

D'Eguilles' List of Jacobite Troops

D'EGUILLES lists the troops of the Jacobite Army on the eve of the Prince's march into England on 3 November 1745.[1]

INFANTRY

Duc d'Athol	2,027	hommes.
Duc de Perth	406	
Les Trois Magdonels	1,851	
Les Camerons	752	
Les Stuards	360	
Les Gordons de Glenbucket	302	
Les Macintosh	563	
Les Phraesers	619	
Les Méphersons	630	
Les Magregors	205	
Les deux Mackinnons	480	
Les Robinsons [Robertsons]	280	
Le Duc de Gordon	350	
Total de l'infanterie	8,825	hommes.

CAVALERIE

Gardes commandés par le Cte. d'Elcho	120	hommes.
Les Gentilhommes avec Mylord Pitsligo	130	
Leurs domestiques formant une compagnie	70	
Gentilhommes volontaires de Pais Bas	197	
Gens de la Maison et societé du Prince	49	
Total de la Cavalerie	566	
TOTAL	9,391	hommes.

Troupes attendues.
Du Duc de Gordon au moins six cens cavalerie montés 600
On aveu que le Macleod et les Magdonels des Isles viennent avec trois milles hommes 3,000

Si ces troupes arrivent, l'armée du Prince Charles Edouard sera de 12,991 hommes, sans compter ce qui pourrar se joindre à ce Prince le long de la route.
Archives du Ministère des Affaires Etrangères, Mem. et Doc. Angleterre, Tome 78, 136.

APPENDIX 3

Foreign Officers Taken Prisoner at Inverness

AMONG the 'officers étrangers prisonniers à Inverness' who signed the *billet d'honneur* were: le Colonel Jean Macdonald; le Commandant François Nugent, le Capitaine faisant les fonctions de Maréchal des Logis des Troupes François en Ecosse; Patrice Nugent; Robert Shee; Thomas Bagot (Capitaines); Philippe Mollet, Quartier-Maître; Barnaval; Jean Nugent (Lieutenants); de Cooke (cornette); Marc Bagot (Aide-Major). Tous du Regiment de Fitzjames. Le même jour, trois officiers et seize cavaliers du même Regiment se rendirent prisonniers au Duc de Cumberland.

De celui de Berwick, le Brigadier Stapleton, Lieutenant-Colonel de la Hoyde, Patrick Clargue, Capitaines; Thomas Goold, Pierre O'Reilly, Eugène O'Keeffe, Lieutenans.

Du Regiment de Bulkeley, N. Commerford, Capitaine; O'Danill, Lieutenant; Thomas Scott, volontaire.

Du Regiment de Dillon: Cusack, Richard Burke, Edouard de Nugent, Jean Dillon, Capitaines; Jean Macdonald, Michael Burke, Edouard de Nugent, Carbery Fox, Lieutenans.

Du Regiment Royal Ecossais: O'Donohu, Douglas, O'Norton, Jean St. Leger, Lord Louis Drummond, Dicconson, Nairne, Damary.

Du Regiment du Roth (Ross): Thomas Macdermott, Dudley Macdermott, Pierre Tauffe.

Du Regiment de Lally: Robert Stack (blessé), Richard Murphi, Alexander Geoghegan (Capitaines); Miles Swiney, Patrice Sarsfeld, Jacques Grant.

Autres officiers françois oui signèrent le même billet. Le Marquis d'Eguilles (Capitaine au Regiment de la Marine); Charles-Guillaume Douglas (Capitaine au Regiment des Milices de Paris); Pierre Colieno (Capitaine au Service d'Espagne); du Saussai (Ingénieur françois); D'Andriou et Charles Bodin (Officiers d'Artillerie); Alexander Gordon (Aumonier des Troupes Françoises).

Liste des officiers du Prince Edouard prisonniers à Inverness: Le Lord Kilmarnock, François Farquharson, André Wood, Alexander Coming, Sprewell, Alexander Buchanan (Capitaines); George Gordon, MacGregor, Jaques Lindsai et Jacques Hai (Lieutenans); Jean Finlayson (Ingéneur); George Law (Aumonier), Nairne (Lieutenant-Trésorier); George Lowther et Jean Rothery (Chirurgiens); le Chevalier Jean Wedderburn (Garde du Corps).

NOTES

CHAPTER ONE

1 Thaumas de la Thaumassière, *Histoire de Berry* (Bourges, 1695). 'En France vinrent au secours de Monseigneur le Dauphin plusieurs seigneurs d'Ecosse avec une grande armée dont étoient conducteurs et chefs les Comtes de Boucain et de Victon et Messire Jean Stuart, Connétable de l'Armée d'Ecosse; lesquels guerroyoient fort contre les Anglois. Et l'année suivante le roi d'Angleterre amena une grande armée en France...'

2 Archives Nationales, J. 677, 20.

3 Archives Départmentales du Cher, 4H, 541, 1.

4 A.N., K. 168, 91.

5 Andrew Stuart, *Genealogical History of the Stuarts*, p. 143. 'En perpetuelle mémoire de tant de signals et importants services les Stuarts étaient accordés le glorieux privilège d'écarteler ses armes de celles de France.'

6 A.N., J. 678, 21, Lettres de créance accordées par Jacques I à ses Ambassadeurs près de Charles VII pour traiter du mariage du Dauphin Louis et de Marguerite d'Ecosse (16 juillet, 1428).

7 Lettres de Charles VII approuvant le mariage de son fils Louis, Dauphin du Viennois et de Marguerite d'Ecosse, ainsi que les conditions et la dot de la princesse (Chinon, 30 octobre 1428).

8 Symphorien Guyon, *Histoire du Siège d'Orléans*, Part II, pp. 186–96.

9 Bib. Nat. Ms. Fr. 14665, 'Le sacrifice des Ecossais à la bataille des Harengs', d'après le Journal du Siège d'Orléans (12 février 1429).

10 La Thaumassière, op. cit. Vol. IV, Chap 1, 'Les seigneurs d'Aubigny de la Maison Royale de Stuart'.

CHAPTER TWO

1 Pierre Sala, *Procès de Jeanne d'Arc*, p. 280.

2 Archives Nationales, J. 409, 57, Lettres closes de Charles VII par lesquelles il autorise son fils Louis, le Dauphin du Viennois à solliciter la dispense d'âge pour son mariage avec Marguerite d'Ecosse (Bourges, 3 juin 1436).

3 Beaucourt, *Histoire de Charles VII*, Vol. II. Regnault de Girard, an eyewitness reported that the King 'se montra moult joyeux et bien content de sa personne'.

4 Archives Départementales, Châlons-sur-Marne, 17 August 1445, G. 463.

5 Obituaire de la Cathedrale de Châlons-sur-Marne. Procès-verbal de la translation du corps de la Dauphine Marguerite de Châlons-sur-Marne à Thouars.

5 Francisque-Michel, *Les Ecossais en France et les Français en Ecosse*, p. 193.

7 Philippe de Commines, *Memoirs*, Vol. II, p. 51.

8 Ibid., p. 75.

9 Archives de La Verrerie, Cote II, Pièce 1, Ordre du roi Louis XI de payer 1,200 livres à Bérault Stuart.
10 Archives de La Verrerie, Cote III, Ordre du Duc de Bourbon à Bérault Stuart de gouverner la ville de Sancerre et la province de Berry.
11 Paulus Jovius, *La Vita del Gran Capitano*, pp. 267–9.
12 Philippe de Commines, op. cit., Book 8, Chap. 1.
13 Paulus Jovius, op. cit., p. 269.
14 Andrew Stuart, *Genealogical History of the Stewarts*, p. 161.
15 Ibid., p. 209.
16 Archives de La Verrerie, Papiers de famille, 1512.

CHAPTER THREE

1 A.N., J. 678, 33, Concession par Louis XII de lettres de naturalité générales pour les Ecossais résident en France. Cette concession d'intéret général fut accordée à la requête de Andréas Forman, archevêque de Bourges, d'origine ecossais et de Robert Stuart, Seigneur d'Aubigny, Capitaine de la Garde Ecossaise. Elle portait exemption pour les Ecossais résident en France de se pouvoir les lettres de naturalité, leur accordant en outre le droit de tester, de succéder et de tenir des bénéfices comme s'ils étaient Français (Amiens, September 1513).
2 Archives de La Verrerie, Cote XXX, Testament d'Anne Stuart (24 decembre 1516). Fondation d'une messe pour sa femme par Robert Stuart (4 avril 1517).
3 La Queulle family, Boulet's *Nobiliaire d'Auvergne* (La Queulle, Culan, Castelnau, Lauzun).
4 Archives de La Verrerie, Cote XIV, Ambassade de Robert Stuart en Ecosse (26 octobre 1520).
5 Archives de La Verrerie, Cote XVIII, Ordonnance du roi François par nommant Robert Stuart lieutenant-géneral de l'armée d'Italie (25 mai 1522).
6 The mother of Anne d'Este was the Princesse Renée de France, younger daughter of Louis XII and Anne de Bretagne. Anne d'Este married Duc François de Guise, and her two elder sons were Duc Henri de Guise (le Balafré) and Louis, Cardinal de Lorraine.
7 Archives de La Verrerie, Papiers de famille, Lettres de François 1 à Robert Stuart sur l'indiscipline de sa compagnie.
8 Archives de La Verrerie, Double de testament de Jacqueline de la Queulle, femme de Robert Stuart (4 juin 1543).
9 A.N., AE. III, 32, Ratification par Marie Stuart du traité d'alliance passé entre ell-meme et François I (Edimbourg, 15 décembre 1543).
10 Archives de La Verrerie, Cote XXII, Jehan Stuart prisonnier à La Bastille (8 août 1543).
11 Archives de La Verrerie, Liasse 10, Cote 86, Inventaire du Châteaux de La Verrerie et d'Aubigny fait par François de l'Aubespine, lieutenant-général du baillage de Berry.

CHAPTER FOUR

1 Jean II, Vicomte de Rohan, married in 1461 Marie de Bretagne, daughter of Francis I, Duc de Bretagne, and the Princess Isabelle Stuart, known as the Duchesse Isabeau.
2 Henri d'Angoulême, fils de Henri II et de Jane Fleming, sa maîtresse écossaise, Governeur de Provence (Musée de Versailles).
3 A.N., J. 679, 56, Lettres de créance données par Marie Stuart pour traiter de son mariage avec le Dauphin François (Fontainebleau, 16 mars 1557).
4 Ibid., 59, Donation du royaume d'Ecosse par Marie Stuart pour le cas ou elle mourrait sans héritier au Roi de France, lors regnant (Fontainebleau, 4 avril 1557).
5 Dispensation accordée.

[6] Archives de La Verrerie, Cote XXIV, le, Paiement de la rançon (5,000 écus d'or) de Jehan Stuart, prisonnier du Comte de Mansfeld (30 mai 1559).

[7] Archives de La Verrerie, Cote XXIII, Pièce 1, Ordre du roi Charles IX s'informer contre certains habitants d'Aubigny.

[8] Archives de La Verrerie, Pièce 2, Lettre du roi Charles IX à Jean Stuart, Seigneur d'Aubigny, l'informant de la sus dite décision.

CHAPTER FIVE

[1] Archives de La Verrerie, Cote XXVII. Contrat de mariage entre Esmé Stuart et Catherine de Balsac d'Entraigues (1572).

[2] Andrew Stuart, *Genealogical History of the Stewarts*, p. 260.

[3] T. Thomson, *Historie and Life of King James the Sext* (Bannantyne Club, Edinburgh, 1825).

[4] Archives de La Verrerie, Papiers de famille. A la demande de Catherine de Balsac Stuart, veuve, le Seigneur de Culan est nommé tuteur de ses enfants (1 août 1583).

[5] Archives de La Verrerie, Cote XXXVII, Homage d'Esmé Stuart à Henri IV (24 avril 1600).

[6] Gowrie conspiracy (5 August 1602).

CHAPTER SIX

[1] *Memoires de Sully*, Tome II, Vol 14, p. 195–204; Vol. 15, p. 213.

CHAPTER SEVEN

[1] Archives du Ministère des Affaires Etrangères (A.M.A.E.), Mem. et Doc. Angleterre, Tome 24.

[2] A.M.A.E., Mem. et Doc. Angleterre, Tome 25, Contrat of Mariage de Monsieur Philippe de France avec Henriette Anne d'Angleterre.

CHAPTER EIGHT

[1] and [2] Chaillot Mss, A.N., K. 1303–1307.

CHAPTER NINE

[1] Frances Jennings married Richard Talbot, Duke of Tyrconnell, one of James's closest friends, and Sarah became Duchess of Marlborough.

[2] Bourbon l'Archambault was the fashionable spa in the seventeenth century, to the west of Moulins, the capital of the Bourbonnais. It is a walled town with the ruins of the main château of the Bourbon dynasty, and in the Cathedral James's great-great-grandfather Antoine de Bourbon married Jeanne d'Albret, the heiress of Navarre, who became the mother of Henri IV. A seventeenth century street opposite the Cathedral is called the Rue Berwick.

[3] A.M.A.E., Mem. et Doc. Angleterre, tome 75, 1, Traitement du mariage du Duc de York.

[4] A.N., Chaillot Mss, K. 1302.

[5] Ibid. 'J'ai été toute ma vie mal logée, étant en Angleterre je logeois à Withal, qui'est come disoit un Ambassadeur la plus laide et la plus incommode maison du monde.'

[6] Four children of James II and Mary of Modena are buried in Westminster Abbey in the same tomb as their great-great-grandmother, Mary, Queen of Scots: (1) Catherine Laura died in 1674 aged 1 month, (2) Isabella died at 4 years old, (3) Charles, Duke of Cambridge, died of smallpox at 1 month and (4) Charlotte Mary died at 2 months old.

[7] Dangeau, *Journal de la Cour* (June, 1688). 'On apprit que la Reine d'Angleterre était accouchée d'un fils et que son père lui donnera blentôt le titre de Prince de Galles.'

[8] These autograph letters from Lauzun to Louvois are preserved in the Archives of the Duc de La Force. Four of the most interesting were published in *Les Caumont La Force* (Fasquelle, 1960) by Auguste de Caumont, Duc de La Force, of the Académie Française.

CHAPTER TEN

1 A.M.A.E., Mem. et Doc. Angleterre, Tome 75. Louis XIV kept himself informed of the movements of his enemy William of Orange through the French Ambassador at the Hague, the Comte d'Avaux, and through the French Ambassador in London, Barillon.

2 Bib. Nat. Estampes, L'arrivée du Roi d'Angleterre en France, 25 décembre 1688. 'Le roi débarqua à Ambleteuse d'une barque de pêcheur le jour de Noel à trois heures du matin. Il se prosterna, remercia Dieu, se coucha quelques heures puis entendit la messe. Reçu magnifiquement à Boulogne et à Amiens, il fut le lendemain à St Germain.'

3 Bib. Nat. Estampes, gravure, Louis XIV accueille Jacques II à St Germain (26 décembre 1688).

4 A.N., AE.111, 83, Rélation des évènements de 1688 écrite àSt Germain, sous la dictée de Jacques II.

5 Soeur Angélique Priolo came from a distinguished Marseilles family of Italian origin.

6 A.N., K. 1302.The originals of these letters are contained in the Chaillot Mss.

7 The present Turkish Embassy occupies the site of the Lauzun house in Passy.

8 A.N., K. 1302, Lettre de Marie de Modène à la Supérieure de la Visitation de Chaillot, après avoir eu connaissance du désastre de la Hogue (St Germain, 14 juin 1692).

9 Arch. Communales, St German-en-Laye, Acte de baptême de la Princesse Louise Marie Stuart, née à St Germain le 28 juin 1692.

10 Dangeau, *Journal* (24 avril 1698). 'Le Roi alla à la chasse au vol dans la plaine de Veziné; le Roi d'Angleterre et le Prince de Galles y étaient. On prit un milan noir et le Roi fit expédier une ordonnance de 2,000 écus pour le chef du vol. Autrefois il donnait le cheval sur lequel il était monté et sa robe de chambre.'

11 James had told Louis XIV that Berwick's rank in the English army was Lieutenant-General and that he hoped Louis could have him confirmed in this rank in the French army. Louis said, after consulting the Maréchal de Luxembourg, that this was not possible immediately but that Berwick would be made Lieutenant-General at the next promotion.

12 Dangeau, *Journal* (9 novembre 1700). 'On apprit la mort du Roi d'Espagne arrivée le jour de la Toussaint.'

13 A.N., K.1302, Chaillot Mss.

14 A.N., Chaillot Mss.

15 Arch. Communales, St Germain-en-Laye, Acte de décès de Jacques II, roi d'Angleterre, d'Ecosse et d'Irelande (16 septembre 1701).

CHAPTER ELEVEN

1 A.M.A.E., Mem. et Doc. Angleterre, Tome 75, Memoire sur la recognition du Prince de Galles comme roi d'Angleterre.

2 Ibid., Text of Bill of Attainder in which William III made it a treasonable offence for any British subject to correspond with or send money to the Pretender.

3 A.M.A.E., Mem. et Doc. Angleterre, Tome 75.

4 A.N., K. 1302,77, Letter with a black mourning seal from Queen Mary of Modena to Mère Priolo (21 August 1702).

5 A.M.A.E., Mem. et Doc. Angleterre, Tome, 207, Pleins pouvoirs de Louis XIV au Sieur Nathaniel Hook, Colonel au service de France pour traiter avec les Ecossais (9 mars 1707). Col. Hook à Dunkerque (8 avril 1707).

6 Ibid., Memoire des demandes des seigneurs eccossais remis au Sieur Hook (7 mai 1707).

7 Ibid., 213, Lettre de recommandation pour M. Hook allant en Ecosse, addressée par M. de Torcy à M. de Gassé. Disposition pour le voyage du Prétendant auquel on donne le nom de Roi d'Angleterre (6 mars 1708).

8 Ibid., Lettre de Louis XIV au Prétendant. Il l'engage à renoncer à son entreprise et à revenir à St Germain et lui annonce qu'il va faire rentrer sa flotte à Dunkerque et ses troupes dans leurs quartiers (11 mars 1708).

[9] Ibid., Lettre de Louis XIV au Prétendant avec compliments de condoléance sur le mauvais succès de son entreprise (11 avril 1708).

CHAPTER TWELVE

[1] A.M.A.E., Mem. et Doc. Angleterre, Tome 75, Lettre du Chevalier de St Georges à la Reine Anne.
[2] A.N., Chaillot Mss., K. 1302.
[3] A.N., Chaillot Mss, K. 1302, 85. 'A St Germain ce 6 octobre 1701. Mon coeur et mon âme sont tristes jusqu'a lamort . . . Il me manque tous les jours d'avantage dans milles sortes de rencontres.' Letter, black-edged with a black mourning seal, addressed to the Superior of Chaillot.
[4] A.N., Chaillot Mss, K. 1302.
[5] Ibid., 165 bis, copie de la lettre du Roi d'Angleterre à S.M.T.C. écrite à Châlons le 19 février 1713. With Madame de Maintenon's comments.
[6] A.N., Chaillot mss, K. 1302.
[7] A.M.A.E., Mem et Doc. Angleterre, Tome 75, 238, 245, 249, 261 (3 mars 1714).
Lettre du Prétendant à l'Abbé Gaulthier.
Lettre du Prétendant au Vicomte Bolingbroke.
Lettre du Prétendant à la Reine Anne (en copie) par laquelle il lui demande de restorer les Stuarts sur le trône d'Angleterre lui assurant la survivance.
Lettre du Prétendant au Comte d'Oxford.
Lettre du Prétendant à Lord Paulet.

CHAPTER THIRTEEN

[1] A.M.A.E., Mem. et Doc. Angleterre, Tome 75, 64, Letter from James III to Torcy, 13 August (N.S.), 1 August (O.S.). The English calendar was not brought into line with the European one until 1751.
[2] Ibid., 169, Protestation solenelle contre l'Usurpation de son droit héréditaire à la couronne d'Angleterre par l'Elector de Brunswick (29 août 1714).
[3] Ibid., 169.
[4] Ibid., 170
[5] *Memoires du Maréchal, Duc de Berwick.*
[6] A.M.A.E., Mem. et Doc. Angleterre, Tome 75, 173, Letter from the Maréchal de Villeroi to Madame de Maintenon.
[7] Duc de La Force, *Les Caumont La Force*, 'La chaise de poste à Nonancourt'.
[8] The Hotel de Serre no longer exists. These houses and the rue St Marc were demolished when the present Avenue de la République was constructed in Napoleon's time.
[9] Berwick made over to his son aged nineteen the title and rank of Grandee of Spain, first-class, with the Duchies of Liria and Xerica.
[10] El Marischal Duque de Berwick, *Letters*. Berwick's children by his second marriage were Henri Jacques de Fitzjames (b. 1702, d. 1721); Henriette (b. 1705, d. 1739); François (b. 1709, d. 1764), who renounced the dukedom of Fitzjames to become Evêque de Soissons and Grand Aumonier to Louis XV; Laure Anne (b. 1710, d. 1766); Henry (b. 1711, d. 1731), who became a priest; Charles (b. 1712, d. 1787), who succeeded Henri as Duc de Fitzjames, and was Marèchal de France; and Edouard (b. 1715, d. 1758), who was at Culloden as Maréchal de Camp in the Regiment of Fitzjames.
[11] The Czar made a point of visiting the tomb of Cardinal Richelieu, the French statesman he most admired, in the chapel of the Sorbonne. A contemporary Russian colour print depicts Peter laying his great hand affectionately on the marble effigy of the Cardinal.
[12] *Letters from Liselotte*, translated by Maria Kroll, p. 195.

13 A.N., K. 1303, Autographe lettre de Jacques III à la Supérieure de Chaillot.
14 Arch. Dép. Seine et Oise, Liste des officiers de la reine d'Angleterre qui demeurent sans emploi par suite de son décès.
15 The composers James most probably listened to were Arcangelo Corelli and Domenico Scarlatti.
16 A.M.A.E., Mem. et Doc. Angleterre, Tome 75, Le Prétendant notifies the Regent of the birth of his son, 'a strong healthy boy', on December 31 1720. Prince Charles Edward Louis John Casimir Sylvester Maria Sobieski. Same official notification to Louis XV, 1 janvier à Rome.
17 Two large paintings in the Louvre by Pannini show the fêtes to celebrate the birth of the French dauphin. One is a gala performance at the Opera with the Stuarts present, and the other shows the fireworks in the Piazza Navone.

CHAPTER FOURTEEN

1 The first Duke of Richmond died in 1723. Arch. Dep. Cher., F.23, 41, A letter written on behalf of Louis XV by Torcy addressed him as, 'très Haut, très puissant Prince Monseigneur de Lenos, Duc de Richmond, de Lennox et d'Aubigny, Pair de France, d'Angleterre et d'Ecosse'.
2 A.M.A.E., Mem. et Doc. Angleterre, Tome 78, 1 A, Lettre de Lord Sempill.
3 Ibid., Tome 76, 2, Lettre de sept seigneurs éccossais au Cardinal Fleury (Edimbourg, 13 mars 1741).
4 Ibid., Tome 78.
5 A.M.A.E., Mem. et Doc. Angleterre, Tome 75, vol 406.
6 Ibid.
7 Ibid.
8 Stuart Papers at Windsor,p. 110.
9 Ibid., p. 112.
10 A.M.A.E., Mem. et Doc. Angleterre, Tome 78, 1, Mémoire sur la situation de l'intérieure de l'Angleterre, 30 janvier 1745 à Paris.

CHAPTER FIFTEEN

1 A.M.A.E., Mem. et Doc. Angleterre, Tome 78, 4, Autographe lettre de Jacques III à M. d'Argenson, Rome ce 22 février 1745.
2 Ibid., 5, Autographe lettre de Jacques II à M. d'Argenson pour introduire Milord Sempill (23 février 1745). 'Milord Sempill de qui vous recevez cette lettre est d'une ancienne famille catholique d'Ecosse et depuis quelques années il a été dans une étroite liaison et confiance avec mes amis dans ce Royaume et même avec ceux d'Angleterre . . .'
3 A.M.A.E., Mem. et Doc. Angleterre, Tome 78. 'Le Baron revint hier soir de Versailles en bonne santé et il n'est pas encore levé.'
4 Ibid., 7, Reflections sur la mort du Chevalier Robert Walpole (mars 1745).
5 Ibid., 8, L'affaire Maclean.
6 Ibid., 9, Lettre à ce sujet du Roi Jacques III (10 mars 1745).
7 Bishop Robert Forbes, *The Lyon in Mourning*, Vol. III, pp. 180–81. January to May, Negotiations of John Blaw of Castlehill in France.
8 Antoine Walsh descendant d'une famille Irlandaise, né à St Malo en 1703, mort à Saint Domingue en 1783.
9 A.M.A.E., Mem. et Doc. Angleterre, Tome 78, 17, le 5 mai 1745.
10 These spelling mistakes are the Prince's.
11 From 1740 until the end of the *ancien régime* in 1789, 24 livres = 1 louis d'or.
12 Fontenoy, the French victory won by the Marèchal de Saxe over the English and Dutch, at which Louis XV was himself present. The English troops were commanded by the Duke of Cumberland, who was three months younger than Prince Charles Edward.

13 A.M.A.E., Mem. et Doc. Angleterre, Tome 78, 23, Autographe letter in French dated 12 June 1745 from Le Prince Charles Edouard to 'Monsieur mon oncle le Roi Louis XV'. On 16 May 1745 Charles had been named Regent by his father.

14 *Une famille royaliste irlandaise et française*, p. 21. 'Vendredi le 2 juillet 1745. Au nom de Dieu et de la très sainte Trinité. Soit commencé le présent journal pour servir à moi, Durbé, commandant de la Frégate Dutillet de Nantes, armée en guerre pour faire le voyage d'Ecosse.'

15 A.M.A.E., Mem. et Doc. Angleterre, Tome 78.

16 Ibid., 16A.

CHAPTER SIXTEEN

1 Arch. de Guerre, A. 3152, Plan de baies de Loknover [Loch-nan-Uamh] and Withs [Uist] et d'une partie de la côte occidentale d'Ecosse. Loch-nan-Uamh is a wild and desolate sea loch between Arisaig and Moidart.

2 *Une famille royaliste irlandaise, écossaise et française*, p. 29.

3 A.M.A.E., Mem. et Doc. Angleterre, Tome 78, 150, Autographe lettre du Prince Charles à 'Monsieur mon oncle, Louis XV'.

4 Ibid., 16, Lettre du Chevalier de St Georges [Jacques III] au Roy Louis XV (11 août 1745).

5 Ibid., 16A, Prince Charles Edward's printed offer of £30,000 reward for the capture of the Elector of Hanover.

6 *L'Ascanius Moderne*, Part I, p. 35.

7 *Une famille royaliste, irlandaise, écossaise et française*, p. 34.

8 Archives du Chateau de Serrant. 'Boradel, le 16 aoust [5 August O.S.] 1745. Monsieur le Chevalier Walsh, non obstant tout ce que je vous-ai dit de bouche, je ne puis vous laisser partir sans vous donner un témoinage par écrit du contentement que j'ai reçu de vos services. J'ai prié le Roy, mon Père, de vous en donner une marque éclatante, et je le ferois moi-meme dès à présent si j'en avois le pouvoir. Ainsi, vous pouvez compter que si jamais je parviens au trône, ou ma naissance m'appelle etc. Votre bon ami Charles P.'

9 A.M.A.E., Mem. et Doc. Angleterre, Tome 78, 76, Letter from Alexandre de Boyer, Marquis d'Eguilles, from Dunkirk to the Marquis d'Argenson for the attention of Louis XV (1 October 1745).

10 Ibid., 77, Letter from D'Eguilles to d'Argenson for the attention of Louis XV (1 October 1745).

11 Ibid., 70, Letter from Henry, Duke of York, to Louis XV, from Avignon (27 September 1745).

12 Ibid., 83, Memoire à Fontainebleau le 8 octobre 1745

13 Ibid., 108. 'Le Prince Charles Edouard de la Maison Royale de Stuart, ayant été proclamé dans Edimbourg en qualité de Regent du Royaume d'Ecosse, et étant ainsi que Sa Majesté Très Chrétienne en guerre avec le Roy George, Electeur d'Hanover, auroit, fait proposer à S.M.T.C. de lui envoyer des troupes auxiliaires pour etre employées contre leur Enemi commun et d'unir leurs interests par un Traité d'Alliance, S.M.T.C., ayant agrée cette proposition, les Ministres soussignés, dument autorisé de part et d'autre sont convenus les articles suivants. . . .'

A.M.A.E., Tome 78, 109, Articles du Traité de Fontainebleau. Le present Traité sera ratifié et les ratifications en serons échangés à Paris dans le temps de 2 mois ou plutôt si faire se peut. Fait à Fontainebleau le 24 octobre 1745.

14 A.M.A.E., Mem. et Doc. Angleterre, Tome 78, 111, Letter introducing the Chevalier James Stuart of Goodtrees as the Prince's agent to Louis XV (24 October 1745).

15 Ibid., 135, Liste des gens considerable qui sont à l'armée du Prince Edouard.

16 Ibid., 136. Liste des troupes composent l'armée du Prince.

[17] A.M.A.E., Mem. et Doc. Angleterre, Tome 78, Letter from O'Bryen to d'Argenson.
[18] The Duc de Richelieu was a friend of the Prince's cousin the Duc de Fitzjames.
[19] A.M.A.E., Mem. et Doc. Angletrre, Tome 78, Letter from Sir Thomas Sheridan to d'Argenson (2 mars 1745).
[20] Ibid., 13, Letter from D'Eguilles. 'En général toutes les femmes jeunes ou jolies sont Jacobites et ne sont la pluspart que depuis l'arrivée du jeune Prince. Ce n'est pas qu'il soit coquet ou galant, c'est peut être au contraire parce qu'il l'est pas et que les Ecossoises, naturellement sérieuses et passionées, en concluant qu'il est véritablement tendre et qu'il seroit constant. C'est une femme qui m'a donné cette explication. Quoi qu'il en soit, il est certain que l'amitié des femmes ne fait pas la plus petite force de son party' (à Inverness, 6 avril 1745).
[21] Arch. de Guerre, A. 3154.
[22] The English calendar was not changed to correspond with the European calendar until 1751.
[23] A.N., K. 1351, 79, Lettre d'Argenson au Comte de Broglie ou il insiste sur la nécessité pour le roi d'Angleterre d'être clément envers les partisans du Prince Charles Edouard (26 mai 1746).
[24] Stuart Papers at Windsor, p. 148.
[25] A.N., K. 1351, 79. On 26 May 1746 the Minister of War, the Comte d'Argenson, had noted that it was necessary to do something for the defeated partisans of Prince Charles.
[26] The Comte Thomas de Lally, of Irish origin, was a naturalized Frenchman who became Governor of the French East India Company, and, as Governor of Pondicherry, capitulated to the English. He was convicted of treason on his return to France and executed in 1761. He was rehabilitated by his son the Marquis de Lally-Tollendal, Thomas de Lally was forty-three at the time of the Forty-five.
[27] Stuart Papers at Windsor, p. 155.

CHAPTER SEVENTEEN

[1] A.M.A.E., Mem. et Doc. Angleterre, Tome 78, Letter from Cardinal Tencin to James III, dated Fontainebleau, 15 October 1746: 'Sire, Je respire. Le Prince est sauvé; il est heureusement arrivé à Rosehof [Roscoff] qui est le vieux rade entre Rennes et Morlaix.'
[2] Ibid., 54, Etat d'officiers écossois passés en France à la suite du Prince Charles Edouard.
[3] Ibid., 39.
[4] Ibid., 40.
[5] Lochiel got his regiment but not his peerage.
[6] A.M.A.E., Mem. et Doc. Angleterre, Tome 80.
[7] Ibid., Tome 78, 41, The Prince protests to Louis XV against the terms of the Treaty of Aix-la-Chapelle.
[8] Ibid., Tome 80, 41, The Prince protests etc. 'Je m'oppose et m'opposerai Absolument à tout cequi pouroit être dit, fait, et stipulé à Aix-la-Chapelle ou ailleurs. J'espère que S.M.T.C. fera toutes les reflections qu'elle prendra à Mon Egard. Je regarde cette Conjoncture come Etant plus critique pour les interests de S.M.T.C. que pour les miens. Je vous prie Sa Majesté de tout Mon Respect et Attachement. Rien ne m'est plus à Coeur que luy Devenir utille un jour, et de luy prouver que les véritables Interests me sont plus Chères que ses Ministres. Charles P.'
[9] A.M.A.E., Mem. et Doc. Angleterre, Tome 80, Lettre du Roi Jacques III à son fils le Prince Edouard, Rome, ce 23 novembre 1748, autographe. 'Quelque soin que vous ayez pris, mon cher fils, de me cacher ce qui s'est passé entre la Cour de France et vous, depuis la signature des préliminaires, je suis, cependant, informé de tout et je vous avoue que je n'ai pu lire sans une vraie surprise et douleur votre letter au duc de Gesvres etc.'

[10] Ibid., Tome 80, 81, Lettre du Capitaine de la Garde à Versailles (10 décembre 1748). 'Monseigneur, J'ai l'honneur de rendre compte à Votre Grandeur que M. de Vaudreuil a arrêté le Prince Edouard dans le cul-de-sac de l'Opéra. M. de Vaudreuil ayant pris la précaution de le faire saisir par quatre sergents. Les gentilhommes de sa suite ont été aussi arrestés.'

[11] Ibid., Tome 80, 82, Lettre du Duc de Fitzjames à Monsieur le Comte de Maurepas, Ministère et Secrétaire d'Etat. Letter acknowledged but marked 'Le Roy n'a pas jugé convenable d'accorder sa permission'.

[12] Ibid., 83, Le Cardinal Tencin est informé de toutes les demandes faites au 11 décembre etc.

[13] Ibid., 93 and 94.

[14] Ibid.

CHAPTER EIGHTEEN

[1] A.M.A.E., Mem. et Doc. Angleterre, Tome 80. 430.

13 juin 1759, Projet militaire pour un débarquement dans les Isles Britannique; M. Mackenzie, M. douglas et le Cte. de Leslie.

15 juin 1759, Réponse du duc de Choiseul.

16 juin 1759, Liste des Seigneurs Eccossois qui sont attachés aux intérêt de la famille de Stuart, et qui se réuniront en Parlement d'Ecosse aussitot que les Troupes Françaises se seront mises en possession d'Edimbourg.

10 septembre 1759, Instructions données par Louis XV au Duc d'Aiguillon, commandant-en-chef des troupes françaises destinées à passer en Ecosse.

23 septembre 1759, Rapport sur l'état actuel de l'Ecosse et les bonnes dispositions de ses habitans pour la France et les Stuarts.

15 novembre 1759, projet de declaration du Duc d'Aiguillon aux habitans de la Grande Bretagne.

20 novembre 1759, Lettre du Duc de Choiseul au Duc d'Aiguillon, approbative de la déclaration précedente.

[2] Stuart Papers at Windsor, p. 218.

[3] Bishop Robert Forbes, *The Lyon in Mourning,* Vol. III, p. 137.

[4] John Douglas was the most usual of the Prince's many pseudonyms during his wanderings in Europe. He also called himself Woulfe, Burton, Thomson etc.

[5] A.M.A.E., Mem. et Doc. Angleterre, Tome 80, 54, Mémoires sur un projet de descente en Ecosse en 1759 par le Duc de Choiseul, le Duc de Soubise et le Cte de Douglas.

[6] On 20 October 1759 King James had written to Sir John Graeme at St Germain: 'You will, I am sure, be concerned for poor Lord Lismore's death. I am myself very much so and with reason; for I have lost in him a true friend, and an old and faithful servant.' As Colonel Daniel O'Bryen, Lord Lismore was James III's accredited agent at the French Court from 1744 throughout the Jacobite Rising. He signed the Treaty of Fontainbleau in October 1745 on behalf of the Prince and his father. James added: 'After serious reflexion I have determined to call for you (Graeme) here to replace Lord Lismore, but without the title of Secretary-of-State.'

[7] This convent, a beautiful decaying eighteenth-century house, still stands hidden in an inner courtyard behind a fish shop and a vegetable shop at 171, rue St Jacques. It has come down in the world and is now let out in rooms, with very little comfort. The fine curving staircase is now very worn. The original windows remain, looking out on the shabby cobbled courtyard.

[8] A.M.A.E., Mem. et Doc. Rome, 841, Extrait du testament du Chevalier de Chevalier de St Georges (1 janvier 1766). Oraison funèbre prononcé en presence du Pape, par le prélate Mattei.

[9] Ibid., Mémoire du Cardinal York su la necessité ou se trouve le St Siège de reconnaitre pour uniques successeurs légitimes au trône d'Angleterre, les Princes de la Maison de Stuart (8 janvier 1766).
[10] Ibid., Lettre du Cd. York à Louis XV sur la mort de son père (8 janvier 1766).
[11] Ibid., Lettre du Prince Edouard à Louis XV sur la mort de son père (29 janvier 1766).
[12] Ibid., 834, Sur la pension annuelle des Stuarts.
[13] Arch. Dép. Oise, Parish register of Fitzjames dated 2 September 1771. Marriage de Charles Fitzjames Stuart, Marquis de Jamaique, petit-fils du Maréchal de Berwick avec Carolin Augusta de Stolberg-Gendern.
[14] François-Jacques Walsh, né à Saint-Malo en 1711, mort à Serrant en 1782.
[15] Contrat de mariage du Prince Charles Edward et la Princesse Louise-Maximilienne de Stolberg (13 avril 1772, copie Comte de Pange).
[16] A.N., K. 1303, 105, Mémoire par lequel Charlotte, fille du Prince Charles Edward, sollicite des secours du Roi de France.

EPILOGUE

[1] Weymouth was the favourite holiday resort of King George III and his six daughters. They stayed in the house belonging to his son the Duke of Gloucester. The King hunted in Dorset, and kept a yacht in Weymouth Bay so that he and his family could make sea trips along the South Coast. Later the Prince of Wales made Brighton the fashionable royal resort, when he built the Pavilion during his Regency.
[2] The Musée Fabre in Montpellier contains several portraits of Louise, Comtesse d'Albany, and also a pastel of Charlotte, Duchess of Albany, by H. D. Hamilton.
[3] In 1790 Thomas Coutts visited the Cardinal York at Frascati as executor of Charlotte's will (Henrietta Tayler, *Letters of Charlotte, Duchess of Albany*).

APPENDIX I

[1] Aeneas Macdonald was in fact with the Prince throughout the campaign, and was the younger brother of Macdonald of Kinlochmoidart.
[2] This was Sir John Macdonnell, who sailed with the Prince from Nantes.
[3] This was John Murray of Broughton, who later turned King's evidence against some of his fellow Jacobites.

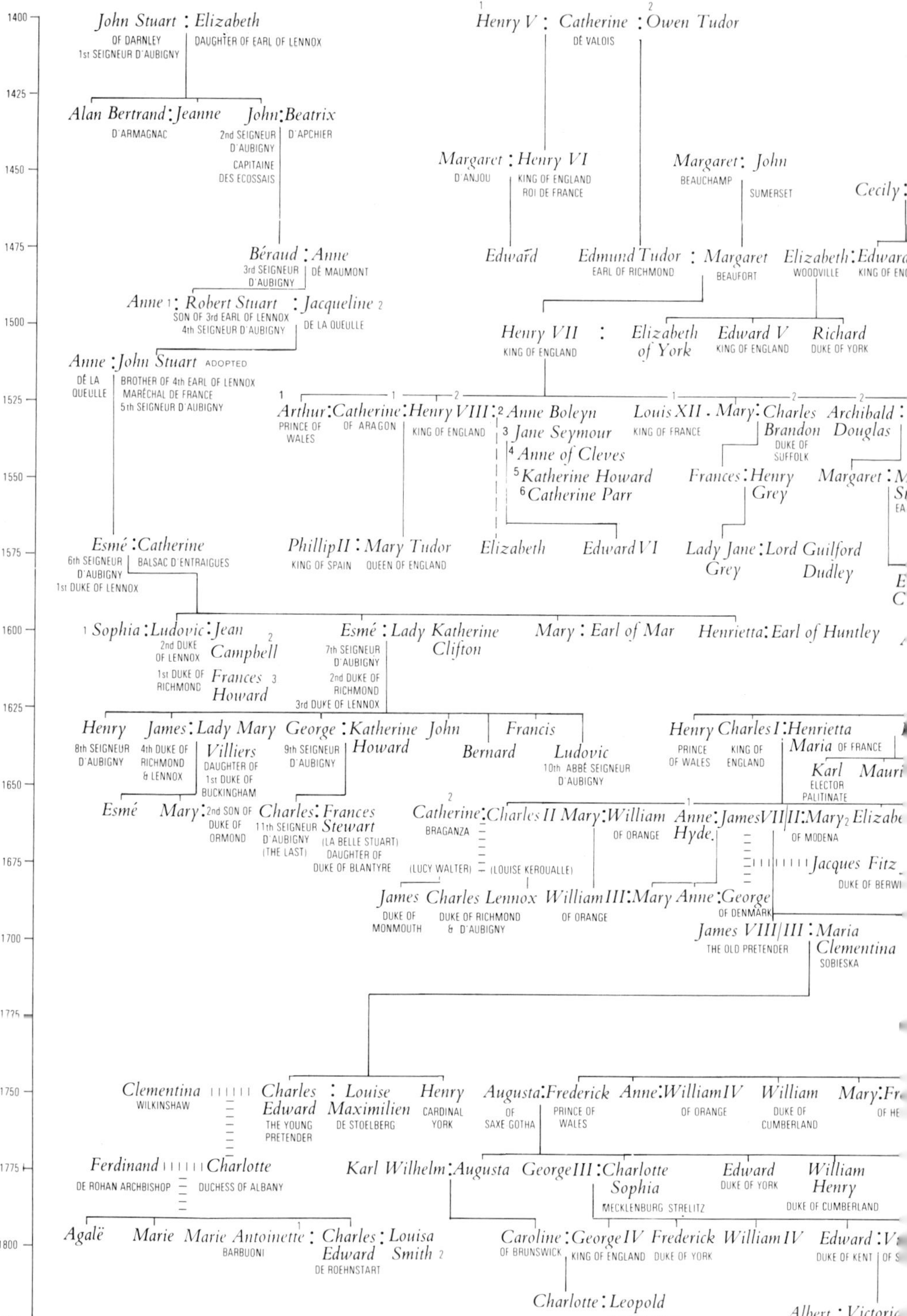

1400
1425
1450
1475
1500
1525
1550
1575
1600
1625
1650
1675
1700
1725
1750
1775
1800
1825
John Stuart : Elizabeth
OF DARNLEY
1st SEIGNEUR D'AUBIGNY
DAUGHTER OF EARL OF LENNOX
1 Henry V : Catherine : 2 Owen Tudor
DE VALOIS
Alan Bertrand : Jeanne
D'ARMAGNAC
John : Beatrix
2nd SEIGNEUR D'AUBIGNY
CAPITAINE DES ECOSSAIS
D'APCHIER
Margaret : Henry VI
D'ANJOU
KING OF ENGLAND
ROI DE FRANCE
Margaret : John
BEAUCHAMP
SUMERSET
Cecily :
Béraud : Anne
3rd SEIGNEUR D'AUBIGNY
DE MAUMONT
Edward
Edmund Tudor : Margaret
EARL OF RICHMOND
BEAUFORT
Elizabeth : Edward
WOODVILLE
KING OF ENG
Anne 1 : Robert Stuart : Jacqueline 2
SON OF 3rd EARL OF LENNOX
4th SEIGNEUR D'AUBIGNY
DE LA QUEULLE
Henry VII : Elizabeth of York
KING OF ENGLAND
Edward V
KING OF ENGLAND
Richard
DUKE OF YORK
Anne : John Stuart
ADOPTED
DE LA QUEULLE
BROTHER OF 4th EARL OF LENNOX
MARÉCHAL DE FRANCE
5th SEIGNEUR D'AUBIGNY
1 Arthur : Catherine : Henry VIII : 2 Anne Boleyn
PRINCE OF WALES
OF ARAGON
KING OF ENGLAND
3 Jane Seymour
4 Anne of Cleves
5 Katherine Howard
6 Catherine Parr
Louis XII . Mary : Charles Brandon
KING OF FRANCE
DUKE OF SUFFOLK
Archibald : Douglas
Frances : Henry Grey
Margaret :
Phillip II : Mary Tudor
KING OF SPAIN
QUEEN OF ENGLAND
Elizabeth
Edward VI
Lady Jane Grey : Lord Guilford Dudley
Esmé : Catherine
6th SEIGNEUR D'AUBIGNY
1st DUKE OF LENNOX
BALSAC D'ENTRAIGUES
1 Sophia : Ludovic : Jean Campbell 2
2nd DUKE OF LENNOX
1st DUKE OF RICHMOND
Frances Howard 3
Esmé : Lady Katherine Clifton
7th SEIGNEUR D'AUBIGNY
2nd DUKE OF RICHMOND
3rd DUKE OF LENNOX
Mary : Earl of Mar
Henrietta : Earl of Huntley
Henry
8th SEIGNEUR D'AUBIGNY
James : Lady Mary Villiers
4th DUKE OF RICHMOND & LENNOX
DAUGHTER OF 1st DUKE OF BUCKINGHAM
George : Katherine Howard
9th SEIGNEUR D'AUBIGNY
John
Bernard
Francis
Ludovic
10th ABBÉ SEIGNEUR D'AUBIGNY
Henry
PRINCE OF WALES
Charles I : Henrietta Maria
KING OF ENGLAND
OF FRANCE
Karl
ELECTOR PALITINATE
Esmé
Mary : 2nd SON OF DUKE OF ORMOND
Charles : Frances Stewart
11th SEIGNEUR D'AUBIGNY (THE LAST)
(LA BELLE STUART)
DAUGHTER OF DUKE OF BLANTYRE
2 Catherine : Charles II
BRAGANZA
(LUCY WALTER)
(LOUISE KEROUALLE)
Mary : William
OF ORANGE
Anne Hyde : 1 James VII/II : Mary 2
OF MODENA
Jacques Fitz
DUKE OF BERWI
James
DUKE OF MONMOUTH
Charles Lennox
DUKE OF RICHMOND & D'AUBIGNY
William III : Mary
OF ORANGE
Anne : George
OF DENMARK
James VIII/III : Maria Clementina
THE OLD PRETENDER
SOBIESKA
Clementina
WILKINSHAW
Charles Edward : Louise Maximilien
THE YOUNG PRETENDER
DE STOELBERG
Henry
CARDINAL YORK
Augusta : Frederick
OF SAXE GOTHA
PRINCE OF WALES
Anne : William IV
OF ORANGE
William
DUKE OF CUMBERLAND
Ferdinand
DE ROHAN ARCHBISHOP
Charlotte
DUCHESS OF ALBANY
Karl Wilhelm : Augusta
George III : Charlotte Sophia
MECKLENBURG STRELITZ
Edward
DUKE OF YORK
William Henry
DUKE OF CUMBERLAND
Agalë
Marie
1 Marie Antoinette : Charles Edward : Louisa Smith 2
BARBUONI
DE ROEHNSTART
Caroline : George IV
OF BRUNSWICK
KING OF ENGLAND
Frederick
DUKE OF YORK
William IV
Edward
DUKE OF KENT
Charlotte : Leopold
OF SAXE COBURG
Albert : Victoria
OF SAXE COBURG GOTHA

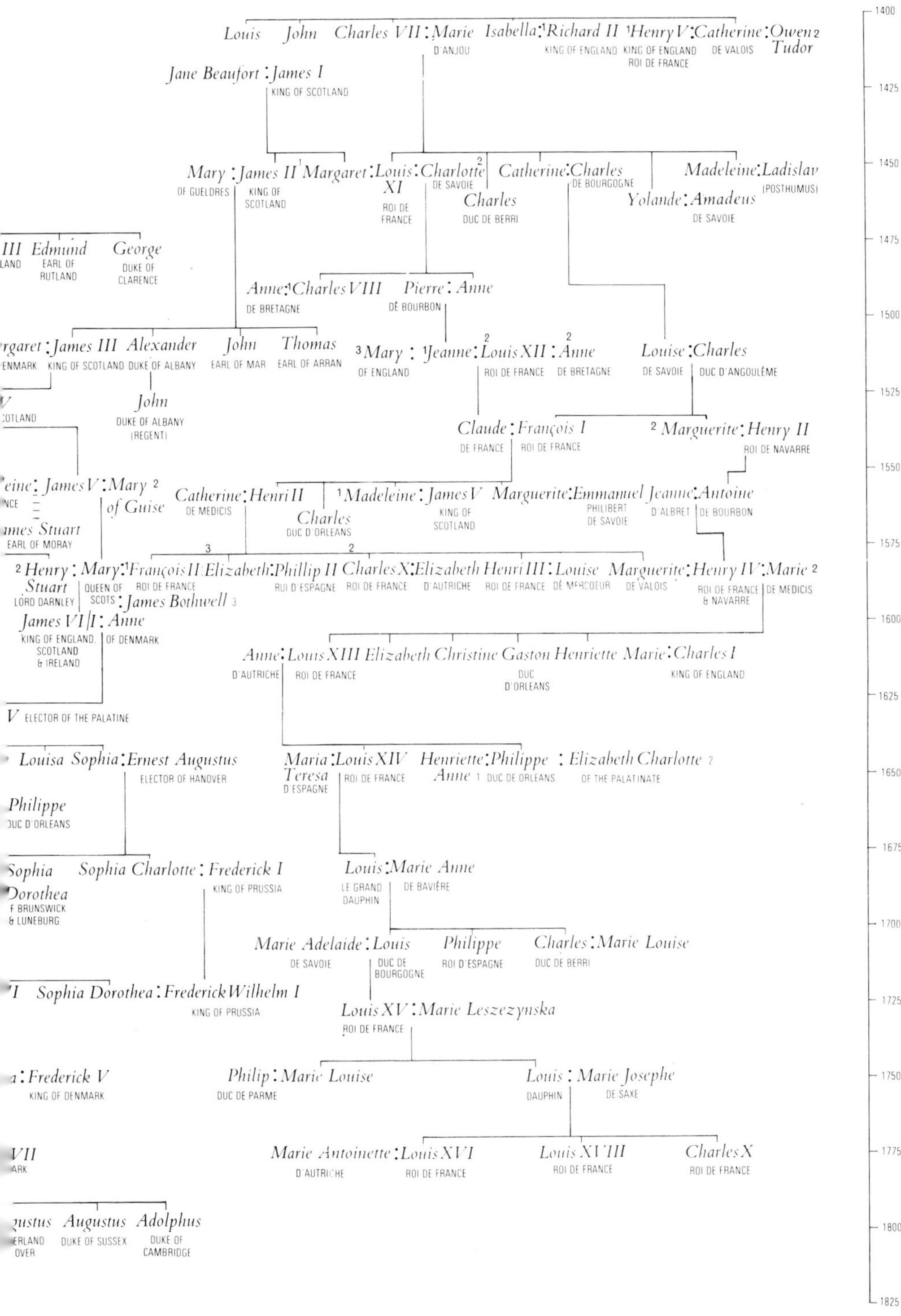

Louis
John
Charles VII : Marie
D'ANJOU
Isabella : Richard II
KING OF ENGLAND
Henry V : Catherine : Owen Tudor
KING OF ENGLAND ROI DE FRANCE
DE VALOIS
Jane Beaufort : James I
KING OF SCOTLAND
Mary : James II
OF GUELDRES
KING OF SCOTLAND
Margaret : Louis XI : Charlotte
ROI DE FRANCE
DE SAVOIE
Catherine : Charles
DE BOURGOGNE
Charles
DUC DE BERRI
Madeleine : Ladislav
(POSTHUMUS)
Yolande : Amadeus
DE SAVOIE
III
Edmund
EARL OF RUTLAND
George
DUKE OF CLARENCE
Anne : Charles VIII
DE BRETAGNE
Pierre : Anne
DE BOURBON
rgaret : James III
ENMARK
KING OF SCOTLAND
Alexander
DUKE OF ALBANY
John
EARL OF MAR
Thomas
EARL OF ARRAN
Mary : Jeanne : Louis XII : Anne
OF ENGLAND
ROI DE FRANCE
DE BRETAGNE
Louise : Charles
DE SAVOIE
DUC D'ANGOULÊME
John
DUKE OF ALBANY (REGENT)
Claude : François I
DE FRANCE
ROI DE FRANCE
Marguerite : Henry II
ROI DE NAVARRE
eine : James V : Mary of Guise
Catherine : Henri II
DE MEDICIS
Charles
DUC D'ORLEANS
Madeleine : James V
KING OF SCOTLAND
Marguerite : Emmanuel Philibert
DE SAVOIE
Jeanne : Antoine
D'ALBRET
DE BOURBON
ames Stuart
EARL OF MORAY
Henry Stuart : Mary : François II
LORD DARNLEY
QUEEN OF SCOTS
ROI DE FRANCE
James Bothwell
Elizabeth : Phillip II
ROI D'ESPAGNE
Charles X : Elizabeth
ROI DE FRANCE
D'AUTRICHE
Henri III : Louise
ROI DE FRANCE
DE MERCOEUR
Marguerite : Henry IV : Marie
DE VALOIS
ROI DE FRANCE & NAVARRE
DE MEDICIS
James VI/I : Anne
KING OF ENGLAND, SCOTLAND & IRELAND
OF DENMARK
Anne : Louis XIII
D'AUTRICHE
ROI DE FRANCE
Elizabeth
Christine
Gaston
DUC D'ORLEANS
Henriette Marie : Charles I
KING OF ENGLAND
V ELECTOR OF THE PALATINE
Louisa Sophia : Ernest Augustus
ELECTOR OF HANOVER
Maria Teresa : Louis XIV
D'ESPAGNE
ROI DE FRANCE
Henriette Anne : Philippe : Elizabeth Charlotte
DUC DE ORLEANS
OF THE PALATINATE
Philippe
DUC D'ORLEANS
Sophia Dorothea
F BRUNSWICK & LUNEBURG
Sophia Charlotte : Frederick I
KING OF PRUSSIA
Louis : Marie Anne
LE GRAND DAUPHIN
DE BAVIÈRE
Marie Adelaide : Louis
DE SAVOIE
DUC DE BOURGOGNE
Philippe
ROI D'ESPAGNE
Charles : Marie Louise
DUC DE BERRI
I
Sophia Dorothea : Frederick Wilhelm I
KING OF PRUSSIA
Louis XV : Marie Leszezynska
ROI DE FRANCE
a : Frederick V
KING OF DENMARK
Philip : Marie Louise
DUC DE PARME
Louis : Marie Josephe
DAUPHIN
DE SAXE
VII
ARK
Marie Antoinette : Louis XVI
D'AUTRICHE
ROI DE FRANCE
Louis XVIII
ROI DE FRANCE
Charles X
ROI DE FRANCE
gustus
ERLAND
OVER
Augustus
DUKE OF SUSSEX
Adolphus
DUKE OF CAMBRIDGE
1400
1425
1450
1475
1500
1525
1550
1575
1600
1625
1650
1675
1700
1725
1750
1775
1800
1825

BIBLIOGRAPHY

As this is the first general history of the Stuart family's connection with France, the majority of the books consulted are by French historians, and naturally the French version of events does not always tally with accepted English accounts. Therein lies the fascination of history. My key source book for the medieval period is the six-volume *Histoire de Charles VII* by G. du Fresne de Beaucourt, who devoted half a lifetime to this study—thirty-five years of research and then ten years to write it. In his introduction he says: 'Pour bien remplir ce vaste cadre il était nécessaire de procéder avec méthode et de bien classer les matériaux.' This is what I have tried to do throughout my book.

Anon. *L'Ascanius Moderne* (Paris, 1760)

Ashley, Maurice, *The Glorious Revolution of 1688* (London, 1966)

Ashley, Maurice, *Rupert of the Rhine* (London, 1976)

Bannantyne Club, *Historie of King James the Sext* (Edinburgh, 1833)

Bapst, E., *Projets matrimoniaux de Jacques V d'Ecosse* (Paris, 1889)

Beaumont, G. du Bosq de, *La cour des Stuarts à St. Germain-en-Laye* (Paris, 1909)

Beaucourt, G. du Fresne de, *Histoire de Charles VII*, 6 vols (Paris, 1881–91)

Berwick y de Alba, Duque de, *El Mariscal Duque de Berwick* (Madrid, 1925)

Bourgeois de Paris, *Journal d'un Bourgeois de Paris 1408–1499*, ed. Alexandre Tuetey (Paris, 1879)

Brantôme, Pierre, *Histoire des Ducs de Guise* (Paris, 1850)

Brantôme, Pierre, *Oeuvres Complètes* (Paris, 1832)

Burnet, Bishop Gilbert, *History of His Own Time* (London, 1840)

Campana di Cavelli, *Les Derniers Stuarts à St. Germain-en-Laye*, 3 vols (Paris, 1871)

Carte, Thomas (ed.), *A Collection of Original Letters and Papers* (London, 1739)

Carte, Thomas, *Life of James, Duke of Ormonde* (London, 1735–6)

Chameau, Jean, *Histoire de Berry* (Lyon, 1556)

Chartier, Alain, *Les chroniques du feu roi Charles septième* (Paris, 1528)

Clark, Ruth, *Sir William Trumbull in Paris* (London, 1938)

Cust, Elizabeth, *Some Account of the Stuarts of Darnley, Lennox and Aubigny* (privately printed, London, 1895)

Dangeau, Philippe de Courcillon, Marquis de, *Journal de la Cour, 19 vols* (various editions)

Donaldson, Gordon, *Memoirs of Sir James Melville of Halhill* (London, 1969)

De Gaury, G., *The Grand Captain, Gonzalo de Cordoba* (London, 1955)

Forbes, Bishop Robert, *The Lyon in Mourning*, 3 vols (Scottish History Society, Edinburgh, 1896)

Forbes-Leith, A., *The Scots Guards in France*, 2 vols (London, 1899)

Force, Auguste-Nompar, twelfth Duc de La, *Les Caumont La Force* (Paris, 1960); *Lauzun, Courtisan du Grand Roi* (Paris, 1960)
Fournernon, H., *Louise de Kéroualle, Duchesse de Portsmouth* (Paris, 1886)
Francisque-Michel, *Les Ecossais en France et les Français en Ecosse* (Bordeaux, 1862)
Fraser, Antonia, *Mary, Queen of Scots* (London, 1969)
Godefroy, M. (ed.), *Mémoires de Philippe de Commines* (Paris, 1723)
Grew, M. and S., *The English Court in Exile* (London, 1911)
Guicciardini, Francesco, *Storia d'Italia*, ed. C. Panigada (Bari, 1929); *Storie Fiorentine dal 1378–1509*, ed. C. Palmarocchi (Bari, 1931)
Guyon, Symphorien, *Histoire du Siège d'Orléans* (Orléans, 1650)
Hamilton, Anthony, *Mémoires du Comte Philibert de Gramont* (various editions, Paris)
Henderson, Nicholas, *Prince Eugen of Savoy* (London, 1964)
Hillairet, Jacques, *Evocation du Vieux Paris* (Paris, 1953); *Les villages du Vieux Paris* (Paris, 1953)
Hume, David, *Histoire de la Cour d'Angleterre pendant les règnes des Stuarts*, 6 vols, trans. par l'Abbé Prévost (Paris, 1754–7)
Jesse, John Heneage, *Histoire de la Maison Royale de Stuart*, 3 vols (Paris, 1840)
Jovius, Paulus, *La vita di Gonsalvo de Cordoba, detto il Gran Capitano*, ed. C. Panigada (Bari, 1931)
Jusserand, J. J., *Recueil des instructions diplomatiques données aux ambassadeurs: Angleterre* (Paris, 1929)
Kenyon, J. P., *The Stuart Constitution* (Cambridge, 1966)
Kenyon, J. P., *The Stuarts* (London, 1969)
Kroll, Maria (ed.), *Letters from Liselotte* (London, 1970)
La Fayette, Mme de, *Histoire de Madame Henriette* (Paris, 1812)
1760)
Latham and Andrews (ed.), *Diary of Samuel Pepys* (London, 1970)
Lobanov-Rostovsky (Prince Labanoff), *Lettres et Mémoires de Marie, Reine d'Ecosse*, 7 vols (Paris, 1844)
Lucie-Smith, Edward, *Joan of Arc* (London, 1976)
Mattingley, Garrett, *Renaissance Diplomacy* (London, 1955)
Morrah, Patrick, *Prince Rupert of the Rhine* (London, 1976)
Montpensier, Anne-Marie de, *Mémoires de la Duchesse de Montpensier*
Motteville, Mme de, *Histoire de la Cour de France* (various editions, Paris); *Histoire d'Anne d'Autriche*
Ogg, David, *England in the Reign of Charles II; England in the Reigns of James II and William III*
Pelligrini, Carlo, *La Contessa d'Albany e il salotto del Lungarno* (Naples, 1951)
Pepys, Samuel, *see* Latham and Andrews
Perroy, E., *La Guerre de Cent Ans* (Paris, 1950)
Petrie, Sir Charles, *The Jacobite Movement* (London, 1953)
Petrie, Sir Charles, *The Maréchal Duke of Berwick* (London, 1959)
Pelissier, Léon, *Lettres inédites de la Comtesse d'Albany* (Paris, 1862)
Pelissier, Léon, *La portefeuille de la Comtesse d'Albany* (Paris, 1869)
Plantavit de la Pause, l'Abbé Margon (ed.), *Les Mémoires du Maréchal Duc de Berwick* (Paris, 1737)
Ranke, Leopold von, *History of England, principally in the 17th century* (London, 1875)
Raynal, Louis, *Histoire de Berry* (Bourges, 1845–7)
Roxburgh Club, *Discours du Grand et Magnifique Triomphe faict du mariage de François et Marie Stuart* (Edinburgh, 1818)
St Simon, Duc de, *Mémoires de la Cour de Louis XIV* (various editions, Paris)
Samaran, Charles, *La Maison d'Armagnac au XVe siècle* (Paris, 1907)

Strickland, Agnes, *The Last Four Princesses of the House of Stuart* (London, 1872)
Stuart, Andrew, *Genealogical History of the Stewarts, made during a visit to France in 1788–89* (London, 1798)
Taillandier, Saint-René, *La Comtesse d'Albany* (Paris, 1862)
Tayler, A. and H. (eds), *The Stuart Papers at Windsor* (London, 1939)
Tayler, H., *Letters of Charlotte, Duchess of Albany* (London, 1951)
Thaumassière, Gaspard Thaumas de la, *Histoire de Berry* (Bourges, 1689)
Trémoille, Duc de la, *Une famille royaliste, française, irlandaise, écossaise* (Nantes, 1901)
Turner, F. C., *James II* (London, 1948)
Thomson, George Malcolm, *Warrior Prince* (London, 1976)
Wedgwood, C. V., *The Great Rebellion: The King's Peace* (London, 1953); *The King's War* (London, 1958)
Wilson, Arthur, *Life and Reign of King James I* (London, 1653)
Willson, D. H., *King James VI and I* (London, 1956)

INDEX

·N·Poilly ex. c·p·r·

Veüe et perspectiue du Jardin de S.t Germ